ENCYCLOPAEDIA OF
SPORTING
SHOOTING

ENCYCLOPAEDIA OF
SPORTING SHOOTING

ROBIN MARSHALL-BALL

B. T. Batsford Limited · London

For my Parents:

My Mother, who nurtured my early years and first faltering steps into field sports.

My Father, whose 30 years of Shikar experiences in India have always been a source of fascination.

First published 1992

© Robin Marshall-Ball, 1992

Typeset by Graphicraft Typesetters Ltd, Hong Kong
and printed in Great Britain by Butler and Tanner Ltd, Frome, Somerset
Published by
B. T. Batsford Ltd
4 Fitzhardinge Street
London
W1H OAH

A catalogue record for this book is available from the British Library

ISBN 0 7134 6547 6

CONTENTS

Colour plates between pages 128 and 129

ACKNOWLEDGEMENTS

The Author and Publishers would like to thank the following for permission to reproduce illustrations:

N.G.R. Baker: page 96; BASC: page 33, colour pages 7, 15; BDS: page 34; BFSS: page 36; Beretta: colour page 3; Arthur Berschenk: page 260; Browning (UK) Ltd: page 161; J.R. Cannings: page 227; R.E. Chaplin: page 121; Churchill Atkin Grant & Lang Ltd: pages 19, 101; Chris Cradock: pages 21, 26, 27, 52, 83, 88, 102, 110, 111, 167, 187, 216, 219, 229, 267; Prudence Cumming Associates: pages 134; 135; D.N. Dalton: page 139; Dan'l Fraser & Co.: page 105; John Dickson: page 81; Game Conservancy: pages 24, 108, 113, 215, 286/7; Gunmark Ltd: pages 212; Roy Harris: page 51; HM Tower of London Armouries: pages 30/1; Holland & Holland: pages 132/3; John Jochimsen: pages 182/3; R.P. Laurence: page 50; David Lloyd: page 144; David De Lossy: page 191; J. Manton: pages 131, 153; Marlin Inc.: pages 29, 142/3; John Marchington: pages 24/5, 63, 185, colour pages 1, 4, 5, 12; Shelagh Marshall-Ball: pages 19, 64, 144; Mark Newman-Wren; pages 85, 95, 118, 150; Parker-Hale: pages 164/5, 232/3; Rodney Paull: pages 11, 13, 15, 22, 23, 32, 41, 46, 54, 55, 56, 99, 103, 141, 149, 175, 199, 233, 238/9, 244, 245, 271, 279; Remington Arms Co.: pages 17, 181; John Rigby & Co.: page 198; Steyr-Mannlicher: pages 150/1, 151; Sturm-Ruger Inc.: pages 208/9, 234/5; John Tarlton: pages 70, 224; US Repeating Arms Co.: pages 100, 181/2; Edward Watson: pages 87, 88/9, 122/3; Weatherby: pages 200, 201, 263, 264/5; Winchester; pages 160/1. The remaining pictures were taken by the Author.

PREFACE

In preparing this book I have needed to call upon the experience and advice of many other people. I count myself fortunate in that during the 30 years and more that I have been an active participant in shooting sports in Britain, I have enjoyed both shotgun and rifle shooting in a wide variety of environments and in the company of a broad spectrum of people. Even so, such is the variety of sport available within these shores that I have not sampled all of the sports described in this book. Hence my reliance on others to fill in the gaps of my own experience.

Among my 'chief advisers' I must name Clive Wordley and Chris Cradock, whose help I gratefully acknowledge. Many others have given of their own skills and experience, and I am grateful to those experts in their own spheres, John and James Marchington, Lea MacNally, Richard Prior, and John Dryden.

I am also grateful for the advice and help I have received from the Game Conservancy, the BASC, and the British Deer Society, together with the large numbers of gunmakers in Britain and overseas who have responded to my requests for information and illustrations.

When I was first approached to write this book I was given a word budget which I felt was really daunting! However, as I got down to preparing the manuscript, I became increasingly aware that there was a very real risk of over-running the planned length by a large margin. Of necessity therefore, I had to prune out some of the items that I felt should be included in a work of this nature. But you should not despair if your favourite entry has been omitted. Wherever possible I have endeavoured to include most of the 'pruned' entries within the text of associated entries.

Air Rifle Air weapons are powered by compressed air and are built in four calibres. The .177 is predominantly a target-shooting calibre, although some hunters prefer the higher velocity and deeper penetration that is achieved by the small pellet. The .20 calibre is confined to rifles manufactured by Sheridan in the USA on a 'pump-up' action. The most popular calibre for serious air rifle hunting is the .22, although some manufacturers also produce small quantities of air rifles in .25 calibre.

Hunting air rifles in Britain are restricted in power to a maximum of 12 ft lbs muzzle energy. There is a very large range of reliable and accurate weapons available at present. Over the past two decades the improvements in air weapon technology have made serious air rifle hunting a sport in its own right and finally dispelled the image of an air rifle being a mere 'toy'. Air rifle shooters are making an increasingly valuable contribution to the control of vermin in many parts of Britain and air rifle shooting constitutes a major growth area in shooting sports.

See also: **Vermin Control; Vermin Shooting – Weapons**

Ammunition Reloading Using the correct tools, reloading components which are compatible, and suitable charts, and by exercising reasonable care at all times, it is possible to produce safe and reliable centrefire ammunition. There is some satisfaction to be gained from shooting your quarry with

A popular hunting air rifle, the Weihrauch HW 80

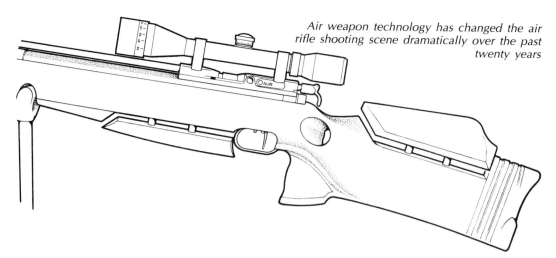

Air weapon technology has changed the air rifle shooting scene dramatically over the past twenty years

ammunition you loaded yourself, and there is the added bonus that the cost of reloading may be considerably lower than the cost of purchasing factory-made cartridges. In addition, by carefully varying the powder charge and the shot load or bullet weight, the shooter can tailor the ammunition to specific purposes. In this way the shotgun shooter can vary the pattern spread through a 'fixed-choke' barrel of the shotgun and a rifle shooter can achieve greater accuracy than is possible with any branded ammunition.

It is virtually impossible for the amateur to reload rimfire ammunition. However, centrefire cartridges for either shotgun or rifle present few difficulties to the careful home loader. The reloading process is the same for either shotgun or rifle cartridges. The first stage is to decap and resize the case to remove the used primer and ensure that the cartridge conforms to the correct chamber dimensions. The case is then reprimed with a fresh primer and the correct quantity of powder added as the propellant charge. In shotgun cartridges the main wadding is then seated on the powder and the shot charge is added. Finally, the end of the cartridge is closed by either a crimped closure or a rolled turnover closure. In rifle ammunition, after the powder charge is added the bullet is seated in the end of the cartridge case and the completed round inspected for correct seating.

Many reloading presses are available to speed up and simplify the reloading process and some shotgun presses, used efficiently,

can produce over one hundred finished cartridges in an hour. Rifle ammunition tends to take longer, as the process needs to be more precise to achieve the exact powder charge and seating depth.

Experimentation with different powder charges is very dangerous, as some combinations of powder and bullet weight or shot charge will produce abnormally high chamber pressures, so variations must be within recommended tolerances only. Nevertheless, with a little care, excellent quality reloaded ammunition can be produced at a

Consistent and accurate ammunition can be made using only simple reloading kits

Though renowned for their bolt-action sporting and target rifles, Anschütz also produce a light self-loading rimfire .22

considerable saving on comparable 'branded' ammunition.

The proof house will, for a fee, test cartridges produced by the home loader. The prudent home loader will always send a sample of his home loads to be tested before he shoots any such reloads through his own shotgun.

See also: **Shotgun Cartridge Design**

Ammunition Storage   Shotgun and rifle ammunition today is far safer and more stable than that which was used earlier this century. The smokeless propellant powders and the ignition caps are less prone to variation or deterioration than in the days of black powder and therefore may be stored safely more easily.

Modern shotgun cartridges usually have plastic casings which make them virtually waterproof and therefore damp storage does not cause them to swell as was the case with the older paper cartridges. However,

A steel ammunition safe bolted to a wall is a very secure method of storage

exposure to heat, e.g. in drying coat pockets, can also cause the composition of the powder to change and produce variable, sometimes dangerous, pressures. Ideally, therefore, ammunition should be stored in a cool dry environment to avoid any risk of the metallic parts of the cartridge becoming corroded through atmospheric dampness. More importantly, though, ammunition should be stored in a secure place in order to keep it out of the reach of others, particularly children, who may find live ammunition of interest. A lockable drawer is sufficient, providing it is kept locked and it is not subject to damp or extremes of heat or cold. However, many metal gun security cabinets are furnished with a lockable ammunition compartment. In addition, separate metal 'ammunition' safes are available on the market: bolted to a wall they offer a high degree of safe storage.

Anschütz   The name of Anschütz is probably most often associated with the manufacture of target rifles. Indeed, such is the quality of their .22 target rifles that this manufacturer has the virtual monopoly of the honours in world-class target competitions.

The skills and expertise that have, over the 130 years of the company's existence, culminated in the production of their outstanding .22 LR target rifles are reflected in the quality of their sporting rifles. Based at Ulm in West Germany, Anschütz specialize in sporting rifles in the light calibres. Thus they produce sporting rifles chambered for .22 LR and .22 Magnum rimfire cartridges in their rimfire range, together with a variety of centrefire rifles chambered for .22 Hornet and .222 Remington cartridges.

Apart from one auto-loading rifle, the Anschütz Model 525, which is itself a robust and reliable weapon, all their other models are based on a precise bolt-action mechanism. The better quality rifles use a bolt of similar design to their target rifles, and this, combined with the legendary Anschütz barrel, is a sound basis for a fine sporting rifle.

The auto-loading Model 525 comes in two versions. Both feature a clip-loading system and a deflector to direct the spent cases away from the shooter, but the standard 525 uses a 24-inch barrel and the shorter 'carbine' Model 525H is mounted with one of 20 inches.

In the bolt-action rifles there is a far wider selection. The less expensive models include the single-shot Model 1388, the five-shot clip-fed 1450 and the 'junior' Model 1449, all chambered for the .22 LR cartridge. The top-of-the-range rifle is the 1422 in .22 LR and the 1522 chambered for .22 Rimfire Magnum. These models, like the centrefire range, are well-finished precision rifles with good-quality walnut stocks and a streamlined bolt action. Amongst this range of .22 rimfire bolt-action repeating rifles are models fitted with straight 'classic' stocks, Monte Carlo stocks, and a 'Stutzen' style full-stocked rifle. This is one of the few rimfire Stutzen rifles available on the market, and to round off the rimfire range Anschütz produce what is, as far as I am aware, the only truly left-handed bolt-action rifle chambered for rimfire calibres.

The centrefire range of rifles is similar to the better quality rimfires with a range of stock styles, a Stutzen full-stocked model and a left-handed bolt-action rifle. All the models are clip-fed repeaters and they are all characterized by outstanding accuracy. It is perhaps less well known that Anschütz also

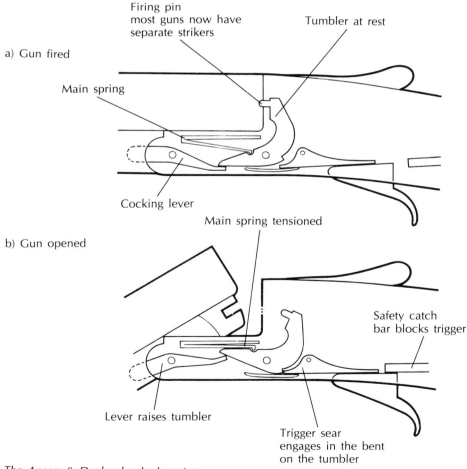

The Anson & Deeley boxlock action

produce both high-quality target and sporting air rifles and a simple 9 mm bolt-action shotgun.

Anson & Deeley   When the first hammerless double barrel guns were being developed in Britain, most gunmakers were devoting their attention to sidelock actions. W. Anson and J. Deeley, two Birmingham gunmakers, decided to concentrate on a simplified design and the action they produced still bears their name. In contrast to the sidelock design, their 'boxlock' housed the four main moving parts in the bar of the action beneath the barrel flats. The beauty of the design lay in its simplicity, and the vast majority of side-by-side shotguns being made today still use the Anson and Deeley boxlock action.

When it first appeared in 1875 this design simplified the process of re-cocking the internal hammers by using the leverage of the drop-down barrels when the gun was opened, and this method has subsequently been adopted even in sidelock designs. The Anson & Deeley action is extremely hard-wearing. The design has stood the test of hard usage for over a century with very little modification; but the main criticism of this mechanism stems from the fact that there is less exposed metal and it is less 'elegant' than a sidelock. Certainly a boxlock action gives the skilled engraver less scope to ply his art, but this is an aesthetic rather than a functional criticism.

Nowadays most of the less expensive double guns are of the Anson & Deeley boxlock design, purely because this action is simpler and therefore less costly to produce than a sidelock.

Some 'best-grade' boxlocks are available from such highly respected gunmakers as Holland & Holland, and the maxim that it is better to purchase a moderately priced boxlock than a 'cheap' sidelock is generally sound advice.

In all the shotgun sports in Britain, except perhaps on driven game shoots, the majority of shooters will be using double barrel guns with Anson & Deeley boxlock actions – a time-tested design, variations of which are still being manufactured in large quantity in many countries.

Antlers   Antlers are the bony outgrowths on the heads of the males of most species of deer. Often (wrongly) called horns, they differ from true horns in that they are grown and shed annually. True horns, on the other hand, are permanent features which usually increase in size with each successive year.

Unlike true horns, antlers are made of bone-like material which stems from the raised pedicles on the head of the deer. Changes in the hormone level in the deer after the breeding season result in a weakening of the antlers at the pedicle, and it is at this point that they finally drop off the animal. Immediately after the antlers are cast the new set begins to grow beneath a strong and flexible protective covering of 'velvet'. The antlers at this time are well supplied with blood vessels and are warm to the touch when 'in velvet'. However, when growth is complete the blood supply is cut off and the velvet shrivels. At this stage it appears to irritate the deer, to the extent that the animal will fray the antlers against saplings and undergrowth in order to remove the velvet and expose the hard antlers underneath. When first exposed the antlers are a pale creamy colour, but they soon colour up to a dark brown as they are stained by vegetation and sap. Just occasionally a hormonal imbalance caused by an injury may interfere with this process and a 'malformed head' is produced – in roe deer this sometimes gives rise to the 'perruque' antler deformities.

The Chinese water deer is the only species of deer without antlers living wild in Britain. As a general rule the larger the deer species the more elaborate the pattern of antlers grown. Thus the small muntjac and roe deer grow short simple antlers, while red deer can grow impressive 'heads' of over twenty points.

Antlers serve two main purposes. They are primarily adornments which denote the status and seniority of the beast, which allow deer to live among their own kind with the minimum of physical competition. During the rut, however, and when confronted by predators, antlers are also used as weapons of defence. The multiple branches of normal antlers reduce their effectiveness as weapons, so that rut contests between male

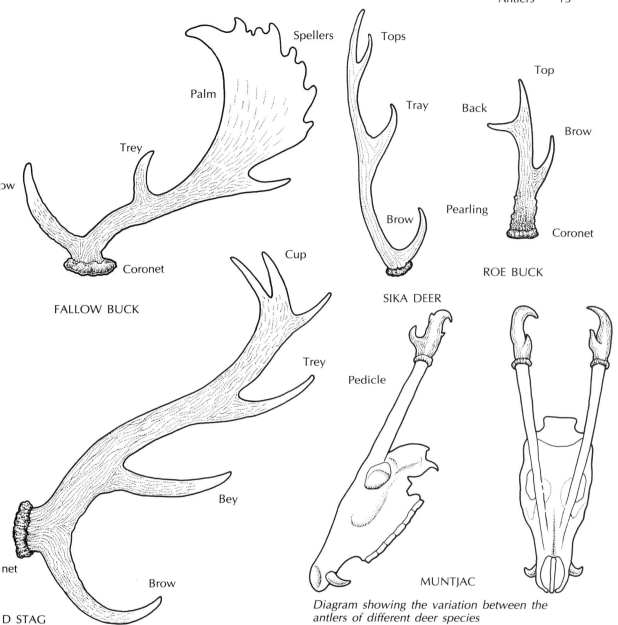

Spellers

Tops

Top

Palm

Tray

Back

Brow

Trey

Brow

ow

Pearling

Coronet

Cup

Brow

ROE BUCK

Coronet

FALLOW BUCK

SIKA DEER

Trey

Pedicle

Bey

net

Brow

MUNTJAC

D STAG

Diagram showing the variation between the antlers of different deer species

deer are settled without serious injury to the combatants. It is for this reason that deer managers are quick to cull out malformed 'switch' red stags or 'dagger' roebucks whose unbranched antlers may cause their competitors serious injury or even death.

Red, sika and fallow deer cast their antlers in spring, and the regrowth takes place in the summer when food supplies are plentiful. By September most males of these species have stripped their velvet and are in 'hard antler', ready for the October rut. Roebucks, on the other hand, cast their antlers in December, and the new growth is usually clean by mid-April. Muntjac bucks do not follow a seasonal cycle but may cast at any time of the year with the regrowth taking up to twelve weeks, depending on the season.

See also: **Deer**

Aperture Sights   The aperture sight on a rifle is basically a small disc which is pierced by a small hole or aperture. When the device is mounted on the breech end of the weapon, the eye of the shooter can be placed so that the foresight and target can be viewed through the aperture. The aperture can be adjusted up and down (elevation) and from side to side (windage) so that the rifle can be accurately zeroed at any suitable range.

Competition target shooters have proved just how effective the aperture or 'peep' sight system is in Olympic and international competitions at ranges up to 1,000 yards. In experienced hands it is much more precise than the standard open sights, and aperture sights can be used for hunting. The system, however, suffers from the disadvantage that it is difficult to use quickly and 'snap' shooting is virtually impossible. Both open sights and telescopic sights are better in this respect, and the aperture sight also fails in low light conditions. As most rifle shooting sports in Britain take place around dawn and dusk the aperture sight is far less effective than a good light-gathering telescope and few sportsmen choose it when hunting live quarry.

Auto-Loading Weapons   Auto-loading or self-loading firearms are often incorrectly termed 'automatic' weapons. As each round of an auto-loader can only be fired by a separate pull of the trigger the weapon is incapable of firing in bursts and is therefore not a true automatic.

Auto-loading weapons generally fall into three main types: recoil-operated, gas-operated, and 'blow-back'. The first reliable recoil-operated shotguns were devised by John M. Browning at the turn of this century and the design has proved to be so reliable that the Browning five-shot auto is still being produced. In a recoil-operated weapon the breech assembly and barrel are mobile. When the gun is fired the recoil moves both breech and barrel to the rear. At the fullest extent of the rearward travel the breech is unlocked and the barrel slides forward under the force of the return spring. As this takes place the spent cartridge is ejected and an unfired one is fed up from the magazine to be pushed home when the bolt moves forward to its closed position. Many self-loading shotguns use the recoil principle but it is less frequently seen in centrefire rifles.

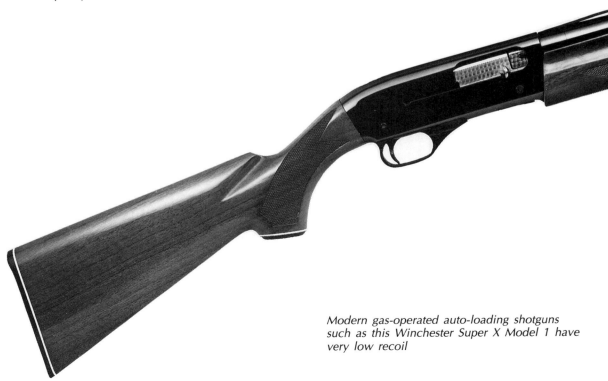

Modern gas-operated auto-loading shotguns such as this Winchester Super X Model 1 have very low recoil

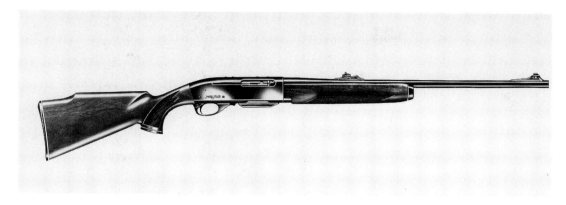

The Remington 'Model 4' auto-loading centrefire hunting rifle is now a prohibited weapon for stalking in Britain

Gas-operated self-loaders use gas pressure from the exploding powder to activate the mechanism. A small hole or gas port in the barrel channels some of the gases into a chamber to move a series of rods that draw the bolt to the rear, extract the spent case, load a fresh one, and return the bolt to the closed position. The barrel is fixed and it is only the breech assembly that moves. Self-loading centrefire rifles tend to be built on this principle and an increasing number of shotguns are now also gas operated. The Remington model 1100 is an example that has been in production for some time and has proved the reliability of the system in sporting weapons.

The blow-back action is restricted to low-powered weapons such as .22 rimfires or 9 mm shotguns. Here the mild recoil is insufficient to throw the whole assembly to the rear as in a recoil-operated weapon, but it is adequate to unlock the breech and activate the reloading sequence. As most rimfire .22 rifles are designed to operate with the Long Rifle cartridge there is a tendency for the mechanism to stick or jam when lower-powered ammunition, such as the .22 Short, is used.

AYA Aguirre y Arranzabal, the gunmaking firm from which the trade mark AYA is derived, are one of the oldest established in Spain, and are of world repute.

AYA have a very large annual output of weapons and the styles of shotguns they produce are designed to suit their destinations. Thus shotguns designed for the American market will have beavertail fore-ends, raised ventilated ribs (even on side-by-side models) and single selective triggers as standard features. Those for domestic and European use may be equipped with sling-swivels, and those for the British market are styled to conform to the specifications of English shotguns.

As a result of this adaptability to individual overseas markets, AYA are now probably leading the sales of shotguns in many countries. Certainly in Britain they were the first of the European gunmakers to reach the popular market during the 1960s and have gone on to exert a strong influence on other competitors wishing to break into the British market.

The range of AYA shotguns available to the shooter in Britain is extensive. At the top of their range of side-by-side doubles is the AYA No 1 sidelock. It is indeed a superbly finished weapon with a great deal of skill and artistry in the elegant line and fine engraving.

These are built to special order and are available in pairs or triples. Modelled on the London-made 'best' gun they offer an alternative at a far lower price.

Other models in their range of sidelock ejector side-by-sides include the popular AYA No 2 at a price below that of a new English-made boxlock.

At the other end of the range is the AYA Yeoman. Although a basic side-by-side boxlock without engraving or embellishment it is nevertheless a well-made and hard-working gun capable of giving a lifetime of service. Perhaps one of the keys to AYA's success in this country is the degree of thought they apply to their gunmaking. This is illustrated by the fact that all their side-by-side shotguns are built on chopper lump barrels, a method traditionally used on the better English guns, and the action faces have disc-set strikers. To cater for the British sportsman, they have produced a 25-inch-barrel gun, modelled on the Churchill guns, and a heavy wildfowling boxlock double, in addition to the standard game and rough shooting guns, which are also styled to suit

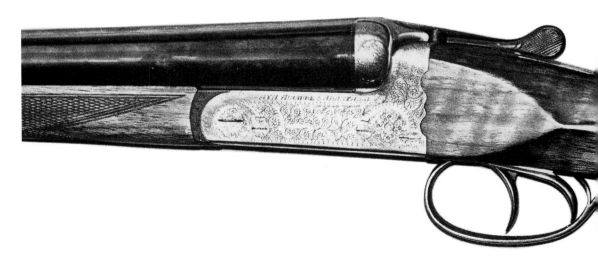

A fine example of Spanish gunmaking, the AYA 'best' boxlock in 20 bore

A Churchill Regal boxlock ejector 12-bore shotgun

British tastes. The short-barrelled lightweight game gun, called the AYA 'XXV', is available in both sidelock and boxlock editions and, like its Churchill counterpart, is fitted with a high, narrow file-cut rib.

AYA also offer a full range of purpose-built small-bore shotguns, and this has perhaps encouraged the recent resurgence of interest in the 20 and 28 bores as sporting guns. Unlike other manufacturers who have in the past produced small-bore guns by merely fitting narrower barrel tubes on an existing 12-bore action – a process that produces a heavy and ungainly weapon – AYA have scaled all the components to the appropriate size and thus produced elegant and well-balanced small bores in both boxlock and sidelock models.

Practically all their side-by-side models for Britain are styled on the traditional English sporting gun. For those who prefer the over-and-under format, AYA also produce a range of shotguns to this design. The Yeoman model over-and-under is the basic rough shooter's gun and the models available include side-plated boxlocks (guns which outwardly look like a sidelock) and at the top of the range a true sidelock over-and-under. Although the choice is less extensive than in the side-by-side shotguns, AYA over-and-unders are also available in small-bore versions.

Although many other Spanish gunmakers now market their weapons in Britain, AYA guns have been used in this country for nearly thirty years and have really stood the test of time.

Their excellent workmanship and reliability have earned them a good reputation and they are unlikely to lose their lead to other competitors from the Iberian peninsula.

Backstop In the context of shooting sports the term 'backstop' may have two meanings.

In lowland driven game shooting the normal procedure is for beaters to drive the game, be it pheasant or partridge, so that when flushed they fly over the waiting guns. Usually the beaters walk in line towards the stands at which the guns await the flushed birds. In most cases the birds are pushed forward over the waiting guns but there are circumstances which cause the flushed birds to curl back over the beaters. In dense thicket it is very difficult for beaters to hold a steadily advancing line and in these instances birds may lie low and then flush after the line has passed them by. These birds invariably fly towards the rear and away from the awaiting standing guns. In this situation the shoot captain may use two backstops in order to cover the birds breaking back. A backstop in this context is therefore a walking gun who follows the line of beaters at a distance of around 50 yards to the rear. Although generally they are likely to see fewer birds than the standing guns, there are occasions when the backstop enjoys a fair amount of sport, particularly if the beaters are working into a strong headwind. Birds flushed forward in these conditions may well gain height rapidly and cut back over the line of beaters. By the time they approach the backstop they are high and travelling downwind at speed – offering him or her a fine testing shot.

In the context of rifle shooting, the backstop or backdrop is the safe ground behind the target which will take the bullet in the event of it passing through the animal, or in the case of a clean miss. In a country as overcrowded as Britain, it is essential, for safety reasons, that shots are only taken with a rifle when there is a clear backstop to receive the bullet. When shooting on level ground this can be extremely difficult, and shots must be taken with great caution. One way round the problem is to shoot from an elevated position such as a high seat. In this way the rifle is pointing downwards, so that the bullet goes to ground and the risk of a missed shot flying wide is minimized.

In undulating land the problem of a safe backstop is eased, with the shooter often able to take advantage of hollows, slopes and earth banks. Here again the golden rule is not to shoot unless the shooter can see where the bullet will come to rest. Thus shooting against a skyline can be very dangerous and should not be attempted.

When shooting in dense woodland it is not safe to assume that the trees will form an effective backstop. The shooter must be sure that there are no other humans or livestock in the area, and that the vegetation is sufficiently dense to stop the flight of a bullet. Ascertaining that there is a safe backstop is an essential duty for the rifle user each time the rifle is raised for a shot.

Badminton Library The Badminton Library series of books was a milestone in sporting book publishing. Supported and indeed edited by the Duke of Beaufort, and published by Longman Green, the books served to bring a very wide selection of sports and pastimes to a far broader readership.

The series was published from about 1885 until just after the turn of the century, and volumes were devoted to such subjects as racing, cycling, boating, cricket, golf, riding, tennis, yachting, athletics and football. Of the field sports, fishing was published in two volumes and there were a total of four volumes devoted to shooting sports. In common with all the volumes, the authors used in the Badminton series were acknowledged experts in their field.

Shooting sports in Britain were treated in two volumes by two of the most famous shooting sportsmen of all time: Lord Walsingham and Sir Ralph Payne-Gallwey. Both volumes were first published in 1889 – Volume One entitled *Shooting Field and Covert*, and Volume Two *Shooting Moor and Marsh*. Following the success of these two volumes came another two-volume set devoted to big game. Written by Clive Phillips-Woolley, Volumes One and Two of *Big Game Shooting* appeared in 1894.

The success of the Badminton Library series of books was such that it was imitated a generation later by the Lonsdale Library, which continued publication until the 1970s whilst other publishing houses attempted to establish 'Library' series of sporting books with varying degrees of success.

In recent years the Badminton Library books devoted to the shooting sports have come to be seen as classics and are sought after in their various editions by sporting book collectors. The great interest in these books, stemming perhaps from the fact that they had illustrious authors and that the text described what many consider to have been the 'golden age' of shooting, has led to recent re-publication of facsimile editions by the Ashford Press.

Ballistic Coefficient The ballistic coefficient of a bullet is a measurement of the bullet's ability to overcome air resistance and so retain its original velocity. Therefore a bullet with a high coefficient will have far better downrange velocity and retained energy than a projectile with a low ballistic coefficient. Basically, the bullet's weight, diameter and shape determine its coefficient. A heavy bullet with a narrow diameter and pointed nose will perform better than a flat or round-nose bullet of light weight and large bore diameter.

The formula often used to determine the ballistic coefficient (C) is:

$$C = \frac{W}{nd^2}$$

where W is the weight, d is the diameter and n is an empirical value indicating the shape of the head.

Barrel The barrel is simply the 'tube' on a firearm through which the charge is fired. In a shotgun the interior of the barrel is smooth bored and the muzzle might be constricted slightly to form a choke. In a rifle the interior of the barrel is cut or forged with spiral grooves known as rifling. Both shotguns and rifle barrels have an enlarged section of the bore at the breech in order to accommodate the cartridge. This enlargement is known as the chamber. The only exception is the air rifle, which lacks a chamber as such, the air rifle pellet being loaded directly into the barrel in the case of 'break-barrel', models or into a loading point in fixed-barrel underlever or sidelever actions.

Winchester side-by-side barrels. Left: with Winchoke tubes. Right: with integral chokes

Battue In the late Victorian era the style of gameshooting among fashionable circles changed from walked-up shooting and shooting over pointing dogs to the driven game shoot. This was initially copied from the traditional style of shooting on the European continent. As time progressed the large estates of the British Isles vied with each other to produce bigger and bigger bags and a 'record' bag was a fashionable and prestigious goal. This quest for large bags was a British digression from the continental shooting style, yet these driven game shoots retained the European term 'battue'.

Nowadays the term is seldom used in the context of the British driven game shoot and more correctly now refers to the large-scale driven shoots that are still popular on the European mainland.

Bead/Blade The term 'bead' has two meanings, depending on whether it refers to a shotgun or a rifle.

The bead on the muzzle of a shotgun is not really a sight. Shotguns are not aimed in the manner of a rifle, certainly not when shooting at moving quarry, so the bead is used as a quick reference point to the general direction in which the gun is pointing. To this end, shotgun beads are generally very small affairs – yet there are instances when they play a more significant role in the process of shooting. Shotguns designed for serious competitive clay pigeon shooting will often have an enlarged foresight bead together with another smaller bead halfway down the top rib. For clay disciplines such as down-the-line or Olympic Trench the gun is already mounted and the alignment of these two beads helps to ensure that the gun is consistently mounted for each target. In the sporting context wildfowling guns often also have an enlarged foresight bead. Since much wildfowling takes place in conditions of very poor light, a large 'blob' at the end of the barrel helps the shooter to discern the direction in which the gun barrel is pointing. Lacking a large bead on my own wildfowling gun, I have often stuck a blob of mud over the existing small bead to achieve the same end! In shotgun shooting, therefore, the bead is simply a reference point or direction indicator rather than a gun sight.

On a rifle, the bead takes on an altogether

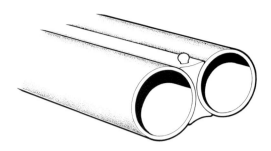

The bead sight on a shotgun is not used for 'aiming'

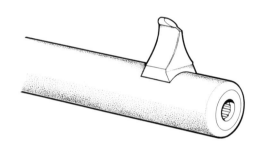

The simple foresight bead on an old BSA air rifle

greater significance. Rifles have two main types of foresight: the bead and the 'blade'.

On the simplest air rifles the bead takes the form of a small conical pillar on top of which there is a sphere or bead. As an aiming device this is perfectly adequate and effective when used in conjunction with the 'V' of the rearsight or the aperture of a peep sight. It does have the disadvantage, however, of being rather delicate, and the bead can be easily broken off. To overcome this the most common form of bead foresight nowadays is bead-shaped in cross section and blade-shaped in long section. When viewed along the axis of the barrel, i.e., along the sighting plane of the rifle, the foresight has a similar appearance to the simple bead, a clearly seen blob on top of a supporting pillar.

Bead foresights are most often and most effectively used with a 'V' rearsight. With such a combination, the bead is rested in the apex of the 'V' to achieve the correct aim for the normal shooting distance. Elevating the bead within the 'V' (known as drawing a full bead) raises the point of impact or extends the range, whilst lowering the bullet's impact point is achieved by sinking the bead into the apex of the rearsight 'V' (known as drawing a fine bead).

The term 'blade foresight' is self-explanatory. A plain vertical metal blade, this type is more often used with a 'U' or notch rearsight. The standard aim is then taken when the top of the blade is in line with the top of the notch and the blade is seen to be equidistant from both sides of the notch. Adjusting the elevation is achieved in the same way as for the bead foresight – showing a full or fine foresight depending on whether one wants the shot to go higher or lower.

Although some foresights have lateral adjustment to enable the sights to shoot to the left or right, the great majority of rifle foresights are fixed, and adjustment for lateral movement (windage) and up-and-down movement (elevation) is carried out on the rearsight, be it aperture or open sight.

See also: **Sights – Rifle**

Beater   In shooting terms a beater is a person employed as part of a team to flush game and drive them over or past the standing guns. In some parts of Britain beaters are also known as 'drivers', 'bramble bashers' or 'bush beaters', the latter terms coming from the habit of supplying each beater with a stick with which to tap on tree trunks, branches and bushes in order to drive game forward.

On informal rough shoots, friends and family may be persuaded to act as occasional beaters in order to work out a patch of cover or a spinney. Even in more formal walked-up shooting there may well be beaters between each walking gun in the line, and these will usually act as dog handlers for the close-ranging spaniels and labradors.

In the case of the formal driven shoot, the head keeper will usually gather together a regular and reliable team of beaters which he will use throughout the season. It is usual for the beaters to be paid for their efforts, and they thoroughly deserve and earn their wages. A day's beating will involve walking several miles over difficult terrain and through dense undergrowth in winter weather conditions, and a good team of beaters

should earn the gratitude of all the guns for the sport they have provided.

Many shoots hold an informal beaters' day at the end of the season, and on these occasions the beaters and guns change roles. It is a time when the guns come to realize just what efforts the beaters have made throughout the season, and a chance for the beaters to prove they can shoot as well (or better) than the guns. A day's beating offers an enjoyable day in good company, whilst participating in the healthy exercise of a countryside sport.

Belted Case   'Magnum' rifle calibres are generally identified as those firing bullets at an appreciably higher velocity than standard for the bullet weight and bore diameter. By way of comparison, a .244 Holland Magnum fires a 100 grain bullet at 3,500 fps, while a standard .243 Win. generates only 3,000 fps with the same bullet weight. The Magnum cartridge therefore has to contain more powder and generate far higher pressure on firing in order to achieve its performance. Under these conditions there is an increased risk of the cartridge case splitting around its base, thereby causing a nasty blow-back into the shooter's face.

In order to prevent this the 'belted case' was devised, in which there is a belt of additional brass around the cartridge base. This in effect serves two purposes: it reinforces the cartridge case in an area where there are very high stresses, and it assists in reducing the headspace between the cartridge, the chamber and the bolt. This reduction in free play also cuts down on the stress put on the cartridge case when it is fired.

When a bird is flushed the line stands

A well-ordered line of beaters is essential to the success of a driven shoot

Beretta Beretta, based in Brescia, are one of the oldest established firearms manufacturers in Italy. Their traditions go back over four hundred years and they are probably the best-known of all the Italian gunmakers. They now produce a wide range of military, competition and sporting guns.

Like many other arms manufacturers in Southern Europe they gear their products to the taste of the overseas market, thus most of their side-by-side shotguns available in Britain are contoured to the English style of weapon with concave ribs and straight stocks. Both their boxlock Model 626 and sidelock 627 are available in a variety of grades, and those on the top of the range have detailed and finely executed engraving on the action and lock plates. Both models are available fitted with single selective triggers rather than the more normal double trigger. Although styled on the lines of a game gun, these shotguns are proof tested to 1,200 kg/cm². which allows the use of the semi-magnum cartridges, if need be. Beretta take great care in their selection of raw materials and the use of stainless steel for the firing pins, and tri-alloy steel for barrels has only enhanced their world-wide reputation.

In the British Isles it is the over-and-under shotguns produced by this firm that have received most popular acclaim. Unlike other competitors, Beretta have been careful to keep the weight of these shotguns down to around 6¾ lbs which, for an over-and-under, is a lightweight gun. The basic boxlock model is the 686, and the range available rises to the luxury sideplated Model 687EELL. They are all equipped with single-trigger mechanism and full-pistol-grip stocks. In addition the barrels may be fitted with Beretta's system of interchangeable choke tubes which are unobtrusive and flush fitting. This reliable system further increases their versatility as sporting guns. Within this range the 20-bore edition has received wide acclaim.

Of the true sidelock models, the Beretta SO series are high-quality and elegant weapons, and can be engraved to the customer's individual requirements.

Beretta have recently produced both boxlock and sidelock over-and-under express rifles, designated the Model 689 and 550 respectively, in a variety of calibres up to the 9.3×74 and these have been received favourably by the European battue shooters for their fast handling and accuracy.

The Beretta 627 EELL Grouse Gun. Only ten guns of this model have been made

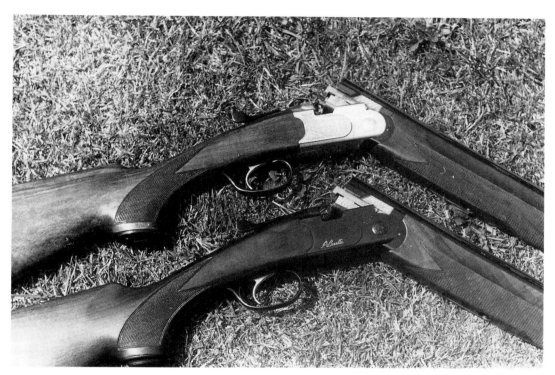

Two boxlock over-and-under 20 bores by Beretta – light and fast-handling game guns

In their sporting-guns category comes the Model 302 gas-operated semi-automatic shotgun. The action is proved to accept 3-inch magnum cartridges. One can buy interchangeable barrels proofed and chambered for the 70 mm or 2¾ inch magnum or interchangeable barrels proofed and chambered for 76-mm or 3-inch magnum loads.

Beretta also produce a range of competition shotguns that may equally be used for sporting purposes, although they tend to be heavier than the sporting range. All are hard-wearing and good-looking weapons that contribute to Beretta's position as one of Italy's most respected gunmakers.

Beretta semi-automatic gun

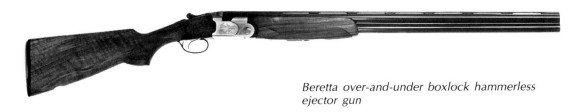

Beretta over-and-under boxlock hammerless ejector gun

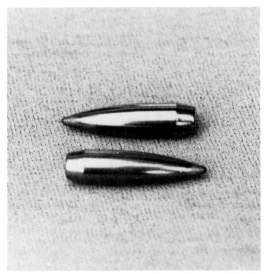

Examples of boat-tail bullets showing the rear-end taper

Bland, Thomas The gunmaking firm of Thomas Bland & Sons was founded in Birmingham in 1840. By 1872 the business had moved to London, where high-quality guns and rifles were produced. By the early twentieth century most of the crowned heads of Europe were listed as customers.

T. Clifford Bland joined the firm in 1906 and it was from this time that the name became increasingly associated with wildfowling guns. Bland improved on the various designs of punt guns and was one of the few London gunmakers to produce these guns in any quantity. The heavy shoulder guns of the wildfowler's armoury were also built and a Bland single 4 bore or double 8 was considered to be among the best wildfowling weapons between the wars. One unusual weapon developed by the company was the double 4-bore punt gun. This weapon could be wielded as a shoulder gun by a powerfully-built person but the stock was bored for a recoil rope and the two triggers were drilled to take a double lanyard so that both could be fired simultaneously.

Bland also produced a range of strong boxlock 12-bore shotguns chambered for the 3-inch cartridge and the best model was named 'Brent'. As with so many other London gunmakers, production of Bland guns ceased in the early 1960s.

Boat Tail One of the main factors that contribute to the deceleration of a bullet in flight is the drag caused by the turbulence behind the base of the bullet. The greater the surface area of the base of a bullet the greater this drag factor becomes. One theoretical way of reducing the drag is to reduce the base diameter by tapering the bullet towards its base. Ballistic tests have proved, however, that this boat-tailed bullet only gains a distinct advantage when it has decelerated to sub-sonic speeds and this, in the centrefire rounds, is well beyond its accurate range. Nevertheless, many bullet makers manufacture boat-tailed bullets and the design has a popular following among many sporting rifle users.

See also: **Bullet**

Bolt Actions   Bolt-action weapons may be single shot or repeaters. The loading cycle involves lifting the bolt handle and drawing the bolt to the rear in order to expose the breech end of the barrel. In single-shot weapons the cartridge is inserted and the bolt pushed home and closed by pulling the handle downwards. In repeaters the fresh round may be fed upwards from the magazine to be pushed home by the forward movement of the bolt. Both shotguns and rifles are built on bolt actions, but it is in rifles that this mechanism really comes into its own. Different methods of locking the bolt in the closed position have produced an action which will safely withstand very heavy chamber pressures. As a consequence, bolt-action centrefire rifles can be built in the heaviest calibres with no risk of a systems failure in normal use. Many modern bolt-action rifles use bolt designs which originated in military rifles in the early part of this century. Thus the Mauser action, the Springfield action and to some extent the Lee-Enfield action are still in regular use in sporting rifles. Newer designs have evolved in the Finnish Sako and the American Wetherby bolt actions, and these perpetuate the reputation for strength and reliability that was established by the military bolt actions.

Bolt-action weapons feature a positive lock-up of the cartridge in the breech, and the headspace is kept to a minimum. This produces outstanding accuracy in most rifle calibres, and it is therefore not surprising that most full-bore competition rifles are built on bolt actions, and bolt-action repeating sporting rifles have become the 'standard' stalking rifle in Britain.

Bolt actions for rimfire rifles range from very simple devices as fitted to the inexpensive BSA 'Sportsman' rifles produced up until the 1960s to the precision bolts fitted to such rifles as the Anschütz and Ruger rimfire rifles. Like centrefire rifles, rimfire bolt-action rifles possess great potential accuracy and are fine hunting weapons. Bolt-action shotguns are robust weapons which do not, however, command the same popularity as other shotgun designs. The main criticism, which can also be applied to rifles, is that the reloading cycle is slower than in autoloading, pump-action and lever-action repeaters. Nevertheless, I once saw a friend shoot a left-and-right at driven partridge using a bolt-action .410 repeater! In rifle sports the slowness of the reloading cycle is more than compensated for by the potential accuracy of the first shot.

See also: **Mannlicher**

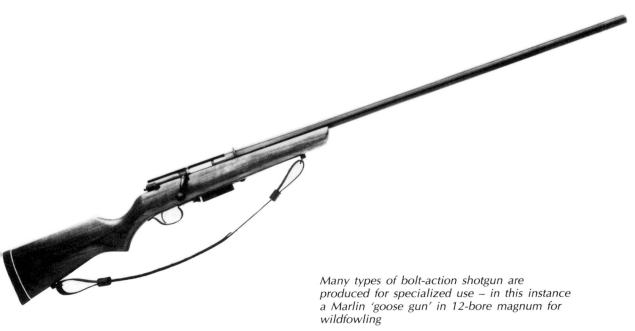

Many types of bolt-action shotgun are produced for specialized use – in this instance a Marlin 'goose gun' in 12-bore magnum for wildfowling

Bore The bore of a firearm is the measure of the interior diameter of its barrel. There is, however, a difference in the way that the term is applied to rifles and shotguns.

In rifles it is usually a direct measurement of the internal diameter of the barrel measured in inches or millimetres. Thus a .22 rimfire rifle has a bore of .22 inches, a 7-mm Remington Magnum rifle has a 7-mm bore diameter. However, the exact bore dimensions may be the same for many different calibres and each calibre is then differentiated by the last figure in its name. For example, the .220 Swift, .22/250 Remington and .222 Remington all have the same bore diameter but very different performances. Calibres with 6-mm bore diameter include the .243 Winchester, the .244 and 6-mm Rem., and the .244 Holland Magnum – for each of these the bore diameter is a constant 6 mm. Going up the scale of rifle calibres there is an enormous variety of .30 cartridges and the big-game rifles extend up to the giant Holland .700 Nitro Express.

A mixed bag of cartridges from .410 to 4 bore including 28, 20, 16, 12, 10 and 8 bore

A double 4-bore heavy rifle firing a 4-oz projectile from each barrel

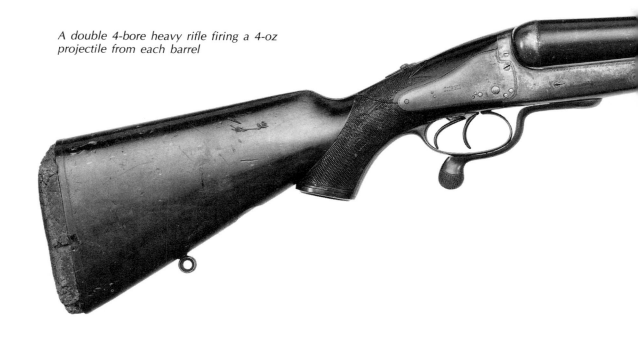

In shotguns, and early rifles which fired spherical balls, the word 'bore' is used in a different way. The weapon was designated by the number of lead balls making up one pound in weight that exactly fitted its barrel. Thus a weapon that fired a lead ball weighing 4 oz would be called a 4 bore (i.e., 4 to a pound). A 12 bore fired a ball weighing $\frac{1}{12}$ of a pound, and a 16 bore fired a ball weighing one oz.

This method of shotgun calibre classification is now used throughout the range of sizes with the exception of the smallest, which revert to the measurement system. Thus the .410 shotgun has a bore diameter of .410 inch and the 9 mm (.360 inch) is a shotgun of that bore diameter.

See also: **Calibre – Shotgun**

Boss & Co. Boss & Co. (Gunmakers) are based in Dover St, London, and are ranked alongside Purdey and Holland & Holland as one of England's premier gunmakers. The company was founded in 1812 by a Thomas Boss, a gunmaker with links to Joseph Manton. Using experience gained with Manton, Boss soon built a reputation for building fine-quality guns. In 1894 Boss was the first gun-maker to develop and market a single-trigger mechanism for a double-barrelled weapon.

Boss & Co. have concentrated all their efforts, throughout the history of the firm, on producing only the finest hand-built guns and they can accurately claim that they have never made a 'second-grade' gun.

As a company, they have concentrated on shotgun production and, although they are still producing fine over-and-under guns to their original design, the bulk of their production is in side-by-sides.

Like the other bespoke gunmakers, Boss & Co. will only build guns to specific order and the time taken to complete each gun may extend beyond two years from the date of the order. Nevertheless, skilled work has never been sacrificed to speed, and a Boss shotgun is today ranked as being one of the world's best.

Double side-by-side shotguns in 12 and 20 bore to show the relative difference in diameters

The Gunmark Kestrel is typical of the lower-priced but reliable boxlock shotguns produced in Spain

Boxlock The simplest and perhaps the most robust of the various actions fitted to double barrel shotguns and rifles. A gun fitted with a boxlock action is usually identifiable by the metal of the mechanism joining the stock in a vertical line just behind the standing breech and in line with the central spindle of the top lever. Thus all the moving parts are 'boxed in' under the barrel flats and the breech. The majority of double side-by-side shotguns are produced on the boxlock action, a mechanism which was first produced in 1873 and which has seen little modification since.

See also: **Anson & Deeley**

Brennecke The Brennecke projectile is a single 'rifled slug' which is fired through a shotgun. Brennecke slugs have a series of angled fins on their leading edge which imparts a spin to the projectile when it leaves the barrel. This spin helps to improve accuracy over short distances, and the Brennecke slug is perhaps the most accurate of all the rifled slug designs.

See also: **Rifled slug**

The Brennecke rifled slug can achieve remarkable accuracy in some shotguns

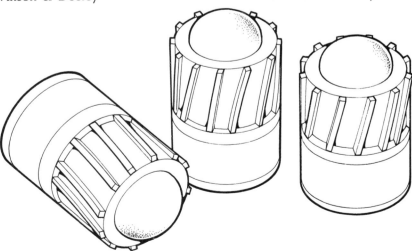

British Association for Shooting and Conservation (BASC)   As early as 1908, Stanley Duncan, a wildfowler on the Humber estuary, became aware of the growing threats to wildfowl and their habitats, and his concern for these prompted him to establish a nationwide association for wildfowlers. Thus the Wildfowlers Association of Great Britain and Ireland (WAGBI) came into being. From its establishment up to the early 1950s WAGBI remained a rather low-key organization, successfully representing the wildfowlers of these countries.

During the 1950s, however, shooting sports were threatened not only by loss of countryside and coastline environments but also by the growing strength of the anti-shooting and anti-field-sports organizations. In order to stem this tide WAGBI embarked on a campaign to recruit a wider section of the shooting public on the premise that the association's strength lay in a large membership. The title WAGBI was first added to with the words 'for Wildfowling and Rough Shooting' but this was later dropped in favour of 'WAGBI – for Shooting and Conservation'. The voice of the association was further enhanced with the incorporation of the Gamekeepers Association of the United Kingdom.

Under the driving force of their director, John Anderton, the title was formally changed in 1981 to the British Association for Shooting and Conservation (BASC), taking under its representative umbrella all those who take part in live-quarry shooting. Membership increased rapidly and in 1991 stood at 110,000.

From its roots as a low-key organization representing a minority shooting sport, BASC has now evolved into a body of high international repute and is a powerful voice for the shooter within Britain. The work carried out by the association reflects the wide variety of shooting sports this country has to offer. The BASC now has national headquarters in North Wales and a number of regional offices covering the entire country (see address below). The national headquarters is the nerve centre of an extremely complex and efficient organization.

A separate department handles all matters concerned with conservation and research, working jointly with other interested bodies

The BASC logo depicts a dog, goose and pheasant

and co-funding various research projects on quarry species and their habitats. The spin-offs to members from the activities of this department include an advisory service in land management for game species, quarry population statistics, and conservation planning.

Another department handles national and international affairs, monitoring the activities in both the British and European parliaments which may affect shooting sports, and acting as the voice of the shooting person in any discussions on these matters. The activities of this department play a vital part. in safeguarding the future of shooting sports.

There are specialized staff who concern themselves with firearms and the law, deer, the press and public relations, and education and shooter training and regional development. The firearms department acts as a helpline for any shooter who encounters difficulties over legislation and certification, and has even taken over-zealous police forces to task over the interpretation and implementation of firearms legislation. It also provides advice on all legal aspects of shooting, based on the Wildlife and Countryside Act and the various other acts concerning quarry species. The Deer

Committee concerns itself with all matters relating to deer and deer control and works closely with the British Deer Society to this end, while representing the growing number of deer stalkers and managers within the BASC's membership.

The education and training staff at headquarters organize a wide number of courses for the membership. Aimed primarily at the newcomer to shooting, there is a nationwide network of volunteer education officers who run the Shotgun Proficiency Award Scheme. In addition there are training courses on deer stalking, gundog training, pigeon shooting, and wildfowling, to name but a few. These are all open to members, whether new to shooting or those with more experience wishing to broaden their expertise. In addition the BASC publishes a series of 'Codes of Practice' leaflets which cover the whole spectrum of sporting shooting in Britain. These form the essential guidelines for controlled, sportsmanlike and safe shooting within this country.

With the BASC's headquarters playing such an important and central role, the regional officers have a primary task of bringing the association to the people. The regional officers therefore have a high profile at country shows and fairs. They also organize local competitions, exhibitions and roadshows devoted to the interest of the shooting public. The regional offices maintain local representation and public relations within their regions and are a channel for two-way communication between local membership issues and headquarters.

All in all, the BASC is the voice of the shooting person in Britain. Members also enjoy automatic insurance cover for all their shooting and conservation activities. I believe that insurance cover is an essential prerequisite for any activity of this type and, indeed, many landowners or shoot organizers insist upon it. The BASC represents all live-quarry shooters in Britain and as such should be supported by all who benefit from this sport.

Address: **BASC National Headquarters**
Marford Mill
Rossett
Wrexham
Clwyd
LL12 0HL

British Deer Society (BDS)   In 1963 the Deer Group of the Mammal Society of the British Isles evolved into a new and completely separate organization – the British Deer Society.

One of the main aims of the new society was to promote a wider interest and understanding of deer in Britain, their welfare and their management; and membership was made open to any who supported these aims.

The BDS now has a permanent headquarters near Reading and a number of active regional branches which cover the entire British Isles. These regional branches are virtually autonomous, organizing their own events and exhibitions in order to keep in contact with the members at 'grass-roots' level and to promote the aims of the BDS to a wider public.

The BDS logo depicts a red deer stag

Organized in this way, the national headquarters is in a position to concentrate on broader issues relating to deer, and the society performs a number of important functions. In terms of bringing deer awareness to the public, the BDS produces information packs and other audio-visual materials for use by schools and other institutions. For stalkers and deer managers, the British Deer Society has established two qualifications. The National Certificate tests the candidate's knowledge of deer and their habitats, safety in the field, the principles of deer management and shooting competence. The Advanced Stalker's Certificate takes this a stage further and covers more advanced deer management and handling techniques. The society also runs various residential courses for those wishing to broaden their expertise in many aspects of deer management at basic and advanced levels. A variety of other stalking courses are organized by branches to cover both highland (open ground) and woodland stalking.

Being a registered charity, the British Deer Society cannot get involved in the political scene, yet it is a respected voice that is consulted when legislation concerning deer is proposed, and as such it is a representative voice through which those concerned with deer can be heard.

The BDS also funds various research projects with the aim of improving our knowledge of deer behaviour, and is also a monitoring body for the effects of agrochemicals and changes in land use on deer populations. When necessary the BDS can call upon expert advisers on legal and veterinary matters and this is yet another valuable service available to members.

Since its establishment, the steady growth of the society has been aided by two factors. The Deer Act of 1963 and subsequent legislation placed deer management and control firmly in the hands of the competent stalker by outlawing the shotgun deer drives, snares and other inhumane and unselective methods of controlling deer numbers. The second factor is the virtual population explosion of the smaller deer species, roe and muntjac in particular, which has resulted in the recent colonization of many parts of Britain by these animals. The spread of these small deer and the realization that their populations must be managed in a more humane and scientific way has led to a growth in opportunities for deer stalking in many parts of the country. This has, and is continuing to happen, at such a rate that deer stalking as a shooting sport and as part of a sound management plan is a significant growth sector in field sports.

The British Deer Society recognizes this. With the interests and welfare of deer as a primary consideration, anyone who raises binoculars, camera, or rifle to deer should be a member of the BDS.

Address: **The British Deer Society (BDS)**
Beale Centre
Lower Basildon
Reading
Berks
RG8 9NH

See also: **Deer; Seasons**

The logo of the BFSS

British Field Sports Society (BFSS) The British Field Sports Society was founded in 1930 as an umbrella organization covering all field sports in the country. From the outset the main brief of the BFSS was to defend each and every type of sport from attack by the anti-sports organizations, from Parliament and, more recently, from European legislation. It is in fact the only society which represents the hunter, shooter, angler, courser and falconer, presenting a united front to those who speak against field sports.

Perhaps more than any other organization, the BFSS is politically oriented in that it maintains a strong lobby in Parliament and the society's headquarters are in London. The BFSS parliamentary committee is composed of both MPs and Peers who support its cause, and the society uses professional parliamentary consultants to brief MPs on issues which affect field sports.

Outside London the BFSS plays a very active role in bringing field sports to public attention through country sports shows and game fairs, actions which seek to put forward the logic and purpose of field sports and to counter the emotive propaganda often heard against them. Like the BASC and the BDS, the BFSS places a strong emphasis on education by expecting high standards of safety and sportsmanship from participants in all field sports and introducing 'Codes of Practice' to this end. In addition it puts valuable effort into educating the young through visits, films and publications.

Membership is open to all who shoot, fish, go coursing or hunting, or who just value the heritage of country sports. Members enjoy automatic liability insurance to £1 million and a £75,000 personal accident cover together with a wide variety of other benefits.

While the BASC represents the shooting sports and the BDS covers the interest and welfare of deer, the BFSS is the overall representative of all British country pursuits. With its strong parliamentary presence and its voice in Europe, the British Field Sports Society is worthy of all our support.

Address: **BFSS National Headquarters**
59 Kennington Rd
London
SE2 7PZ

British Shooting Sports Council (BSSC) This council was formed by the major shooting associations in conjunction with the manufacturers and importers of firearms and ammunition. It safeguards and encourages the safe and lawful use of firearms and ammunition for sporting and recreational purposes within the UK and has become recognized as the central representative body for its member associations.

Address: **The British Shooting Sports**
Council
Pentridge
Salisbury
Wilts
SP5 5QX

Brno The Zbrojovka works in Brno, Czechoslovakia, produces tractors, typewriters, machine tools and firearms. The last of these, the firearms, are marketed under the Brno trade name and exported through the Merkuria organization.

Brno have a long tradition of arms manufacture, and they gained respect in Britain for its innovations in machine-guns and other military weapons. The light machine-gun developed in Brno and adopted by the British Army became known as the Bren gun (Brno/Enfield).

The present firearms output of the Brno works concentrates exclusively on a range of sporting and competition weapons that are exported to many parts of the world. Brno shotguns, centrefire rifles and rimfire rifles are imported by Britain and some of these have quite unusual features which demonstrate the thought and care with which they are made.

The two models of shotguns to reach Britain are a plain and inexpensive sidelock side-by-side 12 bore and an over-and-under of unusual design. The sidelock side-by-side is not often seen in the shooting field. This is not a criticism of its rather robust design but more a reflection of the degree of competition it faces from 'prettier' guns from Southern Europe. The Model ZH over-and-under is different in that it has a two-piece take-down rather than the more normal three-piece. Barrels and fore-end detach from the action as one unit and the mechanism itself is of an unusual design. Rather than a fixed standing breech, as on a 'normal' drop-down shotgun, the Brno model has a sliding breech which moves to the rear on opening the gun. On closing the weapon it is locked in the forward position by a cross bolt with two extensions on the barrels. The action is a non-ejector. Although the shotgun is equipped with a double-trigger mechanism, the rear trigger will fire both barrels (as a single trigger would) if pulled twice, and the safety catch is located at the front of the trigger guard rather than on the top tang. These shotguns are manufactured to such fine tolerances that the barrel and fore-end assembly is interchangeable. It is therefore possible for a shooter to have the choice of skeet barrels with muzzle brakes, normal game-bored barrels or heavily choked and long barrels, all of which can be fitted to the same action and stock.

The ZKK series of centrefire Mauser bolt-action sporting rifles comes in three action lengths. The Model 601 short action is chambered for short cartridge calibres from .222 Rem. to .308 Win., the standard Model 600 is available in the larger calibres up to the .30–06 and the Model 602 is the long-action Magnum model for .375 H & H Magnum, .404 Jeffrey and .458 Win. Magnum. Although perhaps lacking the finish one sees in West European weapons, these are low-priced and very accurate weapons which will give years of hard service. An unusual feature of these is the little aperture sight that is housed in the rear of the action. Normally concealed, it is spring-loaded and will pop up into the line of vision at the touch of a small button. Though of little practical use in these days of efficient and reliable telescopic sights, it does nevertheless reflect the thoughtfulness that goes into the rifle's design and production.

Brno also produce rifles designed specifically for the .22 Hornet cartridge; their Model ZKW proved to be so successful that its production recommenced by popular demand. A neat and light bolt-action repeater this model was recently also made available in .222 Rem. calibre.

Of all their sporting weapons, it is perhaps for their .22 rimfire rifle production that Brno have received most popular acclaim. The Model ZKM 581 is a clip-fed auto-loading rifle weighing 5½ lbs and measuring just over 38 inches. This light and handy rifle competes on equal terms with the rather heavier products of the American manufacturers.

However, the high reputation of Brno firearms throughout the world rests on their .22 rimfire bolt-action repeater the Brno No 2 or Model ZKM 452. Whereas many rifle manufacturers look on the .22 rimfire as a 'fun gun' not to be taken seriously, and design their weapon accordingly, Brno have produced a stylish, well-finished and accurate rimfire weapon which has the appearance of a serious hunting rifle. As a hunting rimfire rifle it is Australia's best seller and probably also holds that claim in Britain. Like all Brno weapons, the Poldi steel barrel is accurately forged and resistant to erosion, the bolt is crisp and smooth in operation, and the rifle balances well. What gives this Brno rifle a great advantage over its serious competitors is its price – the rifle is barely half the price of other 'serious' rimfire hunting rifles from German or American manufacturers.

The Brno Model ZKM 452 has been in production for about thirty years and the fact that it is still in demand speaks volumes for its quality.

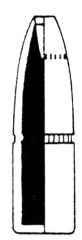

Pointed soft-point (PSP)   Hollow-point (HP)

The four main designs of hunting bullet

Bullet Many people wrongly refer to a loaded rifle cartridge as the bullet. The bullet is only the part of a rifle's cartridge which is fired along an anticipated trajectory to hit a target.

To be effective against live quarry, i.e., to achieve a quick and humane kill, a bullet must conform to a certain set of requirements. Firstly the bullet must be able to penetrate deep into the body cavity of the quarry concerned; then it must expand or deform in order to create the maximum amount of damage to the internal organs. The kinetic energy of the bullet in flight would then be released into the quarry in the form of shock.

Additionally, the bullet must be able to perform these functions over the whole of its effective or accurate range. A deer, for instance, should sustain the same amount of body damage at 250 yards as it would at 10 yards, even though the bullet at the longer range may be travelling considerably slower than at the closer range.

When one considers the wide range of quarry species that are hunted, from rats at one extreme to elephant at the other, it becomes clear that these requirements could not possibly be fulfilled one bullet design. Therefore, bullets are constructed in a variety of ways in order to achieve the required

penetration and expansion throughout the range of species.

Bullets for the rimfire rifles and for some of the low-velocity centrefire calibres fall into two main types. At the low velocities generated in this group (mostly below 1,500 fps at the muzzle) frictional heat on the surface of the bullet as it travels up the barrel is not really significant. As a consequence the bullets are generally made of lead, with occasionally a thin coating of soft copper. These low-velocity bullets are most frequently made in solid- or hollow-point form. The solid bullet has the advantage of more consistent accuracy and deep penetration, but when one considers the size of the quarry hunted with these weapons the latter is not an important requirement. Set against this is the solid's reluctance to deform on impact and its propensity to ricochet even after passing through, for instance, a rabbit and one can conclude that it is not a good hunting bullet.

The hollow point is a far better proposition. Constructed in such a way that the front section of the bullet is hollow, and having a hole at the tip, it deforms easily on impact, with the solid base allowing sufficient penetration to inflict far greater internal damage on small quarry. It is also a safer round to use in the field as its ability to deform means

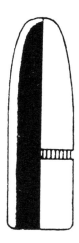

Full metal jacket (FMJ)

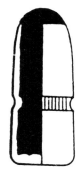

Round nose

that ricochets are far less likely to 'bounce' around the countryside. As to its disadvantages, being lighter than its solid counterpart it sheds velocity more rapidly and is somewhat less accurate, although for hunting purposes the difference is insignificant. An expanding bullet, though, means more meat damage to edible quarry, but this can be compensated for by accurate placement of the shot. These slight disadvantages do not diminish the effectiveness of the hollow-point bullet for hunting small game and vermin.

The medium- and high-velocity centrefire rifles generate far higher frictional heat on the bullet's surface when it passes through the barrel. A lead bullet would melt in contact with the barrel wall, leaving a fine lead coating in the bore and making the bullet's trajectory very unpredictable! Bullets for these calibres therefore have to have some form of outer casing or jacket of harder metal to protect the lead. The most frequently used material for this purpose is called gilding metal. Varying the thickness and extent of this jacket produces a variety of bullet types with different expansion and penetration characteristics.

Where deep penetration is essential, the bullet is entirely enclosed in the jacket except for the base. This is known as the Full

Metal Jacket (FMJ) and, when used in large-calibre rifles, heavy bullets of this design will penetrate deeply into tough-skinned game and are even capable of going through six inches of bone. The release of energy and resulting shock has been known as the 'knock-down' effect and is essential when taking on dangerous game at close quarters. Expansion of the FMJ bullet is negligible, and it relies for its effectiveness on the enormous dissipation of energy during its passage into the animal. For lighter-skinned game – even the largest antelope – the FMJ is far less efficient, as it will penetrate and pass clean through the beast without deformation. The internal wound is therefore smaller and the animal is less likely to suffer the catastrophic internal damage which brings about instantaneous death.

For these animals (and here I would include the British deer species) a lighter bullet is required. By maintaining jacket thickness at the bullet's base, but reducing it progressively towards the front with the jacket ending just before the point, a 'soft point' (SP) bullet is created. Here the lead point of the bullet is exposed at the front end. This effectively means that the front end will break up on impact and the heavy base will ensure good penetration by the deformed projectile.

For soft-skinned game of deer size and upwards this is the ideal hunting round. Penetration by the rear section of the bullet is good and the front-end deformation makes for rapid destruction of the internal organs.

Partition bullets extend this idea further in that the delicate front section of the bullet is separated from a solid base by a partition of some other metal, and other devices have been designed in order to ensure rapid expansion of the front end. Hollow-point bullets are also available in this category, and 'cone points' actually have an insert in the nose of the bullet which drives a wedge into the front section on impact, thereby aiding the break-up.

If one assumes that the soft-point, partition, hollow-point and cone-point bullets are the correct choice for deer and other soft-skinned game, one should also note that bullet weight is important. A very light bullet of this type travelling at high velocity can, if it meets the bone of a shoulder blade, burst and bounce off. Penetration is not achieved and the animal suffers a horrible surface wound which is itself not fatal. The light and very-high-velocity bullets of a .220 Swift or .22/250 Rem. have been known to bounce off animals as small as roe deer in this way.

At the opposite end to the FMJ on the scale of bullet construction is the 'varmint' bullet. This is usually of small calibre and light in weight, the centrefire .22 having an average bullet weight of 50 grains. Very light in construction, the thin jacket and open end ensure that this bullet will virtually explode on hitting anything. For long-range fox shooting in Britain or 'varminting' in America this are ideal. Instantaneous expansion on contact also makes it a very safe round to use, far safer than the .22 rimfire, as ricochets are virtually non-existent.

As the construction of the bullet affects its powers of penetration and disruption, so the shape of the bullet affects its trajectory and its long-range capability. Round-nosed bullets are essentially for short-range work. Their advantage is that the increased frontal surface area of the bullet provides a greater impact shock and their shape makes them less likely to be upset when passing through light foliage. Thus they are known as 'brush-busting' bullets in America, where they are frequently used in the low- to medium-power lever-action calibres. Lacking a point, they are also less likely to ignite each other when jostled end to end in the tubular magazines of these rifles. The heavy African calibres such as the .458 Win. and .470 also use round-nose FMJ bullets for close-range work against dangerous game in thick cover. Again, their resistance to deflection by undergrowth is a distinct advantage. The rounded shape, however, means that they have a relatively high wind resistance and their velocity is shed more rapidly than a corresponding more streamlined shape, and this does tend to restrict them to ranges below 100 yards.

For longer ranges a more streamlined shape is required: the pointed or semi-pointed bullet. These are accurate over ranges up to 400 yards in some calibres and are by far the most frequently used bullet shape. Also known as 'Spitzer' bullets, their advantage lies in long-range accuracy but the disadvantage is that they are more susceptible to wind drift. An accurate shooter would therefore compensate for this when shooting over distance. In addition they are far more likely to be deflected when passing through foliage, and this can produce a clean miss or a poorly-hit animal even at close range.

I have so far concentrated on the shape of the front end of the bullet, as the base is almost uniformly cut off as a flat or slightly concave surface. Research has shown that it is the turbulence behind the bullet's base that has the greatest effect in slowing the projectile down in flight, and the larger the diameter of the base, the greater drag effect. This research led to the development of the 'boat-tailed' bullet in which the base tapers to leave a smaller flat area. While the boat tail does reduce drag, the degree of reduction only becomes marked when the bullet falls into subsonic velocities – usually far beyond its accurate range.

The Brennecke bullet takes the boat-tailed concept a stage further in that the base is actually conical. Its ballistics differ little from those of standard-based bullets but, like all other bullet designs, it has its own supporters among sportsmen who swear by its performance.

See also: **Boat Tail; Brennecke**

Calibres – Rifle The table overleaf shows a selection of the most popular rifle calibres and these have been categorized into six groups. In terms of British sporting rifle shooting, groups 5 and 6 are of little importance. The great majority of rifle sport in the British Isles is confined to vermin control using rimfires (group 1), fox shooting and, in Scotland, roe stalking with the .22 centrefires (group 2) or deer stalking using the group-3 rifles. For red deer, some stalkers opt for calibres that come into group 4.

The table is based on the average performance for each calibre and does not relate to any one brand of ammunition.

Bullet weights are given in grains.

Popular deer stalking calibres (left to right): .22 LR (for comparison only), .243 Win., .308 Win., 7×57, .270 Win., 30.06

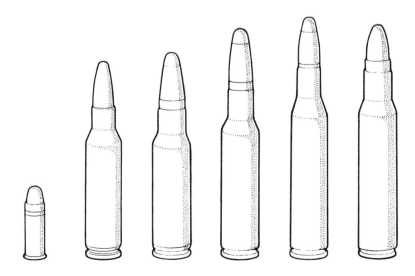

Group 1 The Rimfires					
Name	**Bullet Weight***	**Velocity fps** Muzzle 100 yards		**Energy ft/lb** Muzzle 100 yards	
.22 Short Hp	27	1125	900	74	48
.22 Short solid	29	1090	900	76	51
.22 Long Rifle HVHP	36	1285	1008	130	80
.22 Long Rifle Subsonic HP	36	1050	872	90	62
.22 Hyper Velocity	32	1550	1090	170	87
.22 WRF Magnum	40	2000	1390	255	170
GROUP 2 The .22 Centrefires					
.17 Remington	25	4020	3290	900	600
.22 Hornet	45	2690	2030	720	420
.222 Remington	50	3200	2660	1140	785
.223 Remington	55	3300	2800	1330	955
.22–250 Remington	55	3810	3330	1770	1360
.220 Swift	48	4111	3610	1877	1448
5.6 × 57 RWS (.224)	74	3410	3050	1910	1530
GROUP 3 Deer Calibres					
.243 Winchester	100	3070	2790	2093	1729
6mm Remington	100	3190	2920	2260	1890
.25–06 Remington	120	3120	2850	2590	2160
.257 Roberts	100	2900	2540	1870	1430
7 × 57 Mauser (.275 Rigby)	150	2756	2539	2530	2148
.270 Winchester	130	3110	2850	2800	2390
.280 Remington	150	2990	2670	2800	2370
.303 British	150	2720	2440	2465	1983
.308 Winchester	150	2860	2570	2725	2220
.30–06 Springfield	180	2700	2494	2914	2485

* Bullet weight measured in grains

Table of the most popular rifle calibres

Name	Bullet Weight	Velocity fps Muzzle 100 yards		Energy ft/lb Muzzle 100 yards	
Group 4 The Medium Magnums					
.244 H & H Magnum	100	3500	3230	2725	2320
7mm Remington Magnum	150	3260	2970	3540	2945
6.5 × 68 mm	93	3937	3389	3183	2360
.300 H & H (Super 30)	150	3190	2870	3390	2740
.300 Winchester Magnum	180	3070	2859	3770	3250
8 × 68 mm	185	3080	2761	3896	3132
.338 Winchester Magnum	200	3000	2690	4000	3210
GROUP 5 The Heavy Calibres					
.358 Norma Magnum	250	2790	2493	4322	3451
9.3 × 74mm	285	2365	2260	3530	2578
.375 H & H Magnum	300	2530	2140	4330	3450
.404 Jeffrey	300	2600	2360	4500	4250
.416 Rigby	410	2350	2150	5010	4250
.425 Westley Richards	410	2350	2120	5010	4100
.458 Winchester Magnum	500	2130	1910	5040	4050
.470	500	2125	1910	5030	4060
.500 Nitro	570	2125	1880	5730	4490
.505 Gibbs	525	2300	2020	6180	4760
.577 Nitro	750	2050	1730	7020	5000
.600 Nitro	900	1950	1690	7610	5720
.460 Weatherby Magnum	500	2700	2330	8095	6025
GROUP 6 The Brush Calibres					
25–20 Winchester	86	1460	1180	405	265
32–20 Winchester	100	1290	1060	370	250
30–30 Winchester	150	2410	1960	1930	1280
44–40 Winchester	200	1310	1050	760	490
.444 Marlin	240	2400	1845	3070	1815
45–70 Government	405	1320	1160	1570	1210

Comparison of shotgun cartridges (left to right):
.410, 28, 20, 16, 12, 10, 10 magnum, 8,
4-bore cartridges

Calibres – Shotgun Although in the past there were devotees of the 14-, 24-, and 32- bore guns among the ranks of shotgun shooters, nowadays there are nine shotgun calibres in general use in Britain. Of these the three largest, the 4, 8, and 10 bores, are specialist wildfowling guns seen only in the hands of dedicated foreshore shooters waiting for wild geese in the half-light of icy January dawns. They are heavy and powerful shotguns that encourage restraint due to the cost and scarcity of ammunition.

At the other end of the scale of shotgun calibres, the two smallest, the .360 (9 mm) and the .410 are generally considered to be useful as close-range vermin weapons, and certainly the very small shot charge of the 9-mm garden gun puts a considerable restriction on its effectiveness. The .410, on the other hand, can be a very handy weapon for grey squirrels, bolted rabbits, and even decoyed pigeons if the chamber allows 2½- inch or 3-inch cartridges to be used.

The remaining calibres, from 28 bore, through 20 and 16, to 12 bore, are the general-purpose game and rough shooting calibres. The 12 bore is by far the most versatile, the 3-inch magnum being hailed as the wild-fowlers' 'maid of all work' while the 2½- inch-calibred game gun is considered the standard game gun for all forms of sporting shooting.

The table below gives standard dimensions, chamber lengths and shot loads for all nine calibres.

See also: **Game Guns; Vermin Shooting – Weapons; Wildfowling Guns**

Gauge or Bore	Bore Diameter (in)	Chamber Length (in)	Standard Shot Load (oz)
4	1.052	4	3¼
8	.873	4¼ 3½	2½ 2⅛
10	.775	3½ 2⅞	2 1⁷/₁₆
12	.729	3 magnum 2½ 2	1⅝ 1¹/₁₆ ⅞
16	.662	2½	¹⁵/₁₆
20	.615	3 2½	1 ¹³/₁₆
28	.550	2½	⁹/₁₆
.410	.410	3 2½ 2	⅞ ⅜ ⁵/₁₆
.360 (9 mm)	.360	1¾	³/₁₆

Data chart of the different shotgun calibres

Canada Goose It would be very difficult to misidentify a Canada goose (*Branta canadensis*). With an overall length of up to 40 inches and weighing up to 12 lbs, it is the largest British wildfowl quarry. Both at rest and in flight the black head and neck are distinctive and the bold white chin and cheek patch are visible at a considerable distance. Apart from these features the goose is a large brown-grey bird with a darker back, white tail coverts bordered in black, and paler flanks. No other goose comes anywhere near the size of a Canada, and both young and adults have similar plumage and are virtually indistinguishable in the field. On land the Canada has a slightly more upright stance than the grey goose, but this is perhaps accentuated by its relatively long neck. This species is vocal in flight and its characteristic call is a loud, trumpeting honk, although it has a wide variety of other 'conversation' calls.

The Canada goose is not a native British species, the first specimens being introduced in the seventeenth century. The early introductions on ornamental lakes proved successful and a feral population was soon established. Subsequently birds were released in many parts of the country in the hope that they would develop the strong migratory habits they have in America. The Canada goose, however, preferred the non-migratory life in Britain and even now, two hundred years after the first introductions, only one pocket of these birds in Yorkshire has developed a moult migration to Scotland.

Nowadays feral Canada geese may be found on any open fresh water in most parts of England and their spread continues into Wales and Scotland. Indeed so successful are these birds that in some areas their numbers have increased to the extent that they do significant damage by feeding on arable crops close to their home water.

The Canada goose is an agile bird in the water and a strong walker on land. Its reluctance to fly may be seen by the fact that it will walk to its feeding field if there are no serious obstacles in its way. When on the wing, however, it is a strong and direct flier and flocks will readily form into the characteristic 'V' formation when flying any distance. The Canada goose is predominantly a grazing bird, although it will supplement its diet with insect food during the summer. It will also feed on the water margins and 'up-ends' more frequently than other goose to feed on aquatic vegetation.

During the breeding season the Canada goose can be quite aggressive but at other times of the year it is gregarious and will readily respond to decoys and calling. Even when moving long distances, Canada geese in Britain fly low on deep and powerful wingbeats and, even though they may be tame on the local park lake, when on the wing they are wary and wild.

The only other species that resemble the Canada goose in colouring are the brent goose and the barnacle goose. Both are protected, both are considerably smaller, both have very different patterns of black and white, and both are saltwater birds. The Canada goose, on the other hand, is very much a freshwater species and may feature in any inland shooter's bag. A well-prepared Canada goose makes an excellent substitute for a Christmas turkey!

The Canada goose is now firmly established in many parts of Britain

A cannelured hollow-point centrefire rifle bullet. In this instance the cannelure is used to gauge the depth of the bullet's seating in the cartridge case

Cannelure   Some rifle bullets appear to have a knurled ring or channel around the circumference of the thick section. This is known as the cannelure and serves to identify the bullet manufacturer, and differentiates between bullets of the same weight and calibre.

Otherwise, in centrefire cartridges cannelure serves little purpose, although some manufacturers claim that it helps the bullet to take the rifling and also helps to speed the break-up when hits a target.

In some .22 rimfire ammunition the cannelure may contain grease, wax, or other bullet lubricant which helps to prevent lead fouling in the barrel.

Capercaillie   The capercaillie (*Tetrao urogallus*) is the largest of Britain's game birds. The cock bird measures up to thirty-six inches in length and may weigh up to twelve pounds. The female, though still large, is considerably smaller than the male and measures only about twenty-five inches. Like the black grouse there is a considerable difference in the appearance of the sexes. The cock 'caper' has an overall grey-black glossy plumage with a blue-green iridescence on the breast. The outline is also quite distinctive as the tail appears rather long and broadly rounded. As well as size, this helps to distinguish this bird from the blackcock, and the underparts of the caper may be boldly marked with white flecks. The overall colour of the hen bird is a deep rich brown, and at close quarters the black, grey and cream mottling is visible. The upper surface of the hen's rufous tail is strongly barred with black, a useful identification feature. There is a corresponding rufous patch on the breast which contrasts with light brown underparts. Young birds of this species resemble the adult hen's plumage.

The capercaillie is a quiet bird outside the breeding season but the female's single crow may be heard when the birds are flushed. During the spring the male adopts an elaborate display, with fanned tail and drooping wings, which has led it to be nicknamed the 'European turkey'. At this time of year the male's voice includes a complicated and varied number of percussion-like sounds.

The caper's habitat is mature pine forest in upland areas, and it is generally thought that the species became extinct in Scotland in the eighteenth century as the ancient forests were cleared. It was reintroduced into Tayside in 1837 using stock birds from Sweden, and a number of subsequent introductions are based on the success of these original birds. Nowadays this large grouse is rapidly extending its range in much of Highland Scotland and it is now firmly re-established as a British quarry species.

Its preferred habitat includes areas of dense tree cover interspersed with patches of thick undergrowth and open ground. Though largely sedentary, the young males may disperse during the winter in search of unoccupied territory.

From spring through to autumn it is mainly a ground-dwelling bird, resting in dense scrub and feeding mainly on ground-level vegetation. In the winter capercaillie often spend most of their time in trees feeding on conifer buds.

For such a large bird the capercaillie's flight is unusually and deceptively quick, and when flushed it will tend to fly among the treetops rather than above tree level. This weaving flight makes it a testing target but, like many other game birds, it rarely travels far. Its take-off is very noisy but its flight is surprisingly quiet.

Driven caper shooting is becoming an

established activity on a number of Highland estates, not only for the sport it provides but also to keep capercaillie numbers in check – overpopulation can cause quite considerable damage to conifer plantations. In addition, a capercaillie and black grouse drive may be incorporated into a day's grouse shooting to add variety to the sport. The capercaillie in Britain is regarded as a quarry species for the shotgun shooter and this contrasts with many European countries where the cock caper is considered to be a 'rifle trophy', to be stalked much in the same way as deer.

The capercaillie's large size makes it easy to distinguish from any other game bird species in Britain.

See also: **Driven Game Shooting**

Cartwheel   Not a frequent occurrence in these days of shotgun cartridges with crimped closures, the cartwheel pattern was thrown occasionally by the older rolled-turnover type of cartridge. The characteristics of such a pattern were thought to be produced by the over-shot wad in a rolled-turnover cartridge obstructing or deflecting the central portion of the shot charge a short distance from the muzzle. This, at 40 yards, produced a pattern with a relatively dense edge and an empty centre. A bird could often fly straight through the centre of the cartwheel unscathed. Cartwheeling did not happen very often in reliable cartridges but it was frequently blamed for inexplicable missed shots!

Paradox guns, with the ends of their barrels taking a rifling twist, also had a tendency to throw cartwheel patterns as these gave a slow spin to the shot charge before it left the barrel – this happened regardless of the type of closure used on the cartridge.

With the advent of crimp closures on shotgun cartridges, cartwheel patterns became a thing of the past.

Census – Deer   A deer census serves to ascertain the numbers of deer on a particular area of land. A census involves spending some time in organizing a number of people so that they can move deer from concealment to a place where they may be observed and counted. This activity is usually carried out in late February or March when the ground vegetation is at a minimum.

It is the estimates gained from the annual deer census that the stalker or deer manager uses to work out an annual cull plan in order to minimize damage to agricultural and woodland crops and to maintain a healthy breeding stock of deer.

See also: **Deer; Deer management; Stalking – Highland; Deer Stalking – Woodland**

Centrefire   By far the most frequently used ignition system for shotgun and rifle cartridges is one in which the ignition cap is placed centrally in the base of the cartridge case. This is known as the centrefire system. In order to appreciate its inherent advantages it is perhaps useful to refer to the other ignition systems which have at one time or another competed with it.

From the end of the muzzle-loading days in the late nineteenth century, numerous breech-loading ignition systems arose. These included the Lancaster 'basefire' system, the pinfire and the needle gun. Though each one was an improvement on the percussion muzzle-loading weapon in terms of convenience, ease of loading and rate of fire, either the cartridge or the gun's mechanism contained design faults which rendered the system less than ideal. In many ways the success of the centrefire system can be attributed to the failure of George Daw to patent it. Thus it was readily adopted by many gunmakers and quickly superseded all other ignition systems, except perhaps the low-powered rimfires which also appeared at about the same time.

The advantage of a tight-fitting cap placed centrally in the base of the cartridge were numerous. The cartridge could be inserted into the breech with no need to align it, as in the pinfire. The flush-fitting cap meant that the ammunition could be safely carried in bulk and could stand far more rough treatment than, for example, the basefire devised by Lancaster. With the cap placed centrally in the cartridge base this potential 'weak spot' on the cartridge was in the safest possible location when the gun was fired – flat against the centre of the standing breech.

This increased safety factor allowed the centrefire cartridge to develop more power and the efficient shotgun cartridge on the centrefire system quickly gained acceptance in a variety of standardized calibres.

The centrefire rifle cartridge, like its shotgun counterpart, possessed a far greater strength and safety margin than its competing rimfire, and, as all but one of the rimfire rifle calibres fell into disuse, the centrefire rifle dominated the shooting field. The changes from black powder through cordite to the new 'nitro' powders also saw the development of the 'necked' cartridge case, which had a vastly increased powder capacity in relation to the bullet diameter and weight. The modern high-velocity rifle was born.

The centrefire ignition system is now so dominant that it never appears in any calibre designation – unless the rimfire system is specified (as in .22 Winchester Magnum Rimfire) it is assumed that the calibre uses the centrefire ignition system.

Chamber   On a breech-loading firearm, the chamber is the internal bore at the breech end of the barrel. The chamber is enlarged so that a cartridge of the correct size and calibre can be loaded into the barrel.

In shotguns and rimfire rifles the degree of enlargement is determined by the thickness of the cartridge wall and consequently the chamber diameter is not very much greater than the bore diameter of the barrel. The chamber of a centrefire rifle, on the other hand, usually has to accommodate the 'bottle-necked' cartridge case and this entails a far greater degree of enlargement. In addition, many centrefire rifle cartridges taper from the base towards the shoulder and the dimensions of the chamber have to reflect this to quite a fine tolerance to prevent a bulged or split case.

The normal shotgun and rimfire chamber is parallel, tapering at the front end to the true bore diameter. This taper is known as the chamber cone and it allows a smooth transfer of the shot charge or the bullet from the cartridge into the base of the barrel when the propellant powder is ignited. Some time ago there were a small number of 'chamberless' shotguns made, mostly in the large wildfowling calibres and notably in 8 bore. These were designed to use very thin-walled brass-cased cartridges and although they did achieve some popularity they are now obsolete. The main difficulty with a chamberless 8 bore was that it produced poor obturation and inferior ballistics with 'normal' paper-cased cartridges.

Most firearms have extractors and chamfers cut into the breech end of the chamber in order to facilitate the removal of the cartridge.

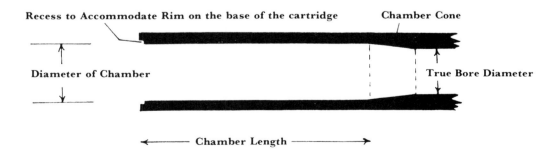

Cross-section of a shotgun's chamber

*Different types of chequering. Left: standard.
Right: skip-line*

Chequering   Chequering is the method used to enhance the shooter's grip on the stock and fore-end of a weapon. To do this, intersecting parallel grooves are cut into the surface of the stock where the hands will be placed when the gun is mounted to the shoulder. The resulting chequering may be cut by hand or impressed by machine but it is the former method which produces the more lasting and better grip. The degree of fineness of the grooves is measured in lines per inch. Very fine chequering tends to be less effective as the grooves very quickly fill with dirt and oil – too coarse a cut and the chequering can look unsightly.

Normal chequering in which two systems of grooves intersect each other at a fixed angle results in a surface composed of small diamond-shaped highs separated by cut grooves. Sometimes the regularity of the parallel cuts are interrupted to produce 'skip line' chequering, which leaves a pattern of larger diamonds between the lines of chequering.

In recent years a number of weapons have appeared with 'Lazer' chequering. This process, pioneered by Weatherby in the USA, cuts the wood to produce a 'stipple' finish.

The roughened timber enhances the grip much in the same way as the more traditional chequering but has the advantage of enabling far more artistic patterns to be produced on the stock.

The Chinese water deer is the only antlerless species living wild in Britain

Chinese Water Deer The Chinese water deer (*Hydropotes inermis*) is the only deer living wild in Britain which does not grow antlers. It is a small deer, standing only twenty inches high at the shoulder, though it may appear to be more heavily built than a roe.

Adult bucks weigh around 40 lbs and does somewhat lighter at 35 lbs, which is heavier than one might expect for a species that is significantly smaller than a roe deer. Although it can easily be mistaken for either a roe or the even smaller muntjac, the Chinese water deer does have a number of distinctive features which aid an accurate identification. The colour of both sexes is similar both in summer and winter. The summer pelage is an unspotted reddish brown which is more drab than that of a roe. In winter this changes to a pale beige-brown coat which is sometimes streaked or flecked with grey. There is a short and barely visible tail and this species does not have the roe deer's distinctive rump patch. Fawns have a background colour which is noticeably darker than their parents' and in the

first four weeks of life the coat is decorated with two rows of small yellowish spots on each flank.

Although the bucks do not have antlers, both sexes have quite easily visible tusks in the upper jaw. Those of the male are longer than the doe's, being almost three inches in length in some instances. These tusks are mobile, and are swept back while the animal is feeding or ruminating but in alarm they are brought forward to become efficient weapons. Chinese water deer are, however, shy and inoffensive animals.

The other facial features of the Chinese water deer are also quite distinctive. The ears are more rounded and smaller than those of either of the other two small deer species, and the black eyes and button nose give the animal the appearance of a cuddly toy.

The necks of both sexes are slender regardless of age, and the fact that the back legs are longer than the front give the animal a forward tilt, although the head is held upright. The forward tilting line of the back differentiates the species from roe and the upright head stance differs from that of a muntjac.

Chinese water deer rut in December and the fawns are born in June or July. They are territorial animals, though this is not as formalized as in the roe. Lacking antlers, Chinese water deer bucks mark vegetation with their facial scent glands and during the rut fights occur between rival bucks. Despite the tusks, serious injury is rare, though much hair is lost and the ears may bear the marks of aggression.

This species has the highest potential breeding rate of all the deer in Britain. Twins and triplets are common and litters of as many as six offspring have been reliably recorded. The survival rate amongst the larger litters must, however, be poor for the simple reason that the doe only has four teats. Nevertheless, where the environment is suitable these deer can colonize and populate an area very quickly.

As the name suggests, the natural habitat of this species in its native land is swamps and reed beds. Without a marked adaptation to the different conditions that exist in Britain we are unlikely to see this species of deer spread throughout the country in the manner of the roe and muntjac.

Their present distribution in Britain is centred on western East Anglia and the Home Counties. The original wild-living population first established itself in Bedford-

Present colonization area of Chinese water deer

shire but the deer have now spread to Norfolk, Cambridge, Northamptonshire and Buckinghamshire. Local colonies do exist in Shropshire, Gloucestershire and elsewhere due to either deliberate release or escapes. Though originating from an aquatic environment, some water deer in Britain have adapted to living in mixed woodland and adjacent arable land. In the fenlands, however, they have colonized what is still their ideal habitat. These deer are mainly grazers, preferring grasses and sedges as a food source though they will browse and take root vegetables if the opportunity arises.

So little is yet known about the water deer that it was ten years after they established a prolific colony at Woodwalton Fen that they were positively identified. Prior to this they were thought to be muntjac.

Although the Chinese water deer are limited by the availability of suitable habitat, they are nevertheless firmly established as a wild species and their range is slowly extending to cover most of East Anglia. In time the isolated pockets in other parts of the country may see a similar expansion, perhaps along the watercourses and flood plains to which they are suited.

See also: **Deer**

The rounded ears and facial characteristics of a Chinese water deer are quite distinctive

Choke The term 'choke' refers to the degree of constriction at the muzzle of a shotgun. Varying the degree of constriction alters the extent to which the shot load spreads on leaving the gun. If we take a 30-inch circle at forty yards as the standard reference, increasing the degree of constriction from nil (true cylinder) to full choke has the effect of reducing the spread of shot. In a well-bored gun a true cylinder barrel is supposed to put 40 per cent of its shot charge inside the 30-inch circle at 40 yards. There are five degrees of choke above true cylinder as in the table opposite:

	Shot spread at 30 yds (in)	% in 30 in at 40 yds
True Cylinder	44	40
Improved Cylinder	38	50
1/4 Choke	35	55
1/2 Choke	32	60
3/4 Choke	29	65
Full Choke	27	70

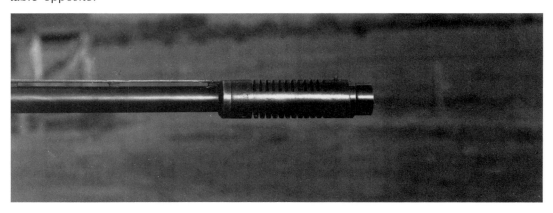

A range of 'external' choke devices is available for single-barrel guns

Comparison of patterns from a 12-bore cartridge loaded with 1 1/8-oz No 5 shot fired through:
1. A full choke barrel – 70 per cent in a 30 in circle at 40 yds (approx 172 pellets)
2. A true cylinder barrel – 40 per cent in a 30 in circle at 40 yds (approx 77 pellets)

1

2

.410 gauge 7/16 oz
No 5/American 6 shot

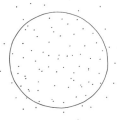

12 gauge 1 1/8 oz
No 5/American 6 shot

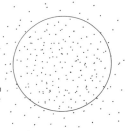

Profile of a
clay pigeon on
the same scale

Comparison of full-choke patterns at 40 yds. 30 in circle. A small target such as a partridge or clay pigeon could fly through the .410 pattern without being hit

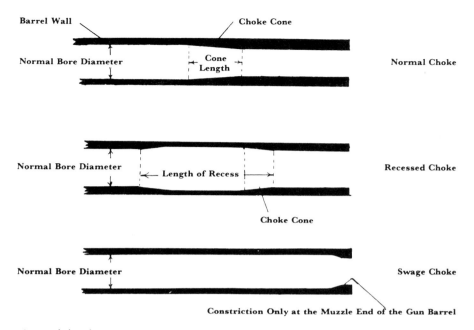

Cross-sections of the three types of choke formation

It can be seen from the table that correct choice of choke really depends on the average range at which the quarry is encountered. A driven game shooter who usually takes his shots at ranges from 25 to 35 yards will be at a disadvantage when using a heavily choked gun as this would restrict his margin of error when aiming and there would also be a danger of meat spoilage if a bird receives the full charge of a tightly choked gun at close range. A wildfowler, on the other hand, would probably need a tightly choked gun, as the average range at which the quarry is taken may be 40 to 50 yards. A denser pattern of shot at long range is therefore desirable, but the accuracy of the shot will have to be that much better to take advantage of this. It is far more difficult to hit a fast-flying bird at 40 yards than at 25 yards.

In order to achieve these chokings the degree of constriction at the muzzle of the shotgun should conform to the table above. These figures are arrived at by comparing the internal diameter nine inches from the muzzle and at the muzzle of the barrel.

These measurements of constriction and therefore choke refer to a 12 bore with an internal bore diameter of around .729 inches.

Choke	Constriction in Inches
True Cylinder	0
Improved Cylinder	.005 to .008
1/4 Choke	.008 to .015
1/2 Choke	.015 to .025
3/4 Choke	.025 to .030
Full Choke	.030 to. 040

The diameter of the total shot charge spread is approximately the same for 12, 16, 20 and 28 bores when the same degree of choke is used; in other words, the dispersion is the same irrespective of the bore size, and depends on the amount of choke. In the smaller-calibre shotguns the degree of constriction is proportionately smaller to achieve the same pattern densities.

Some shotguns intended for very-close-range shooting (and the majority of clay-shooting guns designed for the skeet discipline) may be bored with 'retro choke'. Rather than being constricted at the muzzle, the bore actually opens out to encourage a more rapid spread of the shot pattern.

There are a number of ways in which the muzzle of a shotgun barrel can be choked. The 'standard' choke is one where the

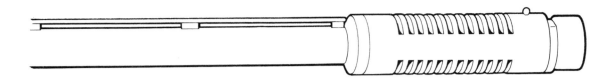

*Detail of an 'external' choke device for a
single barrel gun*

constriction is placed about four inches from
the end of the barrel. The bore of the barrel
narrows down according to the table in the
form of a choke cone of perhaps 1½ inches
in length. From the front end of the cone to
the muzzle the bore is again parallel, but at
the constricted dimension and not at that of
the original bore. This form of choking is
the most frequently used on sporting guns
and it is one which can be carefully regulated by a skilled barrel-maker to produce
excellent shot patterns. Certainly the London
gunmakers of the Boss, Purdey, and Holland élite would spend many hours regulating and modifying the choke cones of their
guns in order that they throw very consistent and even patterns.

Where a shooter desires a greater degree
of choke from an existing barrel, this can be
achieved with some success by creating a
recessed choke in the barrel. By this method
the bore is gently enlarged about four inches
from the muzzle so that the equivalent of a
choke cone will constrict the barrel to what
was its original bore. While not often as
successful a method as the standard choke,
a carefully recessed choke can perform very
well.

In both the methods described so far the
choke constriction occurs some distance
from the end of the barrel. This is an advantage in that the choke cone will remain
unharmed should the end of the barrel receive an accidental knock or dent. Indeed,
in the case of a badly dented muzzle the
shooter can afford to have the barrel shortened an inch or two without significant loss
in performance, and some people see this
as an important advantage over the other
methods of choking.

Swage choking is the most vulnerable. In
this method the choke constriction occurs
at the muzzle. There is no gradual choke
cone and the barrel is simply 'turned in' at

its end. Choke of this kind is quick and
economical to produce on barrel-making
machines and one often sees swage choke
on single barrel repeating shotguns. However, the performance of a carefully swaged
barrel will compare favourably with most
shotguns bored with standard or recessed
chokes.

In the last decade there has been a great
increase in the number of shotguns which
are fitted with choke tubes. The muzzle end
of the barrel is threaded to accommodate
a screw-in tube of two to three inches in
length. The tube fits flush with the internal
bore of the barrel and the choke constriction
occurs within the length of the tube. The
beauty of this system is that the shooter can
decide on the appropriate choking for any
shooting situation and screw in the correct
choke tube. This makes for far greater versatility as a person may shoot driven game
on one day and go wildfowling on the next
using the same gun.

There are, however, disadvantages. A
choke tube, when fitted in the barrel, becomes part of the barrel as a whole. It is
therefore subject to the stresses and strains
that every barrel experiences when a cartridge is fired. Therefore a good and secure
fit is essential in order to prevent the tube
working loose.

There are many accounts of poorly fitted
tubes being blown out of the barrel when
the gun fired and there is even a risk of
further damage to the main barrel if the
choke tube hinders the passage of shot and
wad in any way. Nevertheless, the choke-
tube system adds a great deal to the versatility of any shotgun and a correctly designed
and fitted interchangeable system of screw-
in choke tubes made from the correct material, which has passed Birmingham or
London proof, should give years of first-class
service.

The development of the choke-tube system has led to the decline in popularity of the variable choke devices one often used to see on single barrel repeating shotguns. Unlike the choke tube, which fits inside the barrel, the variable choke device is one which is added on to the end of the barrel. The most frequently used system of varying the choke involved the use of a collet of steel fingers which could be adjusted by turning a knurled ring on the outside of the device. Patterns thrown were generally acceptable but the weight and appearance of the variable choke attachment counted against its use. The extra metal at the end of the barrel usually disturbed the gun's point of balance and therefore its handling characteristics, and the appearance of such a lump of metal did nothing for the aesthetic line of the weapon. Variable choke devices did add versatility to single barrel shotguns, but nowadays the screw-in choke tube achieves the same if not better performance without affecting the balance, handling or appearance of the weapon.

Churchill A London gunmaking firm with a high reputation, Churchill (Gunmakers) Ltd was founded in 1891 by Mr E. J. Churchill. Originally it was the quality and effectiveness of the live-pigeon trap-guns which caused Churchill's rapid rise to prominence among the London gunmakers. However, it was the short-barrelled game gun introduced by Robert Churchill in the 1920s for which the name is chiefly remembered.

By the end of World War One Robert Churchill had come to the conclusion that the modern smokeless propellant powders did not require long barrels and a short lightweight game gun would provide comparable performance. After much experimentation he introduced the now well-known Churchill XXV with 25-inch barrels and a narrow raised 'Churchill' rib. These guns were significantly lighter than their contemporaries and were quickly adopted by a number of driven game shooters. Churchill's production of guns included both boxlocks and sidelocks and they were considered to be of good to best quality. While Churchill recommended 25-inch barrels, he would build guns to his customers' requirements with barrels of any length.

There has been a recent resurgence of interest in these short, quick-pointing shotguns among Britain's game shooters and a number of European gunmakers offer a 'XXV' model in their game-gun range.

After the last war Churchill (Gunmakers) Ltd underwent several changes, finally amalgamating with the fellow London gunmakers of Atkin, Grant & Lang before ceasing production in the early 1980s.

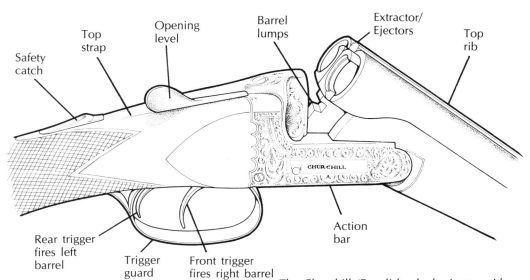

The Churchill 'Regal' boxlock ejector with main features indicated

Closures – Crimp and Rolled Shotgun cartridge manufacturers use two methods of closing and securing the shot load within the cartridge case. In the early days of breech-loading shotguns the shot load was sealed in the cartridge by placing an 'over-shot' thin card wad over the charge and then sealing the assembly by the application of wax around the edge of the wad. This method is still used by those shooters who use and reload cartridges for the 8- and 4-bore wildfowling guns and for punt guns. All other modern cartridges use either the 'rolled-turnover' or the 'crimp' method of closure.

In the rolled-turnover cartridge the shot load is secured by an overshot wad and the end of the cartridge case is folded inwards to secure the wad. When the shot is fired the pressure of the exploding propellant powder unrolls the lip of the cartridge case and the shot and overshot wad are pushed through the barrel. After leaving the muzzle the card wad is overtaken by the shot and falls to earth a short distance from the gun. Over many years this has proved to be an efficient system of cartridge closure and some cartridges are still sealed by a rolled turn-over. The criticism of the system, however, was that the cartridge occasionally threw a 'cartwheel' pattern when the overshot wad interfered with the normal passage of the shot charge through the air and the resulting pattern had an empty centre. This only happened occasionally and a poorly bored gun was more prone to throw cartwheels for which the rolled-turnover cartridge received the blame.

To eliminate this possibility the 'crimp' closure was devised. In this method of closing the cartridge the case was extended so that when pleated into a 'star' pattern and pressed down onto the shot charge it formed an effective seal. The advent of the plastic-cased shotgun cartridge meant the decline of the rolled turnover as this seal was less effective with the thinner cartridge wall, and the crimp closure became the dominant form. Crimping the end of the case in this way made the overshot wad unnecessary and the problem of the occasional cartwheel was eliminated.

See also: **Bore; Cartwheel; Wad**

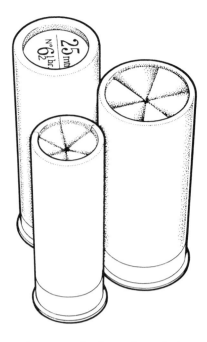

The two closure methods used on shotgun cartridges – crimped or star, and rolled turnover

Clothing Different types of sporting shooting have different criteria for the correct choice of outer clothes. However, there are a number of points which are common to all shooting sports. Clothes must allow the shooter both comfort and ease of movement – shotgun sports after all demand that the gun must be mounted and swung with ease even though the shooter may be in a variety of postures. Many shooting sports involve walking, so trousers must offer freedom of movement and comfort. In addition, the outer garments must offer protection from the elements so that the shooter can remain warm and dry even in the worst weather. Colour is also important, and the shooter should choose outer clothes which, if not actually camouflaged, are at least of a sub-dued 'natural' colour in order to blend in better with the environment. Finally, outer clothes should provide ample storage, in the form of pockets or pouches, for cartridges, knives, and other accesories that the shooter may find indispensable. Within these re-quirements there is considerable variation in what may be worn in the various types of sport.

Game shooting in all its forms is often a social sport, where the shooter is in the company of others. There is therefore some degree of social pressure which requires the clothing to be not only practical but also reasonably smart – scruffily dressed individuals on a driven grouse moor or pheasant covert will look out of place among their companions. The traditional dress for such 'formal' occasions is a tweed jacket and trousers. These, when well-fitting, will give the shooter both comfort and warmth with the required freedom of movement in order to shoot fast-moving targets.

Game shooting in general is a 'disturbance' sport in which the quarry is flushed either by beaters or by walking up, and therefore concealment and camouflage are not essential. The subdued greens and browns of traditional tweed patterns will blend with the scene while allowing the shooter to look reasonably well turned out. Trousers may be of the short 'breeks' type, made of moleskin or corduroy, and these are the modern substitute for the traditional plus-fours or plus-twos. Depending on the type of terrain to be covered, footwear may vary from brogues through walking boots to the ubiquitous rubber wellingtons. In warm weather, on a grouse moor in August for example, the jacket may be discarded and it may be acceptable to shoot in 'shirt-sleeve order' or in a waistcoat. In cold wet weather, on the other hand, the waxed cotton coat is the all-round standby for the gameshooter as it may be worn over tweeds or warm jumpers. Headgear is a matter of individual choice but the flat cap and fore-and-aft deerstalker are popular styles. The latter has a disadvantage if the shooter has to make overhead shots as the rear peak may dig into the back of the neck and dislodge the hat at the critical moment of firing. Again tweed is the traditional hat material: it will absorb a fair amount of rain before becoming saturated yet still helps retain much of the body heat which would otherwise be lost through the head.

In rough shooting the 'formal' dress requirements are relaxed, yet tweeds and waxed jackets are still popular for their warmth and weatherproof properties, and

where a certain amount of walking through beet or kale is necessary waterproof over-trousers or leggings may also be very useful to prevent the trousers becoming saturated from wet vegetation.

Of all shotgun sports practised in Britain, wildfowling takes place under the most arduous and taxing weather conditions. It is essential therefore that the clothing of the coastal shooter be adequate to give protection from climatic extremes. In addition, concealment assumes far more importance than with any form of game-shooting, and the clothing should reflect this need.

The outer jacket of the wildfowler should be of a suitable camouflage or colour to blend into the surrounding environment, while affording the maximum protection from both water and wind. Again waxed jackets, and particularly camouflaged waxed jackets, are a good choice as these will offer both concealment and protection. Underneath this the fowler may wear a number of sweaters above a shirt and thermal vest in order to insulate the body against the cold. Thigh waders are almost essential. The fowler will need to kneel, sit and slosh through foreshore mud and creeks, and calf-length wellingtons are simply inadequate. Trousers and thermal long-johns will keep the legs warm and the waders will keep them dry. Headgear must also insulate as much as possible, and peaked thermal balaclavas of a suitable colour or thick woolly hats are a popular choice. These do not, however, offer protection from driving rain and sleet, and a waxed hat of a larger size than normal may be worn over a balaclava for better protection.

Gloves are very important in wildfowling – I once had one of my hands freeze to the gun barrel through forgetting my gloves. Again the criteria are warmth and protection from the elements. The latter is harder to achieve as waterproof gloves tend to restrict the movement of the hands, so I have opted for a combination of leather shooting gloves worn under sheepskin or woollen shooting mitts. Even when saturated they still offer some degree of protection and retain the hands' warmth.

In contrast to wildfowling, a sport which is often at its best when the weather is at its worst, the vermin shooter is better able to pick and choose conditions in which to shoot. Unlike gameshooting, vermin control is often a sport of stealth and concealment, so camouflage assumes the greatest importance. Ex-military camouflage jackets are available in a number of colour variations and these can be selected to suit the environment. Again there is no formality in the style of dress and the shooter should choose the correct colour scheme for the outer garments and adequate underclothing for warmth. On warm summer days this may mean dressing in camouflaged shirt and trousers with gloves, headgear and footwear to match. In winter, of course, more insulation is required and a number of sweaters may be worn underneath the military camouflaged jacket. Hats should shade the face as much as possible and the cotton 'jungle' hat is ideal. Some shooters go further and use facemasks or veils to conceal the most prominent and easily recognizable of human features, while others use face paint (or mud) to help break up the outline.

The clothing requirements for deer stalking are somewhat different to most forms of shotgun shooting. Again, freedom of movement is important in order to hold a rifle steady regardless of the shooter's posture. However, in hill stalking and woodland stalking, stealth and concealment are the main priorities. Waxed jackets are just about the noisiest of all garments used in field sports. The scraping sound of a sleeve rubbing against the body, or a twig brushing past, is sufficient to alert deer up to a hundred yards away; so a waxed cotton jacket should only be a last resort in very poor weather. At other times jackets of a softer fabric should be worn, and here there is a divergence between the types of clothing recommended for hill and woodland stalking. Tweed suits in the traditional highland patterns blend very well into the heather moorland and they offer comfort and warmth. As in covert shooting there is a certain amount of social pressure to 'dress for the occasion' and one would look out of place on the hill in scruffy ex-army kit. Tweed is relatively shower-proof although it can become quite heavy when wet. The prudent hill stalker therefore carries a lightweight waterproof in case of emergencies. Hill stalking often involves walking several

miles in the course of the day's sport, so good strong pair of walking boots is preferable to rubber wellingtons, although the stalker must accept the fact that the feet will get wet very quickly and remain so throughout the day.

Woodland stalking does not involve the strenuous walking of its open-ground counterpart. Footwear is therefore less important, although soft soles are preferable for silent movement. I tend to use wellingtons in winter or when the ground is very wet, and soft-soled training shoes in the summer. Soft and silent trousers and jacket are very important if a reasonable degree of stealth is to be achieved. The very best are the garments made of green 'loden' cloth. Though soft-textured, loden cloth is hard-wearing and shower-proof. As a more economical alternative, unwaxed camouflaged cotton jackets and trousers are very effective and reasonably silent. As with vermin shooting, a wide-brimmed hat helps to conceal the face and leather shooting gloves will hide the hands and offer some protection from mosquitoes and biting midges.

Woodland stalking does not involve much strenuous exercise, so the winter stalker would consider thermal vest and long-johns to be essential. During the long periods in which the stalker stands still or moves very slowly the body can quickly lose heat, and good insulation is vital for a steady shot.

Cocking Indicator   Cocking indicators may be incorporated into the design of a variety of weapons. Basically they show whether or not the weapon is 'cocked' and ready to fire Bolt-action rifles may incorporate an indicator in the form of a small brass pin which protrudes when the action is 'live', but these are usually used only when the bolt itself is concealed beneath a protective casing.

Some sidelock double rifles or shotguns incorporate cocking indicators in the form of a pin which rotates as the tumblers are cocked. In better-quality weapons the screw slot on this pin may be gold-filled to make the cocking indicator more easily visible.

Collimator   A collimator is a small optical device which fits into the muzzle of a rifle in order to align a telescopic sight to the bore of the weapon. The device is fitted

The small pin behind the bolt handle on this BSA rifle is raised, indicating that the rifle is cocked. The safety catch on the side of the action is on 'safe'

vertically onto the muzzle and it is then viewed through the telescopic sight. A series of lenses within the collimator allows the telescopic sight to focus on the engraved graticule on the ground-glass screen at the rear of the collimator. The shooter is then able to adjust the crosswires in the sight so that they coincide with the desired graticule mark. The use of a collimator in this way has the same effect as optically bore-sighting the rifle, i.e., it provides a rough alignment of the sight and rifle. After using the collimator the rifle still needs to be zeroed to the desired range.

See also: **Zero**

A collimator being used to check the alignment of the telescopic sight

Colour Hardening Colour hardening, or case hardening, is a process which produces a beautiful blue-brown-purple finish on the surface of the action body and sideplates of a weapon. The metal to be hardened is placed in bone ash and heated to a dull red colour. In this state the surface of the metal absorbs carbon to produce the mottled colouring seen on many new guns. In time and with wear and tear the colours tend to fade, so an old gun retaining much of its colour hardening has been well looked after and seen little use.

Combination Any double barrel weapon which has a mixture of shotgun and rifle barrels.

See also: **Drilling**

Conseil International de la Chasse (CIC) CIC is the European body which lays down regulations for the measuring and assessing of trophy antlers.

The formula for antler measurement, now applied to trophy heads in most European countries, varies from one species to another but in general such considerations as antler length, span, circumference, colour, and even volume may be taken into account. In addition, points may be awarded or deducted for pearling, regularity or beauty of the head.

Good trophy heads are awarded bronze, silver or gold medals if they attain certain scores under the CIC formula for the species and it has become the ambition of many European deer stalkers to shoot a 'medal head'.

With this ambition in mind, landowners and deer managers generally vary the fees paid by visiting stalkers according to the quality of the antlers of any deer shot. 'Trophy bucks' will command much higher stalking fees than 'cull bucks' and a stalker wishing to secure a 'Gold Medal' head would expect to pay many hundreds of pounds.

It is the CIC formulae that are almost invariably applied to deer shot in Britain and Europe, but they are only used infrequently in other parts of the world. In the Americas the CIC is supplanted by the Boone and Crocket system of trophy measuring and in Australasia it is the Douglas method that is most often used. The American and Australasian systems publish record books which register all the best trophies that are shot each year but neither system awards medals.

See also: **Medal Head**

Cripple Stopper When a punt gun is fired at a group of sitting fowl, providing the birds are taken in good range, the majority will be killed cleanly. Inevitably, however, there may be a small number of wounded birds which will require despatching as quickly as possible. This is the reason a punt gunner will also carry a shoulder weapon in the punt – the 'cripple stopper'. Previously some gunners used a rook rifle or rimfire .22 for this purpose, but these days when the foreshore is shared with other wildfowlers the risk of a ricochet would preclude the use of any rifle.

For this reason a cripple stopper is usually a shotgun. Although some shooters feel that any old gun will serve as a cripple stopper, the use of hammer guns or single barrel repeaters is to be avoided. This is because a well-equipped punt will contain much equipment which may obstruct the reloading of repeating guns, and an accidental discharge from a hammer snagged in the stowed gear will bring a punting expedition to an abrupt end. I have seen both single-shot and double barrel guns used for this purpose but it seems that a double side-by-side is the ideal.

After firing the big gun the punt gunner quickly moves the punt to the pick-up. For the time being the dead birds can be left to float while attention is focused on shooting any wounded trying to escape. A 12 bore loaded with No 4 shot will perform the duty efficiently and the risk of a wounded bird escaping to a painful and prolonged death is minimized. After the 'cripples' have been stopped the dead birds can be picked up at leisure.

See also: **Punt Gunning; Punt Guns**

Cross Bolt A cross bolt is a bolt positioned just behind the breech face on the action of a double barrel gun. The most frequently seen cross bolt is of the type designed by Greener. The standing breech is inletted so that it can accommodate a rearward exten-

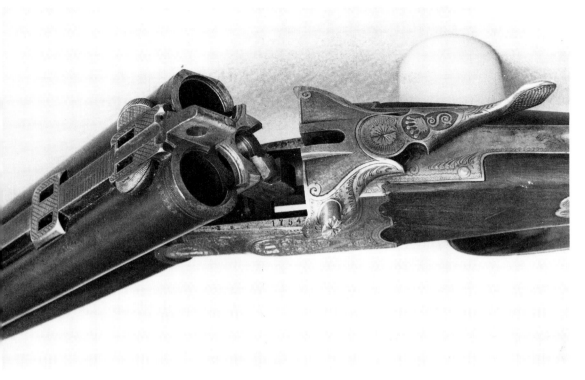

When the weapon is opened, the cross bolt protrudes from the left side of the standing breech. When closed it locks through the top extension to the rib

sion of the top rib on the barrel. When the gun is closed the bolt runs through a hole in this top extension, locking the barrels firmly to the action.

In some early side-by-side shotguns this cross bolt was the only method of locking the barrels to the action, but in later weapons the cross bolt is used in conjunction with other locking mechanisms on the lumps below the barrel flats. On such guns the barrels are locked in the closed position both below and at the top of the barrels and this is perhaps the most secure of all closing mechanisms.

Most modern guns have now dispensed with the Greener cross bolt as the extension of the top rib is considered to obstruct the breech and slow down the rate of loading. The use of a top extension also reduces the arc of the cartridge extractors, although in practice this is of little consequence.

See also: **Barrel; Greener; Lumps**

Crow   Two forms of crow inhabit the British Isles but they are really two races of the same species (*Corvus corone*). By far the most common is the carrion crow (*Corvus corone corone*), which inhabits all of England and Wales and most of Scotland south of the Great Glen. In the Highlands further north and west the hooded crow (*Corvus corone cornix*) takes over. There is considerable overlap of the two races, and hybrids frequently occur.

The carrion crow is a heavily-built, all-black bird which, at nineteen inches overall, is somewhat larger than the rook. Its longer legs, heavy black bill and larger head also make it look more heavily built than the rook, although it is still considerably smaller than the protected raven. In flight it is more direct than the rook and its tail is square-cut rather than rounded. At closer range the plumage of a carrion crow has a purple-green gloss but this is usually visible only in strong sunlight.

The hooded crow has the same heavy bill, head and build as the carrion crow but its plumage shows a marked difference. The head, wings, legs and tail are black but the body colour is a medium to pale grey. As a result a pure-bred hooded crow cannot be confused with any other corvid, but where the ranges of the two birds overlap offspring may show considerable variation from all black to full hooded-crow plumage.

Although Eastern and Central England receive an influx of migrant carrion crows from Europe from November to March, most birds of both types are resident and sedentary in this country. They are found in a very wide range of environments from coastal marshes and the foreshore to pasture and arable farmland, woodlands, and high moorland.

Compared to others in the crow family, both carrion and hooded crows are rather solitary and are most frequently seen in pairs, although family parties may roost together. Wingbeats are slower and stronger than the rook and flight is usually direct and purposeful. Unlike the raven, the crow rarely soars.

Both crows are normally ground feeders, eating a variety of food as the opportunity arises. Grain and other vegetable matter is consumed along with insects, small mammals, carrion, birds and eggs. Though not a true bird of prey, the crow will kill smaller species of bird and mammal and may cause extensive damage among fledgeling songbirds and game chicks.

The crow is a sharp-sighted, cautious and intelligent bird which normally requires a fair degree of field craft to outwit it. When feeding on the ground crows may be stalked with a shotgun, rifle, or air rifle, providing sufficient cover exists for a concealed approach. At other times the static hunter may wait at a known roost to intercept the incoming birds in the late evening. Carrion crows may also be drawn to an owl decoy on some vantage point such as a fencepost and the odd bird can be shot while it is mobbing the owl. At other times crows are a target of opportunity on the rare occasions when the shooter catches them off their guard. When one considers their diet, a reduction in the crow population in an area will have an obviously beneficial effect on wildlife in general and game birds in particular.

See also: **Vermin**

D

Damascus Barrels Modern shotgun barrels are invariably made of high-quality steel. Before this became available, however, barrels were made from alternating flat rods of iron and steel. These were laid together and twisted to form a tight spiral and a number of these spirals were hammered together to form one long flat strip of metal. The strip was then wound around a mandrel of roughly the same diameter as the interior bore of the barrel in much the same fashion as the bandage on the handle of a tennis racquet. The spiral seam was then welded, the mandrel removed and the barrel tube struck down and finished. The term 'Damascus barrel' is derived from the intricate and beautiful pattern which was produced by the twisted alternating iron and steel, as it was reminiscent of the swords produced by Damascus craftsmen. Although generally

A fine old hammer 12-bore with the Damascus pattern clearly visible on the barrels

Mallard decoys will attract most duck species

Full bodied pigeon decoys may be used on the ground or lofted into trees

weaker than steel tubes and therefore less suitable for use with modern high-pressure nitro powders, Damascus barrels had the advantage of bulging rather than bursting if a slight obstruction became lodged in the barrel when the gun was fired. In order to bring out the full beauty of the Damascus twist in the metal, barrels of this type were usually 'browned' rather than blacked, and many fine examples are still in use today.

See also: **Barrel**

Decoys In shooting terms, a decoy is a device used to attract members of a quarry species into shooting range, and in Britain a wide variety of decoys are used. All the commercially available decoys are more or less accurate representations of bird species and they work in two ways. The main group is designed to work on the gregarious habits of the quarry species involved, and a number

of decoys may be set out to represent a flock either feeding or at rest in such a way that a passing bird will approach to investigate. The exception to this is a decoy which arouses the curiosity or anger of a quarry species.

Woodpigeon decoys are by far the most frequently used, and they are made in two forms. The 'shell' decoy is the most convenient and least expensive, and these are designed for setting out in a pattern on a field known to be visited by pigeons. Full-bodied pigeon decoys may also be used in this way but are often 'lofted' on long poles to sit among the branches of a tree. Using these decoys, pigeons may be attracted to a 'feeding flock' of decoys or to a 'perching' tree or roosting area in a patch of woodland. So effective are these decoys that a pigeon shooter without decoys will severely limit his chances of success. 'Flapper' decoys with extended flexible wings are made to represent a woodpigeon on its final landing approach and these can be quite effective at times. By far the most effective pigeon decoy, however, is the dead bird set out in a lifelike posture.

Goose decoys are also made to represent geese feeding and are most often used on corn and potato stubble during the winter, in areas that geese are known to frequent. There are two types available – the full bodied and the silhouette – and both are made in the 'alert' head-up and the 'feeding' head-down postures. Most goose decoys are designed for setting out on land, whereas duck decoys are designed to float on water.

Duck decoys are made to represent a variety of species, but the most frequently used is the mallard decoy. Set out in shallow water they can represent a party of duck at rest or feeding, and in the right conditions can be very effective.

Vermin species such as crows and magpies are also gregarious feeders, and decoys are available for these; but the owl decoy can be equally effective for attracting corvids. A single owl decoy set on a fence post in an easily-seen location may be mobbed by both crows and magpies, and the vermin controller may well be able to account for a good number of birds using this form of decoying.

See also: **Pigeon Shooting; Vermin Shooting – Tactics; Wildfowl Decoying**

Deer The largest land mammals living in the wild in Britain, the deer population of the country is made up of six different species.

Deer lie within the order Artiodactyla (even-toed ungulates). These are basically cloven-hoofed mammals, and deer of the family Cervidae share the order with pigs, cattle and antelopes. They are herbivorous animals that are also classified as ruminants as their digestive system has much in common with domestic cattle. Swallowed food is passed into the first stomach chamber (the rumen) where it is fermented. When the animal is at rest it is regurgitated to be chewed and mixed with saliva before being passed back to the second stomach chamber

(the reticulum). The process has evolved for two very good reasons. Deer species, in common with other small to medium ungulates, form one of the prime food sources for the larger carnivores. Therefore a deer must be able to feed rapidly, thus exposing itself to predators for as little time as possible, and digest at leisure, when it has found safe concealment.

Secondly, plant tissue tends to be deficient or low in the nutrients needed to sustain health, and the ruminating system in which plant material has a longer residence within the animal's body serves to extract as much nutrition as possible from the plant food.

Deer share many visual features with other ruminants such as antelopes. They have slender legs and graceful bodies, short tails and long necks. They all have angular heads, large round eyes which are placed well to each side and large ears set high on the head.

The feature that distinguishes deer from all other ruminants is the growth of antlers among the males of almost all the species. Whereas the horns of cattle, sheep, goats, or antelopes begin growth shortly after birth and continue growing throughout the animal's life, deer antlers are grown and shed annually. In general, these long bony outgrowths increase in size with each successive year until the animal reaches maturity, although this is more evident in some species than in others. As the animal declines into old age the quality and size of the antlers it grows tends to deteriorate.

Of the six species of deer that now exist in a wild state in Britain, only one, the Chinese water deer, does not have antlers, and the size and shape of the antlers of the other five are important aids to identifying and distinguishing them.

In descending order of size, the six species of deer that live in a wild state in Britain today are: red deer (*Cervus elaphus*), fallow deer (*Dama dama*), sika deer (*Cervus nippon*), roe deer (*Capreoleus Capreoleus*) Chinese water deer (*Hydropotes inermis*) and the muntjac (*Muntiacus reevesii*).

See also: **Antlers; Chinese Water Deer; Fallow Deer; Muntjac Deer; Red Deer; Roe Deer; Sika Deer**

Deer Management All animals, including humans, reproduce at a rate which is greater than is necessary for the maintenance of their population. In other words, the population of any species will increase rapidly if there are no external limiting factors.

These factors slow down the rate of growth by the elimination of a proportion of the population, and they include availability of food, disease, shelter, climate, accident, and predation. After the end of the last ice age, Britain was virtually covered with primaeval forest. Red and roe deer flourished in these forests and, as food and shelter were easily available, mortality through exposure during cold weather was not a significant control factor. As always accidental death will occur in any species, but again its importance in population control is negligible. However, predation by the large carnivores that followed the deer over the continental land bridge was Nature's very efficient way of keeping the deer populations in balance. Recent research has shown that in areas of Europe free from human disturbance, roe deer populations are effectively controlled by lynx. These large cats regulate their breeding according to food supply, thus in an area well populated by roe the numbers of lynx will increase in order to harvest the slow, frail and sick. The deer most likely to survive and breed are the strong and quick-witted. When a balance is achieved and prey harder to come by, the breeding rate of the lynx drops to a more appropriate level with many animals moving on to search for fresh hunting grounds.

By the time the land bridge to the continent had been flooded by the rising sea level, Britain's forests and upland willow scrub were populated by elk, reindeer, red deer and roe. Of the predators, the wolf and lynx were the most important although bears also contributed; and of least importance at that time was man. In time, though, humans have come to dominate: firstly by clearing and fencing off areas of forest for farming and thereby reducing the habitat available to deer; secondly by domesticating grazing animals such as cattle, sheep, goats and pigs, all of which compete to some extent with deer for food. Finally, in order to protect his domesticated stock man set about exterminating the predators that posed a threat. The

wolf, lynx and bear were all removed from lowland Britain in medieval times, and the last wolf in Scotland was killed in the 1700s. By this time man's own predilection for meat had eliminated both reindeer and elk from these islands, and by the nineteenth century roe deer only survived in the remoter glens of Scotland. The loss of the large carnivores did not cause an increase in the deer population because man had enclosed most of the habitat suitable to deer and he had also become a far more efficient predator than any wild animal. In every lowland part of the country where deer were not protected they were shot, trapped and snared into oblivion.

From the end of the last century there has been a remarkable turnaround. In the aftermath of the 'Romantic' era and helped by the Victorian revival of interest in deer, the red deer of Scotland were encouraged and roe reintroduced into Southern England began to spread. Both World Wars made great demands on Britain's timber resources and the secondary scrub growth in the felled areas suddenly made much more ideal habitat available to roe and the newly feral muntjac. In Scotland the large estates began to break up into smaller units, and deer stalking on the hill ceased to be a sport for the privileged few.

The establishment of the Forestry Commission led to vast areas of hitherto open ground being converted into coniferous forest. Though not an ideal environment when mature, the young plantations provided sufficient food and shelter to act as a 'springboard' for the spreading deer colonists. By the 1980s all six species of deer living wild in Britain were increasing their range and distribution. A newly conservation-conscious human population encouraged diversification through lowland woodland schemes and set-aside land.

From 1959 in Scotland, and 1963 in England, the Deer Act stopped the indiscriminate and often inhumane methods of deer control: shotgun drives and snares are now prohibited. The shooting and farming population were slow to realise the importance of deer management, with the result that by the late 1980s the deer population of this country exceeded one million animals, probably for the first time since Neo-

Culling the females during the winter is a very important management task

lithic times. Recent estimates put the red deer population at 300,000, with nearly half a million roe deer, fifty thousand fallow, ten thousand sika and a muntjac population well into six figures. Being unable to enlist the aid of lynxes and wolves, around 300,000 deer need to be shot every year in Britain just to keep the population stable, with road deaths and other accidents bringing the total mortality per year up to roughly half the population. Despite the recent growth of deer management and deer stalking, the annual cull figure in Britain does not come anywhere near this and so the deer population continues to spread into areas that have been devoid of deer for centuries.

If sound deer management policies are not implemented quickly the likely eventual control on deer may be the availability of land. There is only a finite amount of countryside, and this land has to satisfy a wide range of needs. Rural land is used for food production, timber, recreation, mineral ex-

traction and a whole host of other functions as well as being a habitat for the wild fauna of the country.

The growth of the deer population has coincided this century with a dramatic loss of rural land – new housing, industries and transport links continue to make inroads into the amount of land available to wildlife in general and deer in particular.

The total amount of countryside is decreasing and it may be said that the expanding deer population is expanding within a shrinking habitat. Inevitably, in these conditions deer will cause agricultural damage in some form, either as direct damage to arable crops by grazing and trampling, or to woodland crops by fraying, bark stripping and browsing. Inevitably, conflict will arise between the deer population and the farmer or forester if damage reaches unacceptable levels, and it is on this cue that the deer manager should enter.

There are three aims of deer management.

Firstly, deer damage to agriculture and forest must be reduced to an acceptable or tolerable level. In order to do this the numbers of resident deer must be reduced by shooting to a level which will reduce damage. Secondly, the manager should plan to maintain a healthy and continuous population of deer on the ground in numbers that are in balance with the cover and natural food available to them. In order to achieve this, shooting to reduce the population must be selective, and the year-to-year cull plan must also be geared to encourage the strongest and healthiest animals while taking out the surplus young, weak and old.

Finally, in order to compensate for the damage that may still be sustained the manager should be able to provide an income from the sale of venison or from stalking sport. Deer are, after all, a renewable resource in the same way as domestic livestock and, as in stock farming or forestry, the deer manager needs to formulate a long-term plan for the control of the deer population of the area even though this may be modified by changing circumstances.

To start with, the manager must realize that an area holding a high deer population will also inevitably suffer much deer damage. A population that has exceeded the holding capacity of the ground can be identified by excessive crop damage and by the general inferior condition of the animals. In the male deer antler growth may be both retarded and of poor quality. If a population at this stage is allowed to go unchecked, damage will increase and the beasts will deteriorate even further, until the stage is reached when starvation, disease or parasitic infestation exerts its own population control. Admittedly, if the adjoining land also holds deer any major reduction in population may serve to attract others in from outside, but careful and selective culling will help to minimize immigration, and even a slight reduction in deer numbers can produce a dramatic reduction in crop damage.

The first task of a deer manager is therefore to arrive at an estimate of the numbers of deer on his ground and to assess the available food resources in the form of grazing and browse. If, as in the case of roe and muntjac, the bucks are territorial, the manager may also map out any existing territories by looking for fraying stocks and scrapes that act as the boundary markers. Arriving at an estimate of deer numbers is largely a matter of frequent observation at dawn and dusk until a rough figure begins to resolve itself. It is said that deer management involves 90 per cent of time spent observing and 10 per cent in stalking, and it is only by using this sort of time allocation that the manager will arrive at a reasonably accurate population figure. A quicker result can be obtained, however, by carrying out a deer census. This is best done in late February or early March because low-growing vegetation is at its lowest ebb and visibility in woodland is therefore at its best. In small woods deer can be moved by two or three people walking slowly and quietly through the wood in order to push the deer past an observer placed at some strategic point. If the observer is correctly placed and the route taken by the walkers carefully planned, then most of the deer will be counted.

In larger blocks of forest a figure may be arrived at by applying the same technique to two or three portions of the forest. The numbers of deer seen may then be extrapolated to produce a population figure for the whole block. Even so, whether in small woodland or in large blocks, the census can never be regarded as an accurate figure. The older and more wily animals are often prone to break back or to lie low so that they fail to get counted and the deer will know of far more concealed escape routes than we could imagine. If planned carefully, though, a deer census in late winter or early spring can produce a rough working figure on which the manager can build.

Once a population figure has been arrived at the next stage is to estimate the annual rate of increase. Observations to this end are carried out in August by counting the number of females with young. In some areas infant mortality can be high from road strikes, fox predation, grass cutting or even cold wet weather. By August, though, it may be safely assumed that the young seen at heel will live to at least their first winter. Careful observation will allow the manager to arrive at a figure for the annual natural increase over the early spring population. In lowland, deer fertility is high and each mature female may be expected to produce offspring every year. If the number of adult females is known quite accurately then the annual increase can be estimated. The females of red, fallow and sika usually produce one offspring per year. Under favourable conditions the roe can produce twins, muntjac produce three offspring every two years and water deer may have multiple births.

In most species the infant mortality rate can be assessed in August by counting the number of mature females without young or, in the case of roe, those with only one rather than two. The biological potential minus infant mortality will produce a figure for the annual increase. The maximum natural mortality is in the spring.

Armed with this knowledge the deer manager is in a position to work out a cull plan. In effect, the deer manager should strive to reproduce the effects of natural predation on the deer population. In countries where wolves and lynx control roe, for example, it is the fittest and strongest deer that survive. Yearlings form a good proportion of the kills made by these carnivores,

with the weak and the old deer taking up most of the remainder. It is therefore advisable in the cull plan to arrive at the total number of deer to be shot that year. Roughly equal numbers of males and females should be culled and these are then subdivided according to age and condition.

A good working proportion, depending of course on the rate of increase and the species, is to shoot yearling males to about 60 per cent of the buck cull figure. If one can be even more selective and shoot only the weaker yearlings, leaving the better specimens to grow to maturity, all the better.

The other 40 per cent of the buck cull may be divided roughly between animals which are well past their prime and, if these are few and far between, the poorer specimens of the mature male population. Owing to the difficulty of estimating the age of female deer beyond the yearling stage, it is not usually possible to cull selectively; therefore a random selection of all ages should be shot up to the cull figure.

Woodland stags can develop very heavy antlers

In order to carry out a cull of this type it is essential for the manager to get to know his deer population very well. By careful observation, the selection of animals to be culled should be made long before the stalker takes to the woods with a rifle. The manager must learn to assess the age and condition of each male deer that is observed so that a picture can be built up of the age/sex structure of the population. In small woodlands this is relatively easy and the manager may well become familiar with each animal in the area. In larger blocks this is more difficult but a cull plan on the basis of the age groups described above is still both possible and practical. As it is, however, where damage is severe the immediate task is to reduce the overall deer numbers. In this case females should form the highest proportion of the early cull targets as this effectively reduces the breeding rate in a short time. The surplus males can then be culled out to redress the balance of the optimum sex ratio for the species and the area.

Many traditional stalkers are reluctant to shoot female deer. Recent research indicates, however, that a surplus of hinds or does adversely affects the antler quality of the males and generally upsets the breeding equilibrium of the herd. In the Highlands of Scotland the red deer population has reached the crisis point where spells of hard weather will produce a heavy mortality. The difficulty of achieving the correct annual quota of hinds in remote areas, during very short hours of daylight and in often atrocious weather conditions, has meant that the red deer population explosion is now out of control.

If the manager intends improving antler quality to be the main priority, then a heavy cull plan may be implemented in order to virtually clear out the resident deer. The cleared woodland will provide abundant food and undisturbed ground where the incoming deer may develop impressive heads. This 'clear out' may have to be carried out once every ten years to establish new bloodlines. In the meantime, however, agricultural and forest damage may be quite severe as young males compete for territories,

The rifle takes a much needed rest while the stalker 'glasses' the hill for a shootable beast

rutting stands, or groups of females. To compensate for this, stalking may be offered on a letting basis in order to gain the sometimes quite substantial income from sportsmen wishing to shoot a 'medal' head.

On the other hand, if the main priority is to reduce forest damage then the stalker should make every effort to preserve the dominant males. In territorial species like roe and muntjac the strongest males tend to establish and hold large territories. Admittedly, fraying damage does occur on the boundaries, but if these bucks were shot out then the area would be subdivided into a greater number of smaller territories by competing young bucks. Damage would increase dramatically. In fallow, sika and to some extent lowland red deer, shooting out the dominant males would also increase fraying damage as the lesser males would feel more inclined to challenge each other in shows of strength.

It should be clear that a cull plan is not merely a matter of shooting a specified number of deer each year. Depending on the importance assigned to each of the three main areas of management, the manager should devise a plan detailing the numbers of deer to be shot, their ages and sex, and, in many cases, which individuals are to be culled. The cull plan is now seen as the practical application of scientific management of a wild population. It is relatively new in Britain, although sound deer management has existed for many years on the European continent. The recent rapid spread and growth of Britain's deer population, together with legislation allowing only humane control with appropriate weapons, has made Britain wake up at last to the importance of proper deer management. In the next few decades the need for proper management will only increase.

See also: **Deer; Medal Head**

Deer Stalking – Highland   When one mentions deer stalking, the image that comes to most people's minds is of remote heather-clad Highlands, red deer, and stalkers dressed in tweeds. The prevalence of this image was brought about by events in the Victorian era and is widely attributed to the activities of Prince Albert, the Queen's consort. Prior to this, red deer were considered to be fair game for laird and crofter alike, and there are many accounts of large-scale hunts in which packs of dogs and beaters drove the herds of unfortunate deer to a slaughtering ground. Mary, Queen of Scots, once participated in a hunt of this type in which three hundred and sixty deer were killed. At that time the deer hound was a prized possession, and they feature prominently in the history of deer sport in Scotland.

Prince Albert brought to Britain his love of shooting sports and, having procured an estate in Victoria's beloved Highlands, quickly set about organizing small expeditions to stalk and shoot deer. Almost overnight deer stalking in the Scottish Highlands became a very fashionable activity for the aristocracy and gentry as other landowners were quick to follow the royal lead. The Victorian era also enjoyed a romantic spectacle and the paintings of Landseer, for example, did much to bring public attention to the new sport. His highly romanticized paintings, of which the 'Monarch of the Glen' is the most famous, also served to attract the English well-to-do from south of the border. They came in such numbers that Highland deer forest owners began to vie with each other for the weight and antler quality of their deer in much the same way as grouse moors competed for record bags. One effect of this growth of interest in Highland stalking was that the deer on each estate suddenly received protection and therefore the overall deer population began to expand rapidly.

As always happens when a species is allowed to exceed the holding capacity of the ground, harsh winter weather resulted in cruel losses and most deer suffered from malnutrition. Estates imported fine specimens of lowland stags to be released and shot by their distinguished guests, and in order to guard their deer miles of fencing was strung across the hills. Thus the wild and romantic sport degenerated to some extent as the Highland estates became virtually 'deer parks'. Long before the principles of deer management were thought out, the absurd spirit of competition between estates assured that only the best stags were shot, and the quality of the herds deteriorated.

Nowadays, thankfully, the scene is very different. The social upheavals brought about by the First and Second World Wars, the changes in the patterns of landownership in the Highlands, and the break-up of many large estates into smaller units have all altered the face of Highland stalking. The rising costs of running estates has led to deer stalking being made available on a commercial basis. Gone are the days when this sport was the prerogative of a privileged minority, as an ever-increasing number of estates let the stalking rights on a seasonal, weekly, or even daily basis. Gone also is the quest for the best trophies, and stalking now is an activity which in the main provides wild sport for the visiting stalker, who is really only participating in the annual cull plan. The accent is now on taking out the weaker stags or ones with undesirable antler growth. The very best stags are now avoided, thus allowing them to pass on their qualities to the next generation of deer.

In theory the cull plan specifies that equal numbers or more hinds should be shot each year, and herein lies a problem. Though let at cheaper rates than stag stalking, hind stalking still has little prestige value to the visiting rifle, and the limited daylight hours, frequently adverse weather conditions and disturbance from walkers and climbers mean that estates often fail to meet their hind quota. It is as a result of this that the population of red deer in the Highlands has now grown well beyond the holding capacity of the ground available to them. Added to this is the fact that the large-scale, and well-fenced, afforestation programmes on the lower slopes of the hills have deprived many herds of their more sheltered wintering quarters. The tragic and shameful result of this combination of factors was only too evident in March of 1989 when a long spell of cold and wet weather resulted in red deer dying in their hundreds in some parts of the Western Highlands. Lessons learned from these tragic occurences should make deer stalking in the Highlands ever more available to the visitor.

Highland deer stalking is the only form of open-ground rifle sport available in Britain. In terms of species, red deer are of course the prime quarry of the Highland stalker but there are an increasing number of locations where sika deer may also be stalked in this

A roesack, slip, binoculars, knives and stalking stick are all essential kit for the roe stalker

way, particularly along the moorland margins of conifer forest blocks. Roe deer may also inhabit open ground on the moorland margins but these are really of secondary importance to red or sika deer.

Highland deer stalking takes place over practically all the mountain and moorland of the Scottish Highlands area. Both the Grampian block south of Loch Ness and north of the Highland boundary fault, and the North-west Highlands further north, boast a large number of stalking estates. Many of the islands off the west coast also carry populations of deer, and stalking is available on these. To the south of Scotland's industrial lowlands, the Southern Uplands and Border country also offer this form of open-ground stalking, with red deer inhabiting the western range into Galloway and an ever-increasing population of sika on the eastern end of the uplands.

In England this 'Highland' style of stalking only takes place in some parts of the Lake District, particularly in the Martindale area, and this is at present the southernmost area where red deer live throughout the year on unenclosed moorland. We are unlikely to see open-ground populations of red deer – natural forest dwellers – extending southwards along the flanks of the Pennines as the deciduous woodland cover and extensive softwood forest plantations on the lower ground is far more attractive. Highland stalking therefore, except in Cumbria, is very much a Scottish sport. The conditions one is likely to meet, the surroundings, and preparations required of the visiting stalker, make Highland stalking quite different from any other form of deer stalking in Britain or, for that matter, in Europe.

Highland deer stalking is not a sport for the unfit or the squeamish. During the course of a day's stalking on 'the hill' a visitor must expect to be subjected to many miles of strenuous hill walking and anticipate returning home soaked through, exhausted, and covered with a fair layer of thick black peat. In contrast to lowland or woodland stalking, though, the day begins in quite a leisurely fashion. Whereas the woodland stalker must be out and ready at dawn, the Highland rifle will have time for a hearty and relaxed breakfast before meeting the estate stalker who will act as the guide.

At the first meeting of the estate stalker and the visiting rifle it is normal procedure for the latter to be asked to 'try the rifle'. This involves the visitor firing two or three sighting shots at a target at a distance of about one hundred yards. Many stalkers have a metal profile of a deer for this purpose, known as an iron stag, and the purpose of the sighting shots is twofold. Firstly, the rifle can ascertain that the weapon has not suffered any knocks in transit that may have thrown the sights out of zero and, perhaps more importantly, the stalker is reassured that the person pulling the trigger is capable of placing the shots accurately.

When the rifle has been tried to the satisfaction of the stalker they are ready to proceed to the hill, perhaps collecting a third person on the way out to act as the 'ponyman'. This name derives from the habit, still practised on some estates, of retrieving shot deer on the back of a garron or Highland pony. The retrieval is more often carried out now with the aid of some form of all-terrain vehicle such as an ATV motorcycle or multi-wheeled Agrocat. The ponyman is dropped off at a point from which he can be summoned after a shot has been taken and a beast killed. The stalker leads the rifle off to some vantage point to survey the surrounding area for a suitable beast for stalking. This may be the rifle's first opportunity for a rest after a gruelling walk of perhaps two or three miles. Most Highland stalkers use a telescope rather than binoculars for this preliminary observation. A magnification factor of around 25 usually enables them to identify a shootable beast at a greater distance than with binoculars, and the stalker will take his time to examine all the deer visible from that point with great care. Once a suitable animal is chosen the stalker employs experience, knowledge of the terrain, and prevailing wind direction to plan an unseen approach to within shooting distance. While this is going on the rifle may sit back and drink in the magnificence of the surroundings. With binoculars raised the pointers given by the stalker may be followed to locate herds of deer that may otherwise not be noticed – red deer can be very difficult to pick out against the vegetation background unless one knows what to look for. Other wildlife of the area appear before the keen observer: birds of prey such as the peregrine or golden eagle, ravens, hooded crows, and a wide variety of waders. Of the other game that may be seen, red grouse and blue hares may be flushed, much to the consternation of those seeking deer, as their alarm may be noted by vigilant animals and the suspicions of the herd aroused.

When the stalker has planned the approach route, both move off, perhaps walking a fair distance to get downwind of the selected animal before working up to shooting range. Initially the stalker will use dead ground and undulations to conceal their movements and they may traverse much ground at a brisk upright walk. The stalker may stop at frequent intervals in order to check for other deer near his planned route. Disturbing these would quickly clear the hill of many others, including the targeted animal. Burns will be crossed, if necessary by wading, and nearing the end of the stalk the walk will change to a crouch and then to a stomach crawl through wet black peat and saturated heather stems. The stalker will move ahead to the final shooting position to ascertain that all is well, then beckon the visitor forward. Tradition dictates that the stalker is also the gun bearer for the day and it is at this stage that he removes it from the gunslip, loads a cartridge into the chamber and hands it to the visitor. He will point out the beast to be shot and estimate the range. It is then all up to the person behind the trigger. The miles of strenuous walking and the final exhausting crawl to the shooting point will have all taken their toll on the visitor, yet the aim must be deliberate and steady for a humane shot.

The satisfaction of seeing the animal collapse is derived from a job well done and only forms a small part of the total experience of being out in one of Britain's last few remaining wilderness areas. The shot is the climax of the stalk, but the task is not yet completed. Within minutes the stalker will have begun the gralloch – cleaning out the internal organs of the carcass before there is any risk of meat spoilage. The beast is rolled onto its back and a slit from sternum to lower abdomen is made in the skin. The abdomen wall is then cut through and the animal is rolled onto its side so that the intestines and rumen can be removed. The

kidneys and liver are inspected and retained. Rolling the animal onto its stomach will allow much blood to drain from the carcass, and there will be time to sit and rest while the ponyman is called up. Red deer are often shot, however, in places inaccessible to even the most determined wheeled vehicle, and this may necessitate dragging the beast. Dragging a heavy carcass across inhospitable country can be likened to dragging two-hundredweight sacks over a variety of rocky, heather-clad or soft marshy ground. Although it is a task shared by both stalker and rifle, it is the latter, unfit and already suffering from the exertions of the walk, who will really experience the agony of the drag! Mercifully, though, the drag will come to an abrupt halt when the ponyman is reached and, unless another deer is to be shot, the rifle can anticipate the homeward journey, downhill for most of the way, and the hot bath that awaits at journey's end.

Writing briefly, as I have done, about a day's stalking on the hill can only convey the bare information. No words can describe fully the total experience of being among the heather and peat bogs in the company of an experienced stalker, and every moment of the day will be savoured again and again. For a day to be successful, though, a certain amount of preparation is essential. It must be remembered that although by European standards the mountains of Scotland are mere hills, the weather conditions pose a very real threat to safety. Even in high summer people have died from exposure and hypothermia among the hills. Weather conditions can deteriorate with alarming speed, and those unprepared are putting themselves at great risk and those sent out to rescue them to great inconvenience.

Selecting the best clothing is therefore very important, and the criteria of warmth, comfort, ease of movement and noiselessness must all be considered. In addition, the rifle's normal stalking accessories should be carried. A wallet containing the ammunition should be placed in a secure pocket. A strong knife, either a lock blade or a sheath knife which may be brought into use for the gralloch or for any number of other purposes, and a pair of binoculars must be carried. Either the stalker or the visiting rifle should carry a length of rope for the drag, and each will have a packed lunch, in Scotland called the 'piece', for Highland stalking is an all-day activity.

The actual weapon used for the stalk must be checked over thoroughly before venturing onto the hill. The average range at which deer are shot is somewhat longer than for woodland stalking, and the choice of a flat-shooting calibre is the norm. The most popular calibres are probably the .270 Win., the 7×57 and the .243 Win. – all these can be zeroed at 200 yards with only a negligible rise in the mid-range trajectory. Virtually the same aiming point can therefore be used at any distance from muzzle to 200 yards and, if need be, a wounded beast may be stopped at a greater distance without excessive 'hold-over'. Having said this, most Highland deer are shot at around 100 to 120 yards and very few stalkers would risk asking an un-

known visiting rifle to take shots longer than 150 yards. A visitor should be closely familiar with his rifle and telescopic sight as it would be very unwise to venture onto the hill with an unfamiliar weapon; a missed beast adds greatly to the stress of the occasion and the risk of wounding or inflicting unnecessary pain on a beast and incurring the stalker's wrath would be too high.

Although longer ranges than woodland stalking are involved, the standard choice of a 4x or a 6x telescopic sight is perfectly adequate, and may well be preferred on the grounds of their resistance to knocks compared to the high-power and variable-power 'scope sights. Finally, all the sight mount screws on the rifle should be checked for tightness.

Thus equipped and fit enough to cope with the rigours of a day on the hill, the visiting

The result of a careful stalk on a crisp winter's morning – a culled fallow buck

stalker may enjoy fine sport in magnificent surroundings.

Many estates now offer stalking on a let basis. In Scotland the stag season runs from 1 July to 20 October although stalking is usually delayed until the stags' antlers are clean of velvet in early August. Although lettings are available on a monthly, weekly or even daily basis, the cost of stalking plus trophy fees can be quite high and it would pay the visitor to shop around.

Hind stalking can be obtained at a very much lower rate and, although it still does not carry the prestige of stag stalking, it is a vital part of red deer management and is pursued in far more rugged conditions in mid-winter. The hind season runs from 21 October to 15 February, and many of the more enlightened estates welcome visiting sportsmen to participate in their hind cull at an almost nominal fee. It is only by really concentrating on the winter culling of hinds that the present population crisis on the Scottish red deer grounds will be alleviated.

See also: **Clothing; Deer; Deer Stalking – Woodland; Safety Catch; Seasons; Zero**

Deer Stalking – Woodland Woodland stalking is a relative newcomer to Britain and has been closely linked with the growth and spread of the roe deer population. Britain has perhaps been slow to learn from its continental neighbours that low ground or woodland stalking is very much a sport in its own right. In Britain deer stalking, both as a sport and as an efficient method of controlling deer populations, has since the Victorian era been focused on the Highlands of Scotland. Indeed, the species of deer that has caused the recent growth of woodland stalking, the roe, was looked upon as very much a 'second-class' animal compared to either red or fallow deer, and was persecuted to extinction in all parts of Britain except the remoter Scottish glens by the eighteenth century.

When reintroduced roe populations in Dorset and Norfolk began to increase and disperse they were often treated as vermin, and even as recently as 1963 they were controlled by shotgun drives and by snaring. Happily, this barbaric situation ended with the 1963 Deer Act and its successive amendments, and this has led to the adoption of the European model of woodland stalking. Before the next century Britain is likely to witness a more rapid growth in woodland deer stalking than in any other type of shooting.

Even before 1963, however, there were individuals who recognized the value of these elegant animals in our countryside, and these were the real pioneers of woodland stalking methods that are now taken for granted. Such names as Henry Tegner, Kenneth Whitehead, Arthur Cadman and Richard Prior were in the forefront of those who strove to alter the shooting person's perception of deer control methods and to promote woodland stalking as the obvious and practical solution. It is largely as a result of the work of such pioneers that woodland stalking as a sport now receives the recognition it merits.

So far in the context of woodland stalking I have mentioned only roe deer, but in different parts of the country this method of pursuing deer as a quarry may equally be applied to any of the six species of deer living in a wild state in Britain today. Since the last World War it has become evident that the deer of this country are on the increase, and in different parts of the country one may encounter increasing woodland populations of red, fallow, sika, muntjac, and Chinese water deer, as well as roe. All are predominantly woodland-dwelling animals, and the recent trends in lowland woodland planting are likely to give them further scope for expansion in the future.

Woodland stalking refers to the pursuit and control of deer using appropriate rifles in lowland areas of the country. Even though there are places where they are encountered and shot on farmland it is the fact that the great majority of lowland deer use woodlands as their 'home bases' that gives rise to the term 'woodland stalking'. This form of stalking also takes place in the many newly-forested upland areas; thus for practical purposes any form of deer stalking that does not involve 'going to the hill' may come into this category. This type of sport differs greatly from Highland stalking and the qualities demanded of the participant reflects this.

Whereas hill stalking involves walking

great distances during all hours of daylight, and demands the physical stamina to do so, a woodland stalker may only cover a few hundred yards in the course of one outing. Again, Highland stalking is an activity in which the deer are intercepted at any time of the day, but the woodland stalker must almost invariably confine his activities to the few hours around dawn and dusk. As night shooting of deer is quite rightly illegal, we can only hope to time our encounters with them at dusk, when they move from rest to the feeding areas, and at dawn, when they move back to their cover. There are times in the year when the woodland stalker must be out at very unsociable hours. Summer stalking involves being in the woods at four o'clock in the morning, and out again to see the sun set after ten at night. At peak periods of stalking activities, for example during the roe rut at the end of July, the stalker must have the ability to abandon a 'normal' sleep pattern in order to frequent the woods at dawn and dusk for a number of successive days.

Although woodland stalking makes far fewer demands on physical stamina than its Highland counterparts, it makes far greater demands on mental concentration and the senses. In woodland stalking one must use one's senses of sight and hearing to the utmost while at the same time using great muscular control to move very slowly and above all quietly. Every inch of one's surroundings must be studied minutely with both naked eye and binoculars for signs of a deer. In woodland a deer seldom appears as a complete recognizable animal, so one has to look between the tree trunks and through foliage for perhaps the outline of an ear, the horizontal line of a partly concealed back, the flicker of a tail or the angle of a neck. Many objects will look like deer and each must be studied intensely for signs of movement before being dismissed. The stalker will also quickly come to realize that only two woodland animals will snap small twigs underfoot as they move – humans and deer. Thus the hearing must be tuned for the subtle difference between the sound of a twig snapping in the wind and one being trodden underfoot. Locating the direction of a sound with any accuracy also takes a good deal of concentration, but detecting the

sound of a snapped twig or heavy footfall can point an alert stalker to the presence of deer. In addition to finely tuned sight and hearing, the stalker must also be able to move with agonizing slowness. The muscular control required to move in this way can be very difficult to achieve, particularly when a deer suddenly perceives a movement and you have to freeze in mid step. After some time the leg and back muscles begin to scream for movement, but a deer can stare at a suspicious object for a terribly long time! It is little wonder that this activity can be every bit as tiring as strenuous exercise.

Most woodland stalking in Britain today will be operated within some form of deer management plan. Even in the instances where a 'medal' buck is sought, the stalker or manager will usually have ascertained that the animal is over-age or surplus to requirements and should be culled out as part of the overall strategy. Even where stalking is run on a commercial basis it would hardly be good policy to shoot out all the good bucks in an area for short-term monetary gain from trophy fees. The sport of woodland stalking can really be broken down to two main strategies, which may be termed 'passive' stalking and 'active' stalking. Passive stalking, known as 'still hunting' in America, is really a sport of sitting and waiting. Essentially the stalker gets into a position where deer are likely to come to the stalker rather than the other way around. Deer in lowland woodland are at their most active at dawn and dusk and the stalker wishing to intercept them about their daily routine needs to be in position well before first or last light. In order to be successful the stalker must know the ground well. He must have a good idea of the areas frequented by deer and must also be able to reach these areas without unduly disturbing the wildlife in the surroundings. These silent approach routes are particularly vital for dawn forays as the route will be negotiated in the dark and the deer are likely to be active. Once the position is reached, having been chosen with due regard to wind direction, the stalker then settles down to wait for the deer.

Inevitably the stalker will disturb wildlife in his approach, no matter how silent and careful he has been, but after about half an hour has passed the early morning life of the woodland will return to normality. For this reason it is essential that the stalker is in position well before the light is strong enough for observing and shooting deer. For this type of stalking the majority of woodland stalkers erect and use high seats. These elevated perches raise the stalker and his telltale human scent above ground level so that wind direction ceases to be such a crucial factor. In addition, high seats usually offer a better field of vision than a seat at ground level and, more importantly, a shot from a high seat is directed downwards and is therefore much safer than a ground-level shot in most instances.

During their rut in October, both red and sika stags may be successfully called by imitating the respective rutting calls of the stags. One must first ascertain that the beast one wishes to shoot is in the vicinity and that the animal is sufficiently established to be actually calling itself. In these circumstances echoing his call with a similar one may convince the stag that he has a challenger nearby. An imitated roar of a red or triple whistle of a sika may cause the resident animal to approach the stalker's position, probably skirting downwind in the process, in order to size up his opposition. All will depend on the stalker's choice of position. If the animal can be brought into view before it can reach a downwind position then there is a fair chance of success.

I have never heard of any cases where fallow bucks have been successfully called by imitating the groaning of rutting bucks, and my own attempts in this line have elicited no response from this species. However, I have watched the reaction of a buck to a pair of antlers being clashed and I believe that a fallow buck's curiosity can be aroused to the extent that he will come and investigate. Roebucks, on the other hand, can be quite effectively called during the rut in late July and early August by imitating the piping of a doe. At this time of year the call of an 'unknown' doe in his territory may well bring the buck out to investigate and many old and reclusive bucks are accounted for in this way.

Calling deer is, however, not as successful as many novice stalkers hope, and if a response is provoked once in ten attempts then the stalker should be well satisfied.

Even in this form of stalking it is essential that the stalker keeps as still as possible. Movement betrays any life in the wood, whether it is partly-hidden deer or a stalker being plagued by mosquitoes on a summer's evening. It is only by sitting as still as possible that the stalker has a chance of detecting the presence of deer before the deer detect the stalker. Still hunting has a magic of its own. Once the stalker is settled he will melt into the environment and is then in a position to witness a wide variety of wildlife without being detected. No two dawns or evenings are the same and the stalker is in a position to become an acute wildlife observer.

Active woodland stalking is essentially going to find deer, rather than waiting for them to come to you. As in still hunting, dawn and dusk are the best stalking times, although in areas where deer are seldom disturbed stalking can continue through the day. In common with passive stalking the active stalker requires a good knowledge of the ground and the likely whereabouts of his quarry. As stated earlier, the ability to move slowly and quietly is vital to success, and active stalking requires a degree of prolonged mental concentration not seen in any other form of sporting shooting. The basic tactic for this kind of stalking is to work slowly upwind to the areas deer frequent and to check each area thoroughly with naked eye and binoculars before moving on. It must be remembered that, even though deer may show a preference for certain parts of a wood, they may be found feeding in adjacent fields or encountered in any other part of the wood as they move about. In many instances the stalker has to be at maximum alertness as soon as he leaves his vehicle.

The success of stalking by this method depends on a number of variable factors. Wind direction is probably the most important one, and the stalker must avoid any risk of alerting deer by moving towards them downwind. Stalks should involve moving up or across the wind direction, but this is not as simple as it at first seems. Within woodland the wind can change direction and eddy to such an extent that the direction of the airstream inside the wood is opposite to that of the wind outside! The stalker must therefore check the wind direction frequently during his stalk. Ground cover is another variable factor. It is all too easy to reveal your presence by making a noise when you move. In autumn the leaf litter can be brittle and crackly when dry, and silent movement is then virtually impossible. Heavy frost has the same effect in winter although a stalker can move very quietly over a light covering of soft snow. Often the most silent movement is along well-worn paths and rides, and every stalker will develop favourite routes which use these as much as possible. Where no such easy routes exist, however, the stalker has little alternative but to traverse the woodland in a very slow and painstaking way, perhaps taking advantage of small areas of silent ground to allow breaks in the intense concentration silent movement demands. Deciduous leaf litter in open woodland after a spell of rain has dampened it down will allow reasonably silent movement, and the deep litter of pine needles in conifer plantations also offers welcome silent ground. The stalker must be wary at all times of cracking twigs underfoot. He may well get away with one or two without disturbing the deer unduly, but a series of twig snaps will be answered by those under the deer's hooves as they crash away through the wood. There are occasions when the stalker can take advantage of other noises to mask his own movements. Heavy rain, high wind, aircraft and nearby road traffic can all be used to advantage.

In still air conditions clothing and equipment can be alarmingly noisy. Loose coins and knives in the pockets, the noise of binoculars against the stalking stick, and the rifle sling on the shoulder can all be quite significant factors. Above all, avoid metallic sounds; natural sounds like snapped twigs are not nearly so alarming as the click of a bolt or squeak of sling swivels on a rifle.

Active deer stalking is a sport of intense concentration, slow movement, and infinite patience. It tests the stalker's fieldcraft and skills of concealment and camouflage far more than any other branch of sporting shooting and success will only come from long preparation and observation.

Woodland deer stalking is now a well-established and growing sport, and the opportunities will grow as the deer population extends into hitherto unpopulated parts of the British countryside. Coming on the heels of lowland deer management has been the growth of woodland stalking as a sport. Like Highland stalking, many lowland estates now let woodland stalking by the day or week, and charges vary with the quality of the animals shot. By and large, most woodland stalking is leased as still hunting from high seats, although some keepers will allow well-established stalkers to stalk unaccompanied. Woodland stalking is available, depending on locality, for all six species of British deer and, as their individual seasons vary, it is a sport that is available throughout the year.

See also: **Deer**

Dickson, John   One of the leading Scottish gunmakers, John Dickson were established in 1820 in Edinburgh. Throughout their successful history the company has seen much expansion and Dickson has bought out many other respected gunmakers – Mortimer in 1938, MacNaughton in 1947, Alex Martin in 1962 and others since then.

Dickson won a good reputation for the quality of their muzzle-loading guns and rifles in the first half of the nineteenth century, and they kept this esteem into the era of the breech loader. The name of Dickson is perhaps most famous for a gun they first patented around 1880. Called the 'Dickson Round Action', the lockwork of this side-by-side double is attached to the trigger plate and the action body is rounded rather than rectangular. By 1886 the ejector mechanism had been added, again contained within the action body, and this elegant design is still being built to order today.

In addition to their round-action guns, Dickson offer a range of shotguns and double rifles as well as their own magazine-fed stalking rifles on either Mauser or Mannlicher-Schoenauer bolt actions.

The firm of John Dickson in Edinburgh is now perhaps the oldest surviving gunmaking company in Scotland and the elegant 'Dickson Round Action' has earned them a place in the history of modern shotgun development.

See also: **Mannlicher**

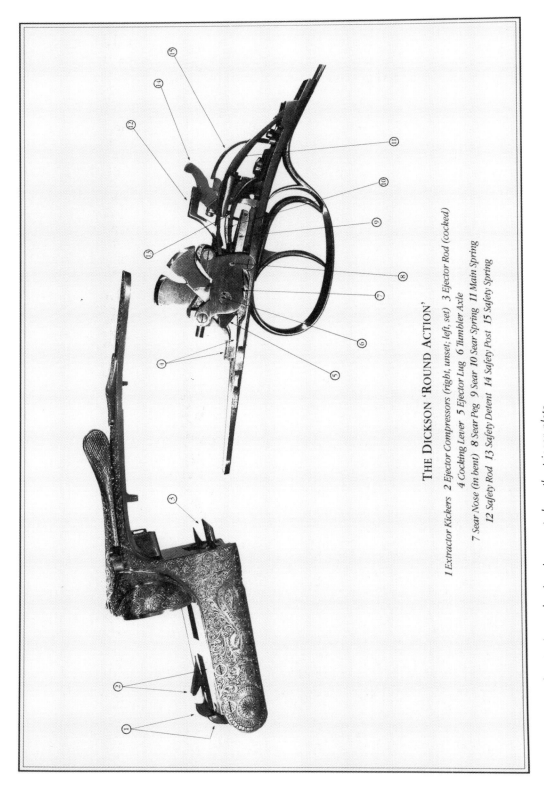

THE DICKSON 'ROUND ACTION'

1 Extractor Kickers 2 Ejector Compressors (right, unset; left, set) 3 Ejector Rod (cocked)
4 Cocking Lever 5 Ejector Lug 6 Tumbler Axle
7 Sear Nose (in bent) 8 Sear Peg 9 Sear 10 Sear Spring 11 Main Spring
12 Safety Rod 13 Safety Detent 14 Safety Post 15 Safety Spring

Most of the round action's mechanism is mounted on the trigger plate

The dollshead extension to the top rib locked the barrels firmly to the breech face in this underlever hammer double rifle

Dollshead Extension   At a time when gunmakers were attempting to improve and strengthen the closing mechanisms of double barrel guns, many opted for a rearward extension of the top rib which was locked into a recess in the action body in a variety of ways. While Greener opted for a cross bolt through the extension, Westley Richards opted for a different method. The top extension ended in a conical 'doll's head' which served to secure the top end of the barrels to the action very effectively.

The dollshead extension was abandoned when improvements were made in locking the barrel lumps to the action.

See also: **Lumps**

Double Barrel   A double barrel firearm is one which possesses two barrels that can be fired either simultaneously or in succession. Both rifles and shotguns are available in the double barrel format and there are even a number of double barrel combination rifle/shotgun weapons on the market.

A weapon capable of firing two shots at will without reloading possesses a number of advantages. In a shotgun each barrel may be bored with different degrees of choke, so the shooter has an instant selection of pattern spread for close-range or longer shots. Further versatility can be achieved by loading each barrel with cartridges of different loads or shot sizes or different types of wad. The main advantage in a rifle is the opportunity to have a quick second shot without removing the weapon from the shoulder. When dealing with large or potentially dangerous game, such as wild boar in Europe or Cape Buffalo in Africa, the advantage of a quick second shot is obvious; however, double rifles are predominately short-range weapons and the accuracy from both barrels beyond one hundred yards falls well below that of a single barrel weapon. For driven game shooting on the European continent many shooters use a 'drilling' multi-barrelled weapon, but these are seldom seen in Britain and the legal restrictions on firearms in this country curtail the ownership and use of shotgun/rifle combination guns.

In the past many English gunmakers experimented with multi-barrelled shotguns in order to increase the rate of fire and some four-barrelled shotguns were produced. They were built on modified boxlock actions but proved unpopular because of their weight.

Modern double barrel weapons come in two styles: the traditional side-by-side in which the two barrels are arranged alongside each other, and the over-and-under in which one barrel is superimposed above the other. Although the side-by-side is looked on as the traditional format for a shotgun it was in fact the over-and-under which was the first double design to be produced in quantity. There are perennial engagements in the shooting press about the advantages of each design – the side-by-side is generally lighter than the over-and-under, the over-and-under offers a quicker and cleaner sighting plane than the side-by-side and so on.

What most people forget is that both designs have the same basic advantages over any single barrel weapon in the instant selection of different chokes or cartridges, and the final selection of the ideal design rests entirely on the individual preference of the shooter. The characteristics of each design can be taken as a merit or a disadvantage according to the shooter's viewpoint. For example, the light weight of a side-by-side game gun can help one shooter in situations where quick reflexes and 'snap' shooting is required, while another shooter may opt for a heavier weapon because the light weight produces punishing recoil with sustained firing. Some will feel happy with the single sighting plane of an over-and-under while others claim that the subconscious picture of side-by-side barrels helps them to swing onto crossing targets.

See also: **Barrel; Choke; Drilling**

Side-by-side game guns (Parker-Hale)

Over-and-unders expose more of their working mechanism than a side-by-side when the action is opened

Drilling Drilling is the family name given to various multi-barrelled rifle/shotgun combinations which are most frequently used when shooting on the European mainland. In many parts of the Continent a standing gun on a driven shoot may expect to be presented with a much wider selection of game species than on a British shoot. In forest blocks the shooter can anticipate raising the gun to anything from woodcock to wild boar, and this calls for a choice of calibres and loads.

'Drilling' combination guns are heavy weapons, but as they are used at a 'peg' or stand the weight factor is of little importance. What is important is that the shooter has available perhaps two different shotgun loads and a centrefire rifle cartridge in order to deal at close range with a wide variety of driven game and these multi-barrelled weapons are the ideal solution.

The term 'drilling' is applied specifically to the double barrel, side-by-side shotgun with a centrefire rifle barrel slung underneath. The 'Doppelbuchsdrilling' is a double barrel side-by-side rifle with a shotgun barrel under, while the 'Bockdrilling' is an over-and-under design with shotgun barrel on top, centrefire rifle barrel below, and a rimfire rifle barrel taking the place of one of the side ribs. Perhaps the most complicated of these designs is the 'Vierling', in which a double side-by-side shotgun has both centrefire and rimfire rifle barrels slung underneath – a four-barrelled weapon with a choice of three calibres! Armed with such a weapon the European sportsman may load one shotgun barrel with a No 6 shot cartridge and the other perhaps with a Brennecke slug. With both rifle barrels loaded he is now in the position to take on a pheasant with the shotgun cartridge, a wild boar with the Brennecke slug, a deer with the centrefire rifle cartridge (usually a 7×57) and a hare with the .22 rimfire. Perhaps the most complicated task is selecting the correct barrel for the target.

These weapons, manufactured by specialist gunmakers such as Heym in Germany, may be built on either modified sidelock or boxlock actions, and usually feature top safety catches and side barrel selector buttons.

The way in which the firearms laws of Britain are framed makes it difficult to own and use such weapons in a sporting context in this country.

See also: **Barrel; Brennecke; Heym**

A Doppelbuschsdrilling: a double side-by-side centrefire rifle with a shotgun barrel slung underneath

Drillings come in a wide variety of barrel combinations

Drilling. Double side by side shotgun with a centrefire rifle barrel underneath.

Doppelbüchsdrilling. The opposite of the drilling. Double side by side centrefire rifle with shotgun barrel underneath.

Vierling. Double side by side shotgun with rimfire and centrefire rifle barrels underneath.

Bockdrilling. Single shotgun, rimfire rifle and centrefire rifle assembled in an over and under form.

Driven Game Shooting Basically, driven game shooting is a sport in which a line of beaters drive the game birds to a 'flushing point' from where they will gain height and fly over the strategically placed guns.

Driven game shooting is the most formalized and most 'labour intensive' of all the shotgun sports in the British Isles. While this form of shooting is also practised in many other parts of the world, the conventions and etiquette of a day's driven shooting in the UK lend it a distinctly British flavour.

Up to fifty people may take part in a day's shoot, each with their own role to play and each an important component in the overall pattern of the day. On most driven shoots the person in overall charge is the head game-keeper. He will be directly responsible for the organization of the team of beaters, the stops, the vehicle drivers and the pickers-up, but the ordering and placing of the shooters – known as guns – and their loaders will be left to the host or the shoot captain.

Stops are placed on the sides of a drive, to turn back any birds that may break out to the sides; and the 'pickers-up', placed behind the guns, use well-trained dogs to retrieve shot, and more importantly wounded, birds. Clearly the guns play a rather small part in the activity of a drive and only rarely serve any other function than shooting the birds. On the larger shoots where each shooting day's bag is expected to run to three figures the shooter may use a pair of shotguns and employ a 'loader' who reloads the weapons – if the shooter and loader work well together the former can achieve a very rapid rate of fire which is important if the birds are being driven over in large numbers.

With so many people involved it is essential that the first consideration is safety, and it is from this aspect that most of the formality of driven game shooting has sprung. The weapons may only be loaded after the host or captain has signalled the start of a drive, and they are unloaded immediately the signal is given for 'drive over'. During each drive it is the shooter's responsibility to determine the exact extent of the 'safe shooting arc' which excludes any low shots that may endanger beaters in front or pickers-up behind, and any shots 'down the line' which could expose a fellow gun to risk as well as taking a bird better suited to a neighbouring shooter.

Driven game shooting takes place in a variety of different environments in Britain. On the wide rolling heather-clad moorland of the Pennines and in Scotland the 'Glorious Twelfth' of August sees the first red grouse of the season killed on many driven grouse shoots.

In response to the environment and the quarry species, a driven grouse shoot differs in a number of ways from the 'basic' driven shoot pattern. The area to be covered is usually much larger than on most lowland

Grouse shooting: at the end of each drive the birds are laid out to cool

shoots, and the number of drives per shooting day is therefore reduced to about six.

However, at the start of a drive the beaters and guns may be over a mile apart, and to keep the red grouse moving in the right direction the shoot may employ walking flankers and flag-men ahead of the line of beaters. These serve the same function as 'stops' on a lowland shoot in that they try to deter any grouse breaking sideways out of the line of the drive.

Again unlike a lowland driven shoot, the lie of the moorland allows for less choice in the direction of each drive, so that the guns will stand in the same positions for each drive from year to year. Driven grouse shoots are therefore able to build permanent 'grouse butts' in which the guns can stand. These are usually drystone-wall semicircles topped at waist height with turf and heather. They can be carefully placed so that they are under or close to the flight lines of birds driven from a particular part of the moor,

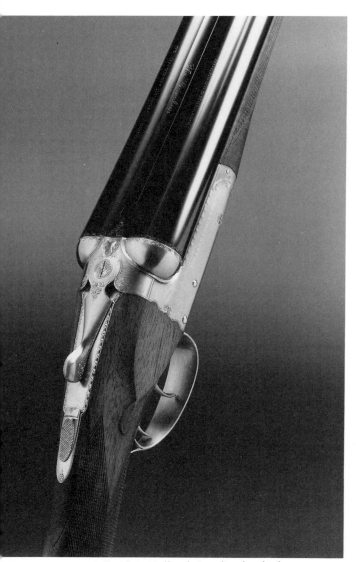

Holland & Holland Cavalier boxlock hammerless ejector gun. The ideal English game gun.

and some shoots even have two or three lines of butts per drive to take account of the wind direction when placing the guns on a shooting day. As the season progresses, grouse that have been over the guns a number of times become 'butt shy' and late-season shoots may eschew butts entirely.

Timing is more important in a grouse drive than in any other form of driven shooting, and portable two-way radios help the head keeper to position all the participants correctly before the beaters move off. As the drive progresses the keeper can adjust the line of beaters to push forward any early flushed grouse so that they will eventually present the guns with low, very fast and very agile targets. He will also adjust the progress of the beating line to control the rate at which the coveys are flushed. Better and

A sight to quicken any shooter's pulse – a covey of red grouse approaching low and fast over the heather moorland

more consistent sport is achieved with a steady flow of grouse over the guns than with one flush of a big pack of grouse near the end of a drive.

Black grouse are birds of the willow- and hazel-clad moorland margins, and a number of grouse moors include a 'black grouse' drive on the fringe of the moor. Here the drive more closely resembles the shorter distances of the lowland and covert shoots, and from this damp scrub environment woodcock may also add variety to the day's bag.

On the wide flat arable land of eastern England, and on the rolling chalk downland of the south, September is often considered to be the best month for driven partridge shooting. Partridge driving encompasses the same principles as driven grouse shooting but on a smaller scale. Unlike grouse shooting, however, the shoot captain is able to take much more account of wind direction in the placing of the guns and the direction of each drive. Partridge should normally be driven downwind, and the guns are usually placed so that their pegs are about forty yards from a hedge over which the birds will pass, so that the birds will appear suddenly as they top the hedge and the action will be fast and furious. A partridge travelling downwind is a very testing target and the guns certainly need very quick reflexes. As with driven grouse, shots are taken at quite low angles, and the shooter must keep rigidly to the safe arc of fire. In addition, when the beaters close in the captain or host may order shots to be taken only after the birds have crossed the line of guns, once the pickers-up have been removed to safety. Again, skilled placing of flag-men and flankers will divert birds breaking out sideways so that they fly towards and over the guns, and the keeper draws on his experience and judgement in altering the pace of the drive to maintain a steady stream of flushed coveys. Both grey and red-legged partridge feature in most driven partridge shoots. Although the mature grey partridge is a hardier bird and posesses more stamina, it is the red-legged which is easier to rear, and many shoots rear and release these in order to supplement the wild stock. The reduction in the use of aphicides on arable crops should have halted the decline of wild partridge in Britain, and the lowland set-aside schemes of land use will certainly help the grey partridge to re-establish itself as an important game species in many British lowlands. In recent years there has been an increase in the number of driven grey partridge shoots, and this is a sign that the long decline of the grey partridge is past.

The first day of October sees the start of the pheasant season. This is the prime lowland game bird, and probably more pheasants are brought to bag each year than all the other game birds put together. Whereas both grouse and partridge are birds of open country, be it heather moorland or lowland pasture and arable fields, the pheasant is more of a woodland bird, and driven pheasants are usually flushed from spinneys and small woods. These environments are known in shooting terms as 'coverts' and driven pheasant shooting is often referred to as 'covert shooting'.

Typically, the pegs for the guns form a line or arc around one end of the covert, which is then driven from the other end by beaters and dogs. The intention is to produce high, fast and testing birds for the guns, and to this end the guns may be placed some distance from the wood. A flushed pheasant may make for shelter in an adjacent patch of woodland so the placing of the guns must be arranged so as to intercept the anticipated line of flight.

In a well-ordered shoot each beater will be armed with a stick to tap on the trees and bushes to push the pheasants towards a flushing point. This may be a cleared ride through the wood or the edge of the wood itself. If the guns have to be placed close to the wood, the pheasants should be induced to flush farther back to gain height and air speed before crossing the line of guns. For this purpose the keeper may well run a line of sewelling across the line of the drive.

Driven game shooting demands certain conduct from the participating guns and is normally organized on a traditional but effective pattern. It is, for example, extremely bad form to arrive late at the appointed venue, and once the guns and beaters are assembled the host and head keeper will brief all the participants on the organization of the day. The beaters will then move off to line up for the first drive of the morning while the guns will draw lots for their peg numbers. Normally between eight or ten guns attend, and the peg numbers on each drive are traditionally numbered right to left – number one being on the right flank of the line of guns and eight on the left. With each successive drive the guns move two pegs to the left; thus, if you draw peg three on the first drive you will stand at peg five for the second, and so on.

When the guns arrive at their allotted pegs the guns are unsleeved and checked prior to the commencement of proceedings. At this time each shooter will make a mental note of the location of the neighbouring guns on either side, of the pickers-up behind the line and of any stops in front. A pre-arranged whistle or horn blast heralds the start of the drive, and only then are the guns loaded.

At the end of the drive the signal will be given to unload and this must be strictly adhered to. Time is then spent picking up the dead and searching for any wounded birds or runners, which are normally accounted for before the party moves off to the next drive. It should perhaps be mentioned here that unless the greatest care is taken there is a risk of harming the shotgun while in transit from one drive to another. A crowded Land Rover or game cart jolting down a rutted farm track has resulted in many a dented gun barrel.

After three or four drives there is normally a lunch break, and this varies from shoot to shoot. On the one hand food may take the form of a sandwich and mug of soup; while on the other hand some shoot lunches are elaborate three-course meals with wine. However, as the hours of daylight are short the break should not last more than an hour before the afternoon drives commence, and indeed later in the season many shoots decide to 'shoot through' the day and take their meal in late afternoon. At the end of each drive the keeper 'braces up' the birds shot and hangs them on the game cart to be taken to a cool storage, and at the end of the day the bag is laid out for inspection by all the participants. The braces of birds, normally a cock and hen tied together, are counted and the overall bag recorded in a game register. At this point each gun is usually presented with a brace of birds and the other helpers are paid according to the host's arrangement. It is customary for the guns to tip the keeper at the end of the day, and a quiet word with the host or shoot captain will identify the appropriate sum. Driven game shooting may be looked upon as a social occasion as well as a good day's sport, and it would only be courteous to thank the host or captain for the day he has provided.

Driven game shooting, whether on rolling moorland on a warm August day or on lowland farmland on a crisp and frosty December morning, can test the shooter's reflexes and skill with a shotgun. Less obviously, though no less important, this form of sport is also a test of gun safety, sportsmanship and courtesy, and a greedy or lax shooter is unlikely to be invited twice.

A driven game shoot in the various forms described here is a very British institution. Ranking alongside foreshore wildfowling and punt gunning as part of Britain's sporting heritage, the driven grouse, partridge or pheasant shoot epitomizes the best in shotgun sports.

See also: **Clothing; Game Shooting**

Ejector The ejector mechanism is designed to throw a spent cartridge clear of the weapon. In many single barrel rifles and shotguns this takes the form of a simple metal bar which fits into a channel in the bolt. When the bolt is withdrawn sufficiently the ejector bar acts on one side of the cartridge case to throw it sideways out of the grip of the extractor.

On double barrel weapons built on the drop-down principle the ejectors are usually incorporated with the extractor so that when the gun is opened the extractors first draw the cartridge a short distance from the breech and the ejector mechanism then kicks it clear of the gun. Automatic ejectors are designed to act only on a fired case; when only one barrel is fired the unfired cartridge is retained while the fired barrel is cleared.

Using the term 'ejector' to describe a double gun implies that it is fitted with this automatic selective ejector mechanism. Although many gunmakers devised their own systems, it is the ejector mechanism designed by Southgate which is most commonly used nowadays on double side-by-side shotguns and rifles.

Elevation Elevation is the up-and-down movement in an adjustable rifle sight. The purpose of this adjustment is to allow the line of sight to coincide with the bullet's point of impact at any distance within its effective range. In a correctly zeroed rifle the path of the bullet crosses the line of sight at close range, then flies above it for some distance before curving down to cross it

again at 'long zero' range. Beyond this the impact point lies below the point of aim, and the distance between the two increases with increasing range.

In order to compensate for the bullet drop the rear sight – be it a mid-barrel open 'V' notch or an aperture sight on the receiver – is raised or elevated. This increases the angle between the line of sight and the bullet's initial path and effectively raises the distant point of impact so that it coincides with the sighting mark.

When the shooter is conversant with the particular brand of cartridge being used, another method for compensating for bullet drop can be used, and this is called 'hold-over'. If, for example, the shooter estimates that the bullet will land six inches below the zero point, it is a simple task to aim six inches high for that particular shot. Hold-over also has the advantage in that the precise zero setting on the sights need not be altered from shot to shot.

Even though telescopic sights are fitted with an elevation adjustment wheel on the top of the 'scope tube, this should be used only for zeroing the rifle at a specific range so should not be moved. The hold-over technique is even easier and more precise when using a telescopic sight than when using open or aperture sights, as the degree of hold-over is easier to assess through a 'scope.

For shots at closer range it may be necessary to either depress the sights or 'hold under' when the bullet is known to be well above the line of sight.

Euston System The Euston system is an effective way of ensuring a good hatch rate in wild partridge broods. Basically, the eggs are removed from partridge nests as soon as the clutches are completed. These are replaced by dummy eggs so the wild birds continue to incubate while their eggs are placed under broody hens. Just before hatching they are put back under the wild bird and the dummy eggs removed; the wild bird then hatches off and leads the brood away.

While not increasing the wild stocks by artificial releases, the Euston system reduces the risk of nest predation and loss of eggs. If the sitting bird does fall victim to a predator the eggs are simply placed in another nest and the overall stock does not suffer.

Evans, William In 1883 William Evans left Purdey and set up a gunmaking company of his own in London. Since that time the firm has established a reputation for the quality of the guns that are produced – living up to the standards expected of a 'London gun' in every way.

Over the year William Evans have built a wide variety of guns and rifles from pairs of best sidelock ejectors to the less expensive boxlock ejector game guns. Specializing in side-by-side shotguns, the firm now makes guns only to order although they offer the shooter a wide variety of repair, maintenance and reconditioning services for all types of weapons.

William Evans is a company that has survived the decline of the London gun trade which has closed so many other small gunmaking businesses in Britain's capital. This is perhaps a reflection of the quality gunmaking and other services the company offers.

Extractor The extractor is a device which extracts the cartridge from the breech of a weapon. In shotguns the extractors are recessed in the breech end of the barrel, but when the gun is opened they engage in the rim of the cartridge to draw it a short distance to the rear. In 'drop-down' guns the cartridge can then be removed by hand.

In rimfire rifles the extractor often takes the form of a hook which is recessed in the bolt. This engages on the rim of the cartridge so that it may be extracted when the bolt is moved to the rear. Most centrefire cartridges are 'rimless' and here the extractor engages in the channel which runs around the base of the cartridge case.

Elevation marks on the side of a Williams rear sight indicate the degree the notch has been raised or lowered

Fallow Deer Fallow deer (*Dama dama*) are perhaps the most widespread of the deer species living wild in Britain at present. They are the second largest of the land mammals after red deer, with mature bucks weighing upwards of 170 lbs (75 kg) and does around 100 lbs (47 kg). They are noticeably smaller than red deer in that the buck stands at about 36 inches at the shoulder. To many people fallow deer epitomize grace and elegance, as they do seem to be better proportioned than the massive and powerful lowland and park red deer. Two characteristics serve to separate fallow as a species from all the other deer in Britain. The antlers are palmated and the coat shows a wide range of colour varieties.

The 'normal' fallow's coat or pelage is chestnut in summer. This is dappled with white spots above a cream-coloured lateral line on the animal's flank. As winter approaches the spotting gradually fades and the coat turns to a grey-brown shade which darkens towards the top of the spine. Throughout the year the underparts remain creamy white and the rump has a whitish patch edged with black, and it is this which helps to distinguish a normal from a black fallow in winter when no spots are visible.

Black fallow are a spotless variety. Throughout the year the coat on the flanks is grey-brown, darkening towards the top of the back to, in some animals, a charcoal black. Underparts are a light grey and there is little seasonal variation in the coat as a whole. The rump patch is medium grey and there

are no black borders to outline it as in a 'normal' fallow.

The light phase is known as a 'menil' fallow. In summer these resemble normal animals as their coats are light brown and heavily spotted. The rump patch, however, is not edged in black and the underparts are white. In the winter menil fallow retain their spots though the thick winter coat produces a darker brown background to them.

Finally there is the white phase, which is not actually albino. The coat of a white fallow only becomes white over a number of years and through successive moults. Fallow fawns of this colour phase initially have a creamy-brown coat and may be taken to be a rather light-coloured menil deer. With each moult, however, the coat grows paler until after about two years the animal becomes pure white. The winter coat of a white fallow can make sheep grazing in the same field look positively yellow by comparison. In a white fallow the nose and eyes are dark but no other black markings are visible. In some lights vestigial spotting can be seen on the coat but this is a result of light reflecting from the deer hair and is not due to colour. The hooves of a white animal are orange-yellow as compared to the dark grey-black of all the other colour phases.

While these are recognized as clear colour variations in fallow, they are by no means the only ones that occur. In a herd of this species, each of the four phases can usually be seen together with animals which grade between the phases. Thus, intermedi-

A big fallow buck rests in a patch of sunlight
during the October rut

ate colour deer exist which may appear to be 'menil–white' or 'normal–black'. This wide diversity of colour within the one species has caused a great deal of confusion to novice deer watchers. However, all fallow do have two common characteristics. Firstly, the tail, at about 12 inches in length, is long for a deer. In normal fallow it is black above and white beneath; in the black phase it is black above and grey beneath. Menil deer tails tend to reflect the colour of the main pelage, varying from pale brown to a dark nut-brown depending on the season, with white underneath. White fallow have pure white tails. Fallow deer frequently shake their tails when moving about their lying-up area. Indeed, the tail movement is often the first indication a stalker receives that he is close to fallow. When the deer is alarmed and running the tail is trailed out horizontally behind. Such a long tail immediately differentiates fallow from red deer, whose

The flattening or palmation of the fallow buck's antlers is quite distinctive

tail is short and stumpy, and from the roe, which has no visible tail.

The second main distinguishing feature is the shape and form of the fallow buck's antlers. Under good conditions, a male fallow fawn will develop small bony knobs on its skull above and behind the eyes. Growth of these knobs begins around the animal's first Christmas and continues through to about April. These are the pedicles on which subsequent antlers will grow, and by the time the fawn reaches its first birthday its first true antlers will have begun growing in velvet. By the end of August the protective velvet will have been cleaned off and the young buck's spikes will be visible. The 'first head' usually consists of two unbranched spikes, reaching perhaps nine inches in length in a good animal. Like all antlers, they are creamy-coloured when freshly cleaned of velvet but soon colour up to dark brown as the buck frays and polishes his antlers on soft vegetation and young saplings. At the spike stage the fallow is known as a 'spiker' or 'pricket'.

By the time the third head is grown the antlers of a fallow will show signs of palmation – the flattening of the main beam of the antler close to the farthest end from the head. With each succeeding year, until the animal reaches maturity at about seven years old, the length of the antlers increases, as does the width of the palmation. Like the antlers of the red deer, fallow antlers are described by ancient terms. In a mature beast the forward-pointing tines just above the pedicle are called the 'brow' points or tines; midway along the beam is another forward-pointing tine known as the 'trez tine'. Beyond this point the antler palmates, and considerable variation in shape occurs. However, the palmation ends with a top point and the trailing edge usually has one large rearward facing 'back point' just above the trez point. Between the back point and the top point the trailing edge of the palmation may show a number of small points and these are known as 'spellers'.

Fallow deer antlers do show considerable variation as a result of genetic factors and quality of feeding. In some parts of the country the deer have deeply-cleft palmations while in others the length of the brow tine varies a great deal. Nevertheless, the palmation is clearly visible on a mature buck and this is a distinctive identification feature for this species.

In the summer months, when the old antlers have been cast and the new ones are growing, fallow bucks may be identified by the prominent tuft of hair growing forward from the penis shaft. This is visible in very young bucks even before their antlers show signs of palmation. The larynx, or Adam's apple, is also prominent in a male fallow deer.

This species walks, trots and gallops, and its gait is elegant compared to a red deer gait. Its fast trot is taken with short strides, unlike the larger species. The one movement which is characteristic of fallow deer is a four-legged bouncing trot known as 'pronking'. This movement, while occasionally seen in the other species, is frequently interpreted as an alarm signal among fallow, and is used by a deer of any age and sex as a means of communicating unease to its neighbours. When moving at speed fallow often adopt a single file, and where unfenced roads exist,

as in the New Forest, this habit often results in road death. The first deer in the file cross the road safely, and later arrivals will dash across regardless of traffic.

Fallow are rather easier to age than red deer, particularly when the growth rates and antler characteristics of a group or herd are known. Like red deer, young fallow bucks will have an upright stance, with their heads carried high on thin necks. As the successive antlers are grown the neck becomes thicker and increasingly muscular. Though the fallow does not grow a mane, the neck fur gets longer and thicker in the lead-up to the rut and this, together with the pronounced Adam's apple, lends a mature buck a strong and muscular appearance. As far as facial features are concerned, a fallow fawn has a short and blunt muzzle. With increasing age the face lengthens, and old does can have a profile reminiscent of aged red deer hinds. It is, however, very difficult to assess the age of a doe older than two years which has not yet reached old age.

Regardless of the colour phase of any particular deer, the winter coat grows through the summer coat during September and October. The spring moult takes place in April and May, during which time the deer look unkempt and ragged, as the winter coat falls out in large clumps. By mid-June most fallow will have attained their full summer coat.

During the summer mature bucks tend to live apart from the does in 'bachelor' groups, but in September these return to the home range of the does in the lead-up to the rut. Prior to this the bucks may wander several miles from their traditional rutting areas, but October sees them gathering for the rut, which reaches its peak in late October and continues on into early November. When they arrive at the rutting stand the bucks indulge in much foliage thrashing with their antlers, and elder, willow and other saplings may be extensively damaged. Older trees are used as anointing posts to mark the buck's territory. Bark scoring may also occur on mature hardwoods, and the buck also produces scrapes on the ground in which he urinates and rolls. These scrapes have a strong 'rutty buck' odour. The rut is a time for frenetic activity by fallow bucks as they attempt to attract does to their particular rutting stand. The bucks produce a deep

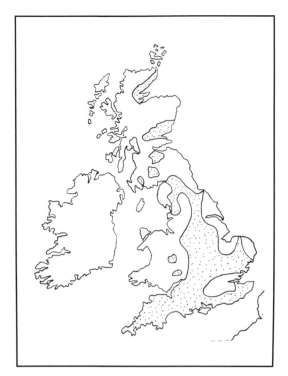

Fallow deer: the most widespread British deer species

resonant grunting or belching sound, called 'groaning', which carries some distance. In an area of mixed woodland and arable land each copse will echo to the groaning of a rutting fallow buck. So busy is the buck with these activities that he will seldom eat and by the end of the rut some bucks will show general weight loss and signs of exhaustion. Fighting between equally-matched bucks occurs when one invades another's rutting stand, and these tend to be short head-on attacks followed by attempts to push the rival backwards. The buck that retreats and gives way is the loser and has to get off the stand and out of the way of the victor's antlers very quickly.

After an eight-month gestation period the fawns are born in May, and join the does' group shortly after. A young buck will often remain with the females until it is two years old and is growing its second head, when it will leave to join the buck parties. Though sexually active by this age, it is unlikely to set up its own rutting stand or attract does until it has reached sufficient size and maturity to compete with the other bucks.

There is evidence that fallow deer existed in Britain before the last Ice Age. However, after the ice retreat the species failed to re-colonize the country before the land bridge from the Continent was flooded by rising sea levels. There is much argument and conjecture as to who eventually re-introduced the species into the country, with the Romans or Normans being the most likely. During Norman times, however, vast tracts of country and forest were set aside as royal hunting grounds, and in these areas both red and fallow deer were regarded as beasts of the chase. As time went on hunting declined, and it became fashionable among the nobility to fence large areas of forest around their houses into deer parks, so that fallow came to be looked upon as decorative adornments as well as meat on the hoof. As the fortunes of the noble families rose and fell so new deer parks were established while old ones fell into disrepair. Both the First and Second World Wars accelerated the process as the large houses were taken over by the military, park fences were broken down, and the deer escaped.

With this historical background it is hardly suprising that fallow deer are at present the most widely distributed of all the wild deer. Fallow can be seen in almost every lowland county in Great Britain and, although some populations trace their ancestry back to the royal forest areas, the majority of wild-living fallow in this country descend from park escapes. Fallow of royal hunting lineage exist in the New Forest, the Forest of Dean, Cannock Chase, Epping Forest and Rock-ingham Forest. Elsewhere, park escapees have established themselves as a wild species and are continuing to spread.

The ideal environment for fallow deer is farmland dotted with mixed or deciduous mature woodland. More than any other deer species these are predominantly grazing animals, preferring grass and cereal crops, although they do also browse hardwood and herb shoots. In severe weather they are also known to strip bark from mature trees, but grazing will remain their main source of food.

Fallow are also perhaps the most diurnal of all British 'woodland' deer, as in an un-disturbed area they will be seen grazing at any time of day. In more disturbed locations, however, they will revert to dawn and dusk peaks of activity: moving to and from their feeding grounds.

See also: **Deer**

Federation des Associations de Chassseurs European (FACE)   FACE represents the views of all the major field sports organizations of Europe. Based in Brussels, it is an important voice in negotiations on hunting legislation formulated by the European Community. FACE-UK is the British branch of the organization and is funded by associations representing anglers, hunters, sporting shooters, and conservation groups. It monitors the changes in European legislation with particular reference to how this affects sport in Britain, and therefore has a very important representational role in the future of field sports in Britain.

Address: **The Secretary**
FACE-UK
Marford Mill
Rossett
Wrexham
Clwyd
LL12 0HL

Feeder   A feeder is a device or construction which is placed at strategic points to provide food for game birds. In its simplest form, a feeder may be a rudimentary shelter under which dredge corn is periodically dumped to feed pheasants. Straw is often strewn about the corn because these birds do like to forage for the grain. However, shelter feeders may be used by other species and several more advanced types are designed to be more discriminating in distributing food.

Drum feeders are simply old oil tins with holes pierced in the base, suspended about eighteen inches from the ground and filled with dredge corn. The pheasants can peck the grain from the holes while it remains inaccessible to squirrels and other species. At the top end of the scale, automatic feeders can distribute measured amounts of grain at pre-determined intervals, sometimes also sounding a buzzer so that the birds associate the noise with a supply of food. Pheasants

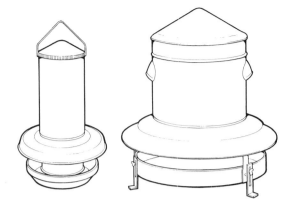

Two models of game bird feeders made from galvanized steel

are notorious for their habit of straying from their release point, and the purpose of any feeder is to hold the birds on the shoot grounds.

See also: **Pheasant**

Firing Pin   The firing pin is the rounded pin which strikes the primer or cap to fire the cartridge. In most 'drop-down' types of weapon the firing pin is spring-loaded and is separate from the hammer or tumbler. When the trigger is pulled these strike the rear of the firing pin, which in turn strikes the cap in the base of the cartridge. The firing pin assembly in these weapons is also known as the 'striker'.

In bolt-action weapons the firing pin is activated by the forward movement of the bolt assembly, and this pin in turn strikes the edge of the cartridge in the case of a rimfire, or the centre of the base in the case of a centrefire

Misfires may arise when the firing pin is broken or worn, or when the tumbler or bolt does not strike the pin with sufficient force.

See also: **Bolt Actions; Hammers;**
Tumblers

Flight Pond   Flight ponds are small areas of open water created for the purpose of attracting wild duck. In some instances a flight pond may be excavated in a damp corner of a field or in a marshy patch of waste ground. In others an existing stream or ditch can be enlarged by damming and excavation in order to produce an attractive habitat for duck. A flight pond need not be large; one on my shoot is roughly circular and barely ten yards across yet it regularly attracts both mallard and teal in the winter months.

Ideally the pond should be sheltered by a tall hedge or trees, and the margins should shelve gradually down to its deepest point, which need not exceed four feet in depth. This will give a shallow-water dabbling zone which can be 'fed' at intervals with dredge corn in order to provide a food source. The hedge or trees will provide protection from the elements, and seclusion, and the bank side may be planted with a variety of reeds and cover plants in order to improve on the natural look of the environment.

For the breeding season, duck nest boxes may encourage an odd pair of mallard to breed, and this will provide a resident population of duck for the following winter. Flight ponds are a valuable micro-habitat for wildlife in general, and different species of warblers may colonize the area round the pond during the summer. Throughout the year it will attract species of birds, insects and animals which might otherwise not frequent the area.

See also: **Mallard; Teal**

Fore-End   The fore-end is the part of any long arm which is supported or held by the shooter's leading hand. Lying under the barrel between the trigger guard and the muzzle, the fore-end is also known as the fore-arm. In sporting weapons the fore-end is usually made of timber to match the stock, and in many single barrel designs of both shotgun and rifle the fore-end and stock form one unbroken unit. In side-by-side double shotguns and rifles the fore-end comes in two main designs and performs a number of functions. In a standard game gun or double rifle the fore-end is a small tapering wedge-shaped piece of timber which secures the barrels to the action and houses the extractor or ejector mechanisms. It can hardly be looked on as as a hand grip as the average shooter supports the gun by cradling the

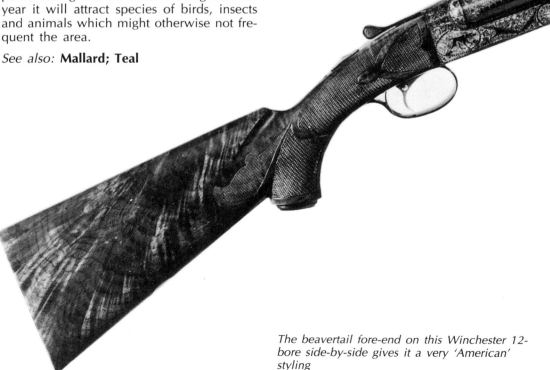

The beavertail fore-end on this Winchester 12-bore side-by-side gives it a very 'American' styling

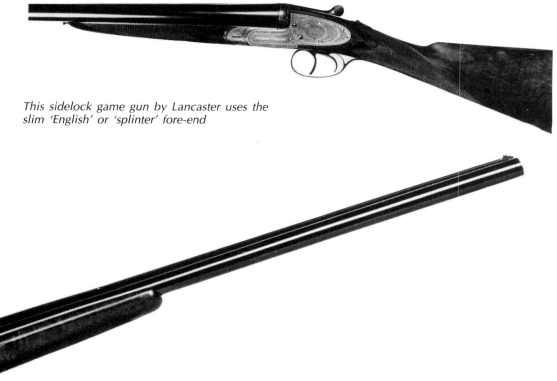

This sidelock game gun by Lancaster uses the slim 'English' or 'splinter' fore-end

barrels on or near the front end of the fore-end. Nevertheless, fore-ends of this design are usually chequered and they do enhance the grace of a gun. In Britain this type of fore-end is the usual choice for the average double shotgun, but in the USA, where they are called 'splinter' fore-ends, they are less favoured than the 'beavertail' fore end.

In the beavertail the width of the fore-end increases from its join with the action so that it wraps around the lower part of the barrels. Unlike the British style this is very definitely a hand grip which, its advocates claim, facilitates the pointing of the weapon.

Additionally, one of the advantages claimed for the beavertail fore-end is that it keeps the hands from coming into contact with the barrel, thus preventing burnt fingers from hot barrels or from barrels at sub-zero temperatures. Fore-ends of this type are therefore often favoured by wildfowlers and by those shooting in warm climates. Another

advantage of the beavertail fore-end is that its greater width prevents the fingers and thumbs of the front hand encroaching over the top of the barrels and thereby encouraging a tendency towards head lifting on the part of the shooter.

In over-and-under and single barrel repeating shotguns the distinction between standard and beavertail is less pronounced, as the fore-end wraps around the bottom barrel and protects about half the top barrel. Like the fore-end of a side-by-side double it holds the barrels to the action when the gun is open, but in the over-and-under the extraction mechanisms are usually housed between and to the sides of the barrels near the breech end. Chequering is standard on over-and-under fore-ends as they are used as a hand grip. Some gunmakers vary this by cutting tranverse ribbing or longitudinal fluting into their fore-ends, claiming that this enhances the shooter's grip and therefore control of the gun. These are, however, cosmetic variations on what is really a standardized part of a shotgun with a set function.

On a single barrel rifle the fore-end shows a somewhat wider variety of styles due to

Beretta over-and-under trap stock with Monte Carlo comb, pistol grip, palm swell, ventilated recoil pad, rounded full checkered fore-end, raised rib, SST

the greater variety of actions used in rifle manufacture. In many self-loading, pump-action and lever-action rifles the fore-end is, like that of a double weapon, a separate piece of wood used as a hand grip.

In bolt-action rifles the stock and fore-end are one piece and the variations come in the form of different lengths, cross-sectional profiles and long profiles of the fore-end.

The more basic pump-action rifles are often fitted with a small, deeply ribbed wooden slide handle which acts as the leading-hand grip and the reloading lever. In better-quality weapons of this design the wooden fore-end is enlarged to cover more of the unsightly mechanisms beneath the barrel so that it enhances the appearance of the rifle while also allowing the shooter greater freedom in where the leading hand is placed.

The term 'beavertail' fore-end is also applied to single barrel rifles and in this case it implies that the width or thickness of the fore-end increases forward of the breech. The cross-section of these beavertail fore-ends varies according to how each manufacturer designs the optimum anatomical grip for the leading hand. The 'beavertail' is also used to differentiate the broad fore-end from the slim and tapering 'AlexHenry' style of fore-end. This elegant style is perhaps the nearest a single barrel rifle's fore-end comes to the traditional 'splinter' fore-end of a shotgun.

The fore-end profile of a one-piece bolt-action stock and fore-end falls into four general categories. The 'classic' English fore-end has a rounded cross profile and is rounded at the front. It has 'wrap-around' chequering where the hand grips and this style is usually associated with the straight or 'classic' stock.

The American style of fore-end owes much to the Weatherby rifles. Here, the front of the fore-end is cut away at an angle and is tipped with a block of contrasting wood (usually rosewood or ebony) which is separated from the main stock by a white-line spacer. In cross-section the fore-end is more square, with a flat base and vertical chequered sides.

The European full stock, also called the Mannlicher or Stutzen, has the fore-end extending to the muzzle of the rifle, where the wood is often tipped with a metal band or contrasting timber without line spacers.

Finally, the lipped or Schnabel fore-end is one in which the gentle forward taper changes to a small elegant bell at the very end of the fore-end. The cross-section is oval or rounded and the Schnabel fore-end usually has a steeper forward taper than the others. Thus its supporters claim that it is the most elegant of the designs described.

No shooter would choose a weapon on the design of the fore-end alone. It is after all simply one minor contribution to the function and appearance of the firearm. The design of the fore-end is, however, tied up with the overall style and it is on these grounds that the selection of a weapon is often based.

Fore-End Catch In many single barrel weapons the fore-end is simply secured to the barrel by means of bolts or screws. In single or double barrel weapons which open by the 'drop-down' principle, however, the fore-end is held on to the underneath of the barrel by a spring catch on the fore-end engaging on a protruding clip – known as the fore-end loop – on the barrel.

In the simpler single barrel weapons and in some of the older double guns the fore-end is held in place by a simple pressure spring. The fore-end is removed by applying leverage to the front of the fore-end until the spring pressure is overcome and the fore-end is dislodged. The fore-end is replaced by engaging its base onto the knuckle of the action and pressing it towards the barrel. In this instance the fore-end snaps into place once the spring pressure is overcome. This is known as the Hackett 'snap' fore-end.

In more modern shotguns this method of securing it to the barrels has been replaced by two other methods. The Anson push-rod device is by far the most common on side-by-side doubles. In this mechanism a rod runs along the fore-end from a small button at the front tip to the spring catch which engages in the loop. To disengage the fore-end the button is pressed and the fore-end removed. Replacing the fore-end is similar

to the Hackett in that it will snap into place without using the button.

The Deeley catch is also used on side-by-sides but is far more common on over-and-under weapons. Fashion in the design of over-and-under shotguns and rifles has dictated that they should be as slim and elegant as possible. As the Anson push-rod device requires a mechanism beneath the bottom barrel it would increase the overall depth of the weapon to an unacceptable level. The Deely catch solves the problem. Instead of using a push-rod from the front of the fore-end, the Deely mechanism uses a ring-pull close to the loop catch. Simple leverage on the ring releases the catch and fore-end, and considerably less depth of fore-end is required to house the device – hence its popularity in over-and-under guns.

Foresight The foresight is a device placed on the muzzle of any firearm to help aim the weapon. On a shotgun the foresight usually takes the form of a small metallic bead which is not really used to 'aim' the gun, but rather indicates the direction the shotgun is pointing. It is the shotgun's bead that the brain registers when the shooter swings the barrels ahead of a flying bird, and as such it is a reference point rather than an aiming device.

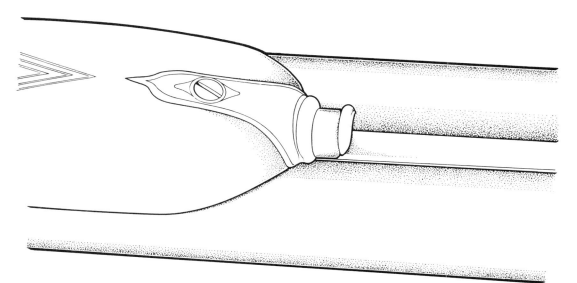

The Anson push-rod button at the tip of the fore-end

The foresight on a rifle takes the form of a bead or blade and is used in conjunction with the rearsight (placed midway along the barrel) or an aperture sight (placed near the shooter's eye) for precise aiming at a target. The almost universal use of telescopic sights nowadays has rendered the foresight obsolete, and many shooters now remove the iron sights on a rifle to achieve a 'cleaner' barrel line. However, this then places total dependence on the telescopic sight, without recourse to iron sights should the optics be damaged.

See also: **Aperture Sights; Bead Blade**

Fouling – Lead   'Lead fouling' is the term used for the residue that is left in a barrel when a weapon is fired. Being a soft metal, lead in contact with a barrel wall when a cartridge is fired will leave a smear due to friction.

Under normal circumstances lead fouling is not a problem and can be easily removed with a phosphor bronze brush. If the barrel is left uncleaned moisture may become trapped between the lead fouling and the barrel, and corrosion may begin. There are some brands of shotgun cartridge which are particularly prone to lead fouling, though this is not a problem if the gun is cleaned soon after use.

Rimfire rifles may have more problems with lead fouling, for two reasons. Firstly, the lead used in .22 rimfire bullets is much softer than the 'hardened' shot used in the shotgun ammunition. This means that friction generated as the bullet is pushed up the barrel is more likely to leave a lead smear, particularly in the higher-velocity rounds. Most manufacturers of rimfire ammunition actually coat the surface of the bullets with wax or a thin copper plating in order to reduce the risk of fouling. The second reason lies in the design of the rifling in some rimfire barrels. Some manufacturers of rimfire rifles cut very shallow rifling grooves in order to minimize bullet deformation and thereby increase accuracy. However, the friction generated on this shallow rifling by the new 'hyper-velocity' ammunition does occasionally cause 'bullet stripping' – a partial melting of the bullet surface in contact with the barrel, with consequent loss of accuracy.

In the high-velocity centrefire rifle calibres lead bullets would certainly strip if they were not protected by the gilding metal jacket, which is always used regardless of the type of bullet design. As a consequence, lead fouling does not occur in high-velocity centrefire rifle barrels.

See also: **Barrel; Bullet**

Fox   The fox (*Vulpes vulpes*) is the largest of the British vermin quarry species. A medium-to-large doglike animal, the fox is characterized by its long body, relatively short legs and long bushy tail or 'brush'. The face is dog-like, with alert ears and pointed muzzle, but the eyes have the vertical slit pupils of the cat family. Colour varies considerably, but the 'typical' fox has a red-brown body and head with black ear tips, lower legs and paws. The tip of the tail may be white. In summer this coat is bright 'foxy' red, but this darkens as the longer winter coat grows through to produce a much greyer overall colour.

Foxes are common over most of the British Isles, and they are often found close to human settlement, although they are truly wild predators. Mainly nocturnal in habit, foxes are somewhat territorial animals, and their nightly patrols follow regular paths. They will keep under cover where possible, and are uneasy when crossing open country in daylight. During the hours of darkness, however, they relax their caution and will frequently raid farms and smallholdings to take waterfowl and poultry. In the wild their main food source is rabbit, but game birds may take up a significant part of their diet when available. Despite this, the fox is an omnivore and will eat fruit and seeds as well as insects, amphibia, and small mammals.

The fox is an alert and intelligent animal which prefers woodland and adjacent farmland as the ideal habitat. They will, however, occupy any environment in Britain, from inner-city parkland and suburban gardens to salt marshes and high sub-alpine slopes of the Scottish mountains. The fox is an extremely adaptable animal, and an overpopulation in any area will severely reduce the numbers of game birds and other ground-dwelling wildlife as well as farm poultry and waterfowl. In severe weather foxes have been observed killing lambs, and in some cases a significant percentage of infant deer will fall to fox predation.

As there is no natural predator on foxes, their numbers must therefore be controlled. Traditionally foxes have been hunted with foxhound packs and in some parts of Britain these work very well. Elsewhere, in areas that are only infrequently hunted or may not be hunted at all, foxes must be controlled by either trapping or shooting.

In some parts of the south-west, fox drives are organized, in which teams of dogs and shooters 'bridge the gap' between hound sports and shooting sports. Elsewhere, foxes are a quarry of opportunity for the shotgun shooter, and many animals disturbed from an above-ground resting place are brought to bag by rough and game shooters.

Lamping for foxes is perhaps the most specialized of all rifle sports. It is broadly similar in principle to lamping for rabbits. The shooter of foxes will use a centrefire high-velocity .22 calibre rifle, and long-range fox shooting at night makes great demands on the accuracy of the weapon and the steadiness of the shooter. When 'hot' calibres such as the .220 Swift or the .22/250 are used in conjunction with very powerful lighting units, I have seen foxes killed at ranges beyond three hundred yards during the hours of darkness. Sitting up over a fox's earth can be productive at certain times of the year and may be useful in eliminating specific animals, but lamping is by far the most effective control method for this wily and intelligent species.

See also: **Lamping; Vermin Control**

Fraser, Dan'l The business of Dan'l Fraser & Co. was established in 1878 and is a good example of a small and successful British provincial gun and rifle maker. Based in Peddieston, Cromarty, in Northern Scotland, it is now a branch of Horton International Ltd.

This company is an example of the bespoke trade in that its craftsmen will build a weapon to the specification and to some extent the price limitations of the customer. To this end it will build both boxlock and sidelock double barrel shotguns either as single guns or in pairs or triples to order. Though meticulously finished to best-quality standards, the price is well below that which would be charged by one of the 'prestige' London gunmakers.

It is, however, for its rifles that this company has gained esteem, and as with shotguns, it will produce rifles to any design demanded by a customer. There are three types of rifle which have almost become its 'standard' production lines, although each weapon will reflect the preference of the individual client. All are handbuilt weapons. They are accurate and reliable and command a pride of ownership.

The first model, the Dan'l Fraser 'Stalking Rifle', is based on the pre-war Mannlicher–Schonauer bolt and utilizes the five-shot rotary magazine seen in big game rifles. The barrel and action are finely finished and the stock is of French or Turkish walnut of high quality. The preferred calibres are .243, .308 and 7×57 (.275) although other calibres may be produced to order. Working with the pre-war actions, the company carry out much modification of both the action and the bolt

to ensure the smoothest and most reliable operation.

Moving up the power scale comes the 'Game Ranger Professional' rifle. This model uses the company's own actions, and each rifle has telescopic sight mounts that are tailored to the choice of 'scope. In this way the sight is mounted as low as possible to ensure very quick sighting of the target. As with the stalking rifle, best-quality materials are used throughout to ensure a lifetime of reliable service and the 'Game Ranger Professional' is available in any calibre up to the .300 Win. Magnum.

The third model offered is the heavy rifle known as the 'Game Ranger African Express'. Based on the Mauser bolt action, this weapon is designed to take the heaviest cartridges and absorb much of the recoil. Careful weighting, balancing and stock contouring will reduce the effect of recoil on the shooter, and the rifle is designed to be used with the traditional three-leaf express open sights. This weapon is built in calibres ranging from the .375 H & H Magnum up to the massive .505 Gibbs, and a wide range of optional extras allows each weapon to be tailored to the customer's exact requirements.

Finally, Dan'l Fraser and Co. will also build double barrel express rifles in any of the heavy calibres, and the quality and accuracy compare favourably with the best and most prestigious in the world.

Frenchman or French Partridge

See: **Partridge – Red-Legged**

Full Metal Jacket   As its name suggests, a full metal jacket bullet (FMJ) is one in which the lead core is completely enclosed in a jacket of gilding metal. It is usually found as military ammunition although some sporting centrefire rifle cartridges are loaded with FMJ bullets for specific purposes. In these the jacket extends to, but does not enclose, the base of the bullet, and they are used where deep penetration with minimum deformation is required. Thus large-calibre rifle ammunition is loaded with full metal jacket bullets for use against thick-skinned African game, as the bullet must be able to penetrate and break heavy bones before disrupting any vital organs. For other game the FMJ round is ineffective as it will pass clear through the body of the animal with the minimum of damage. FMJ bullets are also used in target ammunition.

See also: **Bullet**

Gadwall The gadwall (*Anas strepera*) is probably the most difficult British quarry species to identify. It weighs about 1³/₄ lbs and measures up to 20 inches long, and at any distance or in poor light can easily be taken for a small or immature mallard. There are, however, several points which can aid a positive identification of the species.

The drake gadwall is a medium-sized grey bird. At first it appears to be a medium grey all over, but on its neck and head the colour merges into mottled brown similar to a female mallard. The grey on the back also darkens towards the tail, but this is not often discernible in poor light. When it is airborne more distinctive features are apparent.

The grey of the upper wing surface is broken by bold chestnut shoulder patches and the speculum of both sexes is white – this is the most distinctive feature of the species in flight. As well as this distinctive white speculum, the female may also be distinguished from the duck mallard by its white underbelly but this feature can confuse it with a female wigeon.

The gadwall is not as vocal as some of the other dabbling ducks although the drake does have a nasal creak as its call note and the duck has a short and high-pitched quack.

Although this species may be found on the foreshore, it is predominantly a freshwater duck. Its favoured habitats include sheltered lakes and large and slow-moving rivers. The breeding population is not large but may be found inland of the east coast of England and in the more sheltered glens of Scotland. Outside the breeding season there is a small-scale movement to the salt marshes, but the bulk of the population moves southward to other inland locations, where they are augmented by the arrival of over-wintering birds from the Baltic and the Low Countries in late October.

The gadwall is not as gregarious as other species of duck and has rather secretive and retiring habits. Like the shoveller it is a daytime feeder, although frequent disturbance may make it change to more nocturnal habits. It feeds mainly by dabbling, although it will also visit stubbles for grain and other seeds.

The gadwall moves more easily on land than any other duck species except the wigeon, and its flight is swift and direct. Being rather secretive, the gadwall seldom gathers in large flocks and is more often seen in pairs or small parties flying between feeding grounds and safe resting sites during the day. The distribution of gadwall in winter is very local, and there are large parts of the British Isles from which the bird is absent during the wildfowling season.

Although the white wing speculum is a good aid to identifying the species, in poor light or against the sky, identification is still very difficult.

The gadwall makes a good table bird.

See also: **Inland Waterfowl Shooting; Wildfowling; Seasons**

The Game Conservancy logo depicts a cock grey partridge

The Game Conservancy The Game Conservancy, a registered charity, is an active and practical research organization which aims to ensure the future of game species in the British countryside.

It began life as the Eley Game Advisory Service, but in 1969 was reorganized into an independent research and advisory body. Based at a national headquarters in Fordingbridge in Hampshire, the Game Conservancy is now internationally recognized as a unique authority on game management, and its support comes from a wide section of both the shooting and the non-shooting public.

The research carried out by the Game Conservancy is both wide-ranging and meticulous. The staff are not only highly qualified experts in their own fields but also collaborate with many higher-education institutes on scientific studies of game and wildlife management techniques. Many of the projects are long-term studies. For example, the continuing research into grey partridge populations has pointed quite conclusively to the use of herbicides and other crop sprays at a critical stage of chick growth as responsible for the general decline in Britain's stocks of this game bird. The Game Conservancy grouse project is conducting long-term research into the effective management of grouse moors, and other long-term projects are assessing predator control, headland conservation and wildfowl.

In addition to the long-term projects, the Game Conservancy also conducts research into such subjects as lowland hare populations, woodcock, and many others. It has also collated a great deal of information on game diseases and mortality through the activities of its pathology department, and its findings have gone a long way to solving many of the problems encountered by those who breed game birds.

If the prime function of the Game Conservancy is to conduct research into game management, the most important service it provides is the dissemination of its findings through the Advisory Service. The advice given is not of a theoretical nature, however, as the staff of the Game Conservancy specialize in on-the-spot visits and practical help on all matters concerned with game management and shooting.

Of growing importance in recent years is its consultative role with other field sports organizations and with government bodies. The professional expertise of the Game Conservancy has exerted a considerable influence on the agricultural strategy encouraged by the relevant government departments. Nowadays there is also considerable interchange of ideas and knowledge on an international scale, and the voice of the Game Conservancy is one that is respected.

Membership subscriptions make a substantial contribution towards funding the work of the Game Conservancy, and membership is open to all who have the interests of Britain's varied countryside and game species at heart. It is an organization that deserves support.

Address: **Burford Manor**
Fordingbridge
Hants
SP6 IEF

Game Fairs The spring and summer see a number of country sports or game fairs held in various parts of Britain. Two types of game fair exist – those that are held annually at a fixed location and those that move from one venue to another each year. Of the first type, perhaps the most important are the Game-keepers' Fair held near Birmingham in early August and the Wessex County Sports Fair held in Somerset in early July. In addition to these, numerous smaller field sports fairs are held in most parts of the country through spring and summer.

The largest of all is the County Landowners Association Game Fair. Held in late July/early August it is the premier show for shooting and angling enthusiasts, and it is a touring fair in that the venue changes each year. Once every four years the CLA collaborates with the Scottish Landowners Federation in order to hold the fair in Scotland.

Game fairs and county sports fairs serve the very important role of bringing field sports to the attention of the general public in a way that promotes participation in the sports. In addition they are the 'shop window' of gun and fishing tackle makers and the 'grass roots' platform of the various field sports organizations. These shows give the shooter the opportunity of keeping abreast of all the latest developments on the sporting scene while at the same time participating in a variety of shooting and angling competitions or coaching sessions. They offer an enjoyable day out for anyone remotely interested in the countryside or field sports.

Game Farmers Association   The Game Farmers Association was founded in 1907 with three main objectives:

* To provide the customers of game farms with the best possible stock, as and when required.
* To employ advances in science and veterinary knowledge in the constant improvement of game rearing techniques.
* To play as active a role as possible in the preservation of shooting as a sport and in the conservation of the countryside.

Address: **The Game Farmers Association**
Oddington Lodge
Moreton in the Marsh
Gloucester

Game Guns   To be suitable for the various forms of game shooting practised in Britain, a shotgun has to fulfil several criteria. Most shotgun designs nowadays are reliable, but a game gun, particularly one used for rough shooting, may be required to function in rain and snow, in thick cover and muddy farmland. The shotgun must therefore have a minimum of its moving parts exposed and have a proven reliability in a variety of shooting situations.

The shotgun may well be carried for long periods, and therefore it must be reasonably light and handy. For most shooters, the maximum comfortable weight is probably around $7\frac{1}{2}$ lbs and any reduction on this is a bonus. It must, however, be remembered that in driven game shooting the gun may well be fired over one hundred times in the course of a day's shooting and the lighter the gun the greater the felt recoil. A very light gun, therefore, may well punish the shooter's shoulder to the extent of causing bruising or, worse still, induce a 'flinch' as the triggers are pulled.

In addition to reliability and weight requirements, the ideal game gun also has to be capable of being unloaded quickly and easily, and in this the double barrel shotgun on which the barrels drop down to expose the breech scores over any other design. If the shotgun is fitted with automatic ejectors the time taken to reload is further shortened.

Finally, most game shooting disciplines involve shooting in the company of other people. When not actually loaded and ready for action the gun must not only be made safe, but must also be seen to be safe. Again a double barrel gun scores over the other designs, as an open and unloaded double may instantly be seen to be safe even at a distance.

Tradition has also played a part and the sporting traditions in Britain have all been largely based on the use of the double barrel shotgun for game shooting. Ask any game shooter, therefore, to describe an English game gun and the description will usually be of a side-by-side double barrel shotgun. Not only is it the product of the British tradition, but the double shotgun also fulfils the criteria of a good game shooting weapon admirably. In the first half of this century

Parker Hale, side-by-side sidelock H/E, straight hand stock, splinter fore-end

the side-by-side was regarded as the only acceptable shotgun design for all the different types of game shooting. Since the 1950s, however, the over-and-under shotgun has appeared more and more in the field and is nowadays considered to be just as 'acceptable' as its side-by-side counterpart. Both weapons are of the 'drop-down' design so that loading is relatively easy and free of fumbling, and this opening method also instantly identifies the gun as being open and safe when hooked over the arm.

There are, however, slight differences between the two designs which may influence their selection and suitability for a particular form of shooting. For a number of reasons the over-and-under design tends to be heavier than a side-by-side of equivalent barrel length. The former requires a greater amount of timber for its wrap-around fore-end, the action and breech face requires more metal, and the stock tends to be thicker in the hand, all of which make for a rather heavier gun. This may not in itself be a disadvantage in some shooting situations. On a driven game shoot the heavier gun will absorb more recoil and consequently be more comfortable to use in the course of a full day's shooting, and a rough shooter who has the opportunity to shoot flighting duck or even geese may well require a weapon that will handle heavier-loaded cartridges when the occasions arise. In both these situations the over-and-under may be a good choice even though the wider 'gape' of the open gun makes the reloading rate slower than that of a side-by-side. Apart from these slight differences there is really little to choose between the two designs and the actual choice of weapon is largely a matter of personal taste. I have used both over-and-under and side-by-side shotguns for a wide variety of shooting and both designs func-

tioned perfectly. Having been brought up with the latter design, however, it is with the side-by-side that I feel more 'at home', and this would be my ideal weapon choice.

Game guns have a number of general characteristics in common although different types of game shooting demand certain variations. Most game guns nowadays have either 28-inch or 26-inch barrels. This is shorter than the accepted 30-inch norm of the pre-war years and perhaps reflects the efficiency of modern propellant powders. Indeed, although Churchill, a London gunmaker, pioneered the 25-inch-barrelled shotgun before the last war, the last two decades have seen a great surge in the popularity of side-by-sides with these short barrels. The 'standard' game gun will be a 12 bore, the most popular of all the shotgun calibres, and, even in these days when the smaller bores are experiencing growing popularity, over 90 per cent of all game guns seen in use will be 12 bores. Most game guns of either configuration will have double triggers which allow instant selection of either barrel. The shooter then has an instant choice of different chokes. A greater number of over-and-unders are fitted with single selective triggers, but some game shooters see this as a hindrance rather than an advantage. The 'traditional' side-by-side game gun will also have a straight hand stock. For many shooters this enhances the lines of the weapon, but it also serves a practical purpose as it allows the hand to move more easily from one trigger to the other. No matter how big one's hand may be there is an inevitable slight change in the grip of the stock needed for the front and rear trigger. Where ease and speed of loading are important, both designs of shotgun will be fitted with automatic ejectors which kick the fired cartridge cases clear of the gun. Finally, both types of double may be made on either sidelock or boxlock actions.

If these are the 'common' features of a game gun, what differences do each of the game shooting disciplines create?

In driven game shooting, most shots are taken at either approaching or receding birds. The shooters stand at their allocated pegs and a large number of cartridges may be fired in a short space of time. The average range at which birds are killed on any driven shoot works out at under 30 yards, and in driven partridge or grouse shoots it may be much closer. Game guns for driven shoots therefore need to be open-bored in order to achieve a quick spread of the shot pattern, as this avoids the close birds being 'smashed' and allows a greater aiming margin of error for those further out. For really high screaming pheasants the correct choice of cartridge will give tighter patterns and extend the range effectively.

The barrel length of a gun for driven game is usually about 28 inches, although for both partridge and grouse a shorter and more lively weapon may be preferred. For these low and fast birds many shooters feel that they can react more quickly using a gun with 26- or even 25-inch barrels. The disadvantage of these short-barrelled guns is that they are lighter and prone to increased recoil. The remedy is to use light 12-bore cartridges such as the Eley 'Impax' or others loaded with one ounce of shot. A growing number of shooters have discovered the excellent qualities of these light loads, and there has been a proliferation of one ounce cartridges produced by ammunition manufacturing firms.

Driven game shooting is a sport in which the guns are carried in cases or slips until the shooter reaches his allocated peg and are only then removed and prepared for ac-

tion. Once each drive is over the weapons are again cased or slipped until the party arrives at the next stand. The weapon of a driven game shooter is therefore less likely to receive 'everyday' scratches and bruises and it is at driven game shoots that one usually sees 'best' guns being used. The 'best-grade' boxlocks and sidelocks from the world's most respected gunmakers are at home on a driven game shoot. Where fast and furious shooting is expected the shooter may use more than one gun and engage the services of a loader. Thus it is only at a driven game shoot that one would expect to see 'matched pairs' of guns in use.

The type of shotgun required by a 'walked-up' or rough shooter is governed by a different set of criteria. For one thing, the gun will be carried ready for action for a far greater part of the day than on a driven shoot and will therefore be exposed to far greater risk of knocks and dents. A 'best' gun would seem out of place in these shooting disciplines; the risk of damaging a really valuable shotgun is just too high. The most usual choice for a walked-up shooter is consequently a more moderately priced weapon. Double barrel shotguns, either in a side-by-side or over-and-under format, are again the most popular choice among walked-up shooters. As with most game shooting, the sport is one in which a number of people participate, and a gun that is easily seen to be safe, such as an open double, is to be preferred.

Except when shooting over dogs, which will flush birds quite close to the gun, the average range at which walked-up game is shot is somewhat greater than in a driven shoot. Also, shots will normally be taken at receding targets, and the shooter may well need somewhat tighter chokings than on a gun intended for driven game. There is,

Over-and-under game gun (Lanber)

however, a danger of 'over-choking' a gun and my own personal choice for walked-up shooting would be a gun bored quarter and half choke.

In most walked-up shooting the gun will be carried at the ready for long periods, and the ideal weight will range from $6\frac{1}{2}$ to 7 lbs depending on the individual shooter. Barrel length again averages around 28 inches, but some walked-up shooters argue the case for barrels of 30 inches on the grounds that longer barrels induce a smoother and steadier swing onto going-away birds. There is some substance to this argument and it is reinforced by the fact that competition shotguns for the 'going-away' disciplines of Down-the-Line and Olympic Trench are frequently built with 30-inch or even longer barrels.

A high rate of fire is not a primary requirement in walked-up shooting and one would not contemplate using a 'pair' of guns. Most shotguns seen in this type of shooting are fitted with automatic ejectors, although a soundly built non-ejector is just as effective, and a larger proportion of over-and-unders are seen than on driven days. Again, single triggers do not have the same disadvantage of delaying the shooter's instant selection of two differently choked barrels. The second barrel will almost certainly be fired at a target further away than the first barrel, and the selector button can be set accordingly. With the somewhat longer ranges involved, most walked-up shooters would opt for standard rather than light-load cartridges. With either $1\frac{1}{16}$ or $1\frac{1}{8}$ oz loads a well-bored gun will deal with any sport that is offered in the course of a day's walked-up shoot, and a shooter may even have time to select different loads for the open and 'choked' barrels.

A double barrel shotgun is also the first choice of a rough shooter. As in walked-up shooting, the rough shooter's gun may be exposed to hard work in testing conditions and the rough shoot therefore is no place for a 'best' gun. Indeed, the typical rough shooter's gun would be a double side-by-side boxlock in the low to medium price bracket. Even at this end of the market the gun must be well bored and robustly made to stand up to the demands made of it. Happily, even the lowest-priced doubles

available in Britain satisfy these criteria, and the boxlock 'knockabout' double is well established as the gun for this sport. Generally these guns are bored for full and half choke, but many shooters find their rough shooting performance improves if these are opened out perhaps to three-quarter and quarter choke.

Having stated that the most popular rough shooting gun is a double-barrelled weapon, there are a substantial number of 'solo' shooters who delight in spending an hour or two working a dog down the hedges and ditches of the shoot. They may well have reason to choose a shotgun of a different design and self-loading, pump-action and single-shot can all be used to good effect. For a number of years I have used a 'Rapid' pump-action shotgun for my solo woodcock forays. A fast-pointing and easily reloaded shotgun, the Rapid is an effective woodcock killer.

As for calibre, the 12-bore game gun is the 'maid of all work' used by over 90 per cent of all driven, walked-up and rough shooters. However, over recent years there has been growing interest in the smaller bores and many game guns are now available in both 12 bore and 20 bore. The latter is light, with a side-by-side double weighing between $5\frac{1}{2}$ and 6 lbs. In addition, one hundred 20-bore cartridges will weigh considerably less than the same number of 12-bore cartridges, and this may be an important consideration for a walked-up grouse shoot on a warm August day.

For driven shooting the lighter load of a small calibre is of no great consequence providing a smaller shot size is used, and I know of a number of experienced game shooters who have adopted the 28 bore for their driven shooting.

A walked-up or rough shooter would perhaps find this calibre a little on the light side, although I enjoy using a 28 bore for decoyed pigeon. For my own rough shooting I use a 16-bore side-by-side. Weighing 6 lbs, it is a delight to carry all day and the one-ounce loads are every bit as effective as the larger 12 bore with standard game cartridges.

Although a variety of weapons may be seen in the hands of rough shooters and the over-and-under also has a strong following among other game shooters, the traditional standard game gun in Britain is still a boxlock or sidelock side-by-side double 12 bore.

See also: **Game Shooting; Rough Shooting; Walked-Up Shooting**

Gamekeeping   Gamekeeping plays a vital role in the management of game stocks in particular and of countryside wildlife in general. Whether this role is carried out by a team of full-time gamekeepers, as it is on many of the best driven shoots, or whether by enthusiastic amateurs on evenings or weekends, the general aim is habitat im-provement to benefit the quarry species. If some success is achieved, the holding capacity of the ground will increase and the sporting potential will improve.

Habitat creation and management can be done by planting short-term game cover crops in strips along hedge sides, and long-term cover in the form of spinneys and new hedgerows. This cover increases the potential food sources, nesting sites and winter shelter for game birds, and will help to increase the capacity of the shoot. In providing this cover, the gamekeeper helps wildlife in general, because the variety of habitats created encourages a greater variety of songbirds and wild animals.

The rearing of young game birds is a delicate task

Once capacity is increased the wild game bird stocks may be supplemented by rearing and releasing additional birds. This can be done in a number of ways. A portion of the wild stock can caught up in the early spring and the eggs they produce incubated under hens or artificially. When the poult stage (six to eight weeks old) is reached the young birds are released into the wild in successive stages so that they are better acclimatized to their surroundings.

Eggs can be purchased from game dealers and incubated as above, either artificially if large quantities are involved, or under broody hens if the numbers are more modest. Alternatively, day-old chicks can be bought from the same source and reared by the gamekeeper until they reach release age. Finally, in order to dispense with the rearing stage some shoots buy in birds, either at the poult stage for immediate introduction into their release pens in the coverts, or ex-laying adult birds for immediate release.

The number of birds to be released each year may be as few as a dozen or so or up to several thousand. To a great extent it depends on the area of land, the type of shoot, and the shooter's pocket. Large driven game shoots require much investment of time, labour and money in order to produce a number of 'hundred bird' days in the shooting season. At the other end of the scale a dozen or more birds released onto a small shoot will increase the chance of the odd pheasant adding variety to the rough shooter's bag.

The other main task of any gamekeeper is to control vermin. Here it is game and wildlife protection rather than crop protection which is the main concern, so the gamekeeper will have little to do with pigeon shooting in the course of the job. In gamekeeping terms, 'vermin' is taken to mean predators such as fox, mink, stoat, weasel and the like. All these predate on mature or juvenile game. Of the predatory birds, the true birds of prey are rightly protected by law, so the attention of the keeper will be focussed on corvids such as magpie, jay and carrion crow. As well as taking game chicks these birds wreak havoc among songbirds and other species of wildlife, so active measures to control their numbers benefit a whole range of species.

The gamekeeper may employ a number of methods to control vermin. For the bird predators, shooting is probably the most effective control method, as it is for foxes and grey squirrels. Animals in the mustelid family – stoat, weasels and mink for example – are seldom encountered while out shooting, so tunnel and cage traps are far more suitable. At other times properly set snares can effectively control foxes, and poison can, if handled and set carefully, quickly bring a rat infestation under control.

On small informal rough shoots all these tasks can be shared among one's shooting companions, and the game birds may also need to be held on the shoot by regularly feeding in the coverts. Any time spent on gamekeeping duties will be reflected both by the quality of the environment and by the variety of the bag.

Larger shoots need to employ one or more full-time gamekeepers in order to carry out all the duties described above and on some of the best shoots the team of keepers is led by the head keeper and includes a number of under keepers or beat keepers, each of whom may be responsible for a particular part of the shoot. On shoots that do employ a full-time gamekeeper, it is he who is traditionally responsible for the management of the shooting days. These additional duties include correct placing beforehand of the 'pegs' or stands for each drive, recruiting and organizing the team of beaters for the day, ensuring that pickers-up are present and in position for each drive, and ensuring that flankers and stops are positioned for best effect in each drive. Finally, the gamekeeper is responsible for correct handling and storage of shot game prior to its sale to the game dealer at the end of each shooting day.

As if all these duties were not enough, it also falls to the gamekeeper to ensure that disturbance to game and other wildlife is kept to a minimum by deterring poaching and trespass in areas sensitive to human disturbance.

Behind every successful and enjoyable shooting day on driven, walked-up or rough shoots, there are individuals who strive throughout the year to manage the environment to enhance the quality of the shooting. If the shooters are not themselves involved in these gamekeeping tasks they should make a point of showing their appreciation for those who are at the end of each shooting day.

See also: **Game Species; Vermin Control**

Game Shooting   In the British Isles the term 'game shooting' refers to shotgun sports in which the quarry species are the various species of game birds and animals. It does not, therefore, encompass wildfowling, vermin control or deer management and stalking.

The quarry of the game shooter may be divided neatly into three categories, although there are instances where a particular species may not fit neatly into any category. The lowland game birds form the first and perhaps most important group. Species in this category includes the pheasant, both grey-and red-legged partridge and, in suitable environment, the woodcock. The other category of game birds may be termed the 'upland' species, and includes the red grouse, black grouse, ptarmigan, and in some areas the capercaillie, although this is a bird of the lower coniferous forests. Again the woodcock may well appear in the 'upland' category given any suitable environment. Finally, ground game forms the third category. This will include the lowland brown hare and the upland blue hare, together with the rabbit. This last species occupies an unusual position in that it is considered legally to be vermin unless it is poached or otherwise taken unlawfully, in which case it is considered to be a game species.

Game shooting also breaks down into three broad styles of shooting activity and includes the most formalized and the least formal types of shooting that exist in Britain. The three styles are driven game shooting, the most formal of sports, and walked-up game shooting. Both of these may be subdivided further into lowland and upland activities directed at the different groups of quarry species in the two environments. The final category is rough shooting, which in itself encompasses a wide range of shooting activities from a well-organized rough shooting syndicate to a spontaneous sortie by a shooter and his dog to the hedgerows of the local farm.

The common factor in this great variety of inland shotgun sport is that although wildfowl and vermin species may find their way into the bag it is the game species that are considered to be the prime quarry.

Although the 'Glorious Twelfth' of August heralds the start of the red grouse season and partridge shooting begins on 1 September, for the great majority of game shooters in Britain the first day of October is 'opening day' and for these lowland shooters the season continues until 1 February. The seasons for the upland game birds are earlier in order to minimize disturbance in the harsher months of winter and early spring.

See also: **Driven Game Shooting; Game Species; Seasons; Rough Shooting; Walked-Up Shooting**

Game Species   The game species of the British Isles comprise both winged game and ground game; that is, certain species of birds and mammals are classified as 'game'. Game birds are characterized by the fact that they are ground-dwelling and will fly only when forced to do so. Their take-off when flushed is often sudden and explosive, and their flight is strong on rapid wingbeats. They will glide on down-curved wings between bursts of flapping and will often run for some distance after landing. The one exception to this general characterization is the woodcock, a woodland wader more closely related to the snipe. Of the ground game, the two species of hare, the blue or mountain hare and the brown hare, are considered to be game animals, while the rabbit occupies a peculiar position in that it is considered to be a vermin species for legitimate shooters yet a person caught poaching rabbits may be charged under the Game Laws. Like the rabbit, British deer are classed as game if they are stalked for sport, yet lose this status if the shooter is killing deer in order to protect crops.

The game species of Britain divide conveniently into two groups according to the environment they inhabit. 'Lowland' game includes the pheasant, both grey and red-legged partridge, the brown hare and the woodcock. Of these neither the pheasant nor the red-legged partridge is a true native of this country, having been introduced at various times in the past.

'Upland' game is normally considered to include the red grouse, black grouse or black game, ptarmigan, capercaillie and the blue hare. Of these the capercaillie is the exception in that the species is more a dweller in deep coniferous forests bordering on high ground rather than on the high ground itself, and also because it became extinct in Britain in the late Middle Ages. The present growing population of capercaillie stem from reintroduction from Sweden in the nineteenth century. Unlike lowland game birds, each upland species occupies a separate ecological niche in the upland environment. The red grouse is a bird of the heather moorlands, the black grouse is more restricted to the hazel and willow scrub margins and the ptarmigan is very much a bird of the 'high tops', rarely descending below 2,500 feet above sea level except in adverse weather.

With ten species of game available to the British shooter the variety of environments and styles of game shooting in Britain are interesting and rich.

Goat – Feral   Quite a substantial number of goats live wild in the upland areas of Britain. These animals, descended not from wild species such as the ibex but from the early domesticated strains, have colonized and bred successfully in parts of Snowdonia, the Southern Uplands and the Scottish Highlands and islands. They are wild animals in every way other than their ancestry, and goat stalking is offered by a number of sporting estates as a diversion from red or roe deer.

Goldeneye   Only a small number of goldeneye duck (*Bucephala clangula*) breed in Britain. By late September, however, migrants begin arriving from Scandinavia, and the overwintering population occupy both fresh- and salt-water environments. The drake is a handsome and distinctive medium-sized bird. Its angular glossy black head has an almost circular white cheek patch which is visible from some distance. The white neck and underparts contrast with a black back and wings which fade into a grey tail. In flight the bold white inner wing is very obvious and gives the impression of a strongly

marked black-and-white duck. Both sexes measure about 18 inches in length and may weigh up to 1¾ lbs, although the female is usually the lighter of the two. The female is almost a duller copy of the male: its head is chocolate brown but it lacks the cheek spot, with the neck and underparts a creamy white; upper surfaces of the wings and body are a medium grey but the duck retains the conspicuous white wing patch of the male.

Apart from the nesting season, when its favoured habitat is mature woodland close to deep upland lakes, the goldeneye is a bird of open water and seldom comes to land. It will be found inland on large lakes and reservoirs and also frequents salt marshes and estuaries. A gregarious bird, the goldeneye is most often seen in small groups although in very bad weather these may congregate into larger packs on open water. It is a daylight feeder, diving for most of its food which is predominantly of animal origin. Molluscs, invertebrates and crustacea form a large part of its diet, and these are sought in water up to 20 feet deep. Roosting areas are often some distance from feeding areas and the goldeneye is more likely to participate in morning and evening flights than other species of diving duck. In addition, it often moves about during the day to find fresh feeding grounds and the shooter may be able to intercept this movement.

Goldeneye have an elaborate courtship display in the spring but at other times of the year are generally silent birds. Their pattering take-off from water is characteristic of a diving duck and their flight is strong and direct. The rapid wing beats of a goldeneye produce a distinctive whistling sound which once gave it the local name 'rattlewings' among the east-coast fowlers.

Both birds have quite distinctive plumages and are normally easy to identify. At a distance, however, the drake may be confused with the protected shelduck, but the goldeneye is much smaller, has a more rapid flight, and a different pattern of black and white.

The goldeneye rivals the gadwall in that its overwintering population is lower than the other quarry species and consequently it appears less often in the duck shooter's bag. However, concentrations of goldeneye do occur in some parts of Britain where they are highly regarded as a strong-flying and sporting quarry.

See also: **Wildfowling**

Golden Plover   The golden plover (*Pluvialis apricarius*) is a medium-sized wading bird. Weighing about 9 oz its length is 11 inches from tail to its short straight beak and it has an upright stance. At close range it is distinguished by a strongly-marked gold and black spotted plumage on its back and shoulders. During the winter the face and underparts are a dull white with a faint mottling of brown-yellow, but in the breeding season these parts become black. The crown and nape are strongly mottled yellow and black throughout the year.

The British population of this species is mainly resident, with a seasonal movement from its moorland breeding grounds to lowland pastures in autumn. In October the population is augmented by the arrival of birds in passage from Scandinavia and Iceland to Southern France and the Mediterranean coast. Britain is, however, the wintering ground for a substantial number of golden plover.

Outside the breeding season golden plover are gregarious birds. They fly in small compact flocks and their flight is strong and swift. They often associate with lapwings but their pointed wing shape is quite different from their protected cousins. They are very agile on the wing and their alarm call, a clear bubbling 'tlui', is quite distinctive. On the low wet farmland bordering many British salt marshes, golden plover flocks appear to occupy a 'territory' around which they move during the day, and careful observation may identify a flight line to and from their favoured fields. Being gregarious, golden plover may be brought within shot by using a combination of decoys and calling.

In flight their 'escape' behaviour is to dive to ground level and scatter in different directions, and one ploy used by experienced golden plover shooters is to fire a waste cartridge into the air when a high flock is approaching; the second shot may then be attempted at birds departing very rapidly at low level.

Golden plover are excellent table birds and it must be remembered that their open season extends from 1 September to 31 January regardless of whether they are encountered above or below the tide line.

Greener The gunmaking firm of Greener was first established in Newcastle in 1829 but in 1844 the company moved to Birmingham in order to be closer to the supply of materials and skilled workers. Greener guns and rifles became well known both at home and overseas, and of particular importance at this time was the two-groove 'Cape Rifle', which was perhaps the most effective large-bore black powder firearm against dangerous and heavy game.

In 1879 premises were opened in London and by this time Greener was building a wide range of shotguns and rifles in a variety of qualities and calibres. In order to strengthen the breech-locking system on side-by-side doubles Greener devised the top cross bolt which locks through an extension to the top rib and this cross bolt still bears the Greener name. Another area where Greener gained much acclaim was in the building of both wildfowling shoulder guns and punt guns, and good examples of these command a high price today.

Many side-by-side doubles manufactured by Greener can be identified by the patented Greener 'side safety' catch although this is not a definitive feature – some of this firm's guns were built with the more normal top safety in response to customer's wishes.

One unusual shotgun made by Greener, which after 1920 became known as W.W. Greener Ltd, was the single barrel 'G.P.' model, designed as a 'general-purpose' inexpensive shotgun. The mechanism was a Martini action as used in the earlier military rifles. The breech was opened by operating the underlever which tilted the breech-block downwards to expose the breech end of the barrel. Production of the 'G.P.' extended beyond 1965 when the firm was taken over by Webley & Scott.

The Greener cross bolt through the top extension is still used by many manufacturers

Both William Greener, the founder of the business, and W.W. Greener, his son, were prolific and rather single-minded writers. William Greener was a dyed-in-the-wool advocate of the muzzle loader and his book *Gunnery in 1858* was a scathing criticism of the new-fangled breech-loading guns.

His son, W.W. Greener, was the opposite. A strong advocate of choke boring, his best-known and most popular book was the *The Gun and its Development*, which was first published in 1881, and ran through many editions culminating in the classic 9th edition of 1910. W.W. Greener also published such works as *The Breech Loader and How To Use It*, *Choke Bored Guns* and *Modern Shotguns*, all of which aroused much interest when they first appeared.

Recently the name of Greener has appeared again in the gun trade after the closure of Webley & Scott's gunmaking business and it is hoped that the long and respected tradition for good, sound, moderately-priced English-built guns will be continued.

Greylag Goose   It is from the greylag goose (*Anser anser*) that many domestic breeds of 'farmyard geese' have derived. This species is the largest of the grey geese, and even at a distance it appears heavily-built with its comparatively large head and thick neck. At closer range the plumage appears to be a brownish-grey and the birds have orange bills and pink legs and feet. In flight the greylag shows the prominent pale grey shoulders from which it derives its name, and its wings are broader than other species of grey geese.

This is the only grey goose that breeds in any quantity in the wild in Britain. A variety of wetland habitats are used as breeding grounds and greylags may be found both on wet upland bogs and on lowland marshes and water meadows in central and eastern England and in many parts of Scotland. In parts of the country the wild stock is supplemented by released or introduced birds as this species will also breed readily in captivity. In late October Britain receives an influx of migrating greylags from Iceland and the winter distribution of this bird includes much of eastern England and the coasts of

Scotland with the highest concentrations occurring on the eastern Scottish firths.

The greylag is a stubble feeder during the autumn and winter months and takes off easily from land, though on water the take-off is more laboured. Where their ranges overlap the greylag often mixes with pink-footed geese and it is a gregarious species both on its feeding grounds and on their roosting water. They are daytime feeders, flighting from their roosts in the early morning and returning in late evening, and are strong and powerful fliers. Greylags are most often shot on these flight lines, although they do decoy well. Rough weather tends to upset their rhythm, and the foreshore shooter may well encounter small parties of greylag on the saltings during the day in these conditions. More usually, however, greylags congregate in big flocks and fly in characteristic 'V' formations, although at rest and when feeding they split into family parties within the flock.

Greylags can easily be confused with the other grey geese, including the protected bean goose, but they are vocal on the wing and their calls are unmistakable; anyone who has heard a chorus of farmyard geese would instantly recognize a wild greylag from its calls. They are large and heavy birds, measuring up to 35 inches overall and weighing up to 8 lbs, and the greylag makes an excellent large table bird.

See also: **Inland Waterfowl Shooting; Wildfowling**

Grey Squirrel   The grey squirrel (*Sciurus carolinensis*) is not a native of Britain. Introduced from North America in the late nineteenth and early twentieth centuries, its range has spread rapidly so that it has now colonized most of England and Wales and parts of lowland Scotland. Its rapid spread coincided with the population crash of the smaller native red squirrel, but whether the grey caused the red's crash is still the subject of much debate.

With an overall length sometimes exceeding twenty inches, the grey squirrel is a medium-sized rodent characterized by a bushy tail that makes up half its total length. The fur is grey, although red or yellow tinges do occur on the back and flanks. Ears are short and rounded and the underparts are white. Its thicker winter coat may be more silvery than the short summer coat, and it is the latter which is more prone to show red, brown and yellow tinges.

The grey squirrel prefers mature deciduous woodland and is far less common in dense conifer plantations. This perhaps explains why the population strongholds of the native and protected red squirrel are centred on the vast conifer forests in the Southern Uplands and Highlands of Scotland where the incursion of the grey may pose less of a threat.

The grey is a daytime feeder and is particularly active in the early morning. On the ground it moves with a bounding or loping gait with its tail 'flowing' out behind. In the trees it climbs quickly and is very agile amongst the branches, leaping from one to another with confidence and ease.

As an omnivore, the grey squirrel will feed on grain and other arable crops, on tree seeds such as nuts, acorns and beech mast, and on leaves, buds and shoots. It will readily strip bark off trees and saplings in order to eat the woody tissue, and grey squirrels are perhaps the most damaging of all woodland fauna in this respect. At the appropriate times of year grey squirrels will also take many eggs, nestlings and small birds, causing damage to both the wildlife of a woodland and the wood itself. Some form of control is therefore necessary as a damage limitation exercise, and grey squirrels are hunted by a variety of methods.

Although shotguns are frequently used to shoot squirrels dislodged from their dreys, squirrel control is an area in which the air rifle shooter can excel. Grey squirrels may be stalked in the early hours of the morning, and considerable skill may be needed to approach within airgun range. They are alert and observant animals that will quickly move away from any suspicious movement. Two air rifle hunters can often increase the chance of success because of the habits of a 'treed' squirrel. Very often squirrels will attempt to put the tree trunk between them and the human source of danger on the ground. With two shooters this is made more difficult as the tree can be approached from either side.

As with most air rifle sports, stealth and concealment are vital if the shooter hopes to come within shooting distance of the quarry, and a squirrel scampering through the upper branches of a wood makes an elusive and difficult target.

See also: **Vermin Control**

Grouse – Black The black grouse (*Tetrao tetrix*) is a game bird of the woodland margins. In appearance the male and female of this medium-sized species differ to such an extent that they are often called the blackcock and greyhen respectively. The male, measuring up to 21 inches in length, is noticeably larger than the hen bird, which may reach 17 inches overall. The plumage of the blackcock makes it easy to distinguish from any other game bird. Glossy blue-black overall, it shows conspicuous white wing bars in flight and the outer feathers of the tail curve outwards to form a distinctive 'lyre' shape. The greyhen, on the other hand, is a rich brown on its upper wing surfaces and back, but this colour turns greyer and paler on the flanks and underparts. Overall the plumage is barred and mottled with black and dark browns, and the rather long tail is slightly forked.

In the autumn the male moults much of his breeding plumage and takes on a duller and greyer colouring for a time. Both birds are usually quiet, but during the breeding season the blackcock has a wide vocabulary of sounds which it utters on its display ground. The elaborate display and calling to attract a greyhen is known as the 'lek', and several blackcocks may vie with each other on the same ground.

Black grouse are found in many parts of Scotland, northern England, Wales and the West Country where their preferred habitat exists. Ideal conditions exist where moorland is fringed with scrub, willow and birch woodland, although they will also colonize conifer plantations adjacent to moorland. A variety of ground cover is also required to provide shelter and nesting sites and open spaces for the lek. Although predominantly a ground-dwelling bird, the black grouse will also perch and feed in trees, particularly in winter. Black grouse feed mainly on plant material, taking shoots, seeds and berries in the appropriate season, but the young feed on a higher proportion of insects than the adult birds.

This species will fly readily. Its flight is strong and rapid although it will not often fly far. Compared to the red grouse it will gain more height and is less prone to 'follow the contour', in fact black grouse often fly in a circle to alight close to their take-off point.

Black grouse are gregarious birds throughout the year. Coveys of both males and females may occur, but the males will often collect together in separate groups.

Very few large shoots concentrate only on black grouse, and the most frequent encounter with driven birds of this species is when a moorland shoot includes one or two 'woodland margin' drives. Black grouse are also shot as walked-up birds, and many rough shoots on the fringes of the Scottish Moors regularly include this species in their bag.

The blackcock is quite unmistakable in both plumage colour and tail outline, but the greyhen may be confused with red grouse. However, the notched tail and grey-brown colour will serve to distinguish this bird.

The season for black grouse extends from 20 August to 10 December but, like the red grouse, most birds are brought to bag early in the season.

See also: **Driven Game Shooting; Seasons**

Grouse – Red The red grouse (*Lagopus lagopus Scotius*) is a game bird unique to the British Isles. At 16 inches overall length, it is a medium-sized species characterized by its rounded plump appearance, short 'square-cut' wings and a plumage of a mottled red-brown. The markings of both sexes are similar but the cock bird is slightly larger and the female appears at close quarters to be greyer and more heavily barred. In flight the conspicuous white underwing bar is easily visible and the tail appears longer than that of the partridge species. The male red grouse is a vocal bird and its challenge, resembling 'Kak-Kak-Kak, Gobak-Gobak', is frequently heard on heather moorland throughout the year.

This species is very dependent on heather and is consequently found on moorland in

The red grouse is a bird unique to upland Britain

south-west England, Wales, northern England and upland Scotland. It rarely strays from this environment except when extreme cold and snow compel it to move down onto the fringes of farmland. The highest densities of red grouse occur on well-managed heather moorland where there is ample supply of young, mature and old heather growth, which provide food, nesting sites and shelter respectively.

The red grouse is a ground-dwelling game bird which can run quickly but will fly more readily than partridge or pheasant when threatened. The take-off is explosive and flight very swift, often keeping very low to the ground except when crossing valleys.

Like other game birds its rapid wing beats are interspersed with long glides on down-curved wings and it will seldom fly a great distance before returning to heather cover.

Outside the breeding season it is a very gregarious bird. The young that leave the family coveys in summer collect together, sometimes in packs of over one hundred birds, and may remain like this until late winter. The adult males are strongly territorial in the lead-up to the breeding season often sitting on some vantage point to survey the territory and chasing away other males.

Red grouse feed almost exclusively on heather shoots but insect food forms a higher proportion of the diet of the young.

Now is not the time to fumble while reloading! The speed and agility of red grouse are legendary

The red grouse is the prime sporting bird of the uplands, and driven grouse shooting is a sport unique to Britain. A great deal of time and research has resulted in better moorland management for the wild breeding stock, and this is of great importance as grouse cannot be reared and released in the same way as pheasant or partridge. All grouse that go over the guns are therefore truly wild birds. Grouse populations, despite careful management, will fluctuate from year to year as much still depends on the weather during the breeding season. A cold wet spring will result in high chick mortality and a lower shootable surplus for that year.

As well as being driven, this species may also be walked-up or shot over dogs. The latter method, using pointers and setters to locate the birds, is the oldest and most traditional of grouse shooting sports and an even older variation is to fly falcons to grouse over dogs.

Grouse shooting in Britain is expensive, but it is a unique experience. The season extends from the much publicized 'Glorious Twelfth' of August until 10 December, but most grouse shooting takes place early in the season, the best months being mid-August to mid-October.

See also: **Driven Game Shooting; Walked-Up Shooting; Seasons**

Gundogs Many forms of sporting shooting can be enhanced by the use of a well-trained dog. Indeed, where there is a likelihood that some of the quarry will be injured and not killed outright, the shooter is really morally bound to retrieve and despatch the wounded quarry as quickly as possible. Without a reliable gundog the chances of a quick retrieval are greatly reduced, and this surely is the most powerful argument for using dogs in sporting shooting.

There are, of course, other reasons. A gundog is able to search through dense cover far more efficiently than a human, thereby increasing the numbers of birds that are flushed and producing more sporting opportunities for the shooter. Not only will a dog retrieve dead and wounded quarry, but it will be able to do so from areas inaccessible to the shooter; birds that drop into thick cover or onto open water are two

examples. Finally, a dog makes an excellent companion and enthusiastic partner in the shooting field and this teamwork and companionship will increase the enjoyment of a day's shooting.

A wide range of breeds come under the general heading of gundogs and there are also many individual dogs whose parentage falls well outside the accepted gundog breeds who nevertheless make excellent and amusing companions. However, the main gundog breeds can be classified under generalized types such as questers, retrievers, pointers and all-purpose dogs. Each type has a specific role for which the dogs were bred, although they may perform other tasks equally well, and each breed has its own supporters who swear that their dogs will do everything as well (if not better) than any other breed. As with human beings, there are good and bad dogs in every breed and each dog will have its own personal likes, dislikes, strengths and weaknesses. A good, obedient and responsive dog is a treasure beyond price in the shooting field.

Questing dogs are those which are bred to search for and flush game from all manner of ground cover. Generally, they should range in front of the gun but should not be allowed to stray too far ahead. In this class of dog the spaniel breeds reign supreme. The English springer spaniel is by far the most popular, although one does see other spaniels in some numbers. The largest is the Irish water spaniel and the smallest is the Welsh springer, and the other main spaniel breeds include the cocker, Sussex, field and clumber. They are all keen and enthusiastic animals – keen to get on with their job of rooting out the quarry – and this makes them deservedly popular. Against this, it is rather unfair to expect an active dog to enjoy being cooped up in a pigeon hide for hours on end or to follow steadily and slowly at a deer stalker's heel. They are active dogs and should be employed where this activity will be appreciated in the number of quarry they quest and flush.

Retrievers are of a different temperament. Their main task is to search for and retrieve dead and wounded quarry. They are excellent and steadfast in this task, for which they were bred, and their patience far exceeds that of the spaniels. Retrievers are the favourite dogs of the driven-game shooter and of the pickers-up on formal shoots. They will sit patiently at the peg making a mental note of the location of fallen birds to be retrieved when their handler gives the 'go' signal. They are strong swimmers and resistant to cold, which makes them the favourite choice of the wildfowler. A retriever will, for instance, handle a wounded goose with an authority no other type of gundog can match. The labrador is the favourite in this class although one does see more curly-coated, flat-coated, and golden retrievers than, for instance, the minor spaniel breeds. The strongest and perhaps the best dog for the wildfowler is the large Chesapeake Bay retriever and this breed is slowly growing more popular in Britain.

Like the questing dogs, pointers or setters range in front of the gun, but instead of flushing game they will indicate its presence by adopting a rigid 'point' or 'set'. The guns can then approach, and on command the dog flushes the quarry. As these breeds work this form of controlled flush they are able to range further ahead than spaniels. Pointer and setter breeds include the elegant English pointer and the English, Irish and Gordon setters. They are specialized gundogs for any form of walked-up shooting, and grouse shooting over pointers is a recognized sport in its own right. Pointers are also used by falconers who fly their birds against grouse, and this is one of the more ancient field sports that still survive today.

British gundog breeds tend to be bred for specific roles, although most dogs will be asked to flush and retrieve game. A number of European breeds, however, are bred to be 'all-purpose' dogs with the ability to find, point, flush, and retrieve game. These are sometimes called the HPR dogs (hunt, point,

retrieve) and the most frequently seen dog in this class is the GSP or German short-haired pointer. I have to admit this is one of my favourite gundog breeds; working down the hedgerows on the heels of a GSP is a relaxed and very enjoyable form of rough shooting. Other HPR breeds include the Weimaraner, the Hungarian vizsla, and the large Munsterlander.

All the breeds mentioned in the different classes are recognized gundogs. However, other dogs can be used for a variety of shooting purposes. Jack Russell terriers are frequently used by rat shooters who root out and flush the quarry around farm buildings and they are enthusiastic and tenacious hunters. Jack Russells are also popular among rabbit shooters and may be used in conjunction with ferrets. Terriers are essentially 'flushing' dogs: although I have seen terriers retrieve shot game, this activity does not come naturally to them.

Deer stalkers in Britain use dogs to trail and at times bring to bay a deer that has been wounded. The deer dog needs a placid nature and keen nose so that it will sit immobile for long periods of time at the stalker's feet and be capable of following a wounded deer's scent trail, which may be many hours old. Any breed can be used for this purpose providing the dog has the appropriate temperament and scenting ability. Labrador retrievers can be trained to be good deer dogs, and this breed is most frequently used for this purpose in Britain. On the European continent a wide variety of dogs are trained to trail deer, ranging from the small elkhound to little dachshund.

Regardless of the breed selected by the shooter, a gundog will enhance the enjoyment of the sport and often significantly increase the bag.

Hammers Hammers are the external devices which, when the trigger is pulled, fall onto the firing pins to fire the gun. As the designs of firearms developed from the wheel-lock and flintlock through the percussion muzzle loader to the early breech loaders, the hammers were modified to suit each new system. When centrefire cartridges superseded the pinfire system the days of the 'hammer gun' were numbered and 'hammer-less' actions quickly took over. This advance simply meant that the external hammers were replaced by internal hammers known as 'tumblers'.

While hammerless guns must be cocked by some internal mechanism, the hammer-gun in which the hammers are placed on the side of the action and the 'semi-hammer' gun in which the hammer is recessed within the action are cocked by drawing the hammers back to their cocked position by hand. Some manufacturers still produce hammer guns for sporting purposes, particularly shotguns in .410 calibre.

Hare – Blue The blue, or mountain hare (*Lepus timidus*) is a medium-sized mammal which, as its name suggests, is confined to the upland areas of mainland Britain. It is characterized by its grey-brown summer coat, which in winter turns to pure white except for the black tips to the ears. Compared to the lowland brown hare it is smaller, with a more compact body, shorter hind legs and shorter ears. Nevertheless it is still considerably larger than the rabbit, measuring up to 22 inches overall with the females, or does, slightly larger than the bucks.

Not all specimens grow the white coat in winter and an upland population may show a variety of colours in winter ranging from grey to pure white. In the springtime the summer coat grows through, giving the animal the blue colour from which it gets its name.

The blue hare is confined to the Highlands and Southern Uplands of Scotland in Great Britain, but in Ireland it is far more widespread on low ground. In Scotland the population of the brown hare extends well into the upland range of the blue hare, and there are areas where both species coexist in quite considerable numbers.

The blue hare adapts itself to a wide range of upland environments and will occupy large tracts of coniferous forest as well as open moorland and the higher frost-scoured slopes. Even in very poor weather its thick winter coat will allow it to remain on the higher slopes, providing it can still burrow through the snow for food, which consists mainly of grasses and other vegetation as well as a proportion of woody browse. In new forestry plantations it can, like the brown hare, do considerable damage through bark stripping.

Unlike the brown hare, blue hares are daylight feeders and may be observed feeding at any time of day. During the short daylight hours of winter the quest for food may be extended beyond dusk and feeding activity may begin before dawn.

Where they exist in sufficient numbers, blue hares may be shot either by walking-up or by driving in traditional end-of-season hare shoots. When disturbed they run very fast and often keep low along trackways through the heather or other ground vegetation.

Blue hares may also be considered as a quarry for the sporting rifle user, and stalking this animal with a rimfire rifle can make for fine sport.

Hare – Brown The brown hare (*Lepus capensis*) is the largest mammal which is hunted by shotgun shooters in Britain. Like the grouse and partridge, the brown hare is a game species, and as such the shooter is required to hold a game licence to shoot this species.

The brown or lowland hare is a medium-sized animal measuring up to 30 inches overall and weighing up to 9 lbs. It is tawny-coloured overall, but the coat darkens to-wards the back and becomes lighter on the flanks. The chest and underbelly are white, while the upper surface of the tail and the tips of the ears are black. Of all the related species, the brown hare has the longest ears and longest hind legs, and these are characteristic identification features. At close quarters the eyes are large and golden brown. As winter approaches the additional fur growth on the hare's coat alters the overall colour to grey-brown, but this is usually moulted out by April.

The brown hare is predominantly a low-land species and may be found in most parts of agricultural Britain below the 2,000 ft contour. In some areas, however, its range extends to higher altitudes and it may be found on many high moorlands in Wales and in northern England, and even in the Scottish Highlands there is a considerable overlap in the ranges of the brown hare and the mountain or blue hare. Its ideal habitat, however, is open farmland with arable and

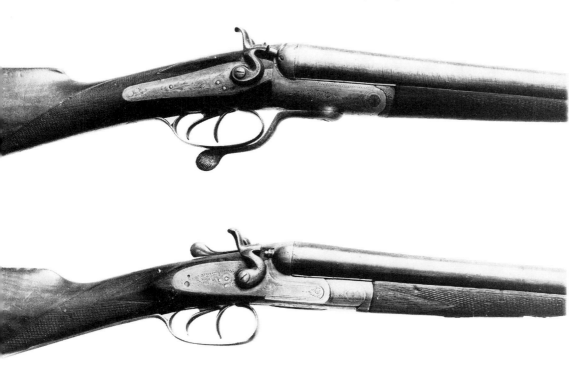

Two good examples of hammer guns. Top: a back-action underlever. Bottom: A bar-action top lever. Note how a 'cocked' right barrel may prevent the gun being opened

pasture fields interspersed with blocks of mixed or deciduous woodland. In such an environment the brown hare is a nocturnal feeder, moving out of cover at dark to feed in the open fields and returning to a lying-up hollow (known as a 'form') soon after first light. Although dense populations of hares do occur, they are generally solitary animals outside the breeding season.

The brown hare is a powerful and athletic animal capable of moving very fast over open ground. When flushed it will often make for any upward slope so that it can use its long and powerful back legs to their greatest advantage, and its uphill acceleration is phenomenal! When first disturbed the hare will often follow a zig-zag course to shake off any pursuit.

The brown hare feeds on a wide variety of vegetation from the bark of young trees to grain and grass. It may also raid rural gardens for vegetables, and will often be seen to work its way slowly along a row of seedlings with frequent stops to sit up and read the surroundings with both its eyes and its large, mobile and sensitive ears. Where insufficient daytime cover exists in the fields, for example in areas of newly-seeded winter grain, brown hares will often retreat to the nearest woodland margins to lie up during the day. I have often witnessed the heavy exodus of hares from the woodland as evening falls.

In recent years the brown hare has suffered a population crash in some parts of Britain. The reasons for this are not yet clear, but there are calls for a moratorium on hare shooting in such areas. Elsewhere, where the brown hare is still abundant, they may be hunted by beagle packs, controlled by end-of-season hare shoots, or form a legitimate target for the rifle shooter. Historically the brown hare was considered to be one of the prime game animals of the British Isles, and this view has not changed, despite the recent population fluctuations.

Hare Shoots In many parts of Britain the traditional end-of-season shoot actually takes place after the game bird season has closed. In these areas the February hare shoot is an event which involves up to 30 guns together with dogs and beaters covering large areas of farmland. Quite often a number of farms will combine, so that the area to be covered may extend up to a thousand acres or more, and a successful day requires much organization.

Nowadays there are fewer hare shoots than in the past – the mysterious decline of the lowland brown hare population in some parts of Britain has contributed to this to the extent that many shoot owners have responded to the call for a moratorium on hare shooting pending the findings of research into the decline. There are, however, still large areas where hares are abundant and in these the hare shoot is still an important event in the sporting calender.

The organization of a hare shoot varies from one area to another but the general pattern is the same. The assembled guns are divided into two teams who alternately act as walking guns or as standing guns. Up to six or seven drives may be attempted in the course of the day and on each the standing guns are placed so as to intercept hares driven towards them by the line of walking guns. At a given signal all shooting forward by both standing guns and walkers ceases, and hares are only shot as they break out of the two converging teams. This safety measure is essential to prevent accidents from ricochet pellets as the line of walking guns draws near to the stands.

A brown hare weighs up to 9 lbs, and carrying two or three over a sticky ploughed field can be quite taxing. Many experienced hare shooters, when allocated to the walking team, will therefore refrain from shooting at any that are driven forward towards the standing guns, on the traditional principle that 'if you shoot it, you carry it!'

Hare shoots have in the past been criticized as risky affairs, with inexperienced and enthusiastic shooters putting others in danger through thoughtless shooting. However, if the instructions are clearly stated in the pre-shoot briefing and these are followed throughout the day, participating in a hare shoot can be both healthy exercise and a sound means of controlling the hare population.

A much wider variety of shotguns appears on a hare shoot than on other game shoots, with single-shot, pump-actions and self-loaders adding to the more conventional double barrel guns. The accent should, of

Beaters driving partridge over September stubble.

The white cheek patch of a Canada goose is visible at quite long range.

Opposite: A stalker taking a shot 'off the stick' at a deer just visible on the edge of the ride.

A good example of fine engraving on Beretta guns.

A high curling pheasant presents a testing target.

Opposite: *Lowland (pheasant) shooting.*

The black grouse cock is a strikingly handsome bird of the willow upland margins.

The greylag, the largest of the wild geese, from which most domestic breeds are derived.

A large proportion of the fallow deer living wild in Britain are the descendants of park escapes.

The Mallard is the most familiar waterfowl quarry in Britain.

The brown hare is considered to be a game species even though it may be shot throughout the year.

During the drive the picker up stands well back and watches where shot birds have fallen.

The summer plumage of the Ptarmigan blends perfectly with its rocky habitat.

Opposite: *The shooter using the sun and hedgerow vegetation — he is directly up-sun of approaching birds.*

Like the other diving ducks, the pochard 'sits low' in the water.

The summer pelage of these deer gave rise to their name – red stags in summer.

Opposite: Red deer in the Scottish Highlands.

Shoveller – an unmistakable species.

Opposite: *Red hind in the snow.*

The distinctive colouring of the tufted duck, the smallest of the diving ducks.

Wigeon, prime quarry of the winter shore shooter.

*The white forehead and black bar on the underparts
distinguish the white-fronted goose.*

course, always be on safety and on being seen to be safe. One friend of mine who always uses a Browning semi-automatic shotgun inserts a large white handkerchief into the open breech of his gun when standing in company. Although the gun cannot be 'broken' in the same way as a double shotgun it is quite visibly 'safe' and this reassures those who regard this type of shotgun with suspicion.

As stated earlier, hares are quite large ground game and most hare shooters would select cartridge loads with a larger shot size, say 4 or 5, in order to achieve good penetration and humane kills.

See also: **Hare – Blue; Hare – Brown**

Hawker, Col. Peter   Born in 1786, Colonel Peter Hawker served with the Royal Dragoons from 1801 until a thigh wound put an end to his military career in 1813. It is not, however, for his army career that he has been called 'the father of sporting shooting'. The diaries in which he recorded meticulous details of his shooting forays from the age of sixteen until his death in 1853 are a detailed account of the shooting methods of the time. He was the first person to describe the sport of wildfowling in detail, and he was an enthusiastic game shooter. Though they were never intended for publication, the Hawker 'Diaries' were edited by Sir R. Payne-Gallwey and appeared in print for the first time in 1893.

During his own lifetime, Col. Peter Hawker published his *Instructions to Young Sportsmen*, the first edition appearing in 1814 and running to a total of eleven editions, which excludes the modern facsimile reproductions. Nowadays the early copies of his books are highly valued by collectors of sporting books.

Headspace   In order to compensate for the expansion of a cartridge case when a gun is fired, the cartridge is made so that it will fit relatively loosely in the chamber and the weapon is built so that there is a narrow gap between the base of the cartridge and the standing breech. This 'headspace' allows the fired case be extracted easily. However, excessive headspace may make shooting the weapon uncomfortable or dangerous.

In a shotgun an excessive headspace gap will usually increase the recoil to a degree where shooting becomes painful. When the striker hits the primer it will in effect push the cartridge as far as it will go into the barrel. Once the powder is burning, however, the cartridge will accelerate backwards to strike the breech face with a powerful blow and this will often increase the recoil dramatically!

In a rifle an excessive headspace may cause the base of the case to perforate and the burning powders may well blow back past the bolt into the shooter's face.

Headstamp   The headstamp refers to the information stamped onto the metallic base of both shotgun and rifle cartridges. It is usual for cartridge manufacturers to stamp their products with their name and logo and the calibre of the ammunition. This applies to most shotgun and sporting rifle ammunition, although .22 rimfire rounds may bear only a logo and code letter for the manufacturer. Sporting centrefire rifle ammunition can be distinguished from military cartridges in that the former invariably is stamped with the calibre and maker while the latter are stamped with military code letters.

Headstamp information should not, however, be taken as the only guide to the origin

Shotgun and rifle cartridges carry information on the calibre and identify the manufacturer of the ammunition

of the loaded cartridge. Many ammunition makers will supply 'primed cases' that are then loaded by someone else. In this instance the headstamp indicates the maker of the case only and not of the completed cartridge.

Heym   Friedrich Wilhelm Heym founded his gunmaking business at Suhl in eastern Germany in 1865. The firm gained public acclaim in 1891 on patenting the first hammerless 'drilling' combination shotgun/ rifle. The company moved to the former West Germany in 1945. By 1952 the factory was established in Münnerstadt and manufacture of sporting firearms had re-started.

Although Heym initially produced weapons that were marketed under other brand names (for example, the Mauser 3000 bolt-action rifle was made by Heym), they later took to firearms production and marketing in their own right. Like many German manufacturers they produce mainly medium-priced weapons, and even their luxury double rifles cost much less then their London hand-built equivalent.

In Britain it is the Heym model SR20 which has received acclaim as a well-finished and good-quality bolt-action repeating centrefire rifle. Chambered for a wide variety of cartridges the SR20 is available as a full-stocked 'Stutzen' carbine, as a standard half-stocked rifle, and as a half-stocked rifle in the magnum calibres. The action is based on the Mauser-type bolt and the rifles are finished to a variety of grades of decoration and engraving. Additionally, these weapons are available in a full left-handed edition with all the mechanisms reversed for a left-handed shooter. Calibres range from the 5.6×57 up to the .375 H & H Magnum, which covers all forms of rifle sport except African heavy game.

Heym also produce a range of double rifles available in both boxlock and sidelock actions and in both side-by-side and over-and-under configurations, again available in a variety of calibres up to .375 H & H Magnum. The other heavy calibres are also available to special order. These doubles are strongly built and elegant weapons which have reinforced Heym's reputation as a producer of accurate rifles.

For the European market Heym make a range of multi-barrelled rifle/shotgun com-

binations in their model 22 and model 33. These are available as double rifles with one shotgun barrel, or as an over-and-under with one shotgun and one rifle barrel, and this type of weapon is ideally suited to the style of driven game shooting that is available in many parts of the European continent.

Heym have also collaborated with the American gunmakers Sturm–Ruger to produce a very accurate single-shot rifle, the model HR 30. Like their bolt-action rifle this weapon is available in standard and Stutzen form, and it marries the precision-forged Heym barrel to the Ruger falling-block action. This underlever action is based on the old British Farquharson rifle and is known for its sturdiness and reliability. Although it resembles the Ruger No 1 rifle, Heym have given their product a distinctly European flavour with a Bavarian-style stock and the option of a round or hexagonal barrel. The Heym–Ruger HR 30 is also available in a variety of grades, some of which employ dummy sideplates which give the skilled engraver even more scope for his art. Standard calibres up to 30.06 and magnum calibres up to the 9.3×74R and .300 Win. Magnum are available and, because of the neatness of the action, these rifles are generally about 4 inches shorter than their bolt-action counterparts.

Heym have quickly built up a good reputation for the quality and accuracy of their weapons, and the high standard of their 'custom' engraved models has made this firm one of the most respected of the European rifle manufacturers.

High Seat   This term is applied to any platform raised above ground level which is used for deer observation, photography or shooting. The presence of high seats in any wood is usually an indication that the deer population is managed or controlled by a stalker.

The advantages of high seats are threefold. With the seat height averaging about 12 feet from the ground the scent of a human is dissipated above ground level, so that the deer are less likely to detect a person's presence. Secondly, when shooting from a high seat the rifle is directed downwards so there is a safe backstop for the bullet to go to ground should a shot be missed, and finally it seems that deer look for danger at ground level and seldom look up – an observer in a high seat is therefore less likely to be detected.

There are many high seat designs. The simplest is a plank resting between two branches of a tree with access either by

A 1938 Manton high seat

ladder or by convenient branches. Next comes the lean-to high seat, either of metal or timber, which rests against and is secured to a tree trunk. This type can be used where there are existing mature trees in a suitable site for observation or shooting, but where mature trees do not exist, overlooking a young plantation for instance, the free-standing seat should be used. The tubular steel or aluminium free-standing high seat is the most convenient in this instance, but if it is likely to be used for a number of years a timber 'German' high seat can be constructed. This is an elaborate and strong affair which looks rather like a child's playhouse on stilts. The seat itself is enclosed by timber or canvas walls into which are cut observation or shooting windows, and the whole affair is roofed over.

The siting of a high seat requires careful consideration of a number of points. To be used effectively the seat must be placed in an area that is known to be frequented by deer. I have seen instances where novice stalkers have placed high seats in a 'likely-looking spot' without first looking for evidence of deer – droppings, browse damage or deer trails. Careful examination of the ground for signs of deer will save many fruitless hours in a high seat.

Access to and from the high seat is also very important; the stalker should be able to approach the seat with the minimum of noise and disturbance so as not to alert any deer in the vicinity and, after spending time on the high seat, he must also be able to 'melt' away from the area quietly. The seat therefore needs to be close to an open path or track so that silent access is made easier.

The third requirement is that the seat be stable. A free-standing seat must be firmly anchored so that the platform from which the stalker shoots is solid. A rickety high seat makes for inaccurate shooting to say nothing of the well-being of the stalker himself. Lean-to high seats should be propped against a mature tree to be as stable as possible. Even so it suprising how much a mature tree-trunk may move about in a fresh wind.

Once the area for a high seat has been chosen one has to decide on the best 'strategic' position. With the above points in mind the ideal location would be downwind of the prevailing westerlies, i.e., to the north or east of the area and overlooking as clear a field of view as possible. Experienced stalkers often avoid placing high seats to overlook clear rides and forest tracks as the deer tend to cross there quickly. From my own observations deer seem nervous about being on a human-frequented path and will dash across only to stop and take stock of the situation when they have put 10–20 yards between themselves and the track. If the cover here is light, a high seat nearby would be far better placed to observe deer at their daily business.

High seats are by no means the only way in which deer can be observed or controlled. Nevertheless their use will aid the accuracy of deer counts, they are an ideal photographic platform, and a safe vantage point from which to shoot.

See also: **Deer; Deer Management**

Holland & Holland This world-famous and prestigious firm was established in 1835 by Mr Harris J. Holland in New Bond Street, London. In 1877 the firm became Holland & Holland, as the nephew of the original founder, a Mr Henry Holland, took over the general management of the firm. By 1883 the quality of the rifles produced by this company was such that in exhaustive field trials, Holland rifles took first place in all classes from rook rifles to 40-bore elephant rifles.

A fine double barrel heavy rifle by Holland & Holland. Note the extended top strap, beavertail fore-end and folding-leaf rear sights

Since that time Holland & Holland have achieved some notable firsts and really pioneered the development of the high-velocity medium magnum rifle calibres. The company succeeded in developing a rifle choke in a shotgun barrel to produce their 'paradox' ball-and-shotguns in 1886. Early in this century they developed the .375 Holland & Holland magnum rifle calibre. Of all medium-to-heavy calibres, this has proved over the years to be the ideal rifle for the tropical big-game hunter. In its original loadings of 270 and 300 grains all cartridges had the same point of zero, and even though the calibre generated over 4,000 ft lbs of energy, their rifles boasted of almost 'varminting' accuracy. Even now the .375 H & H magnum is the medium-heavy calibre against which all the more recent cartridges in this group are judged.

A development from the .375 H & H magnum was the Holland Super 30. Utilizing the former's large-capacity cartridge case necked down to .30, the 'Super 30' took America by storm in the 1920s when it swept all competition before it in the target shoots popular at the time. The post-war American magnum calibres in the .30 calibre class were developed to compete with Holland's Super .30, which is now known as the .300 H & H magnum. In the heavier calibres, Holland developed the still popular .500/465, and rifles in this calibre are still being produced; and in the stalking rifle class the .244 H & H magnum is still the most powerful of all the 6-mm calibres, giving a muzzle velocity of 3,500 fps with a 100-grain bullet.

ESTABLISHED 1835.

GOLD MEDAL INVENTIONS EXHIBITION, 1885.

WINNERS OF ALL THE "FIELD" RIFLE TRIALS, 1883.

HOLLAND & HOLLAND,
GUN AND RIFLE MANUFACTURERS,
98, NEW BOND STREET,
LONDON, W.

GUN AND RIFLE MAKERS, BY SPECIAL APPOINTMENT, TO

His Majesty the King of Italy,

His Imperial and Royal Highness the Crown Prince of Austria.

CASH PRICE LIST OF

ROYAL HAMMERLESS, AND OTHER GUNS	PAGES	3 to 8
PARADOX BALL GUNS	,,	9 to 12
EXPRESS AND BIG GAME RIFLES	,,	13 to 27
ROOK AND RABBIT RIFLES	,,	28 to 39
SWIVEL AND DUCK GUNS	,,	40 to 44
REVOLVERS, AND TARGET PISTOLS, ETC.	,,	44

Telegraphic Address—"ARMOURER, LONDON."

Front cover of early catalogue of Holland & Holland, leading gun and rifle manufacturers, printed 1887

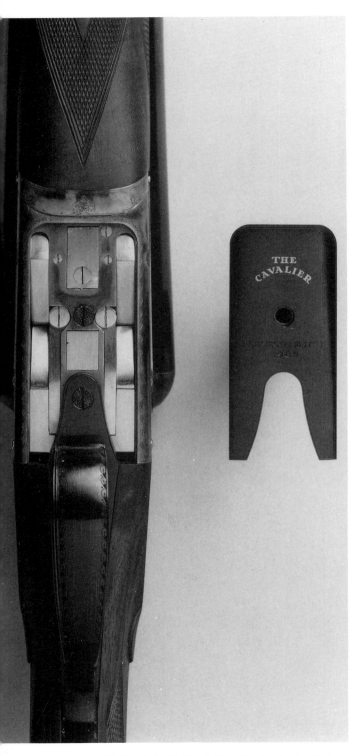

A Holland & Holland Cavalier boxlock ejector showing the lockwork protected by the base plate

It was this company that first developed the 'belted case' for these high-pressure magnum cartridges which has been copied in all other magnum calibres, and it may be said that, while Purdey's reputation rests with their shotguns, Holland & Holland have gained international prestige through their rifles.

Nowadays Holland still produce a wide variety of best-quality sporting firearms only to order. The Holland 'Royal' is a double barrel sidelock ejector built either as a shotgun or as a double rifle. As with the other top London gunmakers these are hand-built weapons of the very highest quality and may take up to three years to complete. Each weapon is unique and tailored to the customer's exact specifications, with the shotgun available in 12, 16, 20, 28 and .410 bores and the 'Royal' double rifle available in .577 Nitro Express, .500/465 H & H, .375 H & H magnum and Super 30 calibres.

Like other top London gunmakers, Holland & Holland also produce bolt-action magazine rifles of the highest quality to any calibre for which ammunition is available, but, unlike their competitors, this company has always been prepared to build lesser-quality and therefore less expensive weapons. In this context 'lesser quality' is of course a purely relative term and the Holland 'Badminton' sidelock ejector double shotgun, for example, is still a very fine weapon. Recently Holland & Holland have introduced a range of shotguns built on the boxlock action. Although they are a fraction of the price of a 'Royal', these boxlocks still are made with the skilled craftsmanship of which Holland & Holland are justly proud and they have brought a 'London' gun within the pocket of a great many more people.

In producing their double-barrelled weapon, this company have concentrated on the production of side-by-sides, and these are offered with single or double trigger mechanisms.

At their present address in Bruton Street, Holland & Holland have incorporated the business of Rowland Ward. This firm specialized in publishing books and other literature on the world's big-game hunting, and the Bruton Street shop therefore houses a comprehensive stock of new, antiquarian, and collector's books on all aspects of field sports as well as a wide range of clothing and shooting accessories.

It would be futile to compare the quality of weapons produced by London's premier gunmakers, but in terms of international prestige Holland & Holland are part of the 'big three', with Purdey and Boss, in the production of best double shotguns and rifles. Their initials have been enshrined in the most highly respected and popular of all the medium-heavy rifle calibres, the .375 H & H magnum, and their most recently developed calibre, the .700 H & H Nitro Express, has put the company back in the lead as the builder of the world's most powerful sporting rifle. This mighty calibre generates an energy of 9,300 ft lbs from its 1,000 grain bullet at a muzzle velocity of only 2,100 fps!

Hollow Point This term refers to a rifle bullet with a cavity towards its point. Very often this cavity is visible through a hole at the point of the projectile. In hollowing out the point of a bullet the thickness of the bullet wall is decreased, and it is therefore much more prone to deform and break up on impact than its solid or full metal jacket counterpart. Hollow-point bullets are not designed for deep penetration, therefore, but are intended to cause the maximum disruption to the internal organs of relatively thin-skinned game. In the case of the centre-fire rifle calibres, hollow-point bullets are designed for deer and medium to small vermin species.

In the .22 rimfire class, hollow-point bullets are designed for hunting all live game within the scope of a rimfire hunter and should always be chosen for this purpose in preference to a solid bullet.

See also: **Bullet**

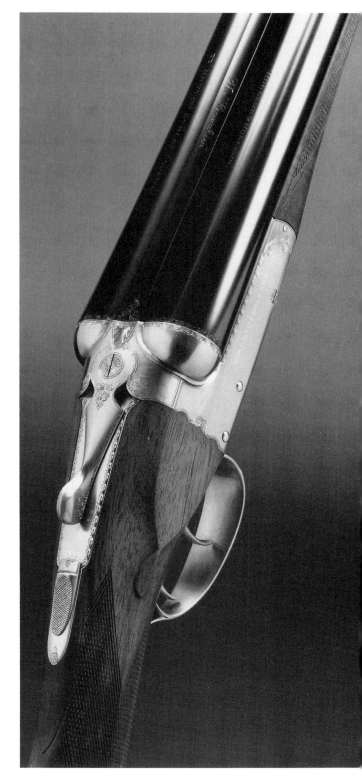

Holland & Holland now produce 'best' boxlock ejector shotguns

Inland Waterfowl Shooting Shooting wild-fowl inland of the foreshore does not qualify for the term 'wildfowling'. Nevertheless, inland waterfowl may be encountered in a wide variety of environments and the sport can take a number of forms.

As on the coastline, the stocks of inland wildfowl change with the seasons. At the start of the season the sport centres on the resident and breeding population. In most parts of Britain the ubiquitous mallard makes up the vast bulk of the birds brought to bag, but as the season wears on the influx of migrating flocks of geese and duck adds considerable variety to the sport.

Every river, pond or lake will hold its own overwintering population of wildfowl, even though in places these may be supplemented by a stock of released mallard. In this season wigeon and other species more usual-ly encountered on the coast will be found on many freshwater marshes and wild geese may well flight many miles inland from their coastal roosts in order to find suitable feeding areas.

The three main strategies used in inland waterfowl shooting are walked-up shooting, flighting and decoying.

Walking-up is a flushing sport. More often than not walked-up shooting nowadays involves placing a number of standing guns at strategic points; the walking guns and dogs then attempt to drive the birds towards the stands. This strategy can be used when shooting on rivers, ponds and small lakes such as gravel pits, but is not practical on the larger expanses of fresh-water. Known as 'jump' shooting in America, the sport condenses a great deal of excitement and anticipation into a short time, unless one has a long stretch of river or many small expanses of still water to cover. Once the birds have been flushed they will not return to the locality for some time, particularly if they have been shot at! In many instances, therefore, a walked-up duck shoot will be seen as an interesting brief diversion during the course of a shooting day on a rough or game shoot.

Shooting flighted wildfowl inland is very similar to coastal wildfowling in that the birds are intercepted either at dawn or dusk as they flight to and from their feeding areas to the waters where they wash and rest. If the shooter is aware of these rest areas on a stretch of river, flight pond or lake, and also knows the birds' routes to and from them, then the wildfowl can be intercepted somewhere along the flight lines. This is a static sport in that the shooter uses some form of cover or hide which affords a clear view of the direction from which the birds are expected, and sits and awaits their arrival. As shooting takes place in poor light both sight and hearing must be tuned for indications that duck are on the move. As the light fails in the evening, hearing gradu-ally becomes more important in locating the whereabouts of the calls and wingbeats of the birds, and shots are generally very hurried and instinctive.

In many parts of Britain, Canada geese

can be most effectively intercepted at twilight and a good flight of these birds is a memorable event. In Scotland this tactic is also often used for wild grey geese as they flight from the coast to the stubbles and potato fields inland, and this is the only occasion which may justify the use of a shotgun of larger calibre than a normal 12-bore game gun. Inland goose flighting is an established sport in its own right on the low ground bordering many of the Scottish firths, and a considerable number of shooters make the trek north in the winter months to participate.

Duck and goose decoying is predominantly an inland sport, although it can also be practised to good effect on the foreshore at certain times. The inland duck shooter will often use decoys to attract birds returning from their feeding grounds. On rivers a pattern of decoys laid out on some calm water and the adjacent river bank can draw birds within range of the concealed shooter when they would otherwise disperse to different parts of the river. At times like these the judicious use of a duck call will add to the realism of the decoy pattern and therefore its attractiveness to the flighting birds.

Inland goose decoying, on the other hand, is much more of a morning activity. If the shooter knows where to find the feeding grounds of the geese, be they grey geese or Canadas, a pattern of decoys set out before dawn may serve to focus the incoming birds onto the area covered by the shooter. There are occasions when the sport can be fast and furious, but the birds soon become accustomed to decoys and learn to avoid the area. Grey geese are often said to be very wild and wary when on the foreshore and on their flight lines, but then become very silly at their feeding grounds. There are many accounts of these birds becoming 'programmed' to go to one feeding field, which they will then return to with almost suicidal determination even though they are aware of disturbance by gunshot. At times like these the shooter must exercise control and impose a limit on the number brought to bag. To go for an unsporting slaughter in order to produce a record bag is both unethical and very short-sighted, and will only bring the sport into disrepute.

Inland waterfowl shooting is a sport when the average range of the shots taken differs little from other game or rough shooting. As such it does not demand heavy loads or big-bore wildfowling guns, and any game or rough shooting gun will suffice. For my own shooting I tend to increase the shot size from the standard all-round No 6 to No 5 for duck and No 4 for geese. In a standard game-choked gun these throw killing patterns to 40 yards which is all that is required, and provided they are used within their limits the small-bore shotguns from 16 bore to 28 bore can be used with good effect. Compared to the foreshore wildfowler, the inland shooter puts the gun to far less risk of damage by mud and salt water so that the shooter has a freer choice of shotgun type. I have used pump-actions and auto-loaders for my inland duck shooting and they have functioned reliably, though my favourite side-by-side double still remains my first choice.

Insurance Every person who takes a gun of any kind out for sporting purposes ought to be covered by insurance. Much as we make every effort to prevent them, accidents do occur. A ricochet bullet may injure a farm animal, a careless shotgun shot may cause a dead bird to fall on a public road to the surprise of road users, and there have even been instances when domestic stock and pets have been disturbed or shot by mistake. All these instances would generate a third-party claim against the shooter, and the shooter's insurance should provide third-party cover! In addition, it must be accepted that shooting is a sport which, if not conducted properly, may involve physical injury to the shooter. A shooter's insurance policy should therefore cover personal accidents, not only while shooting, but also while engaged in gamekeeping or conservation work.

While the shooter may choose to take out a personal insurance policy to cover the sport, it is far more convenient and inexpensive to obtain insurance cover automatically through membership of one of the shooting organizations.

Finally, many of the weapons used in sporting shooting in Britain would be very expensive to replace. A prudent shooter may therefore seek to insure the weapons against accidental damage and a number of insurance companies provide specialized policies for the shooter's guns and other equipment.

Jay The jay (*Garulus glanderus*) is perhaps the least frequently seen of all the common crow species. It is a medium-sized bird measuring about fourteen inches overall, which from a distance resembles a stocky and short-tailed thrush. It is, however, a much more colourful bird. In flight the white rump and wing patches are very prominent at a long distance. Closer observation will also reveal a bright blue wing bar at the base of the primaries, and this is also visible when the bird is at rest. The body is pink-brown but this merges into a dirty white below the black tail. The head is large with a white crest streaked with black, a pale chin and a marked black moustache running back from the base of the bill. The jay's voice is more often heard than the bird is seen, and its harsh and loud screech is a feature of mature lowland oak woods

Indeed this is a bird of lowland woodland, its favoured habitat being mixed deciduous woodland in which oak is the predominant species. It will also happily occupy younger stands and copses in which there is much secondary shrubbery, and it even occurs in some coniferous forests. Like its relative the magpie, this very wild and retiring bird has adapted well to urban environments and populations exist in many of the larger inner-city parks which include mature woodland.

The British Isles contain a substantial resident and sedentary population, but an influx of migrants from Eruope often arrives in late autumn. These do not conform to a regular migration pattern and some believe that they are the result of population irruptions on the continental mainland which trigger a mass movement westwards into Britain. With its short and rounded wings and its rather laboured flight the jay does not appear suited to long migrations, and most of the European migrants arrive in south-east England where the sea crossing is at its narrowest.

Though not adapted for long-distance flights, the jay is a quick and agile bird in the upper branches of mature woodland. Flitting from tree to tree and frequently doing long 'hops' from branch to branch, small parties of jays will scour the woods for food. During autumn the main food source is acorns, and jays have even been observed storing acorns in caches for winter feeding. At other times the jay is an opportunist feeder on both vegetable and animal matter. It will take fruits, grain and other seeds as well as insects and carrion. In the breeding season its main food source changes to eggs and fledglings, and it is because of this damage to the populations of other woodland bird species that the jay has been classed as vermin.

Parties of feeding jays seldom remain in one place for long, so stalking these birds is very difficult. They can, however, be driven towards a waiting shooter by careful stalking by a 'beater', and many jays are accounted for during the course of a game or rough shoot 'drive' through woodland. For the air rifle hunter, 'still' hunting in an area known to be frequented by jays is probably the best method of shooting this species, but

the quarry is keen-sighted and very wary and the shooter must bear this in mind when calls herald the approach through the branches of a feeding party. Stealth and concealment are the essential ingredients for success.

See also: **Vermin Control**

The jay is more usually detected by its harsh call than by sight

Knife Of all the accessories to shooting in the field, a knife is probably the most useful and important, in the form of either folding blades, pocket knives or sheath knives. There is an enormous variety to chose from, so it is easiest to select the correct style of knife by considering the job you wish it to do.

The game and rough shooter will usually find that a simple folding knife will satisfy all his normal requirements. The everyday jobs of cutting baler twine, cutting open feed sacks, and the various occasions when a blade is needed are well within the scope of a penknife. When carrying out heavier work, cleaving rides and undergrowth, arranging foliage around a hide, etc., a more specialized cutting tool may be required. There are occasions when a heavy-bladed machette is very useful and the curve-bladed pruning knife can save time and effort.

The deer stalker may need two knives, one with a short light blade and one which is somewhat more robust. The short blade is for gralloching a deer and for skinning the carcass. In the latter, some delicate knifework is called for and this requires a short blade. The heavier knife is often required for cutting through the ribs at the sternum and for cutting through the tough sinews and skin at the deer's neck. Whereas a small blade may do this job adequately on the smaller deer species, the sternum ribs and neck of fallow and red deer are beyond a small blade's strength, while a strong-bladed sheath knife will perform well.

Folding knives come in many shapes, sizes and costs. To be useful to the shooter the knife must have three qualities. It must be able to take and hold a very sharp edge, it should be sufficiently sturdy to withstand a good deal of twisting when in use, and it must have a means of locking the blade open. Knives conforming to these qualities range in price from a few pounds to those costing over £100, so the choice depends largely on the buyer's taste and pocket.

Knives are easily lost, so it is useful to own a good general-purpose folding knife such as an Opinel No 8 made in France. Though the blade of the Opinel is not stainless steel it conforms to the three criteria listed above, and replacements do not dent the pocket too badly when one is 'mislaid'!

A useful sheath knife to use is of the 'Bowie' type in which the blade is double-edged from the tip to the point where the back of the blade thickens. Again this is not an expensive knife but it is strong and holds a good edge. With its six-inch blade it has sufficient penetration to stick and bleed a suspended deer carcass efficiently. Like the pocket knife the choice of a sheath knife largely depends on preference and pocket.

Recent legislation has classed knives as offensive weapons. Ownership and possession of knives with blades exceeding three inches has to be justifiable. A sporting shooter or stalker should have no problem providing he only carries them when engaged in shooting or conservation work.

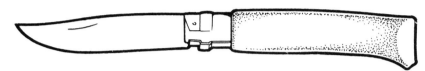

Two examples of inexpensive lock-blade knives for general use (above)

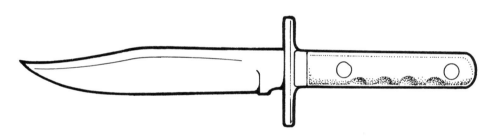

A heavier sheath knife, useful for cutting through the sternam of a deer during the gralloch (above)

A filleting knife is useful for boning joints (above)

The Opinel knife, inexpensive and excellent (above)

Lamping The sport of 'lamping' is a relative newcomer to the vermin shooting scene. Resulting from the development of high-intensity quartz halogen lamps that are both light and portable, lamping is now an effective way of controlling the rabbit and fox population.

See also: **Vermin Shooting – Tactics**

Lee-Enfield Sporter After the Second World War a considerable number of British Army service rifles were converted to sporting use. The short Lee-Enfield bolt provided a smooth working action for sporting purposes and the styling of the Lee-Enfield military rifles was altered to produce stalking or hunting rifles in .303 calibre.

The military sights were replaced by sporting open sights and the stock was re-shaped to produce a half-stocked sporting rifle which was also drilled and tapped for telescopic sight mounting. The resulting weapon, known as the Lee-Enfield Sporter, was a robust and accurate .303 calibre stalking rifle and a considerable number were sold throughout the world. Lee-Enfield Sporters were available in a variety of grades from the basic conversion to deluxe models which were restocked in high-quality walnut with completely reworked barrels and actions. In the immediate post-war years they were the mainstay of the deer stalker in Britain and were only displaced as new weapons in more modern calibres appeared on the market.

Most Lee-Enfield Sporters retained the ten-shot military box magazine, so they can easily be identified by this feature.

Lever In weapons other than those fitted with bolt actions, the lever is the metal arm which is moved to open the breech. In double barrel weapons the opening lever may be placed on top, at the side, or under the action to produce top-lever, sidelever, and underlever firearms respectively. Nowadays the majority of double rifles and shotguns are fitted with top-lever opening, although some semi-hammerless .410 double and singles are still made with sidelever actions.

In the days of hammer guns the sidelever and underlever actions had the advantage that the hammers could remain cocked while the gun was opened, but nowadays this advantage has been lost in the 'hammerless' designs. Most gun manufacturers have therefore opted for the quicker and more convenient top-lever opening.

See also: **Underlever**

Lever Action A 'lever-action' gun is a weapon in which the reloading cycle is operated by a metal hand lever which lies behind the trigger guard along the 'hand' of the stock. The lever is usually shaped so that the three fingers of the 'trigger' hand fit through an enclosed loop. When the lever is thrown forward the bolt is withdrawn and the spent case ejected. At its rearmost extent the bolt cocks the hammer, and pulling the lever back to its closed position feeds a fresh round into the chamber and pushes home and locks the bolt.

Although in the past some lever-action shotguns were produced, the mechanism is now confined to low- and medium-powered rifles. Lever-action rifles first became famous through the American Winchester Model 73, and this pattern has been copied by other arms manufacturers both in America and in Europe. The positive lock-up of the bolt produces an inherently accurate rifle, but the lever action is not designed to withstand very heavy chamber pressures and recoil, and would be unsuitable for use with the heavy 'African' rifle calibres.

Nowadays lever-action rifles are available from a number of manufacturers in calibres ranging from .22 rimfire to the most powerful of lever-action calibres, the Marlin .444. Left-handed shooters find the lever action more convenient to use than bolt actions, as the lever can be operated with equal ease shooting from either shoulder, and lever-action repeaters in .22 rimfire calibre make good vermin-hunting weapons.

The Marlin model 336 is typical of the lever-action repeating rifle

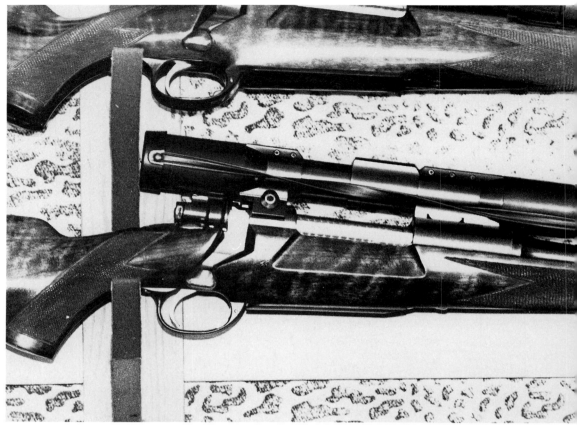

The bolt action of the Lloyd rifle is both functional and elegant

Lloyd, David   One of a small group of custom rifle makers in Britain, David Lloyd has gained an international reputation for his innovative rifle design.

In the majority of bolt-action rifles, the rifle is built first and the telescopic sight is added almost as an afterthought. Despite the many excellent designs of telescope mount, it is this which is the main weakness of the rifle/scope combination. An accidental knock or the rifle falling over is usually enough to throw the rifle out of zero and render it unusable. In addition, the screws of the scope mount can work loose under the effects of recoil and this will again throw off the point of aim. Such delicacy in most rifle/scope combinations necessitates frequent checks and careful handling if one is to keep the weapon accurate.

The David Lloyd bolt-action rifle goes a long way toward overcoming this problem. In this design, the telescope mounts are a solid and integral part of the receiver. It is, in effect, a telescopic sight of the best quality around which rifle is built. The bolt action, using either a Mauser or a Sako bolt, and the telescope are produced as one solid unit. The action is then barrelled to the required calibre, and the weapon is finished using best-quality walnut. The final result is an elegant rifle which is far more resistant to everyday rough handling than a rifle of more conventional design.

David Lloyd rifles are produced in any modern calibre as the customer requires, but they really come into their own as accurate long-range weapons. Thus one is likely to see Lloyd rifles chambered for high-velocity small-calibre magnum cartridges such as the Holland & Holland .244 Magnum or the

.264 Winchester Magnum. Lloyd rifles in these calibres have seen service, and won much praise and admiration, in many parts of the world.

The David Lloyd rifle is a real departure from normal bolt-action centrefire rifle design

Loader   On some of the larger driven game shoots, particularly those where the daily bag is expected to run well into three figures, each shooting guest may require the services of a loader. On these occasions the role of the loader is to keep the shooter supplied with a loaded gun and thereby increase the rate of fire of each sportsman.

Even when the shooter uses one shotgun only, a loader standing nearby with a ready supply of cartridges can greatly increase the firing rate. When the shotgun is fired, the shooter opens the weapon, thereby ejecting the spent cartridges, and the loader quickly slips two fresh cartridges into the gun, which is then closed ready for action. This saves the time normally spent in fumbling for cartridges in a pocket or cartridge bag, aligning them correctly and loading them into the gun, and good teamwork between the loader and shooter can easily double the potential rate of fire.

When the shooter uses a pair of guns the rate of fire can be increased further providing both he and the loader devise a system whereby the guns can be exchanged quickly without the risk of clashing the barrels during what may often be hectic change-overs. A smoothly working team of gun and loader makes it possible to take two birds from a covey of grouse in front, change guns as they cross the line, and take another two behind, providing, of course, the shooter is up to the task.

In the past some of the biggest shoots, whose prestige rested on their large bags, required the use of two loaders per shooter and trios rather than pairs of shotguns were used by each guest, but nowadays this is a very unusual sight.

See also: **Driven Game Shooting**

Lock   The lock is the mechanism for firing the gun. Nowadays the term is usually applied only to double-barrelled weapons, when describing the type of mechanism that has been built into the action. Most double guns, be they rifles or shotguns, are built on either boxlock or sidelock actions. In the former, also called the Anson & Deeley action after its inventors, the mechanism or lockwork is housed within the action body. Sidelock actions come in two forms. In the back-action sidelock the main-spring which acts on the tumbler is housed at the rear of the lock plate. This mechanism has now been largely superseded by the bar-action sidelock in which the main-spring is located in the bar of the action under the barrel flats. As the name suggests, the locks of a sidelock are situated on either side of the weapon, thus exposing more metal on the lock plates and giving the engraver more scope for embellishing the weapon. This is one of the reasons why most 'best' double guns are built on sidelock actions.

See also: **Boxlock; Sidelock**

Lock Time   The time delay between pulling or squeezing a trigger and the weapon discharging is known as the 'lock time'. In the days of flintlock weapons this delay was quite significant, as it depended on the sparks generated by the fall of the flint igniting the priming powder in the pan and the flash from this igniting the main charge. Nowadays the lock time is measurable only in hundredths of a second, as the ignition systems of both centrefire and rimfire cartridges do not depend on any primary ignition outside the main charge. However, some of the older bolt-action weapons do have a lock time which may be sufficiently long to upset an accurate aim. For the majority of modern weapons lock times are no longer significant although some arms manufacturers still use a 'fast lock time' as a selling point for their products.

Lonsdale Library   A series of sporting books first published from the late 1920s by Seeley Service of London, the Lonsdale Library derived its name from association with the Earl of Lonsdale. All in all over thirty titles were published in a variety of different editions ranging from large leather-bound to the standard buckram editions. Subjects covered included most British competitive sports and athletics as well as many types of angling and shooting.

Each book was edited by a noted authority of the time and contained contributions by many other experts in the field. As such the books were highly regarded as authoritative instruction books for use by the new entrant to the sport and as standard reference works for those with more experience.

Of particular interest to the sporting shooter are the titles:

Shooting by Moor, Field and Shore (Vol. III) ed. Eric Parker
Wildfowling (Vol. XXIX) by T. Bland *et al.*
The Lonsdale Keeper's Book (Vol. XXVI) by Eric Parker
Game Birds, Beasts and Fishes by Eric Parker
Big Game – Africa (Vol. XIV) by Major H.C. Maydon.

All were substantial books in their own right, containing a wealth of information on their own particular subject.

Although the series appeared from the late 1920s onwards, reprints and new titles continued to appear until the early 1970s when the original publisher, Seeley Service, was taken over first by Lee Cooper then by Frederick Warne. Much that was written in these volumes is still applicable today and they are considered even now to be good reference works.

Loop In a three-piece takedown double barrel weapon, the fore-end is held to the barrel by a catch which engages on a hook brazed onto the underside of the barrel. This hook, which takes many forms depending on the design of the fore-end catch, is known as the 'fore-end loop'.

Lumps The lumps of a double side-by-side weapon are the metal bars which protrude below the chamber between the two barrels. These lumps slot into the action and lock the barrels in their closed position. The front of the lump is hooked so that it can hinge on the cross-pin at the front of the action when the weapon is opened. Behind the hook the lumps may have a number of 'bites', recesses into which fit the action bolts that lock the gun in its closed position.

Lumps are produced in two ways. In a set of barrels with dovetailed lumps, the lumps are shaped and fitted to the barrels after they have been shaped and are nearing completion. In chopper lump barrels the lumps are an integral part of each barrel forging and are worked on at the same time as the barrels are being made. Chopper lumps are used on the better-quality weapons, although nowadays the new mass-production methods developed by the larger manufacturers have allowed the use of chopper lump barrels on even their basic-grade weapons.

Some over-and-under shotguns have lumps brazed onto the bottom barrel, but this requires a greater depth to the shotgun's action. In order to reduce this the lumps have been moved to the sides of the barrels where they pivot on pins that protrude from the action. These over-and-unders have a slimmer action which enhances their elegance. The lumps on either side of the barrel are known as 'bifurcated lumps'.

Magazine The 'magazine' is the reservoir of ammunition stored in a repeating firearm. In sporting weapons magazines fall into two main types: tubular and box.

The majority of tubular magazines in both rifles and shotguns are slung under the barrel. The tube is spring-loaded so that any cartridges are pushed towards the action to be fed into the breech during the reloading cycle. Pump-action and self-loading shotguns are almost always fitted with tubular magazines which are partially concealed by the wood fore-end. The magazine is loaded through a loading port on the base of the action and, once the magazine is full, the bolt is worked backward and forward to feed a cartridge into the chamber.

Tubular magazines are fitted to some self-loading and pump-action centrefire hunting rifles, but the choice of calibre is restricted by the cartridge and bullet shape. A pointed bullet would increase the risk of a magazine explosion if the rifle's recoil caused the point of one bullet to strike the primer of the next round in the magazine. In addition, if the calibre is prone to producing heavy recoil there is the risk of the bullets being deformed as they are jolted around in the tube. Therefore, tubular magazines tend to be fitted only to 'mild' centrefire calibres which use round- or flat-nosed bullets. Perhaps the most frequently seen tube-fed centrefire repeating rifles are the lever-action models produced by Winchester and Marlin.

Since they lack the problems associated with a central ignition cap and heavy recoil, all manner of .22 rimfire weapons are fitted with tubular magazines. Again, the magazine tube is normally fitted underneath the rifle's barrel, but some weapons, the Remington Nylon 66 for example, have the magazine tube built into the stock. Bolt-action repeaters, auto-loaders, pump-actions, and lever-action rimfire rifles may all feature tubular magazines to give a capacity of up to fifteen shots without reloading.

Tubular magazines have the advantage of being able to hold a larger number of cartridges than other types, but the fact that they are slung along the axis of the weapon in front of the ideal point of balance can affect the gun's handling characteristics. What is more, as the number of rounds in the magazine is reduced the balance and handling of the weapon can change.

Box or clip magazines are placed beneath the breech of the weapon immediately in front of the trigger guard. The vast majority of bolt-action weapons, whether shotgun, rimfire or centrefire rifle, are fitted with this type of ammunition reservoir. Here the cartridges are stacked on top of each other and a spring-loaded base plate pushes each round up to the breech in turn. 'Box' magazines usually refer to a fixed cartridge reservoir while a 'clip' implies that it is removable. Both have the advantage that they hold each round securely and prevent the bullet tips being 'mashed' under recoil. A removable clip makes the process of unloading the weapon much simpler than unloading one with a tubular magazine, and the reduced magazine capacity helps the shooter to keep a check on the number of rounds remaining in a loaded weapon.

One criticism levelled at box magazines

is that they protrude below the line of the stock and fore-end, particularly in shotguns and heavy-calibre rifles, and this tends to spoil the look of the weapon. One development from the vertically stacked box magazine gets over this problem. The 'rotary' magazine can store an equal number of rounds without protruding to the same extent. In this design the magazine rotates during the reloading cycle to present a fresh cartridge to the breech each time. Centrefire rifles from such makers as Mannlicher and Savage feature rotary magazines, the latter gunmaking firm using them for a high-power lever-action rifle.

Due to the size of the cartridges, it would be impractical to fit a rotary magazine to a shotgun, but one .22 rimfire rifle has established the use of this design for the calibre. The Ruger auto-loading rimfire rifle uses a ten-shot rotary magazine which operates on a combination of rotary and spring action to feed each round into the chamber.

Magpie The magpie (*Pica pica*) is a strikingly marked medium-sized member of the crow family. The bold black and white plumage and the characteristic long, wedge-shaped tail of this species make it unmistakable. Although the bird measures up to eighteen inches overall, the tail accounts for half this length. The head, upper back and breast are a glossy black and the bill is large and powerful for the size of bird. The shoulders, lower back and underparts are white and these contrast sharply with the glossy black tail and rump. On the ground the mag-

pie's relatively long legs give it a bounding gait and in flight its short rounded wings make the bird very agile but rather slow. The plumage of both sexes is alike but the immature birds lack the 'gloss' of the parents and their tails are less elongated. The call of the magpie is an unmistakable loud and harsh 'chak' repeated a number of times, and this sound can carry some distance.

Magpies occur throughout Britain except for the extreme north-west of the Scottish Highlands, although recent evidence indicates that the population is increasing rapidly and spreading. Its preferred habitat is farmland or open country which includes tall hedges, thorn thickets or woodland. Like the woodpigeon it has adapted well to city life and will be found in most parks and around suburban gardens.

In the countryside magpies are very alert and wary birds, often found feeding in small family groups. Their diet includes vegetable matter, insects, carrion and fruit. In the spring and summer magpie food consists mainly of eggs and nestlings from a wide variety of both songbirds and game species. When feeding on the ground magpies will rarely move far from tree or bush cover and the small family parties will often work their way along hedgerows searching for food.

Magpies are notoriously difficult to approach and most birds are shot on 'chance encounters'. However, magpies are challenging birds to stalk with either shotgun or air rifle, and their numbers may be controlled by 'still hunting'. Although they will be attracted by a magpie decoy, it is usually

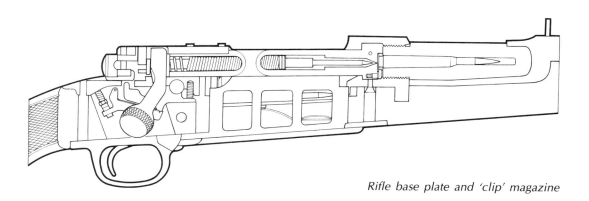

Rifle base plate and 'clip' magazine

to chase off an unknown intruder in their territory.

The magpie is an adaptable and therefore successful species. However, if this handsome bird is allowed to proliferate, its predation on the nests and young of many other species will reach an intolerable level.

See also: **Vermin Shooting – Tactics**

Mallard   The mallard (*Anas platyrhynchos*) is the best known British wild duck, and it is from this species that many domestic ducks have been bred. The wild bird is also the largest British quarry duck, with the adult weighing up to 2¾ lbs and measuring 23 inches in length.

The winter and breeding plumage of the drake is characterized by the glossy green head and pale yellow green bill, a white ring on the neck and a rufous purple chest. The underparts are pale grey merging to a white-bordered black tail. The upper parts are a darker grey with a black band running down the back. The duck (adult female) is a uniformly dull mottled brown, which affords excellent camouflage, and its head shows an eye stripe and an orange-edged brown beak. Both sexes have a bright metallic blue/purple speculum which is bordered with white.

In the summer eclipse plumage the drake resembles the duck more closely but still retains the male's beak colour. The male's call is a creaking nasal quack and a high-pitched whistle, while the female has a vocabulary of chattering quacks. The characteristic female call, however, is the loud deep quack repeated often and dying away gradually.

The mallard is the most widespread British duck species, and its adaptability has allowed it to breed in every location from municipal boating ponds to mountain tarns. It is Britain's most numerous breeding waterfowl. In spring and summer it is predominantly a 'freshwater' species, occupying a wide variety of wetland sites from woodland ponds to the banks of large res-

Many shoots rear and release some mallard to supplement the wild stock

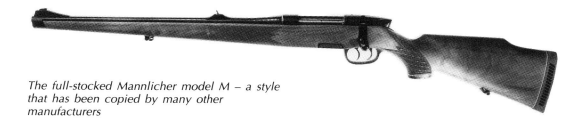

The full-stocked Mannlicher model M – a style that has been copied by many other manufacturers

ervoirs. It is the most easily reared of all the duck species, and large numbers of captive-bred birds are released to supplement the wild stock. The population is further augmented in the autumn as migrants from Iceland, Scandinavia and Russia arrive at their British wintering grounds. Although the British breeding populations are parochial in their movements, there is a movement from freshwater to coastal sites in the early winter, so that mallard may be found, and thus figure as a quarry species: in practically any wetland environment in Britain.

Like all other dabbling ducks the mallard is usually a nocturnal feeder and daytime rester. When flushed it will climb steeply and tend to fly in loose groups rather than in large flocks. It is a very gregarious species, readily attracted to decoys. It takes a wide variety of food from both vegetable and animal sources. In shallow water it frequently up-ends to feed on aquatic plants and insects which it sieves through its beak, and it is also partial to grain stubbles and flooded pasture.

The male in winter plumage resembles the drakes of two protected species, the red-breasted merganser and the goosander, and to the novice it may even be confused with the much whiter shelduck. It is essential therefore that the species be positively identified before the gun is raised.

Finally, the mallard is perhaps the best eating of all the duck species, and a September mallard fresh off the corn stubbles has an excellent flavour.

See also: **Inland Waterfowl Shooting;
Seasons**

Mannlicher   Mannlicher is a branch of the Austrian Steyr-Daimler-Puch group, and its sporting rifles have a well-established reputation. From pre-war days up till the 1960s the bolt action developed by the company was the feature of the rifle. The Mannlicher-Schoenauer bolt-actioned repeating rifle used a bolt in which the handle was drawn back through a bridge at the rear of the action to expose the magazine and breech. Like the Mauser bolt that eventually replaced it, the action was cocked by lifting the bolt handle from rest. The action was both simple and effective and this is borne out by the fact

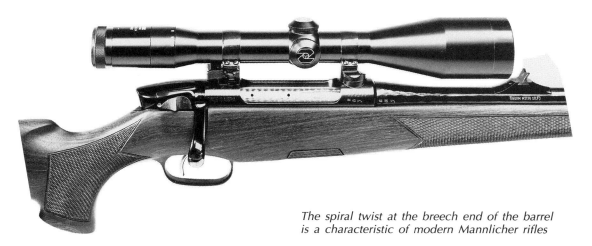

The spiral twist at the breech end of the barrel is a characteristic of modern Mannlicher rifles

that many custom rifle makers still use pre-war Mannlicher-Schoenauer bolts in their modern rifles. The one disadvantage of this mechanism lay in the fact that a telescopic sight had to use a side-mount at the rear in order to avoid obstructing the bolt. In the days when a telescopic sight was looked upon with some suspicion this was of little consequence. Nowadays, however, when a 'scope sight is the norm, the inconvenience of using a side-mount has led to an undeserved neglect of the Mannlicher-Schoenauer bolt action. This is a great pity as side-mounts are in every way as reliable as top mounts and the Mannlicher-Schoenauer bolt is an elegant mechanism.

Another feature which departed from the norm was Mannlicher's use of a rotary magazine instead of the usual straight clip. By loading the rounds into a rotary drum the depth of the magazine can be reduced and the rifle built to a more elegant line. In addition the rotary magazine can be totally enclosed within the fore-end of the rifle and this helps to prevent the ingress of water, dust and grit. The feature is continued in today's Mannlicher rifles.

The modern products of the company, known as Steyr-Mannlicher, are all bolt-action repeating rifles which use a bolt of the Mauser pattern. This action allows a top-mounted 'scope but retains the traditional 'butter-knife' shape of Mannlicher's bolt handles.

Steyr-Mannlicher rifles are available in a wide variety of calibres and five basic models. The model SL is the 'Super light' rifle chambered for the centrefire .22 calibres, the model L for the short-case 6 mm family plus the .308 Win. Both of these use a short bolt appropriate to the length of the cartridge. A longer bolt action is produced for the model M (medium) to accommodate cartridges of the .270, .30–06 and 7×64 length and the models S (strong) and ST (strong tropical) with long magnum bolts for the medium- to heavy-calibre cartridges.

Apart from the models S and ST, all rifles are available in normal style with a 24-inch barrel and the 'normal' type of stock and in 'full-stocked' style with a 20-inch barrel and the European-style 'Stutzen' stock. Such was their lead in developing these European-style carbine rifles that the Stutzen style of rifle is often referred to as a 'Mannlicher' and the style has been copied by many arms manufacturers in other parts of the world. As a light and quick-pointing weapon for use in woodland stalking the Mannlicher-style short rifle has been gaining popularity.

All in all the Mannlicher name is associated with many important developments in rifle design. The rotary magazine, the Mannlicher-Schoenauer bolt and the full-stocked carbine have all contributed to both the practical function and the elegance of sporting rifles. As a final refinement, all Steyr-Mannlicher rifles have a distinctive spiral on the breech end of their barrel. This reflects the unique forging process of the barrel

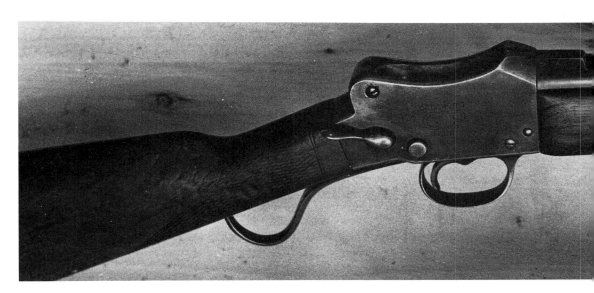

Manton's Standard Hammerless ejector high-velocity rifle from 1938

which was patented by Steyr and adds a touch of elegance to the weapon.

Manton, J. The name J. Manton may relate to one of two brothers. John Manton (born 1752) served his apprenticeship with gunmakers in Leicester and London before opening his own business in the capital in 1781. Having learned the skills of building double guns from John Twigg, Manton quickly established a high reputation for the quality of his guns, rifles and pistols, receiving royal patronage. Taking his son George Henry into partnership in 1814, the company traded as John Manton & Son until it finally closed in 1878.

Joseph Manton, at one time apprenticed to his elder brother John, established his own business in 1792 at 25 Davies Street, London. Joseph was one of the pioneers of percussion systems to replace the flintlock gun. In 1816 the Manton pelletlock was patented and 1818 saw the arrival of Manton's tubelock. The business moved several times and by 1822 was trading under the name Joseph Manton & Sons after his two sons Frederick and Charles had joined the firm. Frederick went on to establish Manton & Co. in Calcutta, India, while the London business went through several financial crises, finally being bought out by Henry Egg in 1838.

In the mid-nineteenth century the Calcutta business was also bought out but has continued to trade under its original name.

Joseph Manton is remembered not only for pioneering inventions in percussion ignition, but for the quality of the barrels on the double guns they produced. Throughout the last century 'Manton barrels' were synonymous with the very finest available.

Martini Action The Martini action is single-shot mechanism originally used in the nineteenth-century Martini Henry military rifles. This action used an underlever opening system which unlocked and pulled the breech face downwards. The breech block itself was actually hinged at its rear so that when the weapon was opened the block tilted rather than dropped. The Martini is therefore a 'tilting' rather than a 'falling' block action. Though it was only a single-shot mechanism, a skilled shooter could produce up to fifteen shots per minute from a Martini-actioned weapon.

The single-shot 12-bore Greener 'G.P.' was produced up until the early 1980s

Though the original military rifle was superseded by the more rapid-firing bolt actions, the Martini action is still used in a number of target rifles manufactured today. However, before the Second World War a considerable number of single-shot sporting rifles were built on Martini actions and many are still in use. The action has the advantage that it locks the breech firmly in the closed position and this positive lock-up greatly enhances accuracy.

Greener produced a Martini-action shotgun as their 'G.P.' model and this remained in production until the 1970s. They were noted for their strength and reliability: my first wildfowling gun was a 'G.P.' and it endured considerable mistreatment without malfunction.

See also: **Underlever**

Mean Point of Impact In a shotgun, the mean point of impact (MPI) can be defined as the centre of the shot pattern. Ideally this point should coincide with the aiming mark at any given distance, but 40 yards is the usual reference range. The MPI in a shotgun depends on a number of factors. If the shooter uses a gun with a badly-fitting stock then the MPI may well change with every shot that is fired. This is due to inconsistent gun mounting, i.e., the sighting line down the barrel to the aiming mark may vary to produce changes in the MPI. If the stock is brought to rest high on the shoulder the gun may shoot low of the aiming mark, and conversely if the shooter crouches over the stock the pattern will go high. A left-handed shooter using a gun cast for the right shoulder may have to cant his head in order to sight down the barrel and this will also produce inconsistencies in the mean point of impact from shot to shot.

In double barrel shotguns it is a relatively simple procedure to align both barrels to shoot to the same point but subsequent alterations in barrel length or choking may cause the barrels to shoot to different points. In practice, however, this is usually of little importance as the difference of, say, six inches in the mean point of impact from the two barrels is effectively compensated for by the actual spread of shot.

Some shotguns, in addition, are deliberately constructed so that they do not shoot to the aiming point. Over-and-unders and, to a lesser extent, side-by-sides that are designed for 'trap shooting' tend to shoot high of the mark. In the clay pigeon disciplines of Olympic Trench, or Down the Line, the target is rising when it is being shot at, and as a consequence a gun that shoots 'high' can be a positive advantage. This is achieved in trap guns by reducing the drop in the stock so that when properly mounted the shooter's eye is raised from the 'normal' sighting line; the MPI is therefore placed above the sighting line from the eye through the foresight head to the target.

Some game guns are also designed deliberately to shoot high. Where a shooter intends to shoot mainly low-flying driven birds, for example partridge or grouse, then the gun that shoots high will reduce the degree to which the approaching birds need to be 'blotted out' by the barrels. Again this is often seen as a positive advantage, and many of the light and short-barrelled 12-bore game guns used for this type of shooting will be designed to shoot high.

In shotguns, therefore, the mean point of impact depends on the way the barrels are aligned (in a double gun) and on the way the stock fits the shooter. If the MPI lies some distance from the aiming mark it is usually a simple matter to alter the stock and bring it more into line.

In sporting rifles the mean point of impact is far more critical when shooting at long range. If one assumes that every cartridge, no matter how carefully loaded, will produce slightly different ballistics, and that each bullet on leaving the barrel will be subjected to differences in wind interference, it can be seen that it would be virtually impossible to put all shots through the same bullet hole on a target. Slight variations in the shooter's aim will further decrease the likelihood of this happening.

At close range and in controlled conditions the shooter should be able to produce very tight groups of bullet holes on a target, but as the range increases so the group will spread. A centrefire rifle, for example, should produce a three-shot group at 30 yards in which the bullet holes intersect each other, but at 100 yards even the best ammunition and well-bored rifle can be expected to spread the group to 1½ to 2 inches in ideal conditions. If the same rifle is zeroed for 200 yards the same group of shots will have spread to just over 4 inches at the longer range. Again this is under theoretically ideal conditions. In practice the greater the range the more wind has a chance to play around with each bullet trajectory, so the group of bullets is usually far more widely spread. It is in situations like this that the mean point of impact assumes much importance. Even in a perfectly-zeroed rifle the number of bullets that actually hit the exact aiming mark at 200 yards will be lower than those that have been spread about by the wind or ballistic variations from cartridge to cartridge. The mean point of impact can therefore be taken as the centre of the group and it is this point which should coincide with the aiming mark.

When the shooter wishes to zero a rifle for 200 yards it is easiest to consult the ballistic tables of the cartridge manufacturer and work out where the MPI should be at 100 yards to be on zero at 200 yards.

According to the ballistic tables supplied with the ammunition, the rifle should be shooting 1½ inches high at 100 yards in order to be on zero at 200. In diagram 1 the MPI of the rifle lies at the same elevation and to the left of the aiming mark. Adjusting the sight up and to the right brings the MPI into line with the desired point and the three-shot group at 200 yards on a calm day confirms that the MPI is on the aiming mark of that range – the rifle is thus zeroed for 200 yards even though no bullets actually hit the bull!

The mean point of impact can be accurately drawn for a three-shot group by drawing straight lines between each of the three bullet holes to form a triangle and then bisecting each line with a line to the opposite bullet hole. Thus the MPI can be determined and the sight adjusted accordingly.

Medal Head   A 'medal head' is the term frequently used to describe a buck or stag whose antlers are of such quality that they would merit the award of a bronze, silver, or gold medal according the CIC formula for antler measurement.

See also: **Conseil International de la Chasse (CIC)**

Millais   Two generations of the Millais family are worthy of mention for their achievements in wild sports. Sir John Everett Millais, one of the great painters of the Victorian era, a contemporary of Sir Edwin Landseer and founder member of the 'Pre-Raphaelite Brotherhood' of artists, was also an accomplished game shooter, angler and deer stalker. His love of the wild sports of Britain was often reflected in his paintings.

In breadth of shooting experience, however, he was surpassed by his son, John G. Millais who, though also an artist and illustrator, became more renowned for his books. He was an eminent zoologist of the time with a comprehensive collection of Britain's breeding species. His books include *Game Birds and Shooting Sketches* (1892), *British Deer and their Horns* (1897) and *The Wildfowler in Scotland* (1900). Travel and sport abroad were recorded in *A Breath from the Veldt* (1899), *Newfoundland and its Untrodden Ways* (1907) and *Far Away up the Nile* in 1924.

Like the works of other leading naturalists and sportsmen of his era, the books by J.G. Millais are becoming increasingly scarce and sought after by sporting book collectors.

Muntjac Deer   The muntjac deer (*Muntiacus reevesii*) is perhaps the most remarkable of all British deer species. It originates from escapes from Woburn Park early this century, but such is its success in the wild that it is now widespread.

It would be very difficult to mistake a muntjac for any other species of deer. To begin with, this animal is very small, standing only eighteen inches high at the shoulder even at full maturity. Even so muntjac appear muscular and are quite heavy for their height – a mature animal weighs 30–35 lbs. There is little difference in size between the sexes and the does are frequently heavier than the bucks as they are usually at some stage of pregnancy throughout their adult life. The fawns are tiny when born, weighing only around 2½ lbs, but they grow very rapidly.

Muntjac deer are spreading more rapidly even than roe deer

At birth the fawn's coat is a light brown and heavily spotted, the spots running in lines along the flanks. It also has a darker brown line running from the nape along the spine to the base of the tail. Perhaps due to its diminutive size the muntjac fawn appears more 'fluffy' than the young of other species, with longer hair beneath the chin and on its underparts, and small rounded ears.

By the time the fawn is five weeks old the spotting will have faded and been replaced by a coat resembling that of the adult. Overall, the summer coat of an adult muntjac is bright chestnut fading into white on the chin and upper throat and under the tail. Although really a sub-tropical species, these deer have evolved a winter pelage of thicker greyer hair. The forelegs are dark brown on the outer surface with a pale leading edge. All four legs seem 'spindly' for an animal that appears to be so muscular. The tail is also an important identification feature. At about six inches in length it looks disproportionately long for the animal's size, and it is brown on the upper and white on the underside. At ease the deer carries it in 'tail

down' position but once it becomes curious or alarmed the tail is raised to vertical to show the very distinctive white. Naturally, for an animal that is active at night or in poor light, the eyes are large and fluid, and their best binocular vision is obtained above the line of the nose. When moving, therefore, the muntjac often adopt a 'head down' position.

The ears are ovoid in shape and covered with a relatively thin coat of hairs – against strong light they are translucent enough to appear pink – and the other facial features also serve to make identification easy. Both sexes carry canine teeth in the upper jaw; in the female these are not very obvious but in the mature buck they are long and prominent. There are numerous reports of these being used as very efficient weapons during confrontations with foxes, badgers and dogs, and there are instances of humans being attacked by cornered deer.

The old name given to this species was 'rib-faced deer', which arose from the prominent bone ridges on the skull running from above the nose, taking in the eyebrows, and ending above the ears in a doe and as the pedicle of the antlers in the buck. These 'ribs' are covered with darker hair than the rest of the face and are therefore easily visible and quite distinctive. At close quarters the large pre-orbital scent gland just in front of the eye is also visible, and it is more pronounced than on any other deer.

The antlers of the buck are also quite distinctive. Unlike the other antlered deer, the pedicles of a muntjac are long continuations of the forehead ridge and the antlers themselves are usually simple spikes which curve inwards towards each other at the tip. On older animals there may also be the vestige of a forward-facing brow tine on each side, but this rarely develops a definite point.

Antlers are grown and cast annually, but the timing of the cycle varies from one buck to another. Unlike other deer there seems to be little link between the growth of antlers and the ability of the buck to mate, and a buck whose antlers have been recently cast will still be capable of impregnating a doe. Recently there have been reports of more and more muntjac bucks evolving a seasonal cycle of casting and antler growth, with the old antlers cast in May and new ones completed and stripped of velvet by September.

As final aids to identification, the gait and social habits of this species are also distinctive. The muntjac has a hog-like hunched back and, as mentioned earlier, its head is carried low. It is understandable, therefore, if the species is mistaken for a badger rather than another deer in poor light, but the peculiar rapid run of a muntjac is unmistakable. This low gait is an adaptation to life in dense undergrowth, a habitat preferred by this species, and dense bramble patches in a muntjac-colonized area will be criss-crossed by a network of tunnels showing the well-worn trackways used by the deer.

Pair bonding and family life is far more developed than in other deer species, and frequent grooming and other physical contact occurs between bucks and does. Observers have noted that the bucks also have a greater degree of contact with the fawns, at times preening and even playing with their offspring. The breeding cycle is not seasonal and there is no 'rut' as in other deer. The doe produces a fawn roughly every seven months, coming into season within days of the birth. There are therefore very few times of year when the doe is not actually at some stage of pregnancy. It also seems that the development and growth of the fawn from birth is very rapid. The doe lactates for about six to eight weeks after birth and the young become sexually mature at about six months old.

The bucks are territorial animals, and a resident will confront any other male that ventures into his territory. Since most clashes are in dense cover there is little usual build-up to conflict, which takes the form of a 'head-to-head' pushing contest. Antlers and teeth are also used and bucks in a well-populated area often show head and neck scars resulting from these weapons. Living in cover which often restricts vision to a few feet, muntjac rely on scent and noise to communicate. Scent glands are found not only on the head, but also in the urinary tract and between the clefts of the hind feet. Presumably these last ones enable deer in a family group to track each other through dense undergrowth.

In India the muntjac is known as the 'Karkar' or Barking Deer. This reflects their main vocal communication: they bark like a small terrier dog. All deer bark, but the muntjac will bark repeatedly for a long time, on occasion barking at four- or five-second intervals for up to an hour. Both sexes bark and they will do so to locate each other, in alarm, or in challenge. In addition they have a vocabulary of squeaks, grunts and clicks which, however, are heard far less often than their barking.

The history of the muntjac is surprising. It is an extremely primitive animal, in that fossil evidence has shown the species to have existed about twenty million years ago during the Miocene period. Thus the muntjac, in its present-day form, existed long before any of the other deer species began evolving, and this little deer can certainly be looked on as a 'living fossil' in the same way as the coelacanth.

The recent history of the muntjac's colonization of Britain is equally astonishing. Within the eighty or so years from its original escapes from Woburn in Bedfordshire the muntjac has colonized the whole of the Home Counties and the Midlands. It can now be found as far west as Cornwall and throughout London's green belt as far as Essex north of the Thames and Kent to the south. Wales is being invaded from the Midlands and Gloucester, and on the east coast all of East Anglia now holds resident muntjac. At present they are colonizing northwards into Lincolnshire, and their rate of advance has been stated as averaging over two miles per year. The pioneering colonists tend to be young bucks that have been evicted from their birthplaces by the territorial bucks, and it may be a year or two before they are joined by does to set up a new breeding colony. Sexual activity at an early age and the capability to produce a fawn every seven months all contribute to the rapid growth and expansion of Britain's muntjac population.

Another significant factor in their expansion is the unobtrusive nature of the deer. They are seldom seen and have until recently been thought to do little damage to either agricultural or woodland crops. Consequently they were not seen as a nuisance in the same way as roe deer and they were often overlooked. Indeed it may be some years before the presence of an established colony of muntjac is even detected. However, new evidence seems to indicate that they do browse young trees, particularly conifers, and at a height which causes damage to be attributed wrongly to rabbits or hares! It is also now recognized that they can create serious damage to horticulture, showing a decided preference for root crops and brassicas.

They are generally disease-free and therefore losses in overpopulated areas through infection and parasitic infestation are negligible. On the other hand, despite the loyal defence of the fawn by both parents, losses of the young to predation by cats, dogs and foxes in some areas are often high. Motor traffic also takes its toll and this deer is particularly susceptible to harsh weather conditions in winter. A severely cold winter may produce a population crash which for a time halts the spread of the species.

Nevertheless, it seems very probable that this fascinating and truly remarkable little deer will continue to expand its population range. In time all the deep valleys of Wales and the low ground in the northern parts of England will boast resident populations of muntjac.

By the 1980s the spread of roe deer had been recognized and the characteristics of that species understood well enough for foresters and landowners to devise sound and workable management and stalking plans. The muntjac, on the other hand, is still little understood beyond a superficial level.

As the population level away from the 'pioneering frontier' builds up, every available niche will in time be occupied and subsequent overpopulation is then inevitable. It is at this stage that some form of population control by man is essential for the general well-being of the deer in the area. Predation and road-strikes by this stage are insufficient to stem the population increase, and deer stalking is the only humane and realistic alternative.

Deer management of muntjac as a species is still in its infancy. As the distribution of these deer throughout the country grows ever more widespread, Britain is likely to witness, in the next decade, the elevation of muntjac as a valuable addition to its wild fauna, to the same status as the roe deer. Muntjac stalking as a sport in its own right will arise in areas that have not known resident wild deer for many centuries, and the present research into this species will form the basis of the future management policies for this, Britain's smallest wild-living deer.

See also: **Deer**

Muzzle Energy   The power of a shotgun charge or a rifle bullet is calculated by measuring the energy it possesses as it leaves the barrel. This is known as the muzzle energy and it is usually measured in foot-pounds or metre-kilograms. Muzzle energy may also be calibrated in joules. In ballistic tables the down-range power of a bullet is indicated by its energy at 100 yards or metres.

See also: **Calibres – Rifle**

Muzzle Velocity   When a cartridge is fired, the exploding gases of the powder charge push the shot load or bullet through the barrel. This push is a rapid and violent acceleration with the maximum velocity reached just as the charge leaves the muzzle of the weapon.

The muzzle velocity is therefore the maximum velocity of the shot load or bullet. The instant the load of a shotgun cartridge of the rifle bullet leaves the barrel, air resistance acts upon it and it starts to decelerate.

With the high-efficiency powders that are used in modern cartridges, there are only marginal differences in the muzzle velocities produced by short or long barrels, although this is more pronounced in rifles. As a general rule, the muzzle velocity data produced by ammunition manufacturers is based on a standard-length barrel of 28 inches in a shotgun and 24 inches in a rifle. Velocities are usually calibrated in feet or metres per second.

Necked Case The term 'necked case' refers to a cartridge, usually for a centrefire rifle, in which the bullet diameter is considerably smaller than that of the cartridge case at its base. In order to hold the bullet firmly there must be some method by which the cartridge case tapers down towards the bullet. This is normally achieved in two ways.

A tapered cartridge case is one in which the diameter of the brass case tapers rapidly from the base of the cartridge down to the diameter appropriate to hold the bullet. Many older, and now obsolete, rifle calibres used this type of cartridge case, and the only modern example is the .22 Hornet. Even so, this little cartridge still shows some degree of 'necking'.

In a necked case, on the other hand, the brass case tapers only gradually from the base to a point where there is a marked shoulder, beyond which the neck of the case is parallel and of the correct diameter to hold the bullet.

The rate of taper in the main body of the case, the angle of the shoulder, and the length of the parallel neck vary between each calibre. The sharper the shoulder the more propellant powder can be loaded into the case. Many of the magnum calibres can therefore be distinguished by a very gradual body taper combined with steeply angled shoulders. Milder centrefire rifle castridges tend to have a steeper body taper and more rounded shoulders, and some examples, such as the .22 Savage and the .303 British, appear to be a combination of tapered and necked form.

See also: **Centrefire**

Obturation In order to propel a charge through a barrel, an efficient gas seal must exist behind the shotgun pellets or the rifle bullet. This seal, known as the obturation, is essential in order to use the power of the exploding propellant powder to its maximum efficiency.

In rifles it is the bullet itself which forms this gas seal. In the .22 LR rimfire this is achieved by making the bullet skirt exactly match the bore diameter of the rifle. The base section of a .22 rimfire bullet is reduced slightly in diameter in order to fit into the cartridge case, but it is the main section of the bullet which is skirted in order to provide good obturation.

Centrefire rifle bullets are not skirted in this way and it is inevitable that some gas will blow past the bullet. However, sufficient obturation is achieved if the cartridge fits the chamber with a minimum of free play. The very small difference between the diameter of the bullet and the neck of the cartridge is compensated for by the deeper-cut rifling found in high-velocity rifles and the probable slight deformation of the bullet itself as it undergoes dramatic acceleration through the barrel.

It is in shotguns that problems may arise from poor obturation, and these are usually associated with using cartridges of the wrong length for that shotgun's chamber. When a shotgun cartridge is fired the crimp or rolled turnover folds out into the end of the chamber and the shot charge and wadding is pushed through the chamber cone and on up the barrel. If the wad is of sufficient thickness the front end of the wad will enter the main bore before the rear end has cleared the mouth of the cartridge. When

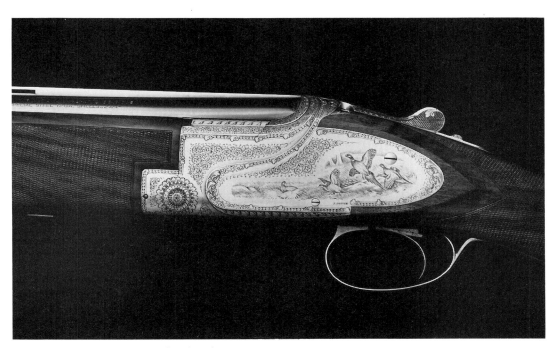

*An over-and-under shotgun fitted with
sideplates to increase the scope for engraving.
This is a fine example by Browning*

this happens there is very little gas leakage round the wadding and obturation is good. Different types of wadding achieve this in different ways. Felt wads are loaded into the cartridge under compression so that when the cartridge is fired they expand to fit the bore diameter to make a good seal. Plastic wads have a skirt around the base which flares slightly to give good obturation when the cartridge is fired.

When a short cartridge is used in a long-chambered gun, however, the risk of 'blow forward' is very much increased. If, for instance, a two-inch cartridge is fired in a standard-chambered 12-bore gun the wad column is too short to prevent gas blowing forward around the wad as it enters the chamber cone, and this problem is even more acute when a two-inch .410 cartridge is used in a gun chambered for the three-

*An over-and-under, popular with both game
and clay shooters, the Winchester pigeon-grade
trap gun*

inch case. The effect of poor obturation in these examples is seen as consistently poor shot patterns, loss of velocity, and increased barrel fouling. In extreme cases portions of the wad may be left in the barrel and this will obstruct the next shot – causing the barrel to bulge or burst and risking serious physical injury to the shooter.

Poor obturation can also be a problem in some of the older 8-bore wildfowling guns. Early this century a number of 'chamberless' 8 bores were made specifically for the thin brass-cased cartridges. As the walls of these cartridges were so thin the wads expanded quickly enough to provide a gas seal despite the fact that the barrel lacked a chamber or chamber cone. Paper, and even plastic-cased, cartridges have much thicker walls so that there is a greater difference between the outside diameter of the case and that of the wad. When these cartridges are used in a chamberless gun the gas seal is therefore much less efficient and the gun throws inferior patterns.

Over-and-Under   An over-and-under is a double-barrelled weapon in which the barrels are superimposed one on top of the

A cut-away over-and-under shotgun showing much of the mechanism

other. Both rifles and shotguns are built to this design. Over-and-under shotguns are popular among clay pigeon shooters for two reasons. The depth of the action required to house the two superimposed barrels demands greater quantities of metal so that the over-and-under gun tends to be rather heavier than its side-by-side counterpart. This increased weight absorbs more recoil and firing the gun is therefore less punishing on the shooter's shoulder when large numbers of cartridges are used in a relatively short time. Secondly, the single 'uncluttered' sighting line along the top rib is favoured by many who claim that it makes pointing or aiming the weapon both quicker and easier. Perhaps for this latter reason, the last two decades have seen the over-and-under shotgun gaining rapidly in popularity among live-quarry shooters and it is now probably the more widely used of the two double barrel configurations.

Over-and-under rifles have found favour on the European continent where large or potentially dangerous game such as elk or wild boar may be encountered at close quarters. Built in the 'medium' calibres such as the 9.3×74, these are effective weapons for close-range shooting, and a double rifle has the advantage of allowing a very quick second shot if needed.

Paradox Guns In the early days of African and Indian exploration the hunter would require a shotgun for use against winged game and a large-bore rifle for use against plains game and other large mammals. At that time rifles were designed to fire a spherical ball or conical slug through rifled barrels, but apart from this there was little to distinguish them from their shotgun counterparts.

The demand arose for a weapon which would fulfil the role of both rifle and shotgun, i.e., one that was capable of throwing a large single projectile with some degree of accuracy at close quarters while still producing shotgun patterns effective enough to fill the pot. A ball-and-shotgun was therefore required.

The paradox gun was developed to answer this need. Usually of double barrel side-by-side design, the paradox barrels were smooth-bored for most of their length but the last nine inches or so were rifled. Although the design did achieve some degree of success it never caught on for a number of reasons. The new high-velocity rifles were evolving rapidly and the ballistics of these new weapons were far superior to the 'ball' rifles.

The rifling at the end of the paradox barrel tended to throw very inconsistent shot patterns, and the 'rifled slug' was developed to produce comparable accuracy from a smooth-bored shotgun. Faced with these developments the 'ball and shot' 'paradox' gun quickly faded from the field.

Parker-Hale In 1904, A.G. Parker and his nephew A.T.C. Hale, formed the gunmaking company of A.G. Parker & Co., but in 1936 this was changed to Parker-Hale Ltd. The company was well established, marketing a wide range of firearms, accessories, and ammunition for both the sporting and the target shooter. In addition, Parker-Hale concentrated much of their attention on developing and perfecting a system of re-rifling barrels based on the idea of the earlier 'Morris Tube' barrel insert. The resultant 'Parkerifling' process involved boring out the existing barrel and inserting a precision-bored tube. Such was the success of this process with .22 rimfire barrels that most target rifles of the day were 'Parkerifled', and a great many service rifles were also converted to .22 calibre in this way for practice and cadet use between the two World Wars.

During the decline of Britain's gunmaking trade after the Second World War, Parker-Hale diversified further in the range of accessories they marketed while at the same time adapting their own rifle production to suit the contracting market. In the early post-war years the firm converted large quantities of Lee-Enfield service rifles to sporting use, as the military .303 calibre made a fine hunting weapon with suitable loads. 'Sporterized' Lee-Enfield rifles were available in a range of grades and finishes but only, of course, in .303 calibre. Parker-Hale's own production of sporting rifles was designed from the outset to appeal more to the slowly growing band of British deer stalkers, and

The classic-style English rifle – this one a Parker-Hale Model 81

the success of this is borne out by the enduring popularity of Parker-Hale stalking rifles to this day.

The post-war years saw considerable redevelopment take place in the Birmingham gun trade, and in this period Parker-Hale moved to their present address on Golden Hillock Road. In this period also the firm took over the Midland Gun Co., a gun-making firm that specialized in lower-priced but hard-wearing and reliable guns. Such was the good reputation of the Midland Gun Co. at the lower end of the market that the brand name has been continued by Parker-Hale.

Nowadays Parker-Hale still live up to their old catalogue claim that they can supply 'everything for the shooter'. The range of accessories available from them is extensive and they import a wide range of sporting and competition firearms from both Europe and the USA. Under their own brand name and that of the Midland Gun Co. they import an impressive range of soundly constructed and good-looking shotguns from such Spanish gunmakers as Ugartachea. In side-by-side configuration these shotguns are available in a variety of grades from a 'Midland' boxlock non-ejector up to a sidelock ejector that has a high degree of hand finishing and elegant engraving. The guns are also available in a range of calibres from .410 up to 12 bore. All these side-by-sides are built to the English style of game gun, with narrow fore-ends and straight stocks, and since their introduction a decade

ago they have been well received on the British game shooting scene.

Parker-Hale also import a range of over-and-under shotguns under their own name. Models are available for live quarry shooting and for the different clay pigeon disciplines, and again these are nicely balanced and reliable shotguns with the cheapest in the range coming under the 'Midland' brand name. Parker-Hale guns in the over-and-under configuration originate from a number of manufacturers in Southern Europe.

At an international level, the reputation built up by Parker-Hale between the wars has been maintained by the performance of the centrefire rifles they manufacture at their own works in Birmingham. The Parker-Hale '1000' series of rifles is probably the most popular range of stalking rifles in Britain. For one thing, their barrels are forged to very fine tolerances to give excellent accuracy, and all the rifles use Mauser bolt actions which are renowned for their strength and reliability, yet they still remain probably the least expensive of all stalking rifles available in Britain. The one exception to this general pattern is the Midland rifle, which uses a modified Springfield bolt instead of the Mauser pattern. Nevertheless this does not detract from the accuracy of the barrel – I used a Midland 2100 rifle in .270 calibre for many years and could not fault its performance.

Parker-Hale centrefire rifles are available in a variety of styles and grades, and are

bored and chambered for calibres ranging from the .22/250 Rem. up to the heavy .458 Win. Magnum. Heavy-barrel 'varmint' editions, lightweight and standard rifles add variety to a range that may also be supplied with walnut or laminated stocks.

If one agrees that the most vital component in an accurate rifle is a well-bored barrel, the Parker-Hale range of centrefire rifles cannot be faulted, and this perhaps goes some way to explain why they are Britain's best-selling stalking rifles.

Partridge – Grey At one time the grey partridge (*Perdix perdix*) was considered to be the prime game bird of Britain. Since the second half of the last century the methods of rearing and release of pheasants have contributed to the change in the status of the grey partridge. In addition, the increasingly widespread use of agrochemicals on farm crops up to the 1960s has also contributed to the decline in numbers of this

Parker-Hale import a wide range of shotguns and market them under their own name. Here is their basic model 601 12-bore non-ejector

truly native species, and it is only in recent years that the decline has been halted.

At around twelve inches long overall, the grey partridge is a small plump game bird with stout rounded wings and short tail. Although the cock bird is slightly larger than the female, the plumage of each sex is similar. Both have a characteristic orange-brown face, pale grey neck and underparts, and chestnut-barred flanks. The upper parts, wings, shoulders and rump are patterned with brown, grey and black; and the tail feathers are rich fawn brown. The male is distinguished from the female by a dark brown and conspicuous horseshoe patch on its lower breast. While the female may have odd flecks of this colour the mark is not as well-formed or as conspicuous as on the cock bird.

The grey partridge is a vocal bird and both sexes utter a loud grating creak from which it gets its Latin name. This call is often heard when the bird is agitated or when flushed, although when at rest it has a varied vocabulary of quieter cheeps and squeaks.

The most favoured habitat for grey partridge is mixed farmland with areas of grassland fringed by thick hedges. It is a bird of the lowlands and is rarely found above the 1,500 ft contour. Where they do occur above this altitude they occupy heathland adjoining cultivated land. The bird is resident through-out lowland Britain and rarely moves far from its established 'lone areas' although the young do tend to disperse in late winter before the cock birds establish their breeding grounds.

This species is almost entirely ground-dwelling and will normally walk or run rather than fly. The normal walking gait shows a head-down posture, but when alarmed it runs with head stretched upwards. It will often crouch to escape detection, but when flushed its explosive take-off develops into a strong and speedy flight with frequent glides on down-curved wings. Grey partridge often flush in groups or coveys and these keep close together in flight with much criss-crossing of flight paths of individual birds in the covey. This manner of flying often helps to confuse both airborne predators and shooters!

Outside the breeding season this is a gregarious species, and a considerable number may roost together on the ground. They are daylight feeders, taking seeds, grain, and other vegetable matter, although the chicks also take a wide variety of insects. Recent research has pointed to the use of aphicide crop spraying in May and June as the cause of high chick mortality, and this may be a significant factor in the areas where this species has declined since the last war. In the breeding season the males are strongly territorial and the female will often join in the defence of a nesting territory.

Of the two partridge species, the grey is the more difficult to rear, although some shoots have achieved considerable success in this field. In other areas management of the wild partridge population has succeeded using the Euston system of artificial incubation of the eggs before replacing them in the nests of wild birds to be hatched.

Where grey partridge numbers are sufficient the shooting may take the form of partridge driving, and there are nowadays a growing number of driven partridge shoots in the eastern counties of England. Elsewhere partridge may be walked up or even shot over pointer dogs.

The grey partridge may be easily confused with the slightly larger red-legged or French partridge, but its call is distinctive and its colouring quite different at close range. Both species are considerably larger than the small, rare, and protected quail.

See also: **Driven Game Shooting;
Walked-Up Shooting**

Partridge – Red-Legged The red-legged partridge (*Alectoris rufa*) is not a true British species. After a number of unsuccessful attempts at introduction in the eighteenth century, eggs were imported from France in the mid-1800s, and a successful population was established in East Anglia. The source of these eggs has led to this species also being called the 'French partridge'.

The red-legged partridge is a small 'dumpy' game bird which has 'square-cut' wings in flight. Measuring around 13½ inches in length it is slightly larger than the native grey partridge, but this is not really apparent unless the two species are seen together at close quarters. Like the grey partridge both male and female plumage is similar, although the male is a slightly larger and heavier bird. The adult bird has a distinctive black eye-stripe which separates a white eyebrow from a large white cheek and throat patch. This patch is bordered in black, but this grades downwards on the neck to black, brown and chestnut. The upper surfaces are a rather uniform grey-brown, but the buff underparts are strongly barred with chestnut, black and white on the flanks. The beak, the eyelids and the legs are a rich red. The contrasting colours and strong barring give the red-legged partridge a more striking and colourful appearance than the native grey partridge.

The voice is another aid to identification. The cock bird utters a loud and repeated 'chuck-kor' and the barking 'cuk cuk' call is used by both sexes, especially when the bird is flushed.

The red-legged partridge is a bird of low-lying farmland. Since its introduction to East Anglia, the wild stock has spread to most of southern and eastern England and as far west as Devon and the Welsh border. It is an easy bird to rear and release and this fact is responsible for its presence in other lowland parts of Britain. It occurs on a variety of different types of farmland, including open woodland, but its preferred habitat is areas of low vegetation and light soils; it is, after all, a native of Mediterranean Europe and Asia Minor. However, as an introduced species it will flourish in very different surroundings, and in recent years the scale of releases to newly established partridge shoots has increased.

Like other species the red-leg will run rather than fly, but when flushed the coveys tend to scatter into twos and threes. Its fast and direct flight, with rapid wingbeats interspersed by frequent glides on down-curved wings, is typical of the partridge family, but unlike the grey it may roost in trees as well as on the ground.

Outside the breeding season it is more gregarious than the grey partridge and may often congregate in coveys of over fifty birds. Even on this scale it will tend to creep away quietly and unobtrusively if a threat appears and this may give the advantage to a staggered flush – sending twos and threes over the guns rather than one big covey.

Like the grey partridge the red-leg may be driven or walked up and it is this species which has helped to re-establish specialized partridge shoots after the decline of the grey partridge. Nowadays many lowland pheasant shoots may include a partridge drive or two as more and more shoots are discovering that rearing red-legged partridge is almost as easy as pheasant rearing

Where the two species of partridge exist in the same area there is no visible competition and they seem to co-exist very amicably. On one Lincolnshire shoot roughly equal numbers of both species have been shot each season for the last ten years and the bags have increased steadily throughout, perhaps related to the steady decline in the use of insecticide crop sprays on the shoot.

Though not a true native species the red-legged partridge, like the pheasant, has become a well-established and very important game quarry species in Britain.

See also: **Driven Game Shooting; Walked-Up Shooting**

Pattern Plate Shotguns are test-fired at a pattern plate in order to test the alignment of their barrel or barrels, and also to ascertain the quality of the pattern thrown by a given combination of cartridge, choke and load.

The term 'pattern plate' is derived from the use of a large steel plate for a test-firing target. In order to be effective the pattern plate should measure at least six feet square and be thick enough to prevent penetration by the shot charge. Nowadays many people use a brick wall for the same purpose. The plate is whitewashed and an aiming point is daubed in the centre. The shot is then fired at this aiming mark from 40 yards and a 30-inch diameter circle is drawn round the centre of the pattern, even though this may not coincide with the aiming mark. The pattern is assessed by counting the pellet strikes within the circle and comparing this with the number of pellets in the shot charge. The number within the circle depends on the choke of the barrel, the quality of the boring, and the quality of the cartridge; and the actual results may be checked against the statistical norms. For the shooter the time

Full choke. Such patterns ruin game at close ranges

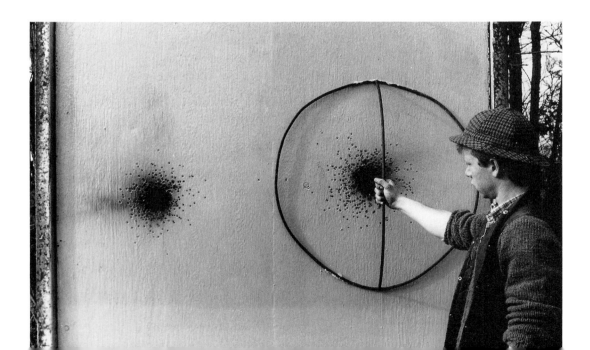

spent on the pattern plate may identify the best shotgun/cartridge combination – the one that throws the most consistent and evenly-spread patterns.

The pattern plate may also be used to ascertain that both barrels of a double gun are correctly aligned to shoot to the same point and whether it is high, on, or below the aiming mark. Some shotguns are designed to shoot high, and this may not be evident until they are tested on the pattern plate.

Payne-Gallwey, Sir Ralph   Born in 1848, Sir Ralph Payne-Gallwey was hailed throughout his adult life as Britain's greatest all-round sporting shooter. As well as excelling in every discipline from grouse butts to the half-decked wildfowl punt in a January gale, Payne-Gallwey was a prolific writer whose works inspired the rapidly-growing numbers of sporting shooters.

The first book, *The Fowler in Ireland*, was written in 1882 and was a product of exhaustive research and exciting experiences. In the late 1880s his *Book of Duck Decoys* appeared at the same time as his collaboration with Lord Walsingham on the two Badminton Library shooting volumes. This was followed by the book *Letters to Young Shooters* in 1890 written in a bright and enthusiastic style and produced as three volumes: *On the Choice and Use of a Gun, On the Production, Preservation and Killing of Game* and *Wildfowl and Wildfowl Shooting.*

His last book, *High Pheasant in Theory and Practice* (1913), reflects the exhaustive research he conducted and the breadth of experience from which he could draw before putting pen to paper. Sir Ralph Payne-Gallwey died in 1916 at the age of 68, but his books have been in demand to the present day.

Peg

See: **Driven Game Shooting; Gamekeeping**

Pelage   This ancient hunting term refers to the coat of a live deer. Most deer species in Britain grow two distinctively different coats. These are known as the winter pelage and summer pelage. In general terms the hair of the summer pelage is brightly coloured and short. During autumn the longer-haired winter pelage grows through the summer coat so that by mid-November the deer are in their more sombre-coloured and thick winter pelage. In the following April or May the long hair is moulted very rapidly, often falling out in big clumps, and the deer at this time look decidedly scruffy and bedraggled. By June, however, the moult is usually complete and the deer are again in their sleek summer pelage.

See also: **Deer**

Pheasant   The ubiquitous pheasant (*Phasianus colchius*) is not a native of Britain. The Romans are generally credited with the introduction of this bird into the country, and by the early eighteenth century the Southern Caucasus or 'blacknecked' pheasant had become known as the 'Old English' pheasant in order to distinguish it from subsequent introductions. The Chinese ringnecked pheasant arrived in the late 1700s and the Japanese southern green pheasant was introduced by Lord Derby in the mid-1800s. Early this century came introductions of the grey Prince of Wales pheasant and the dark melanistic or 'black' pheasant became established in the 1920s. All these strains belong to the same species and have interbred freely, so that nowadays there are very few 'pure-bred' bloodlines among the pheasant population in Britain.

The pheasant is a large game bird, the cock bird measuring up to thirty-six inches in length and weighing up to 3½ lbs. Unlike many other game birds there is a considerable size and weight difference between the cock and hen bird. The latter will seldom exceed twenty-five inches in length or 2⅓ lbs in weight, but both sexes are easily identified by their characteristic long and pointed tail. As a result of the free intermixing of the different races, the plumage colouring in both sexes can show considerable variation.

The 'average' cock pheasant has an iridescent copper plumage with a dark bottle-green head and a red face wattle around the eye. This green head may be separated from the coppery body plumage by a conspicuous white neck ring, although this is often incomplete or absent. The shoulders are a blue-grey colour and the wing feathers are browner. The central tail feathers are very elongated and barred with dark brown or black on the upper surface. The one real departure from this general colour scheme is the melanistic or 'black' pheasant; the cock bird in this case is an overall dark green with a gradual change to a glossy purple along the flanks and lower breast.

Hen pheasants are pale mottled brown overall, with a less elongated tail, and the melanistic hen is considerably darker, with a rich dark-brown ground colour that is strongly barred with black. Although the melanistic hen resembles a red grouse, the tail remains an easy identification feature.

The cock pheasant is a vocal bird, its familiar double crow a common sound in Britain's woodlands, but when flushed its alarm call is an oft-repeated deep chortle. The hen bird is much quieter, using a range of soft calls when attending to its chicks. Its alarm call, most often heard as the bird is flushed, is a single grating squeak.

Within its native population range in Asia, the pheasant is a bird of the water margins and reed beds, but in Britain it has adapted well to life in lowland woodland, hedgerows and farmland. Pheasants breed in the wild in all areas of the country except in the mountain areas of Scotland and North Wales, and in most places the wild stock is supplemented by birds released for sporting purposes. It is the easiest of all game birds to breed in captivity. For this reason millions are bred and released each year in all manner of environments and in all types of game shoots from the smallest rough shoot, where perhaps twenty or so birds may be 'put down' in the woods, to the large driven shoots whose annual release may number many thousand birds. Released pheasants are notorious wanderers and each shoot may go to elaborate feeding strategies in order to keep the birds happy and thus prevent the stock birds from wandering off the ground. Ideally, pheasants like mixed woodland with sufficient undergrowth for shelter, adjoining arable farmland on which they feed during the day. Although basically ground-dwelling birds, pheasant need tree perches for roosting, particularly on land frequented by foxes,

and the cock birds are very vocal as they fly up to roost.

Pheasants will far rather run than fly, and will only take to the air when danger threatens. Their take-off is explosive and they possess a phenomenal rate of climb. Having achieved sufficient height to clear trees and other obstacles the bird levels out and the flight usually continues as a series of long glides interspersed with bursts of rapid wingbeats to maintain its high forward speed. Pheasants seldom fly far, however, and when flushed they will usually make towards some other cover either by going forward or by curling back into the patch from which they were flushed. These high 'curling' pheasants are among the most difficult and testing of targets for a game shooter and many shoots attempt to present their driven birds in this way.

Outside the breeding season pheasant are sociable birds and often feed and roost in the company of others. However, they are not really flocking birds in the same way as woodpigeons or partridge, and a flush of birds going over the guns is usually the result of a number of birds congregating at a good flushing point and taking to the air together.

When one thinks of lowland game shooting in all its different forms it is always the ubiquitous pheasant that features as the prime quarry species.

See also: **Game Shooting**

Picker-Up   A picker-up has a very important role on a driven game shoot. As the term implies, his main function is to mark down birds that have been shot by the gun so that they can be retrieved at the end of each drive. A picker-up usually uses two or tree retrieving dogs for this purpose, and any head keeper knows the value of a team of observant and steady labradors under the command of a reliable handler.

In normal circumstances the picker-up will be stationed some distance behind the gun on each drive. From this position the fall of dead birds can be noted and those lying close to the guns will be left to the guns and their dogs to retrieve. It is the wounded bird that receives the special attention of the picker-up. These birds, if their wings remain undamaged, may glide a long distance before landing and it is there that the picker-up's dogs will be sent to retrieve. Even after landing a wounded bird will run, and these runners make great demands on a dog's observation, scenting powers, and stamina. It is these runners that really test the quality and performance of a retriever. Although procedures vary from shoot to shoot, it is normal to hold up the next drive until the pickers-up have accounted for all 'downed' birds of the previous drive.

It is not surprising, therefore, that a dog handler with two or three well-trained and reliable retrievers will always be welcomed and valued at any driven game shoot, and the role of picker-up has a status all of its own.

Pigeon Shooting   The sport of wood-pigeon shooting serves the dual purpose of controlling the most damaging agricultural pest in Britain while at the same time providing a testing and enjoyable activity for more shotgun shooters than any other shooting discipline. The wood-pigeon is a strong and agile flier and a voracious eater of farm crops; it is possessed of a strong instinct for self-preservation and keen eyesight; and it is also a delicious table bird. As for its general habits, in winter it will often congregate in large flocks to roost and feed, and during the breeding season in spring and summer each breeding pair may raise a number of broods. Weighing up to 2 lbs, its metabolism is such that it will eat its own weight of food per day, and it takes little imagination to envisage what a flock of two or three hundred birds will do to a farm crop over a period of a few days.

The wood-pigeon is a gregarious bird which is always keen to investigate what others of its kind are up to, and this curiosity has led to the development of decoying pigeons as the main strategy for the shooter. Pigeon are daytime feeders, flighting from their roosting woodland to the feeding areas in the early morning and returning at dusk. Even during the breeding season when the large flocks have broken up into pairs, the birds will still congregate in some numbers on their favoured feeding fields throughout the daytime, and any surface water such as ponds, streams, and even cattle troughs will

be regularly visited because the pigeon also drinks a great deal of water. At times the birds may develop established and regular flight lines between roost and feeding area, particularly in winter, and intercepting them en route is often a successful tactic.

The three main tactics used in pigeon shooting are therefore flighting, decoying, and roost shooting.

Basically, flighting shooting involves identifying a pigeon flight line from roost to feeding area and concealing oneself underneath it in order to intercept the passing traffic. In order to ascertain the track of the flight line, the shooter should spend time observing the movements of the birds, identifying the feeding areas and the most frequently used route between these and the roosting woodland. Flight lines are not fixed, and routes frequently change as the birds select a different food source, so the successful flight shooter should glean the relevant information almost on a day-to-day basis before venturing out with a gun and a bagful of cartridges.

Flight lines are usually more difficult to identify in the spring and summer as the birds are dispersed into breeding pairs. However, well-marked flight lines may still exist if the roosting woodland is large enough to hold a good population of breeding birds, but the chances of making good bags are certainly slimmer than in the winter.

In the cold months, when food sources are more restricted and the birds have collected into large flocks, flighting shooting can be fast and furious and, with the birds battling and sliding against a headwind or screaming downwind on a gale, the sport can be very testing indeed. Generally a morning flight is more productive than shooting in late afternoon and evening. When the birds leave their roost for the feeding grounds they tend to move in twos, threes, and small flocks, and the shooter will be presented with a regular stream of birds in a flight which may last for an hour or more.

In the evening, on the other hand, pigeons tend to lift off the field in one large flock to return to roost, so the shooter may only have one 'flock shot' as they pass overhead. Pigeon flighting as a sport is not restricted to morning and evening because there may well be considerable movement of birds between the woods and feeding fields throughout the day. Odd twos and threes may use the flight line between spells of feeding and these birds can provide a steady stream of shooting opportunities in the late morning and early afternoon. On arrival at their feeding field the pigeons will fill their crops as quickly as possible and then retire to a tree perch to digest this first meal. Once this is done they return to feed again. It is these birds that provide the daytime flighting.

When selecting the correct location for a hide, the flight shooter needs to take the weather conditions into account. Rain and mist tend to make the birds fly lower than usual but it is strong wind which has the greatest effect on the flight pattern. A strong headwind will disperse the flight line over a wider area as the birds 'tack' upwind against it. A crosswind will push the flight downwind from its 'normal' line and in strong wind the pigeons will use the shelter afforded by taller hedges to fly low along the lee side. If correctly placed the shooter may intercept a stream of birds beating along the hedge side at low level. A following wind will accelerate the birds' flight and may give them extra height, and a high downwind pigeon can be a very exacting target.

For concealment, the flight shooter may take advantage of any natural cover such as a hedge or grass-lined fence or ditch. The most important qualities a hide must have are that it must break up the outline of the shooter, as flighting pigeons are quick to identify any human form as a potential source of danger, and it must afford the shooter a good all-round view and a clear field of fire. Obviously it is physically impossible to look in all directions at once, but a watch must be kept on the direction from which birds are expected and on the opposite for returning birds. All too often the shooter relaxes vigilance only to be taken by surprise by a bird sneaking through the 'blind' spot.

In terms of choice of shotgun, any well-bored gun of 28-bore or larger can be used to good effect. The choice of calibre and type of weapon is largely a matter of individual preference – if I expect that the birds will be flighting low then my double 28 is my first choice. If, on the other hand, the birds are expected to be flying high and fast then I use a 16- or 12-bore. My own preference is for a double side-by-side shotgun but there may be occasions when more firepower is useful. Some years ago I witnessed a friend take five birds out of one flock using a Browning five-shot autoloader. Nowadays these weapons and pump actions are restricted to three shots, which reduces the temptation among novices to blaze away into a large flock while still offering an increase in firepower over a conventional double gun.

The pigeon shooter would not expect to shoot as many birds at flighting as when decoying them on their feeding grounds, and a bag of twenty pigeons or more is a good flight indeed. In many ways, though, flighting shooting is more rewarding because of the challenge of intercepting a wily and strong-flying bird, dependent on long periods of observation and planning in order to achieve success. The variety of shots offered by flighting birds makes greater demands on the shooter's skill than birds dropping in to a pattern of decoys, and a good pigeon flight can be as enjoyable as a stand at a driven pheasant or grouse shoot.

Many pigeon shooters have developed the sport of pigeon decoying to almost a science, and certainly the great majority of pigeons killed in Britain each year will fall over a pattern of decoys. Pigeon decoying exploits the wood-pigeon's natural instinct to feed, rest, and sleep in large groups. So strong is this gregarious instinct that the birds can be drawn to very unlikely areas by the use of an effective pattern of decoys. However, the heaviest bags of pigeons are usually made when they are decoyed onto a field on which they have been feeding for some time, and the purpose of using decoys in this case is to draw the birds onto that particular part of the field which is within range of the concealed shooter. Essentially, the shooter sets out a number of pigeon decoys in lifelike poses in order to imitate a flock of feeding birds and then retires to a suitable hide to await any birds that are drawn into range.

As in other forms of pigeon shooting preliminary observation is an essential prerequisite for a successful decoying foray. The shooter should note not only the fields that are being used by the feeding birds but also their line of approach and the parts of the field that are most frequented. The location of any 'sentinel' or 'sitty' trees from which pigeons can spy out the ground before committing themselves to a ground landing, and the location of any ground cover in which a hide can be prepared, are also important considerations in planning a decoying foray.

To be successful against such a naturally wary bird, effective concealment is very important. Perhaps the most comfortable of all hides is the bale hide, and these have the added advantage that they can be placed on any part of the field and are not dependent on hedge-side cover. On the other hand, the use of bale hides demands the complete support and cooperation of the farmer and once built they are static structures. The presence of a group of straw bales in a field will go largely unnoticed by wood-pigeons, and the concealment and comfort a bale hide affords a shooter cannot be bettered. However, after a field has been heavily shot the birds may well become 'bale hide shy', and will only alight well away from such constructions despite a convincing pattern of decoys that the shooter may have laid out. If bale hides are not available, perhaps the most valuable accessory for the pigeon decoyer is a camouflage net. Thus equipped the shooter can dispense with any dependence on bale hides and effective concealment is possible in a wide variety of situations. In winter, when field boundary cover is particularly sparse, a camouflage net hide can be rigged up against a low hedge, a tree trunk, or even a barbed wire fence. Suitably garnished with dead grass and other vegetation it will effectively break up the outline of the shooter. In the summer, the net may be disposed of if there is sufficient hedge-side cover to provide effective concealment, but it is still very useful in more open country.

When pigeon shooting from a hide, many novices make the mistake of looking over the net, or concealing foliage, rather than through it. A wood-pigeon will spot a human face at a considerable distance and it is therefore essential that the shooter's face be kept well hidden until the moment to shoot. When constructing a hide, the shooter should arrange 'spy holes' so that a clear and unrestricted view of the expected approach route is possible without exposing the face. With gun at the ready the shooter will only need to 'straighten up' from a crouched position in order to swing the gun clear of obstructions for a flying shot. This of course assumes that the gun in question is a shotgun, but a good many pigeons can be accounted for by shooting over decoys with an air rifle or a .22 rimfire rifle. Bags are not usually as heavy as when using a shotgun for the simple reason that the birds must land before the shot is taken and this will restrict the chances presented to the shooter. When using a rifle the weapon can be aimed through the net or foliage rather than swung over it as in the case of a shotgun, so the need for a clear field of fire is of less importance. On the other hand the need for effective concealment is even more important because a pigeon will usually inspect its surroundings very carefully immediately after landing and before it begins to feed – a combination of still decoys and a suspicious 'lump' in the hedge will often be too much for its nerves!

There is no great art to setting out an effective pattern of decoys but a few points need to be considered. When feeding on the ground, wood-pigeons tend to move slowly upwind, though they will frequently turn to peck at food on either side. When setting out decoys the shooter should therefore avoid pointing all into wind as this regimented look appears very unnatural. Similarly, decoys should be dispersed as single birds or pairs, for two reasons: wood-pigeons seldom bunch together in tight groups and any incoming birds must be given landing space between the decoys. I always find it useful to use two decoys as distance markers – when using a shotgun I place one decoy in a prominent position at 20 yards and another at 40 yards so that I have a guide to the minimum and maximum ranges at which I can shoot. When using a rifle the distance markers are set at different ranges according to the power of the weapon being used, and I find them an invaluable aid to estimating the range of alighted birds.

On many occasions I have observed feeding wood-pigeons 'fanning out' while they move upwind so that an established and settled feeding flock shows an arc pattern. New arrivals tend to land behind the arc then walk forward to join the 'front line' of advancing feeders. Setting out decoys in a rough arc pattern will focus the attention of an incoming bird on the landing area behind the arc and this can be quite useful when using a rifle. If birds can be enticed to land at a predetermined spot then the rifle can be pointed in that direction to minimize movement and the time taken to aim and fire. Wood-pigeons almost always make their landing approach upwind and this must be borne in mind when siting the decoy pattern in relation to the location of the hide. From a bale hide in the centre of a field the decoy pattern can be set so that the shooter is presented with either head-on or crossing shots as the birds make their approach. A hedge-side hide offers less versatility but the decoys can be set so as to present approaching birds from one direction.

Every bird shot should be added to the decoy pattern but the shooter should wait a minute or two after a shot in case the disturbance has alerted any more birds in the vicinity. Once it is safe to emerge, the dead bird is set out in a lifelike pose among the other decoys before the shooter resumes his place in the hide to await further pigeons. Dead pigeons make the best decoys, particularly if they are set out so that their heads are supported in a more lifelike pose by propping them up with a small twig. Artificial decoys in all shapes and sizes just do not seem to have the same pull as the natural decoys, although they are very effective.

Commercially-manufactured decoys come in three basic types – the full-bodied decoy, the shell and the 'flier' or 'flapper'. As its name implies, the full-bodied decoy, often made of plastic or rubber, represents the complete bird, and this type is useful not only for ground decoying but also for setting on fences and lofting into trees. The shell decoy represents the top half of the bird and is designed to be visible from above. In most circumstances they are as effective as the full-bodied decoy and have the additional advantage of being far less bulky as they readily fit inside each other for carrying convenience. Five shell decoys can easily be carried in the pocket of a shooting jacket, for example, whereas the same number of full-bodied decoys would require an additional bag. On the other hand, shell decoys are limited to field settings as they do not have the body silhouette of a wood-pigeon and they are also prone to blow over in a strong wind. However, I have used shells for any years to good effect and their portability more than makes up for their limitations.

Static 'flapping' decoys have been on the market for many years. Basically these are decoys with wings outstretched as if in flight. The wings are flexible and attached to a string which is manipulated from the hide by the shooter. Unlike the normal 'peg' decoys, the flappers are mounted on stakes approximately three to four feet long so the bird appears to be airborne and making its final approach. A flighting pigeon is quick to notice movement and the prominent white wing bars on the flapper increase the distance from which the decoy can be seen. A flapper decoy placed downwind of a static pattern can add greatly to the attractiveness of the layout and can thus draw birds in from greater range. Recently, 'flapper cages' have become available. These are basically wire cradles arranged so that a dead bird can be mounted with its wings attached to drawstrings. Again, when these are pulled by the shooter the dead bird's wings will open and close, thus producing movement and increasing the chances of attracting a passing bird. The 'free-flying' decoy has also recently appeared on the market. This rather resembles a frisbee but is painted in wood-pigeon colours. When a pigeon is seen a 'flier' is thrown from the hide to land among the static decoy pattern, and this will convince the bids that there is something worth investigating. Both flapper and free-flying decoys are intended to support a static ground pattern and should not be used on their own. If flappers are used at all, certainly no more than two should be added to the ground display. Any more and one has visions of the shooter frantically pulling at many different cords and having little time to prepare for any approaching quarry.

At times when food is abundant and the pigeons are more dispersed, setting a couple of full-bodied pigeon decoys on the edge of a cattle trough may draw a few birds to this source of water. Bags will seldom exceed a dozen birds, but a few hours' sport on a summer day can be had. Pigeons can also be decoyed into trees when they do not show a preference for any feeding fields. For this form of shooting the decoys must be full-bodied and they are lofted into the branches either by throwing a rope over a suitable branch and drawing the decoys upwards or by using lofting poles. These are long sectional poles much like a chimney-sweep's rods. The decoy is mounted on the end of the first pole and other sections are added to this until the desired height is reached. The disadvantage of this is that the height is restricted by the strength of the poles but it is easier to place the decoys in a prominent position among the branches. In summer the decoy can be pushed beyond the foliage so that it can be easily seen by any passing wood-pigeon, and when the trees are bare the lofted decoy should be placed among the outer branches of the tree. Large numbers of decoys are not necessary, and two or three lofted decoys will usually act as a good draw to passing trafic. Both air rifles and shotguns may be used in this sport; the air rifle shooter of course waits for the incoming birds to settle on a perch before shooting, whereas the shotgun user has greater freedom either to take the 'sitter' or to intercept the bird on its final approach. As in shooting over a water trough, bags will not be as high as for the field decoy shooter, but the birds offer a wider variety of testing targets and shooting over lofted decoys is another useful tactic that adds variety to the sport of pigeon shooting.

Pigeon decoying in a variety of environments should be timed to coincide with the habits of the pigeon. When shooting over a food crop, many shooters find that the peak feeding times change with the seasons. In the winter when daylight hours are short the flocks will commence feeding shortly after first light and continue throughout the day. It is important that the shooter is set up and ready before the first arrivals in the early morning. The steady stream of birds can then be intercepted as they come from their roosting woods. If the shooter arrives later the chances are that he will disturb a large feeding flock which may then fly off to search for food elsewhere. In the summer the feeding of wood-pigeons is a more leisurely affair, with the peak feeding time in the late afternoon. The shooter can thus delay his arrival to midday and still anticipate a steady stream of birds arriving over the decoys. The feeding activity may reach a peak in late afternoon but birds may continue to come in until sunset. When shooting over water or when lofting, the middle part of the day is often the best time. By then the birds have finished their 'breakfast' and may be searching for drinking water or a suitable tree to rest and digest their meal. This happens in both summer and winter so the shooter does not need to alter the time of the foray with the seasons.

Roost shooting is the final method by which pigeons are shot, and again it is a sport for both the air rifle and the shotgun user. Basically the idea is to shoot the birds in the late afternoon and evening as they come back to roost and it is a sport which on occasions can usefully employ a large number of shooters. Although the solitary pigeon shooter may account for a few birds in an evening shoot, two factors tend to work against the chance of making a large bag. Firstly the pigeons returning to roost often arrive en masse, and the sound of gunfire will drive them all away again. Secondly the landscape over much of Britain offers the pigeons a choice of roosting sites, so if they are disturbed from one they will quickly find an alternative and more peaceful venue. Admittedly, the shooter may be able to pick off the odd early arrival or late straggler, but once the main flocks have been disturbed they will seldom return that night.

In this situation an organized pigeon roost shoot may be the answer. If sufficient guns can be assembled to cover all the woodland in an area the flocks can be pushed from one gun to the next as they search for a peaceful roost. At times these organized roost shoots can account for a large number of birds, and each shooter may be presented with a steady stream of birds which makes the sport both exciting and, for the farmer, a very useful way of reducing crop damage. Due to the disturbance caused by such shoots, they are normally delayed until February or March in order to minimize the disturbance to other quarry species and particularly game birds.

Pigeon shooting does not have the 'status' of wildfowling or game shooting yet more people shoot pigeons than any other quarry species in Britain. The wood-pigeon is a fast and agile flier and is both keen-sighted and very wary. It can provide challenging and enjoyable sport and it tests the shooter's skills in fieldcraft and concealment as well as his accuracy with either shotgun or rifle. Pigeon shooting in addition provides a valuable service in protecting agricultural crops, and due to this it is more freely available than any other live quarry sport.

See also: **Decoys; Vermin Shooting – Weapons; Wood-Pigeon**

Pin Feathers   The pin feathers are very fine pointed feathers found on the forewing of the woodcock (*Scolopax rusticola*). Only one is found on each wing and the pin feathers are often considered to be the trophies of the species; certainly the various national woodcock clubs use them as a logo on the badges awarded to the shooters who achieve a left and right at woodcock.

Pin feathers are also prized by artists. Their fine point and stiffness make them useful for painting fine detail in oil and water-colour paintings.

See also: **Woodcock**

Pinfire   The pinfire system was the first practical ignition system introduced when breech-loading firearms were developed in the mid-nineteenth century. A wide variety of both shotgun and rifle calibres were produced on the pinfire system, but these rapidly fell into disuse when the modern centrefire cartridges were developed.

The pinfire cartridge provided for the first time a reliable and relatively quick system of breech loading, and the ignition system was a great improvement on the percussion-cap muzzle-loaders it superseded. Basically, the pinfire derived its name from the pin which protrudes at almost right angles from the base of the cartridge. When this pin was struck it ignited the primer in the base of the cartridge which then fired the powder charge.

Though basically the same in principle as the centrefire system that eventually replaced it, the pinfire suffered from some disadvantages inherent in the design of the cartridge. Each time a cartridge was loaded into the weapon its pin had to be aligned with a recess in the breech face before the gun was closed. In the newly-developed driven game shooting this made for quite a slow rate of reloading. In addition, the protruding pin was delicate and prone to deformation or even breaking if the ammunition was roughly handled, and there were even instances of the cartridges exploding when the ammunition case received a jolt. Even so, the pinfire system enjoyed a heyday lasting perhaps twenty years before it was replaced by the present centrefire cartridge.

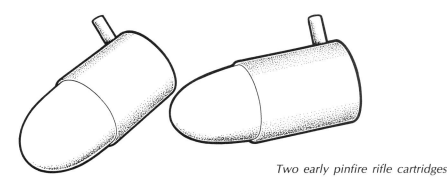

Two early pinfire rifle cartridges

Pink-Footed Goose   The pink-footed goose (*Anser brechyrhynchus*) is mainly a winter visitor to Britain, and very few remain to breed. It is a medium-sized goose measuring up to 30 inches in length and is noticeably smaller and more slender than the greylag. At close range the small head and neck appear a dark grey-brown, but this shades into blue-grey on the wings and back. The bill is short and dark with a pink band across it, and the feet and legs are pale pink.

The breeding range of the bird is dispersed well into the Arctic Circle from Eastern Greenland and Iceland as far west as Spitzbergen, but the overwintering population in Britain comes mainly from the western parts of its breeding range. These migrants arrive in early October and settle in their favoured haunts in northern Britain. Pink-feet seldom come south of a line from the Mersey to the Thames estuaries, and the greatest concentrations occur on the Scottish Firths, the east coast and the Wash.

They are daytime feeders, grazing on stubble and pasture sometimes many miles from their roosting areas, and flighting to and from these areas at dawn and dusk. The autumn and winter flocks may amount to many thousands of birds and a dawn or evening flight is a memorable spectacle. In settled weather pink-feet will continue feeding into the night under a full moon and they sometimes reverse their normal habits by roosting during the daylight hours and feeding under the moon. Their choice of roosting site varies with the location within the British Isles, and they will use freshwater lakes and reservoirs as readily as coastal mudflats and estuaries. Their pattern of feeding changes as the stubble is ploughed and by late winter they will feed almost exclusively on grassland although brassicas and root crops are also frequented.

They are strong and fast flyers, with the flocks often assuming a 'V' formation when travelling some distance, and they are often very vocal in flight. The characteristic call is a short high-pitched yelp, although they also use lower nasal calls, and it is the voice which helps to distinguish the 'pinks' from other grey geese, especially in the poor light of an early morning or late evening flight. In many parts of Northern Britain the pink-footed goose is the prize quarry of the wildfowler although, like other geese, it can be attracted by a pattern of decoys on feeding areas. When a full moon is shrouded by a thin veil of cloud, flighting pink-feet 'under the moon' is perhaps the most evocative and magical of all shotgun sports.

See also: **Seasons; Wildfowling**

Pintail   The pintail (*Anas acuta*) is an elegant bird. Weighing up to 2 lbs, its overall length is about 22 inches although much of this is the long tail. It has a long neck and slim body profile which ends in two elongated tail feathers from which the species derived its name. The adult plumage of the drake is quite distinctive. The head is a chocolate-brown colour which darkens slightly towards the rather narrow slate-grey beak. Running from the back of the head down each side of the nape is a pronounced white stripe which joins in the front to form a white breast. The upper surface of the body and wings are a light grey but the upper wing coverts and tail are black. In the drake the two centre tail feathers are very elongated, tapering to give an easily visible 'pin' in flight.

Both sexes have a dull green speculum which is edged with black on either side and white on the trailing edge. In good light the speculum forms a distinctive wing pattern on the male but is less obvious on the female. The duck resembles the female mallard, though its dull brown mottled plumage tends overall to be greyer, and in flight it appears an altogether slimmer bird. Although lacking the 'pin tail' of the drake, the duck nevertheless has a relatively long and pointed tail which adds to the slim appearance of this bird in flight.

Unlike some of the other duck species, the pintail is a quiet bird. However, its calls are heard when it congregates in flocks: the drake has a low double-note whistle and the duck a purring quack. For most of the time, however, it is not a very vocal species.

Britain holds a rather low breeding population of pintail, and their choice of nesting habitat shows more variation than the other species. They will rest on lowland marshes and rough pasture, on lake sides and on high damp moorland; however, they are a predominantly coastal species and the autumn sees a general movement from their inland nesting areas to sheltered estuaries and salt marshes. Migrants from Iceland, southern Scandinavia and the Kola peninsula begin arriving on Britain's shores in late September and they often delay their northward departure until April.

Like the wigeon, the pintail is a very gregarious species and will at times gather in great packs several thousand strong where the food is plentiful. They are night feeders and tend to be rather inactive during the day, although rough weather does have an unsettling effect. Although pintail will forage on stubble for corn, they gain most of their food from dabbling and up-ending in shallow water where their relatively long necks can be used to advantage.

The flight of a pintail is fast and direct on rapid wingbeats, and they are often seen flying in lines rather than in bunched groups. Pintail will respond readily to decoys, not only of their own species but also of other surface-feeding duck. Despite being predominantly coastal this duck makes an excellent table bird.

The shape and colouring of a drake make it quite easy to distinguish in flight and the only other silhouette that can cause confusion is that of the protected long-tailed duck. The plumage of the latter is, however, quite different. The female pintail can be more easily confused with the other species of dabbling duck but its slimmer profile is an aid to identification.

See also: **Inland Waterfowl Shooting;
Seasons**

Pochard   The pochard (*Aythya ferina*) is a 'stocky' medium-sized diving duck, weighing up to 2 lbs and measuring about 18 inches in length in an adult bird. The drake is readily identified from its chestnut head, black neck and breast, and pale grey body and wings. The beak is black with a broad central band of blue-grey and the upper tail surface is also grey-black. The female is a uniform brown-buff colour with pale flanks and underparts and both sexes can be identified by the absence of any form of wing bars when in flight.

Outside the breeding season they are usually silent birds. Compared to other species, a relatively low number of pochard breed in Britain, and these tend to be concentrated on shallow inland water with thick marginal vegetation in the south and east of the country. They will also occupy slow-moving rivers and streams, but tend to move to larger and more open expanses of freshwater with the approach of winter. Most of Britain's nesting population will remain resident throughout the winter and their numbers are increased by the arrival in October of others from northern Europe. At this time of the year great concentrations of pochard occur on the larger waters of central Scotland and south-eastern England. Even so, this gregarious bird will be more often seen in small groups of up to 20 to 30 birds.

Like the tufted duck, the pochard is a bird of freshwater environments and will seldom be seen on the coast except in adverse weather conditions, but unlike its smaller relative its diet is largely vegetarian. Pond weeds and aquatic seeds form the bulk of its diet and it will seldom be seen on land, where it walks with a decidely ungainly gait. Most of its food is acquired by diving to depths of about 10 feet, but in shallow margins it will also be seen dabbling and up-ending.

On the wing its flight is swift and direct but take-off involves pattering some distance over the water. Flocks usually fly in tight groups but will spread into echelons or 'V' formations for longer distances. Like the other diving ducks it has relatively short wings which produce a strong whistling sound in flight and they are not as manoeuvrable as dabbling duck species of comparable size.

Being gregarious by nature, pochard will respond readily to decoys, and a well set-out decoy pattern of assorted species will attract pochard from some distance away. The contrasting chestnut-red head and black neck of the drake makes the bird easy to identify both in flight and at rest, but the female resembles both the protected female scaup and the shootable female tufted duck. Unlike the latter species, however, the pochard is mainly a nocturnal feeder, and it spends most of the daylight hours roosting on open water. When disturbed it will attempt to swim away from the threat and will only take to the air if grave danger threatens. Pochard will also dive to escape danger, and they can stay submerged for some time. They do not come to shore except to rest if the water is uncomfortably rough, and will only rarely be seen feeding on land.

Pochard makes a good table bird.

See Also: **Inland Waterfowl Shooting; Seasons**

Powder   All propellant powders used in modern cartridges are nitro-cellulose based and are therefore termed 'nitro powders'. These powders, when first introduced early this century, were a significant advance over the previous black powder and cordite propellants. Nitro powders produced a clean burn and far less smoke, hence the term 'smokeless' powders. They were also less susceptible to extremes of temperature and produced far more consistent ballistics. They were safer to load because the loose powder ignites in a flare rather than as an explosion, and they took up less bulk than the older powders so that ballistic performance was increased with the same size of cartridge case.

The one disadvantage of nitro powders is that they produce significantly higher chamber pressures in order to achieve their best ballistic performance and this renders them unsafe to use in firearms that have not been proved to 'nitro-proof' standard. As late as the early 1900s some guns were still being proofed to black-powder standard and many of these are still in existence. Unless the weapon has been subsequently certified as nitro-proof it would be foolhardy to use nitro cartridges in such weapons.

A wide variety of nitro powders are available for those who reload their own ammunition, and it is important to match the burn characteristics of the powder to the calibre and load of shot and bullet weight. Different powders have different rates of burn, from slow and progressive to fast-burning, each suited to a particular type of ammunition, and a 'home loader' should select the correct powder with great care. It is also essential that the percussion cap chosen is also fully compatible with the powder being used.

At the time of writing new legislation is being formulated for the purchase and storage of powder for home loading purposes. Any person considering taking up this hobby should consult the police for an appraisal of the restrictions that apply at the time.

Predators   In the context of sporting shooting the term 'predator' is usually taken to mean those birds or animals that prey on the young of game birds and whose numbers therefore need controlling. These predatory vermin species can be simply categorized into the avian predators of the crow family – magpies, jays, and carrion/hooded crows – and ground predators of the mustelid family such as stoat, weasel and mink.

The variety of weapons and tactics that may be used for controlling the winged predators listed above are described under 'Vermin Shooting – Tactics' and 'Vermin Shooting – Weapons'. Ground predators of the stoat family are more efficiently controlled by the use of tunnel traps than by shooting, and the weasel, stoat, and increasingly the mink are usually only 'opportunist' quarry for the sporting shooter. In effect they are so infrequently encountered during the normal course of a shooting day that they should be shot whenever an opportunity presents itself. Of the other two mustelid species, the polecat and pine marten, there are certain legal restrictions on the way in which they are controlled. For example, they may not be shot by artificial light or with semi-automatic weapons: no such restrictions apply to the other three species.

Owls and the true birds of prey are of course fully protected by law, but rats, grey squirrels, and foxes also predate not only on game species, but also on a whole variety of eggs and nestlings; the shooting of these is also described under the 'Vermin' heading.

See also: **Vermin; Vermin Shooting – Tactics; Vermin Shooting – Weapons**

A gunsmith can check if barrels are still 'in proof' by using a barrel gauge

Proof The Gun Barrel Proof Act and sub-sequent legislation established two proof houses in Britain – one in London, the other in Birmingham. In order to safeguard the public, it was made illegal to make up any weapons using barrels that had not been tested (or proved) at one of the proof houses. Thus every barrel that has been submitted to and passed proof will bear the stamp marks on the barrel flats (if it is a side-by-side shotgun) or near the breech and on the action on other designs.

At one time every weapon imported into Britain also had to be submitted to British Proof, but nowadays the proof houses have reciprocal arrangements with the proof authorities in Spain, Italy, Belgium and other countries which render this unnecessary.

Every weapon should be stamped with a

The variety of proof marks from the Birmingham Proof House stamped on the barrel flats of a Webley & Scott 16 bore

BRITISH
1954 Rules of Proof.(effective 1-2-55)

NITRO PROOF
London   Birmingham

MAGNUM
London   Birmingham

Additionally arms will bear markings to indicate the maximum mean pressure* of cartridges for which the arm has been proved together with the nominal gauge (in a diamond, as ◇) and chamber length Shotguns will also bear marks to indicate the nominal bore diameter, as found at 9 in. from the breech, shown in decimals e.g. ·729 in.

*In exceptional cases maximum service loads may be marked in lieu of service pressures.

1925 Rules of Proof.
London   Birmingham

Rules of Proof prior to 1904.

Birmingham Company Proof words: NITRO PROOF

Rules of Proof from the London and Birmingham proof houses

variety of proof marks to indicate the calibre, chamber length, cartridge load and maximum working pressure. Importantly it must also bear marks indicating it has been tested for nitro powders, and the nominal bore diameter of the weapon will also be shown.

There are strict limits to the allowed variation from the information shown in the proof marks. For instance, if the bore of a shotgun becomes enlarged through fair wear and tear, there are very strict limits beyond which the enlargement would render the gun 'out of proof'. Even though it may still be in good condition, the gun must be submitted for re-proof using its new bore diameter.

With safety being the most important factor, Rules of Proof are naturally very strict, and it is illegal to sell any weapon which is out of proof; it is the proof houses themselves who will bring prosecution.

There is a multitude of proof marks from many nationalities and I would suggest that any person contemplating buying a weapon should first have it checked over by a good gunsmith in order to ascertain that it is 'in proof' and therefore safe to use. The two proof houses publish a fine booklet *Notes on the Proof of Shotguns and Other Small Arms*, which can be obtained from most gunshops or the proof houses at a low cost. This is essential reading for every sporting shooter.

Ptarmigan   In terms of its habitat and plumage, the ptarmigan (*Lagopus mutus*) is quite unusual. At fourteen inches overall this is a small- to medium-sized grouse which is distinguishable at all times of the year by its pure white wings and underparts. The outer tail feathers also remain black through the

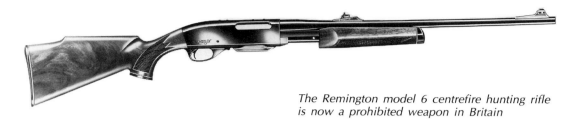

The Remington model 6 centrefire hunting rifle is now a prohibited weapon in Britain

seasons, but the head, neck and upper body surfaces undergo three distinct colour changes. In winter both sexes assume a pure white plumage except for the black tail feathers. During spring the new plumage grows through so that the summer colouring is dark grey-brown. The male appears greyer than the female, though both have strongly mottled and barred body plumage. In late summer and early autumn the dark plumage turns considerably lighter as the white feathers grow through and this 'pale phase' lasts until mid-November. Juveniles differ from the adults in that their wings are a pale brown.

The alarm call of a ptarmigan is a repeated cackle which is often uttered when flushed or when about to land. At other times a low croak may be heard.

The ptarmigan is a bird of the sub-arctic and alpine environment and therefore in Britain it is restricted to areas of the Scottish Highlands above the two-thousand-feet contour. In the summer its preferred habitat is rocky upper slopes with abundant bilberry and cranberry ground cover. During severe weather and in winter the birds may move to lower ground but will soon move up-slope again when conditions improve.

Like the woodcock, the ptarmigan relies heavily on its effective camouflage for its safety. Therefore it only flies reluctantly and will rather creep away and crouch when faced with danger.

In popular hill-walking and mountaineering areas and in areas where they are not hunted the ptarmigan is a tame and confiding bird which may be easily approached. However, the flight of a ptarmigan is typical of the grouse family in that it is fast and direct with whirring wingbeats interspersed with frequent glides. Unlike the red grouse which inhabits the lower heather-covered slopes, the ptarmigan will often fly either downhill or up-slope when flushed.

This species feeds almost exclusively on plant matter, taking shoots, buds and seeds in season, and it will dig through snow to reach its food plants.

Ptarmigan shooting does take place on many Highland estates, and they are usually walked-up or shot over dogs. Numbers rarely merit large-scale shooting of this species, and they are most often encountered as a part of a day's driven or walked-up grouse shoot. Compared to the other game bird species, the number of ptarmigan shot each year is low, a reflection not only of their population

A Winchester 12-bore pump action – a good pigeon decoyer's gun

densities, but also of the remote and often inaccessible areas frequented by these unusual upland game birds.

Ptarmigan on the wing cannot really be mistaken for any other game bird, and in the summer months their camouflaged plumage can easily be overlooked among the lichen-covered boulders and bilberry herbage. Like the red grouse season, the ptarmigan shooting season extends from 12 August to 10 December.

See also: **Game Shooting**

Pump-Action Weapons   Pump-action weapons are single barrel repeaters in which the unloading sequence is activated by pulling the fore-end slide to the rear to eject the spent case, and pushing it forward again to load a fresh cartridge and lock the breech closed. Because of the back-and-forward motion of the loading hand they are also called 'trombone actions'.

Pulling the trigger fires the weapon then unlocks the breech so that it can be opened by the rearward movement of the fore-end slide, and as the sequence is manually

controlled there is no real limit to the type of cartridge that can be used. Consequently there are a number of pump-action centrefire and rimfire rifles and shotguns in current production. The styling of the fore-end varies between manufacturers and the amount of slide movement varies with the calibre and case length.

Punt Gunning Punt gunning is a stalking sport. Essentially the shooter uses a very large and long-barrelled shotgun which is mounted on a small boat designed for the purpose. This craft is called a wildfowling or gunning punt, and the basic principle of the sport is to sail, row, paddle or push this boat into range of wildfowl at rest on the water or on an adjacent riverbank. The punt gun is designed for flock shots, and with a spread of about 6 feet at 70 yards a pattern of No 1 shot provides a good kill area. In the past enormous numbers of geese or duck have fallen to single shots from a punt gun, but nowadays the gunner would be content with half-a-dozen duck brought to bag for each shot.

A punt gun can weigh up to 70 lbs and in order to keep the small craft stable the barrel is always aligned to shoot along the axis and over the bow of the boat, and is firmly fixed in this position. 'Aiming' the punt therefore also aims the gun, although some elevation of the barrel is usually possible. As the muzzle of the gun is barely 12 inches above the water level the pattern tends to be very concentrated. At such a low angle the pellets striking the water will ricochet, so a bird may be hit by both direct and ricochet pellets. Although in days past many of the inland fens and washes echoed to the sound of punt guns, the sport is now confined almost entirely to the large estuaries and salt marshes. Punt gunning was at one time the main revenue earner of the professional 'fowler' but by the end of the Second World War, these men were having to seek other means of earning their living. Nowadays punt gunning, like shore shooting, is in the hands of the hardy and enthusiastic amateur.

Originally gun punts were flat-bottomed and open-decked craft, and on the freshwater washes and fens they survived in this form up till the 1930s. As a craft for estuaries and open sea they were very unstable and far too inclined to fill up and sink in any moderate sea. It was that eminent Victorian gentleman 'fowler Sir Ralph Payne-Gallwey who perhaps did most to improve the seaworthiness of a gunning punt. His design made the craft look very like a kayak canoe at first glance, with decking extending from the bows to the stern except for the cockpit. His designs were adapted for both single- and double-handed punts with a minimum length of 16 feet and a maximum of around 25 feet. Unlike a kayak, however, the punt has to absorb the recoil of a heavy gun and the most usual material used in punt construction is solid timber planking, although nowadays some are made from marine ply. To increase seaworthiness the cockpit was lined with a coaming to reduce deck wash entering the craft, and the decking itself sloped down from the cockpit to the gunwale.

Under the decking and in the cockpit the fowler can stow a great deal of equipment. Apart from ammunition for the big gun there will also be a 'cripple stopper' and its own ammunition. Buoyancy bags and other lifesaving equipment are also essentials that should be stowed so that the shooter has instant access to them should the need arise. A cockpit cover, baling bucket, and sponge should also come in the list of stowed essentials, and lastly the means of propulsion.

When crossing open water these craft may be sailed, so a mast and rigging together with a lee-board may be included in the list. When approaching fowl, on the other hand, the fowler must have oars, hand paddles and a variety of setting poles easily to hand and, just as importantly, they should be stowed in such a way that they can be picked up without making a noise. Finally, a landing net makes picking up the shot birds that much easier.

As mentioned previously, the gun is mounted along the axis of the boat, with the breech inside the cockpit area. A sliding barrel-rest on the fore-deck keeps the muzzle lined up over the bow and also allows some degree of adjustment in the elevation. The recoil of the weapon is taken on breeching ropes which are about 3 inches thick and looped around the gun's trunnions and secured to reinforced mounts on the stem of the craft.

The gunner or gunners lie prone in the cockpit when stalking a group of wildfowl, and a great deal of seamanship and skill is required to move up surreptitiously in full view of the quarry. When 'setting to fowl', as this form of stalking is called, the gunner will be as far back in the boat as possible, with his feet wedged under the stern decking. In deep water the punt can then be propelled by hand paddle – the curve of the hull will hide these movements if the fowler is lying sufficiently far aft – but in shallow water he will resort to setting poles to push the punt along. It must be remembered that the punt is at this time heavily laden with all its operational equipment; running it quietly and gradually towards a flock of wildfowl demands a great deal of physical effort, particularly when a crosswind or running tide is constantly trying to turn the craft.

The 'bows-on' approach is the most effective, as the punt then presents its smallest outline to the quarry, but it may not always be possible. Some punters have devised outrigger boards that can be swung out from the hull to mask the hand movements for a 'quartering' approach, and these boards are sometimes even decorated with driftwood and other material to break up the outline of the craft still further.

Gunning punts tend to be painted in a light shade of 'battleship grey', and the barrel of the big gun also receives this colouring. Pale grey has been proven by long experience to be least visible in the wide variety of lighting conditions on an estuary in winter.

There is very much more to this sport than jumping into a punt and paddling off into the wild blue yonder to search for flocks of unsuspecting wildfowl. Before the gunner is in a position to decide on any tactics he must acquire a sound knowledge of the estuary in all states of tide, of the daily habits of the wildfowl, and of the effects of different weather on both tides and wildlife.

A gun punt fully loaded is a heavy craft which cannot be lifted or even dragged any great distance over the mud. Its launching and recovery site must therefore be accessible at any state of the tide, and the fowler must be prepared for the inevitable occasions when he is left stranded by a receding tide far from the main river channel.

Tactics vary from estuary to estuary and only sound local knowledge will ensure that the novice gunner has even a chance of success.

Many shooters who have not experienced punt gunning at first hand criticize the sport on two points – disturbance and wounding.

As far as disturbance is concerned, a successful punt gunner would only fire the big gun perhaps twice in the course of a day's fowling, and many days would go by without one report from the big gun. Compared to the shore shooter, who on a good flight may well use a box of cartridges or more, the punt gunner creates far less 'disturbance'. I do question the tactic of setting to fowl in their traditional roosting areas on some of the northern firths, but this practice is declining as some of the more unscrupulous post-war gunners are being replaced by more conservation- and environmentally-conscious punt gunners.

As to the wounding issue, I must agree that after each shot the most immediate task is to despatch the cripples. However, with a load of heavy shot in the charge – No 1's should be the smallest – and with careful choice of target group the number of cripples can be kept very low. The number of birds 'pricked' is considerably lower for a punt gun shot than on a foreshore flight. When one considers that a bird hit by a BB or two or three No 1's at 70 yards will suffer considerably more shock than a flighted bird hit at 55 yards by an over-zealous shore shooter using No 5 shot, the chances of a wounded bird flying away from a shot from a big gun are very much lower.

Punt gunning is an old and unique part of Britain's sporting heritage. It is a sport of the hardy few who are prepared to spend long hours afloat in the hope that one day they will get an opportunity for a good shot. It tests all the qualities of seamanship as well as demanding a fine understanding of the estuary environment and the wildfowl it harbours, and it demands sportsmanship of the highest quality. A punt gunner is a wildfowler in the true sense of the word.

See also: **Punt Guns; Wildfowling**

Punt Guns   Punt guns are in essence large-bore shotguns. They are the 'heavy artillery' of the wildfowler in that they are fired from a secure mounting rather than from the shoulder, and as the name implies they are usually mounted on streamlined boats called 'duck punts'.

The gun itself is designed to fire a heavy shot load to produce killing patterns at betwen 70 and 80 yards, and its weight dictates that it be only fired horizontally at groups of wildfowl at rest on the water or on adjacent sandbanks.

The smallest punt gun does look like a shoulder gun in that it has a stock and fore-end and the action is a drop-down breech-loader. However the double 4 bore is too heavy for efficient use as a shoulder arm and these guns usually have a hole drilled in the stock through which a rope is passed and secured to the gun's deck mounting. This is the recoil shock absorber. The triggers of the double 4 bore may also be drilled and a lanyard connected to both so that the two barrels may be fired simultaneously. The double 4 bore used as a punt gun weighs around 30 lbs and has the versatility of being able to fire one barrel or both, thereby discharging from 3 oz up to 8 oz of shot depending on the number of barrels fired and the cartridge load. Guns of this design were produced and made popular by Bland & Co. in London, and the barrel lengths range from 42 to 48 inches.

Moving up the scale of calibres to the true punt guns, there are a number of characteristics which are common to nearly all. They are all single barrel guns with the barrel length varying from 7 feet to 9 feet overall. As a rough guide they are weighted to approximate to the ratio of 6 lbs gun weight per 1 oz of shot load, and the majority of punt guns still in use today are breech-loaders. By the early years of this century a considerable number of muzzle-loading punt guns had been produced, but those that survive today have been successfully converted to a breech-loading system.

The smallest of the true punt gun calibres is the 1⅛-inch gun (the measurement relates to the bore diameter). This weapon matches the top capability of a double 4 bore in that its standard load is ½ lb of shot, and the gun should weigh between 50 and 60 lbs.

Next comes the 1¼-inch gun, with an all-up weight of around 70 lbs and firing an average 1¾-lb shot load. This increase in shot load does not extend the range of the gun, but rather increases the density of the pattern in a 6-foot circle at 70 yards.

The '1 lb' gun with a bore of 1½ inches has always been one of the most popular calibres, and the law restricts punt guns to an upper calibre limit of 1¾ inches, which normally carries a shot charge of 1½ lbs. In times past punt guns were built up to 2¼-inch calibre firing up to 3 lbs of shot, but it

Both ends of a punt gun – the fowler stands over the gun's muzzle holding the screw breech and cartridge

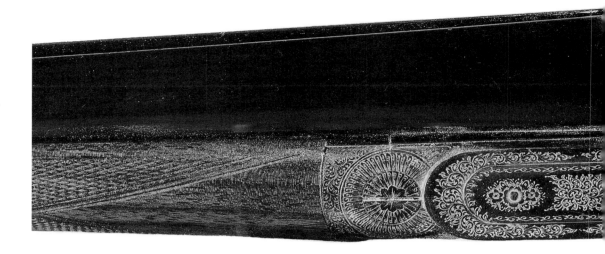

A Purdey sidelock ejector gun. A fine example of a 'best' London gun

was evident that the larger the bore diameter the greater number of pellets were distorted and the patterns did not show much improvement over the smaller-calibre weapons.

Punt guns use large shot sizes ranging from No 1 into the 'lettered shot'. The two most frequently used are No 1 for duck and BB for geese, and unlike normal shotguns it is the striking energy of the shot rather than the pattern density that restricts the range of all punt guns to between 70 and 80 yards. In the case of a 12 bore, for example, the density of the pattern deteriorates long before the striking energy of the individual pellet, yet in a punt gun the pattern at long range may still be good even though the pellets have lost their effective penetration.

Second-hand punt guns do appear on the market from time to time, and they are much sought after by those wishing to take up a fascinating and unique shooting sport. Recently, however, 'Adams Punt Guns', a new

business in southern Scotland, have begun making these guns to order and are also able to supply ammunition and many of the other punt gunner's requisites.

Despite this, punt gunning will still remain a sport carried out by a handful of dedicated wildfowlers. It is unlikely ever to recover from the decline it experienced with the demise of the professional 'fowlers between the two World Wars, and the punt gun is considered to be a mere curio of a bygone age by all but a few sportsmen in the British Isles.

See also: **Punt Gunning; Shot**

Purdey In 1814 James Purdey established his own gunmaking business in London and in 1882 his son moved into the address in South Audley Street from which the business still operates.

Purdey took a lead in the production of

the then new percussion-cap mechanism in the early nineteenth century, and he also quickly demonstrated his ability to build guns and rifles of the highest quality and finish. In an era when the British Empire was expanding, his guns were taken to all parts of the world and proved their durability under extreme conditions.

Successive generations have built upon this esteem, so that a Purdey gun is generally acknowledged to be one of the finest in the world. Nowadays each weapon built by James Purdey & Sons follows the same principle of hand craftmanship that established the firm's early reputation; the guns are truly hand-built and may take up to three years to complete. Although Purdey will build magazine bolt-action rifles to order, it is for their double barrel weapons, and particularly their sidelock, hammerless, easy opening best-quality shotgun, that they are justly famous.

Basically there are four stages involved in the production of a double barrel firearm. In the sequence in which they are usually carried out they are called barrelling, actioning, stocking and finishing. The best London gunmakers take a pride in the fact that on receipt of the rough forgings the building of the gun is then accomplished by skilled hand rather than by automated machines. In Purdey's case they receive raw tubes of the finest steel which will eventually finish as the barrels. These are cut to the appropriate length, and pairs of tubes are trued up to be alike, at the same time being straightened and turned so that the wall thicknesses are even and the outside diameter concentric with the bore diameter of the tubes. Once this has been done the tubes are 'struck down' in order to reach the required weight for the style of the weapon. All these processes are carried out by hand to the satisfaction of the master gunmaker, after which the tubes are brazed together, either in the side-by-side or in the over-and-under configuration, and the ribs are laid and silver-soldered between the barrels.

It is at this stage that the barrels are sent for provisional proof to the London proof house. This proof serves to identify any flaws in the metal, and when the barrels pass this test their wall thickness is adjusted, within stringent safety margins, to achieve the final weight and balance.

The actions on Purdey guns are received as rough forgings and a considerable amount of effort is expended to produce a mechanism finished to extremely fine tolerances. Each part is shaped, polished, and tempered to an exact degree of hardness before being assembled into the finished article. All the work is done by hand and the skill employed in actioning ensures a weapon of the utmost dependability in the field. When the action reaches its final proportions the barrels are fitted to it – again a painstaking and time-consuming task. When both are fitted to-

gether the process of 'sooting and filing' takes place. The points of contact between the barrel and action are covered in soot from a paraffin lamp and then put together. On any high spots the soot will be rubbed off, and these spots are carefully filed in order to achieve an even contact between the two components.

The final definitive proof test is carried out when work is completed and the proof marks are then stamped on the action and barrel flats – the whole assembly is then ready for stocking.

The walnut used on Purdey weapons is of the very best quality. Stock and fore-end blanks are received after ageing for five years and are then stored for a further six. They are weighed periodically to ensure that no weight loss has occurred and that they are in a stable condition. Again the rough stock and fore-end blanks are shaped and cut by hand to fit the barrelled action perfectly, as any undue 'tight spots' will put an uneven strain on the timber when the gun is fired. Detailed measurements of the customer are

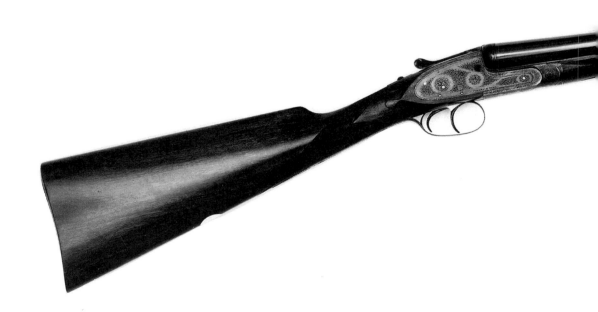

transferred to the stock dimensions so that the weapon is a perfect fit, and a considerable time is spent on chequering and hand polishing to achieve the finish expected of a 'best' gun.

At this stage the gun can be assembled and fired, although the action is still unadorned and the barrels are 'in the white'. The barrels are now regulated by adjusting the alignment of the muzzle. In a double rifle the weapon must shoot to the same zero with both barrels, and the regulation needed to achieve this is a highly skilled task. In shotguns the adjustments need not be as precise, but the barrels must throw dense and even patterns to the same point of aim. It is during this finishing stage that the action receives the attention of a skilled engraver, and the degree of embellishment again depends on the customer's wishes. The barrels are blacked and polished and the weapon receives the final inspection by the master gunmaker before it is declared fit for release to the customer.

Double barrel shotguns are the mainstay of Purdey's output, and they will build these to both side-by-side and over-and-under format. They also build double rifles to the same configuration in the heavier calibres, and their only limitation in this field is the availability of ammunition.

Their magazine rifles, built either in the deer stalking calibres or in the heavier 'African' calibres, also reflect their skill and patient production methods, as they are also hand built and finished. Purdey also produce a rather unusual single barrel shotgun designed for American-style trap shooting. This again is a sidelock shotgun based on the double barrel's 'drop-down' action and it is not often seen in sporting circles in Britain.

It is time, effort and a high degree of skilled craftsmanship which set London-built guns apart from any others. The weapons are built to order and no 'off the shelf' weapons are produced. These guns are considered to be the ultimate exhibition of the gunmaker's craft, and Purdey's weapons will be coveted wherever sporting shooting takes place.

A Purdey 'best' London gun in the classic style of an English game gun

Rabbit The rabbit (*Oryctolagus cuniculus*) is probably the most important quarry species for both the air rifle hunter and the .22 rimfire user. It is a medium-sized mammal which shows considerable variation in the size of the adult and in the colour of the fur. A large buck rabbit may measure up to 20 inches and weigh up to about 4 lbs, whereas a small or weak specimen may not reach half this weight. The rabbit is characterized by long ears, white 'bob' tail and long hind legs. The white on the underside of the tail is a true diagnostic feature which is easily visible as the rabbit moves with its normal bounding gait. Overall the rabbit is still considerably smaller than either species of hare, and the rabbit's ears are also relatively short compared to the larger species. Body fur colour is normally a light grey-brown and there is no darkening on the tips of the ears. However, a wide range of colour phases do exist and, in some parts of the country, black, white, grey or fawn specimens may be quite common. In all these colour variations the underbelly and lower chest fur is white with an 'undercoat' of grey.

Before the introduction of myxomatosis in the 1950s Britain supported an enormous rabbit population which in turn caused serious agricultural losses. The disease effectively wiped out 99 per cent of all rabbits and also caused a population crash amongst rabbit predators, notably buzzards. The lack of grazing rabbits for a decade or more resulted in permanent changes in the vegetation cover on many chalk downland areas in southern England.

Nowadays, however, the rabbit is again widespread throughout Britain, although they are unlikely to reach pre-myxomatosis numbers, since fresh outbreaks of the disease act as a control where population density is excessive, and effective control may be achieved through the growing numbers of rabbit shooters that use equipment and weapons unavailable in 'pre-myxi' days. Modern telescopic sights, reliably accurate hunting air rifles and high-intensity lamping equipment all make today's rabbit shooter more effective than his predecessors.

The rabbit is most active in the evening when it emerges from its burrows in order to feed. Feeding and other above-ground activities continue throughout the night and into the early morning. In areas where they are relatively undisturbed rabbits may also feed sporadically throughout the day, returning between times to the shelter of the burrows to rest. Gregarious by nature, rabbits will often develop 'colonies' or warrens which may number several hundred animals. Rabbits can breed throughout the year and the potential rate of population increase is quite staggering. The availability of food and the presence of wild predators do, however, limit most local populations.

Rabbits feed on a variety of green vegetation including vegetables and grain plants. They will also strip bark in winter to extract minerals contained in the bark at a time when other food resources may be depleted. Saplings are the main target for bark stripping and rabbits may cause serious woodland, as well as farmland, crop damage.

Rabbits offer a wide variety of sport, from ferreting to stalking, still hunting, and lamping with either shotgun or rifle. What is more, rabbit flesh also provides a succulent and healthy meat source.

See also: **Lamping; Vermin Control; Vermin Shooting – Weapons**

Recoil   Recoil is the sudden rearward motion of a weapon as it is fired. This motion is felt on the shooter's shoulder and, in extreme cases, by the side of the face resting on the stock. In determining the force of the recoil, two general rules apply. The heavier the weapon, the more recoil will be absorbed by the weapon's weight, and the more powerful the cartridge, the more recoil will be produced in the first place.

The capacity to absorb recoil varies from person to person and is probably linked more to psychology than to physique. Thus, some slightly-built shooters can happily use strongly recoiling weapons that a more powerfully built person may find too punishing, and a person forced to use a weapon beyond their recoil tolerance is almost certain to develop 'gun flinch' when firing. In extreme cases the shooter may even close his or her eyes at the moment of firing and even in mild cases of gun flinch the aim will be upset as the shooter tenses up for the discharge. The amount of recoil felt by the shooter, therefore, depends on the cartridge being used, the weight of the weapon and the shooter's awareness of the recoil this combination produces. In rifles, the weight of the weapon, the fit of the gun, the shape of the butt compared with the shape of the shooter's shoulder, whether or not a recoil pad is fitted and its efficiency, and the power of the cartridge available for each calibre

Rabbits are now firmly re-established in most parts of Britain

show relatively little variation: a general figure can be put on the force of recoil from each calibre and this can act as a guideline for selecting a calibre to suit each individual. Shotguns, on the other hand, show a far greater variety of gun weight and cartridge loads so it is more difficult to make a general assessment of the recoil power.

One measurement used in assessing recoil is called 'Free Recoil Energy'. The table below may be used as a guide to the recoil produced by the most popular calibres.

Calibre	Free Recoil Energy (ft/lbs)
.22 LR	0.4
.22 Hornet	1.2
.22–250 Rem.	8.2
.243 Win.	12.7
.270 Win.	21.3
.300 Win. Mag.	33.2
.375 H & H Mag.	42.2
.458 Win. Mag.	68.4

A standard-12 bore game gun weighing 6³/₄ lbs and firing a 1¹/₁₆-oz game load generates about 14 ft/lbs free recoil energy.

Red Deer The red deer (*Cervus elaphus*) is the largest wild land mammal of the British Isles. It is also a true native, crossing the land bridge from the Continent during the last Ice Age to colonize the lowland forest that flourished as the ice retreated. The deer in those times grew to great size and developed enormous antlers, feeding as they did on the abundant food supplies provided by this type of natural vegetation. Evidence provided by Neolithic antler tools shows that the red deer was the mainstay of the early human settlers of these islands, both as a provider of ment and 'by-products' like hides and antler tools.

The forest was gradually cleared as the human population turned to agriculture rather than hunting, and the loss of habitat

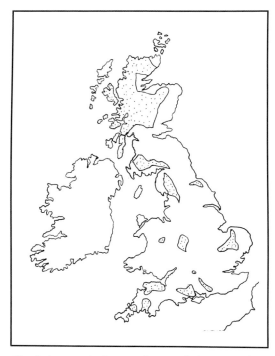

Shaded areas indicate where red deer may be encountered in the wild

in lowland Britain has restricted the red deer of today to isolated pockets around the few remaining forested areas. In the north of the country a combination of climatic change and human clearance would have exterminated this species in the uplands were it not for the deer's ability to adapt to new environments with surprising ease. Thus over much of Scotland and northern England the red deer became an animal of open moorland and fells. A price had to be paid for this adaptability, however, and the Highland deer are now considerably smaller than their lowland counterparts, a fact that reflects their more restricted and less nutritious diet. Genetically, though, they are still the same animal, and a youngster taken from the Highlands to a lowland environment will grow to a size comparable with a lowland 'native'.

Mature forest stags from lowland England average about 350 lbs (160 kg) in body weight, with some reaching up to 500 lbs with a corresponding heavy antler growth, while hinds from the same area would grow to 200–300 lbs weight. In the Scottish

Highlands, on the other hand, mature stags and hinds may only reach half the body weight of lowland animals with the same antler growth.

A mature stag will stand four feet high at the shoulder while hinds are somewhat shorter. In summer the coat varies from foxy red to brown, thus giving the deer its name. The coat darkens towards the spine and there is often a quite pronounced line of dark hair along the backbone from the neck to the base of the tail. The rump, belly and inner thighs are generally lighter creamy yellow. The six-inch-long tail is easily visible as it is outlined by the caudal disc, the light patch on the buttocks.

As winter approaches, the coat of a red deer will change gradually in colour from its summer rufous shade to a dark brown or grey. As the winter coat grows through the summer one during the autumn, the colour change takes several months. In spring, however, the winter coat is moulted in a short space of time. From April to June, depending on the environment and the animal's state of health, red deer will look very scruffy as the bleached winter coat comes off in patches and clumps.

The stag, as he reaches maturity, will develop an increasingly impressive mane in early autumn during the lead-up to the rut. Large antlers and a shaggy mane are important visual factors which contribute to a stag's ability to gain and hold a group of hinds at this time of year.

Like the newly born of most deer species, the coat of a red deer calf is heavily spotted at birth, but within about six weeks only vestiges of these spots appear in the uniform brown-grey second coat which becomes thick enough to see the calf through the first winter. Very occasionally, spots are visible along the spine of adult red deer.

The antlers of a red stag are far more of a status symbol than a weapon of defence. They are cast and regrown annually and their size and weight help to establish the stag within the hierarchy of the herd. No two sets of antler are identical, and they may also aid recognition of individual animals, not only within the herd, but also by human observers.

Basically the red deer's antlers are round in cross-section and have a varying number of forward- and upward-pointing points or tines. A typical twelve-point head will have three tines along the main beam of each antler, and a 'crown' of three points at the end. This gives six points per side – therefore a twelve-point or 'royal' head.

Starting at the pedicle on the skull from which the antler grows, each of the front-pointing tines is given a specific name. The brow tine lies closest to the head and is usually the most forward-pointing although the point does tend to curl upwards. Close to the brow tine comes the bez or bay tine, and about midway along the main beam of the antler is the trez or tray tine.

Beyond this third tine the antler may break into a 'cup' or coronet of three or more upward points. The length and weight of a stag's antlers are less an indication of age than of the quality and mineral content of the animal's food intake.

The growth cycle of a red deer's antlers is timed to make maximum use of vegetation growth in spring and summer; thus old antlers are cast in April and regrowth begins immediately. By August the antlers are fully developed and the protective covering of velvet dries and is frayed off by the animal to reveal the new set. Newly exposed, antlers are a creamy white colour, but they quickly colour up as they absorb the natural dyes in the vegetation frayed by the stag. By September the antlers are dark brown or black with only the points retaining the original colour. Antler growth depends to a great extent on the availability of protein, calcium and phosphorus, and in areas deficient in these elements the antlers of the red deer population are correspondingly small.

On the exposed Scottish hills antler growth tends to be restricted, and even mature animals in some areas fail to produce antlers of more than eight points. On the other hand, some park-bred deer grow prodigious sets even before the stags reach full maturity, and animals barely thirteen months old have been known to produce fourteen-point heads.

The initial development of a red deer's antlers follows a set pattern which subsequently becomes more complex as diet and genetic quality exert a greater influence. A red stag calf begins to develop bony lumps or pedicles on its skull by its first Christmas, but antlers do not start developing until its first birthday in the following May. These vary from tiny knobs in areas of poor grazing to long and unbranched spikes extending in some cases to over 12 inches where the diet is rich. By the following April, when the animal is approaching its second birthday, these spikes are cast and the 'second head' is grown. Hill stags at this age may show a small brow tine and even a trez tine.

From this stage on the quality of food has an important influence on the length and weight of the antlers, while each animal's genetic pattern will influence their shape and layout. Each animal will grow similar-shaped antlers each year so that individuals can be easily identified. Some, of a poor genetic strain, may never develop the full set of points, and a 'switch' head is one in which the antlers are single long and unbranched spikes beyond the brow tine. Some stags fail to grow any antlers at all, and these 'hummels' often achieve greater body weight than their antlered brethren. Red deer stags reach full maturity at about seven years and it is unlikely that the antlers will show any improvement beyond this age.

Red deer, in common with most other quadrupeds, can walk, trot, canter and gallop. They move with remarkable speed in dense woodland for an species of such weight and size, but it is in open country that this ease of movement becomes apparent. The characteristic loping trot of a red deer, in which the head is held upright and steady while the rest of the deer appears to 'flow' over the ground, enables the animal to traverse very rough ground with astonishing ease and speed. At the same time this characteristic gait is graceful, dignified and effortless. In dense woodland a heavily-antlered stage will throw his antlers back on either side of his neck in order to pass more easily through cover.

Red deer are good swimmers, and open water, be it river or still water, is no obstacle to them. They are also powerful jumpers, and several eye-witness accounts recall the ease with which they will clear a six-foot fence. On other occasions the deer have appeared to 'belly flop' onto a fence deliberately in order to break it down.

It is often very difficult to ascertain a deer's age accurately by observation alone. However, the gait and deportment of a red stag do give some indication of the age group to which it belongs. A young stag will hold its head up in an alert way, his neck will be thin and the mane almost non-existent. With each year towards maturity his antlers will grow longer and heavier and his neck muscles must keep pace with this development. Thus a mature animal will carry his head somewhat lower than a youngster and the neck will be noticeably thicker. This apparent thickening of the neck will be enhanced by a more developed mane and the appearance of a dewlap. Generally the body of a mature animal will be deeper and more rounded than a young stag, although at the end of the rut many stags will have lost much body weight. In old age the stag will show a well-defined dewlap and pronounced withers. Though the antlers may show signs of deterioration, the very thick neck and deep body will indicate an animal of advanced years.

Lacking the muscular development necessary to carry antlers, red deer hinds are less easy to categorize into age groups. However, a young hind will bear some of the vestiges of the calf stage in that its face will be shorter and less pointed than a mature or old hind. As the hind ages the profile lengthens so that the heads of some old hinds look markedly 'wedge-shaped'. With advancing years the hind's ears also change shape from the rounded ears of the young animal to a pronounced pointed shape in old beasts.

The red deer rut reaches a peak around 20 October, although this may vary with location and weather, and does not peter out until mid-November. The red stag is unique among British deer in his habit of acquiring and holding a harem of hinds while keeping other competing stags at a safe distance. On open ground, as in the Scottish Highlands, the rut has evolved into a complex and spectacular drama. A master stag will devote much of his energy to rounding up straying hinds and chasing away inferior males. It is when he is challenged by a stag of equal standing that a complex and ritualized threat and counterthreat is seen. The stag will roar and scythe nearby vegetation with his antlers. As an alternative to vegetation fraying he may roll on the ground or attack turf and peat with his antlers, frequently carrying this material on his tines in order to enhance the impression of strength and ferocity. If the challenger still remains undeterred the final intimidation involves the resident stag standing broad-side-on to his opponent. This 'showing the profile' is the final stage before open conflict; the two opponents walk slowly alongside each other then swing inwards to clash antlers with terrifying suddenness and ferocity. Though lasting only a few seconds, these clashes drain the physical reserves of the animal enormously, but, surprisingly, actual injuries are rare.

In woodland habitats the rut tends to be a quieter affair altogether, though the roar of a rutting stag echoing down a deep wooded valley in southern England is an unforgettable sound. Perhaps the dense woodland undergrowth prevents the build-up of the visual stimuli that have caused the ritual scene during the rut on open ground.

Although the population stronghold of this species undoubtedly lies in the Highlands of Scotland, red deer breed in the wild in a number of other localities. Populations decended perhaps from aboriginal stock inhabit the New Forest in Hampshire and the English Lake District. Another well-established and growing population is centred on Exmoor in south-west England. From this base red deer spread eastwards to the Quantocks and south-westwards to Dartmoor and the deep wooded valleys of eastern Cornwall. Elsewhere park escapees have established viable breeding populations in Thetford Forest in Norfolk, in various parts of the Home Counties, in Staffordshire and in Yorkshire. The growing use of red deer on venison farms will inevitably lead to the establishment of further colonies of wild-breeding red deer in the future.

At present the deer population in the Scottish Highlands numbers about 300,000 deer and a combination of factors has caused some observers to maintain that red deer are at crisis point. Over the last twenty years the red deer population in Scotland has doubled while the break-up of traditional estates and widespread conifer afforestation has effectively reduced the habitat available to the deer. Elsewhere the populations are stable, as in the New Forest, or slowly expanding, as in the south-west peninsula and the Lake District.

See also: **Deer; Deer Management; Deer Stalking – Highland; Deer Stalking – Woodland**

Reticule   The reticule is the aiming device which is built into a telescopic sight. When properly adjusted the reticule appears at the same focus as the target when viewed through the 'scope. It gives this sighting system a distinct advantage over both iron and

Normal   Wide-angle

Dual-X. Also called the '30–30'. By far the most widely used. Fine crosswires can be used for range-finding.

Crosshair. Fine crosswires may become difficult to see in poor light. Otherwise good for precision aiming.

Post and crosshair. More popular in Europe. Vertical aiming post remains visible in low light.

Dot. A more recent development. Intensity of the central light dot can be varied.

Four examples of telescopic sight reticules most frequently used for hunting

Firearms Permitted for Killing Deer in the United Kingdom

	ENGLAND & WALES	SCOTLAND	NORTHERN IRELAND
RIFLES	Calibre of not less than .240 ins or Muzzle energy of not less than 1,700 foot pounds		Calibre of not less than .236 ins
RIFLE AMMUNITION	Bullet must be soft-nosed or hollow-nosed	Roe deer: Bullet of not less than 50 grains AND Muzzle velocity of not less than 2,450 feet per second AND Muzzle energy of not less than 1,000 foot pounds AND All deer: Bullet of not less than 100 grains AND Muzzle velocity of not less than 2,450 feet per second AND Muzzle energy of not less than 1,750 foot pounds All bullets must be designed to expand on impact	Bullet of not less than 100 grains AND Muzzle energy of not less than 1,700 foot pounds Bullet must be designed to expand on impact
SHOTGUNS	Not less than 12 bore See important NOTE 1 below	Not less than 12 bore See important NOTE 2 below	Not less than 12 bore See important NOTE 3 below
SHOTGUN AMMUNITION	Rifled slug of not less than 350 grains or AAA shot	All deer: Rifled slug of not less than 380 grains or Shot not smaller than SSG Roe deer: Shot not smaller than AAA	Rifled slug of not less than grains or AAA shot
PROHIBITIONS	Any air gun, air rifle or air pistol	Any sight specially designed for night shooting (The above ballistic requirements eliminate all handguns and all air and gas weapons)	Any handgun, air gun, air rifle, air pistol or gas weapon Any artificial light or dazzling or night sighting device
	NOTE 1 A shotgun may be used only by the occupier and certain others, who must be able to prove serious damage (see Deer Act 1963, as amended, s. 10A)	*NOTE 2* A shotgun may be used only on arable or enclosed land and only by the occupier and certain others, who must be able to prove serious damage (see Deer (Firearms etc.) (Scotland) Order 1985, No. 1168).	*NOTE 3* A shotgun may be used only be the occupier and cetain others, who must be able to prove serious damage (see Wildife (NI) Order 1985, No. 171, art. 20).

aperture sights, where the aiming eye has to change focus rapidly from the sights to the target in order to achieve an accurate shot. A wide variety of reticule styles is available from the telescopic sight manufacturers, and the diagram on page 195 illustrates the four most popular types. Each type has its own attributes and disadvantages and there is really not much to choose between them in potential aiming accuracy. As in so many other aspects of sporting shooting, selection of reticule type is largely a matter of personal taste.

See also: **Telescopic Sight**

Rifle   A rifle is a weapon which is designed to fire a single accurate projectile which is made to spin during its path through the barrel. The spin is induced by cutting or forging a series of spiral grooves in the bore. The bullet is made to fit sufficiently tightly to the bore diameter that these spiral grooves spin the bullet as it moves up the barrel, and it continues spinning after it leaves the muzzle. Accuracy is enhanced by this spin because any uneven weighting in the bullet is effectively displaced through 360 degrees with each rotation. A non-spinning projectile would veer off its predicted path very quickly, which is why a slug fired from a shotgun is not accurate beyond about 50 yards whereas some rifle calibres can maintain good accuracy out to beyond 300 yards.

Rifles can be classed into three main groups depending on the method of propulsion or the method of ignition. Air rifles are the lowest-powered weapons used for hunting purposes, and as their name suggests the projectile (the air rifle pellet) is powered by compressed air. The 'powder' rifles fall into rimfire or centrefire classes according to whether the ignition mixture is located inside the rim of the cartridge case or in the centre of its base. Rimfire rifles are less powerful than the centrefire as they are limited by the need to have a rim which is soft enough to be heavily dented by a blow from the firing pin or striker. With an increase in power and resulting increase in

pressure when the cartridge is fired comes the risk of the case perforating and 'blowing back' into the shooter's face.

The most powerful of the rifle calibres fall into the centrefire class and these range from the little .22 Hornet up to the mighty .700 Holland Nitro Express.

See also: **Centrefire; Rimfire; Vermin Shooting – Weapons**

Rifled Slug   In the early days of big-game shooting the hunter would often be armed with a smooth-bored gun loaded with a cartridge containing a single lead ball. While accurate at close range its performance fell away very rapidly beyond 50 yards. Even though the performance of the newly-developed rifles quickly rendered such 'ball and-shot' guns obsolete, there were still occasions when a single heavy projectile fired from a shotgun was more effective at close range.

The single spherical ball load was therefore replaced by a 'rifled slug'. This projectile was more elongated and included two or more collars which fitted the bore of the weapon. These collars had angled grooves cut into them so that a spin was induced as the slug travelled up the barrel, thereby improving accuracy at somewhat greater ranges. Rifled slug ammunition is used nowadays in such sports as driven wild boar shooting where a potentially dangerous target is moving rapidly at close range. The knock-down effect of a rifled slug is greater than a high-velocity rifle bullet in such circumstances. Rifled slugs are produced to many different designs, but perhaps the best is the Brennecke slug produced by RWS in Germany.

Rifling   'Rifling' is the term used for the spiral grooves which run the length of the internal bore of a rifle barrel. The rifling is composed of lands and grooves. The latter are the depressions in a cross-section of the rifling, and the lands are the 'high' ground between each groove.

The rifling inside the barrel may be forged in two ways. Cut rifling is produced by using a very accurate bore cutter to gouge the metal from the surface of the bore to produce the required spiral of lands and

Firearms permitted for killing deer in the United Kingdom

grooves. Skilled gunsmiths can produce rifled barrels of very precise dimensions in this way, and at one time most rifle barrels were produced by the cut rifling process.

Nowadays the majority of rifle barrels are produced by the 'hammer forged' method. In this process the gunmaker produces a very accurate and hard rod to the exact dimensions of the internal bore of the eventual barrel. On this rod, called a mandrel, the rifling is cut so that it is the 'negative' of that which will appear after the forging process. The mandrel is then placed inside the rough barrel blank and this is then hammered from all sides to reduce it onto the mandrel. When the forging process is completed the mandrel is removed and the 'imprint' of the rifling remains accurately forged in the interior of the barrel.

When a calibre is first devised by a gunmaker, careful experimentation is required to establish the exact degree of twist that the rifling requires in order to provide maximum stability to the projectile. In muzzle-loading days some rifles were bored with a slow twist of about one in forty inches whereas nowadays many of the high-velocity calibres require a very rapid spin to provide bullet stability. Consequently the twist in the rifling may be as rapid as one in twelve inches and the bullet when it leaves the barrel may be spinning at about 30,000 r.p.m.!

Rigby John Rigby & Co. are as well known as any firm in the rifle building trade. Established in 1735 in Dublin, the firm opened in London in 1865.

Whereas the premier gunmakers such as Purdey and Holland & Holland have based their reputations on the production of both shotguns and rifles, Rigby have tended to concentrate on the latter, so that it is the 'Rigby rifle' which is synonymous with all that is best in this type of weapon. It was Rigby who pioneered the first Nitro Express rifles using the then new nitro-cellulose-based propellant. The increased velocity from a much smaller bullet gave startling results compared with the existing large-bore black-powder rifles – the .450 Nitro Express, for example, developed power equal to an 8-bore black-powder rifle firing a two-ounce ball!

BY APPOINTMENT TO HER MAJESTY THE QUEEN
RIFLE AND CARTRIDGE MAKERS

John Rigby & Co.
(Gunmakers), Ltd
66 GREAT SUFFOLK ST.
LONDON SE1 0BU
ESTABLISHED 1735

To this day the Nitro Express rifles are the favoured choice of big-game hunters in the tropics, with calibres ranging from .375 H & H Magnum up to the .600. Though the bullets tend to seem 'slow-moving' compared to the more recently developed high-velocity rifle rounds, these Nitro Express calibres usually show greater penetration and increased consequent 'knock-down' power. Rigby, over the years, have tended to specialize in the production of fine double barrel and bolt-action rifles in these heavy calibres. The calibre they developed, the .416 Rigby, is one of the recognized favourites when dealing with dangerous African game.

Like all the best London gunmakers, Rigby's weapons are hand built using only the finest materials and the skilled traditional methods of making barrels, actions and stocks. As a result the time taken to build a double rifle may extend to two or three years, and a bolt-action rifle may take up to fifteen months to complete, although the average delivery time is around nine months.

Rigby will build rifles in any calibre according to the customer's requirements but there do tend to be certain practical restrictions on matching the type of rifle to the calibre. Double rifles intended for use at close quarters against dangerous game are usually built in the 'heavy' calibres. Their obvious advantage of being able to fire twice without reloading far outweighs the fact that over longer distances they could not hope to compete with a single barrel rifle for accuracy. It would be impractical, on the other hand, to build magazine bolt-action rifles in the really heavy calibres. The magazine storage space required for the enormous cartridges would produce an extremely ungainly weapon and reliable reloading would also pose a problem.

Magazine bolt-action rifles tend to range downwards in calibre from .458 Winchester to the .375 H & H Magnum. Rigby will readily concede that these do not look as elegant as some other rifles on the market, and they place their emphasis rather on functional accuracy and resistance to rough usage. The very high regard with which Rigbys rifles are held would seem to indicate that this is more important than elegance.

Below the medium/heavy bolt-action rifles, Rigby also produce stalking rifles to the same design and have even recently collaborated with Parker-Hale to produce the Parker-Hale–Rigby rifle. This model is basically a mass-produced rifle which undergoes its final stages of completion in Rigby's own workshop. Thus, for a far lower cost than a hand-built weapon, the purchaser can still obtain a reliable, accurate and well-finished rifle bearing Rigby's stamp.

Although this manufacturer's reputation rests on the production of rifles, Rigby also make shotguns of the highest quality. Matching the products of Purdey, Holland, or Boss, the Rigby sidelock ejector shotguns are built with the same skill and care as their rifles. Like the double rifles, the Rigby double shotgun may, however, be identified from the others by the indented line of the top edge of each lock plate. Like the other top London gunmakers, Rigby have access to the finest engravers in the country, and some of the weapons can fairly be described as both functional and accurate while at the same time being real works of art.

When one considers the care and skill that Rigby put into producing the weapons it is hardly surprising that it is the ambition of many rifle hunters to own a Rigby rifle.

Rimfire At one time there were a wide variety of rimfire rifle calibres available. With the coming of the centrefire cartridges and improved ballistics, however, the great majority of the rimfires sank into obscurity.

In a rimfire cartridge the ignition mixture is situated around the rim at the base of the cartridge. When the rim is struck by the firing pin this mixture ignites and the cartridge is fired. The very nature of this system, however, precludes using high-power charges in the cartridge. The rim has to be soft enough to be dented by the firing pin so any increase of stress on the rim by a greater powder charge inevitably blows the base of the cartridge off.

Rimfire calibres are therefore relatively low-powered compared to other centrefire rifle and shotgun calibres. Within the shotgun category the 9-mm 'garden' gun uses a rimfire cartridge to the Flobert design. This low-powered weapon is often used for close-range vermin shooting where the use of more powerful calibres would be dangerous; for example, ratting around grain silos and farm buildings. Where quick shooting at short range is the norm they can be very effective. Also available is a .22 rimfire shot cartridge for use in smooth-bored weapons of this calibre. Using minute quantities of shot and powder, these are of very limited effectiveness.

By way of contrast to the shotgun rimfires, the .22-calibre rimfire rifles dominate the rifle shooting scene in terms of numbers in use as a sporting weapon. There are two basic calibres in this field – the .22 rimfire and the .22 Rimfire Magnum. Both are of markedly lower power than their centrefire counterparts and yet display considerable versatility.

Ammunition for rimfire rifles (left to right): bulleted cap, .22 short, .22 long rifle, .22 magnum

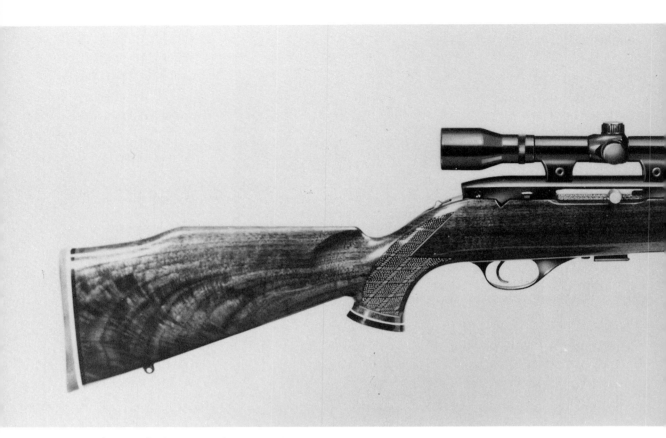

*The Weatherby .22 mark xxii, a rifle at the
luxury end of the rimfire market*

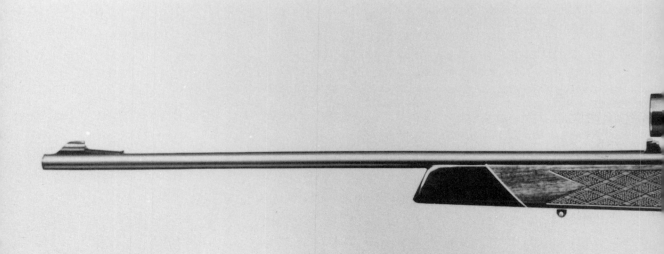

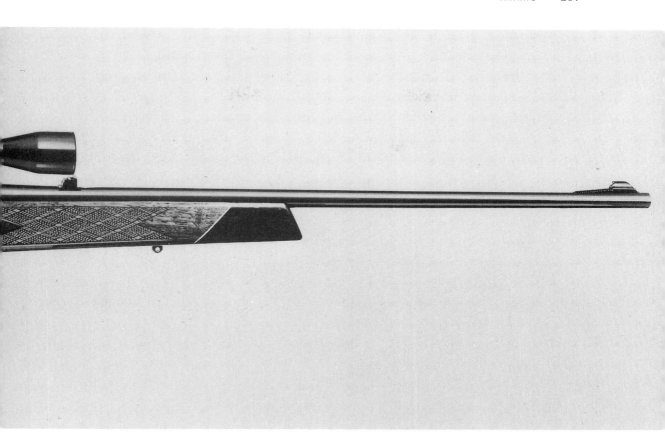

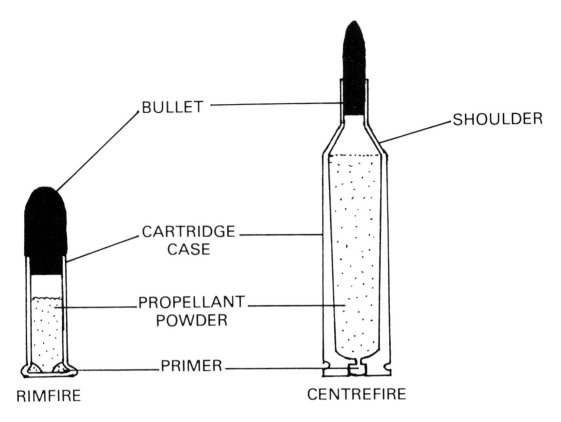

Cross-sections of rimfire and centrefire rifle cartridges

The .22 rimfire in particular, having a parallel-tube cartridge case, achieves a great variety in its range of loadings. The lowest, using a very short case, is the BB Cap, then comes the .22 Short, the .22 Long (now of declining importance), and the .22 Long Rifle. At one time this was extended to the .22 Extra Long but this is now obsolete. All these cartridges can be fired through the same weapon and the range of bullet weights, velocities and muzzle energies is remarkable for so small a calibre. (See calibre tables pages 42–43.)

The .22 Rimfire Magnum is altogether a more powerful round, although it still falls far short of the lowest-powered centrefire, the .22 Hornet. Lacking the versatility of the .22 LR, it is the less popular choice of the two yet it has found its own niche as a rabbit rifle at ranges beyond 70 yards, and it is certainly an appropriate weapon for fox control at ranges up to 120 yards. (See calibre tables pages 42–43.)

Some years ago Remington produced an even more powerful rimfire which they labelled the 5 mm Remington Magnum. This calibre used a cartridge with a necked case and the increased power capacity produced, for a rimfire, quite startling performance. Unfortunately, the round suffered frequent case splitting and the calibre was subsequently dropped.

Roe Deer Roe deer (*Capreolus capreolus*) are small and slightly built. All but the oldest roebucks will appear very dainty compared to the other deer species. A large roebuck will stand about 28 inches high at the shoulder and the doe slightly less. For their size they are long-legged and their weights vary from about 45 lbs to 70 lbs. Does are smaller and lighter than bucks, but the difference is not as pronounced as in the larger deer species.

Except for a newly born roe kid, this species has an unspotted coat. In summer the pelage of both sexes is a bright foxy red but this changes to a grey-brown in the thick winter coat. In both seasons the underparts are paler, the nose is black and the chin is white. One major identifying characteristic is that the roe has no visible tail but does have a distinctive rump or caudal patch. In the winter this appears to be a dirty white which changes to pure white when the deer erects the rump hairs in alarm. In summer the patch takes on some colour and here regional variations do occur. Scottish roe retain the white but those in the south of England turn a pale lemon yellow, or, in the case of my own roe in Wiltshire, a beige-cream colour. Bucks and does have different-shaped rump patches and this may be the only way to differentiate the sexes in winter when the buck's antlers have been cast. The buck's patch is a horizontal 'kidney' shape while the doe has a prominent vaginal tuft pointing downwards from the centre of the rump patch. Occasionally a roe in winter coat will also have whitish patches on the throat but this is not diagnostic. The nose of a roe is short, giving even an old animal a 'young' look, and the ears are large with black borders. The young, which are born in May, are heavily marked at birth with large irregular white spots. By August these will have virtually disappeared. The spring moult may begin in March and I have seen the occasional roe still moulting in late May. During April most roe will look very shabby as the long winter hair falls out in great clumps to reveal the sleek red summer pelage underneath.

The cycle of antler growth is the opposite of the other larger deer species, with the old antlers being cast in November and December and the new ones cleaned of velvet in March or April. Antler growth takes place at a time when food reserves are at their lowest ebb and it is all the more remarkable that young roebucks can achieve their first complete set of six-point antlers before comparable sika or fallow are out of the pricket stage.

Typical mature roe antlers are about nine inches long with three points on each side.

Nearest the skull is the forward-pointing brow point, above which is the back point, and the antler ends in the top point. In mature bucks there are other irregular growths on the main beam of each antler, starting at the base and sometimes reaching beyond the brow point. There growths are known as pearling, and take on importance when the antlers are being assessed for their trophy quality.

Male roe kids by late September in their first year will have grown bony pedicles on their skull upon which their antlers will subsequently develop. Indeed, there are many occasions when these pedicles are capped by antler 'buttons' in the animals' first winter. After these are shed in February the youngster grows his first head. This usually takes the form of a single spike about four inches long on each side, but a good animal with adequate food supplies through late winter may even produce a short six-point head much like a miniature version of the adult head. In an adult buck 'abnormal' heads sometimes have more than six points, and perruque antlers are much sought after by trophy hunters. These are often caused by some physical injury which affects the supply of male hormones during antler growth. Perruque heads grow very rapidly and the formation is uncontrolled, producing a wig-shaped mass of antler tissue which remains covered in velvet. However, infection of this growth is common and usually results in premature death. Should the buck recover from the injury he is likely to grow a 'normal' head again the following year.

Roe deer can be distinguished from other small deer species by their gait. They have an upright and alert stance and their back is horizontal. This distinguishes them from a Chinese water deer, whose back slopes forward, and the muntjac, which has a rounded or hunched back. Their movements are generally dainty and graceful but when in full flight they have a bounding or undulating gallop.

Roebucks can also be roughly aged by their stance and their markings and body proportions. A young buck appears to have a long neck which is carried almost vertically; with advancing age the neck shortens and thickens and the angle at which it is held decreases. Mature bucks therefore carry their necks at about 45 degrees, and in an old buck the neck is almost horizontal, practically continuing the line of the body. In the same way the depth of the body and the strength of the hindquarters increase with age so that it is relatively easy to discriminate between a slim and alert youngster or a heavy-bodied and, for a roe, ponderous old buck. Roebucks mature at around four to five years, and after this age the antlers may begin to deteriorate. They tend to become shorter and thicker as the animal passes into old age and he is then said to be 'going back' but there is great variation between years and between individuals. For a roe living in the wild an eight-year-old is a veritable pensioner. Does are very difficult to age once they have passed their first birthday as there is no pronounced elongation of the face with age.

Roe differ again from the larger deer species in that the rut occurs in late July and early August. From February onwards the stronger bucks become territorial, marking out their bounds with fraying stocks and by scenting foliage from the various scent glands on the head and between the cleaves of their hooves. The size of the territory depends on the environment and the amount of competition with rival males, and fraying of saplings can be quite serious along the boundary of a buck's territory. As the rut approaches any other males will be vigorously chased away, and the territorial buck will frequently patrol his boundary. The roe rut is not a vocal affair as in the larger deer, but the buck will be very attentive to any doe whose home range overlaps his territory.

The antlers of the larger deer species are essentially for adornment or symbols of status; the roebuck's antlers, on the other hand, are very efficient weapons. Fights between equally-matched roebucks do not have a lengthy build-up: they are sudden, short and very vicious. By the end of August some bucks will have succumbed to infections and sepsis of injuries to the neck and head sustained during these fights.

Roe does are unique among British deer in that the ova fertilized by mating in July or August will lie nearly dormant in the uterus until December. This delayed implantation shortens what would otherwise

be a ten-month gestation period. In December the ova embed themselves and development proceeds in the normal way over the next five months.

Roe deer can double their numbers each year, depending on the sex ratio. Twin births are normal and there are frequent reports of triplets. The young are born in May, but mortality may be high in cold and wet weather. Predation by foxes and dogs and deaths caused by silage cutting machines may limit the population growth in some areas. Roe deer have strong inhibitions about overcrowding and the young are chased away in the following March or April, before the new twins are born. It is these youngsters which are responsible for the expansion of the species into new and previously unoccupied areas.

The roe deer is a true native species in Britain. Along with the red deer it colonized the lowland forests of Britain during the Great Interglacial and after the retreat of the last Ice Age. With the passage of time loss of habitat led to their decline and lack of legal protection accelerated the process. Being strongly territorial animals roe could not be hunted in the same way as red deer were by the Norman kings. Thus the red deer was afforded royal protection as a 'beast of the chase' but the roe deer was relegated to the status of a 'beast of the warren' with no legal provision for its conservation.

By the eighteenth century roe were probably extinct or at least very rare across Britain except for the remoter Scottish glens. The 'Romantic' revival of the nineteenth century was the turning point in the roe deer's fortunes, when an increased interest in deer hunting by the nobility led to some Scottish roe being released in Dorset. Attempts to hunt them merely served to spread the population and nearly all the roe living in southern England trace their ancestry back to this introduction. Other introductions took place at Windsor and in Norfolk and later (in 1913) in the Lake District.

Unlike sika deer, these introductions were very successful and breeding populations were quickly established in each of these areas; yet it was the effects on the countryside of the First and Second World Wars that provided the roe deer with the spring-

Roe deer are often seen feeding on the edges of woodland in spring

board that it needed. During both conflicts many areas of woodland were felled to supply timber for the war effort and the secondary scrub growth in the felled areas was ideal habitat for roe. In addition, the replanting of forest and woodland in both upland and lowland Britain after the last war provided even more suitable areas for recolonization. Young plantations of both conifer and broad leaves can harbour and support a high roe density, but the numbers decline as the trees mature. The young then tend to move on to find other suitable cover, and in this way the roe deer has 'leapfrogged' across the countryside. The Deer Act of 1963 put an end to the inhumane snaring and control by shotgun 'deer drives' and gave the roe, for the first time in its history, some degree of protection. At that time woodland stalking was in its infancy as a technique of deer management and population control.

This allowed the roe additional 'breathing space' to continue their recolonization of the country.

At present the original Dorset population has colonized as far west as Cornwall, north to Oxfordshire and Gloucester, and east as far as Kent. The Norfolk population, once centred on Thetford Forest, has now reached down along the Chilterns to link up with roe crossing the Thames from the south.

With the afforestation of the Scottish Highlands and Southern Uplands came a massive population irruption, and roe have moved southwards on the flanks of the Pennines, crossing the Humber in the east and reaching the Welsh border in the west. The introduced population in the Lake District has been virtually swallowed up in this southward movement. Recent reports suggest that the roe are spreading into the upland forests and deep wooded valleys of

Arrows indicate the direction of new colonization by roe deer

walking along a few hedgerows is rough shooting, as are the group of friends who get together for a day's mixed shooting on any patch of land likely to hold the odd head of game or other quarry species. The acreage covered is no criterion, and some of the best rough shooting can be found on very small plots of land.

When two or more rough shooters meet for their sport the accent is on informality and collective decision. Rough shooting does not involve the authoritarian control of the day's events seen in both driven and walked-up shoots, and the rough shooter must be adaptable if he is to make the maximum use of the land available to him. Most rough shooters gather in groups of three or four friends who between them have access to a small plot of land for their shooting. Few rough shoots exceed 200 acres, and the majority fall well below this area. Nevertheless, a suprising variety of species will find their way into the bag during the course of a season and it is the joy of the unexpected which lends rough shooting much of its charm.

Over a number of years the members of the group may expend much energy and effort on improving the the shooting available. With the farmer's consent and coop-eration, a flight pond may be excavated in a damp corner of a field and the edges planted with shrubs and rushes to offer cover for waterfowl. Field boundaries may be left uncut and set-asides may be left to provide both shelter and food for the odd pairs of partridge, and the group may even decide to rear a small number of pheasant to en-hance the winter's sport. Small blocks of woodland may hold the occasional wild pheasant and yield a woodcock or two in cold weather, and roosting pigeons will add variety and challenging shooting to an evening's sport. Pasture and arable land may hold hares and partridge, and the hedge boundaries may harbour rabbits; any small streams and ditches may attract snipe in winter. The more varied the habitat the greater the variety of game that may be met, even on a very small acreage.

To make the most of the sport available, the rough shooters must adapt to the con-ditions they meet on each shooting day. Not

Wales at a rate of three miles per year, and it is possible that the 'northern' and 'southern' populations may meet before the turn of the century. Recent EC incentives to plant lowland woodland will probably accelerate what is already a rapid spreading of the roe population.

The increasing amount of woodland habitat available together with the deer's intolerance of overcrowding and capacity to double numbers each year have all con-tributed to what must be one of the major widlife success stories of the twentieth century.

See also: **Deer; Deer Management; Deer Stalking – Woodland**

Rough Shooting   Rough shooting is the main shotgun sport in Britain and the term en-compasses great variety both in quarry species and in the different environments that offer rough shooting sport. A person who takes his gun and spaniel for the odd hour

for them the well-tried succession of game drives of a covert shoot, but their sport is not diminished by this want of 'order'. Much time will be spent informally discussing tactics, and a consensus plan of action will be evolved. Much of the pleasure of rough shooting is derived from working the gundogs over the land, and tactics will often revolve around the particular skills of the dogs available on the day.

Unlike the other game shooting disciplines, each of which has dogs for specific purposes, the rough shooter's dog must be an 'all-rounder'. The labrador and the springer spaniel are by far the most popular breeds for this purpose, as the dog will be required to seek out and flush the quarry, and to retrieve the fallen, and anyone who has watched a strong springer work through dense bramble and bracken will appreciate its value to a rough shooter. Other breeds may also be used to good effect and there are a growing number of HPR (hunter–pointer–retriever) breeds in evidence on rough shoots. Among these the German short-haired pointer (GSP) is perhaps the most popular.

To illustrate the quality of sport available from a small area I will describe a shoot that I shared with two close friends. The total area of land was a mere 40 acres but of varied habitats. It included a ten-acre mature deciduous wood bordered by drainage ditches that connected to a small pond about 30 feet in diameter and a five-acre spinney through which a spring-fed stream had cut a narrow valley dammed at its lowest point to provide irrigation water. Downstream of this, the outlet stream was bordered on one side by a wet pasture field and on the other by a five-acre withy bed; the remainder was arable land used mainly for grain and potatoes. The whole shoot was bordered on one side by the main London-to-Westbury railway line and on the two other sides by country lanes.

The three of us shot the ground six times each season, and the sport was both exciting and varied. During the first season the spinney yielded woodcock, rabbits and pheasant, while the wet meadow provided both snipe and partridge. The arable fields produced hares, partridge and pigeons and

the wood produced many flight-shot pigeons and a small number of pheasants. During that first season no duck were shot, although some mallard were seen. The following summer we were much occupied building a release pen in the wood and establishing feeders in both the wood and the spinney. The flight pond was cleared of much rubbish and the margins fed with tailcorn. The number of pheasants released subsequently averaged 25 per season, and these did add a little more weight to our bag. We also spent time in the summer on vermin shoots and reduced the magpies, jays and grey squirrels to some extent; and I spent many hours sitting up for the local fox before finally settling the previous winter's accounts.

In terms of variety and the magic of the unexpected, perhaps a brief narration of the end-of-season shoot will illustrate the potential of a small rough shoot. Meeting at 10 o'clock on a crisp January morning, we walked up the withy bed, but the dogs found nothing of interest. As we reached the irrigation dam, however, a big cock pheasant clattered out of a thick tussock: this was cleanly missed with both barrels. Any ribbing was interrupted by a pair of snipe that whipped out of the ditch, and the first bird of the day came to bag after it had splashed onto the half-flooded corner of the water meadow.

With one 'standing gun' by the dam, both sides of the spinney were brought down and a rabbit was accounted for as it broke sideways out of a bramble patch, while two hen pheasants cut back and were lost over our boundary. The ten-acre wood was next on our list and we silently closed in to our flight pond from three sides. Although we had expected that any duck would already have been put out by our previous shots, three mallard splashed out of the reed margin, one of which, a drake, cost us two barrels. Taking the wood in two halves, our spaniel broke out a hen and then a cock bird and the latter was accounted for as our first pheasant of the day. On the second leg of the woodland beat the GSP went on point to flush, in turn, a moorhen (which we left), a hen pheasant (which we killed), and a rabbit – which was missed with both barrels. As we neared the end of our ten-

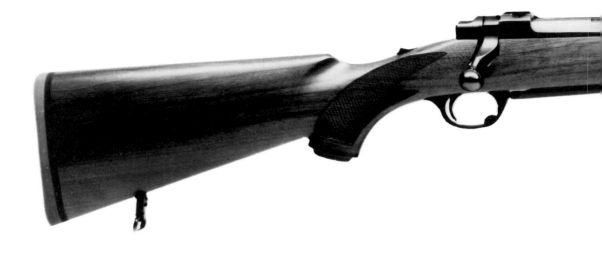

acre wood a winter flock of pigeons came over at tree-top level and two of these were added to the bag before we halted for lunch.

In the afternoon we traversed the fields, walking in line and wheeling at the boundaries or hedges in order to cover the ground as thoroughly as possible. Two coveys of partridge yielded two of their number to our bag; the second was seen to drop out of the air about 150 yards away even though it showed no signs of being hit, and the retrieve of the dead bird severely tested our labrador's skills. Four hares were seen but none shot, and another unobservant and suicidal pigeon was brought to hand. The sun was setting when we took up positions, for which we had tossed a coin, for the 'evening flight': one gun by the dam wall, one at the further end of the wood and one by the flight pond – claimed by the others to be the best location of the three.

As the evening declined into a frosty winter twilight, snipe calls were interrupted by the whistle of mallard pinions, a gunshot, and a solid thump as my friend at the dam took the second mallard of the day. Just then a loud swish and multiple splashes startled me as a party of teal dashed into the flight pond. Before I could move they were airborne again, standing on their tails, but by

great good fortune I had a left and right with which to end my season.

A few minutes later I thought I heard a goose call on the freshening breeze, and two shots from the far end of the wood were followed by a wild whooping from my companion. We hurried over to investigate the commotion, and found our friend dancing a jig in the twilight and proudly holding aloft his first ever Canada goose!

What other shooting sport could boast at the end of the season a bag that included snipe, rabbit, partridge, pigeon, pheasant, mallard, teal and a goose – all from barely 40 acres of land! Admittedly our shoot did not always produce such variety, but the anticipation of the unexpected is all part of the enjoyment of rough shooting, and any variety in the bag adds its own spice. Of all forms of game shooting, it is rough shooting that gets the shooter most involved, not only in organization and participation on the shooting day, but also throughout the year in habitat improvement, amateur game keeping, vermin control, and all manner of other activities related to his sport. I am sure this all goes to enhance the rough shooter's appreciation of whatever his little patch of land may provide.

See also: **Game Shooting**

A Mannlicher-style rifle made in America. The Ruger M77 International

Ruger Sturm, Ruger & Co. Inc. was established in 1949, and from relatively modest beginnings has developed into one of the most notable of United States arms manufacturers. The stated philosophy of the firm is 'to produce the world's best sporting arms at a reasonable and fair price to the consumer'. How well they have succeeded in this is reflected by the fact that the company now employs over 1,500 people at its headquarters and factory in Southport, Connecticut, and at Newport in New Hampshire.

In America, Ruger have made a name for themselves by heading the field in the design and manufacture of heavy, powerful revolvers. The Ruger 'Blackhawk' and 'Redhawk' models, chambered for the most powerful revolver cartridges such as the .44 Magnum and the .41 Magnum, are firmly established as leaders in their class of weaponry.

In Britain, though, it is their sporting rifles that have gained a good reputation for reliability and accuracy. In the centrefire calibres they offer two basic designs which are supplied in a variety of models. The M77 bolt-action centrefire rifle is a box-magazine-fed repeater which is based on an action similar to the Mauser. Unlike many other arms manufacturers, however, they produce all their own components, and do not 'buy in' parts from other sources to be assembled under their brand name. The model 77 is typical of the good-quality medium-price bolt-action rifle and is available in two action lengths to accommodate various lengths of cartridge. The short bolt action is used for the many post-war 'mild' cartridges such as the .243 Win. and the .308 Win., in addition to the .22 centrefires. The magnum action copes with the longer cases, such as .30/06 and .270 Win. as well as the heavier calibres. There are four basic styles in this model. The standard rifle, designated the M-77 RS, uses the magnum action and a barrel length of 24 inches. The stock is of the 'classic' design, in that it lacks a raised Monte-Carlo cheekpiece, and the rifle is available in a variety of calibres ranging from the 7×57 to the .338 Win. Magnum. In the 'short' action, it is also available in .243 and .308.

The lightweight version uses a 20-inch barrel and the same basic stock design, and is available in a variety of non-magnum calibres, while the Tropical edition, chambered for the .458 Win. Magnum, makes use of a heavy barrel and magnum action. Catering for the growing popularity of the European style of Stutzen rifle, Ruger produce a full-stocked version on the short stroke action with a 20-inch barrel for .22/250, .243, .250–300 and .308 calibres. This model is designated the M-77 RSI International.

Perhaps the rifle that has drawn the most attention to this manufacturer is the Ruger No 1 single shot. This is unique among contemporary sporting rifles in that it uses a falling-block action based on the Farquarson design and it has all the attributes of positive lock-up and accuracy for which the old design was famous. Available in editions similar to the M-77, this rifle overcomes the problems of a left-handed shooter using a right-handed bolt, the opening lever of the No 1 being placed below the trigger guard.

The firm also produces two auto-loading carbines, of which the .22 rimfire model 10/22 uses a ten-shot rotary magazine and an 18½-inch barrel. A recent addition to the rimfire range is the bolt-action M-77/22. Utilizing experience gained in producing the centrefire M-77 models, the rimfire variant is a high-quality and accurate rifle which competes well with the top models from such manufacturers as Anschütz and Brno.

Ruger also produce the 'Red Label' over-and-under shotgun in 12 bore, again a sound and reliable weapon, but it is for rifles that the company has gained a good reputation in Britain.

Rut   The rut is the term for the time of year when any deer species reaches its peak of sexual activity. In most deer species this mating season is confined to a fairly narrow period spanning two or three weeks, and is characterized by much more daytime activity than normal. In Britain, red, fallow, and sika deer rut in the autumn. Depending on the weather and the region in which they live, the rut may reach a peak from early October to November. Roe deer, on the other hand, rut in late July and early August; the doe then delays the implantation of the fertilized ovum until around mid-December, after which the foetus develops normally. Chinese water deer rut in late November and December, but the muntjac does not have a specific rutting season. This species breeds every seven months or so throughout the year and the buck is capable of fathering offspring at any time in his antler growth cycle.

See also: **Deer Management**

Sabot A sabot cartridge is used in medium- or large-bore rifles in order to achieve very much higher velocities using a light bullet. Basically the bullet is encased in a disintegrating cup which fits the normal bore of the rifle. When the cartridge is fired this sabot case takes the rifling and imparts a spin to the projectile. On leaving the barrel the cup disintegrates and falls away leaving the bullet to continue on its way. Using a sabot cartridge can extend the versatility of a rifle by providing a light high-velocity bullet for fox shooting in a calibre which would otherwise be suitable only for deer or other medium game. For example, the Remington 'Accelerator' cartridge fires a 50-grain .22 calibre bullet from a .30–06 rifle at around 3,500 fps.

Safety Catch A safety catch is a device which prevents a cocked weapon from firing when the trigger is pulled. In many rifle designs the safety catch actually de-activates the trigger mechanism, although the weapon remains cocked. In most shotgun designs the safety catch mechanism simply blocks the trigger so that it cannot be pulled. Again the weapon remains in a cocked state, and many shooting accidents have occurred when a knock or jar has moved the sear nose out of bent and fired the weapon without the trigger being touched or moved in any way.

Safety catch mechanisms may be divided into manual safety and automatic safety devices. Manual safety catches are found on most rifles and on competition shotguns. In this type the safety catch has to be set to safe once the weapon is loaded and cocked. Automatic safety catches are found on most sporting shotguns and on some hunting air rifles. In these the safety catch automatically resets itself to the 'safe' position when the weapon is opened.

In any branch of sporting shooting, the safety catch should remain on 'safe' until the weapon is being raised to the shoulder for firing, and every shooter should develop the habit of releasing the safety as the gun is raised. This considerably aids safe gun handling as it minimizes the period during which the weapon can be fired by any pressure on the trigger.

The 'top tang' safety catch, which is standard on most double barrelled weapons

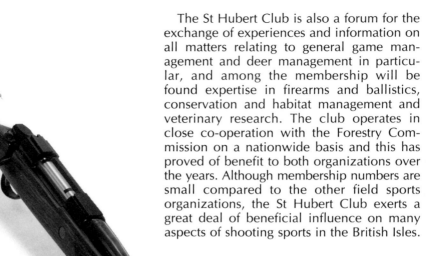

The Sako deluxe model rifle, medium-priced but of very high quality

The St Hubert Club is also a forum for the exchange of experiences and information on all matters relating to general game management and deer management in particular, and among the membership will be found expertise in firearms and ballistics, conservation and habitat management and veterinary research. The club operates in close co-operation with the Forestry Commission on a nationwide basis and this has proved of benefit to both organizations over the years. Although membership numbers are small compared to the other field sports organizations, the St Hubert Club exerts a great deal of beneficial influence on many aspects of shooting sports in the British Isles.

St Hubert Club   As part of an international organization the St Hubert Club of Great Britain was founded in 1953. Among its most important aims are to encourage the conservation of game and the pursuit of all game in a sportsmanlike manner. As a branch of what is a worldwide association it also seeks to promote the spirit of international fraternity among all field sports enthusiasts.

In Britain the St Hubert Club is concerned primarily with deer and their effect-ive management and control. It has acted as an advisory body for much of the current deer legislation and it now works closely with the British Deer Society. It was the St Hubert Club that first initiated a stalker training programme in this country. Under skilled guidance the new entrant serves an apprenticeship of many months' continuous assessment before he or she can gain the status of a 'trained stalker'. It is a carefully planned and thorough course and the final qualification has international recognition.

Sako Oy Sako Ab is a rifle manufacturer based at Rühimäki in Finland. Manufacturing mainly for the medium-priced market, Sako produce bolt-action rifles in four basic models, although three of these are available in a wide range of styles.

Starting with their .22 rimfire, the 'Finnscout' is a plain bolt-action repeating rifle which is fed from a five-shot clip magazine. It is available in two models, the lightweight 'Sporter' and the 'Heavy barrel' version. Both are fairly straightforward rifles which will withstand much hard work without losing their innate accuracy.

The lightest of their centrefire rifles is termed the 'Vixen', and as its name suggests it is designed for hunting small to medium game and vermin. Available in standard, deluxe and super deluxe grades, this model can also be supplied with a heavy barrel or in the Stutzen full-stocked format. The Vixen is available only in the .22 centrefire calibres and the .17 Rem., and is built on a short bolt action which gives a quick and crisp reloading cycle for these short cartridges.

Moving up the scale of calibres to those used for deer stalking, Sako provide the 'Forester' model. Using a medium-length bolt to accommodate the longer cartridges in .243 Win. and .308 Win. calibres, these are the 'all-round' woodland rifles. The Forester is built in three grades, like the Vixen, and is also offered in full-stocked, heavy-barrel and classic styling. The butt of the last has a straight comb stock rather than the raised Monte-Carlo cheekpiece of the other models.

The rifle the company builds for the larger calibres with relatively long cartridges is the 'Finnbear' model. Although not available in a heavy-barrel variant, the range of Finnbear rifles is enhanced in their heaviest calibres by the 'Safari' model. As its name suggests this is a rifle chambered for the medium magnum calibres from the .300 Win. magnum to the .375 H & H magnum. Other rifles in this range take the long-cartridge calibres in the .25–06 to .30–06 range and include the European calibres of 7×57 and 6.5×55.

Not only are Sako rifles accurate and ruggedly built, but in the luxury grades they are also very attractively finished. A great deal of skill and attention is devoted to their construction, and Sako rifles have a justifiably good worldwide reputation.

Scott, Sir Peter (1909–1989) Son of Captain Robert Falcon Scott, Peter Scott won international recognition in a number of fields. He won early acclaim as a wildlife artist, particularly for his paintings of wildfowl. He first exhibited his work when he was 24 years old. A keen game shot and wildfowler at that time, his experiences led him to publish such books as *Wild Chorus* and *Morning Flight*, in which he recounted many of his experiences. His gift for communicating his love of wild places led him to a successful broadcasting career in both radio and television, but he also had many other talents. In 1936 he won an Olympic bronze medal for sailing and was the British Gliding Champion in 1963.

In 1946 he established a wildfowl collection on the Severn estuary at Slimbridge; this later developed into the Wildfowl Trust and more recently the Wildfowl and Wetlands Trust. With a steadily growing international reputation as a conservationist, he worked closely with the International Union for Conservation of Nature (IUCN), becoming the Chairman of their Species Survival Commission. In 1961 he helped found the World Wildlife Fund (now the World Wide Fund for Nature) and designed their famous panda logo. In 1982 he became the Honorary Chairman of their International Council, and held many offices in other conservation societies and organizations. It was hardly surprising that in 1973 he was knighted for his services to conservation, stemming from his early love of shooting in wild and lonely places. Peter Scott grew in stature to be acknowledged as the world's finest ambassador for wildlife and conservation.

Statutory Close Seasons for Deer in the United Kingdom (All dates inclusive)

Species	Sex	England and Wales	Scotland	Northern Ireland
Red	Male Female	1 May–31 July 1 Mar–31 Oct	21 Oct–30 June 16 Feb–20 Oct	1 May–31 July 1 Mar–31 Oct
Sika	Male Female	1 May–31 July 1 Mar–31 Oct	21 Oct–30 June 16 Feb–20 Oct	1 May–31 July 1 Mar–31 Oct
Red/Sika Hybrids	Male Female	*1 May–31 July· 1 Mar–31 Oct	21 Oct–30 June 16 Feb–20 Oct	1 May–31 July 1 Mar–31 Oct
Fallow	Male Female	1 May–31 July 1 Mar–31 Oct	1 May–31 July 16 Feb–20 Oct	1 May–31 July 1 Mar–31 Oct
Roe	Male Female	1 Nov–31 Mar 1 Mar–31 Oct	21 Oct–31 Mar 1 Apr–20 Oct	

The British Deer Society also recommends that both sexes of Chinese Water Deer and Muntjac be given a close season from 1st March to 31st October.

Exemptions – Deer may be killed outside the open season in order to:

a) Prevent suffering, i.e. dispatching an injured animal

b) Prevent serious damage to crops. In this instance permission must be obtained from the appropriate government department.

Note – Night Shooting. As a general rule, only foxes, hares and rabbits may be shot by authorized persons during the hours of darkness. With the exception of hares, no other game species may be taken at nigh. Deer may not be shot at night.

(The above tables were compiled by John Hotchkis, Hon. Legal Adviser to the British Deer Society, by whose kind permission they are reproduced here.)

The following dates are inclusive and indicate the open season for shooting the species:

Game Shooting Seasons:	
Pheasant	1 October–1 February
Partridge	1 September–1 February
Red Grouse/Ptarmigan	12 August–10 December
Black Grouse	20 August–10 December
Woodcock (England & Wales)	1 October–31 January
Woodcock (Scotland)	1 September–31 January
Capercaillie	1 October–31 January
Waterfowl Shooting Seasons:	
Ducks and Geese (inland)	1 September–31 January
Ducks and Geese (foreshore)	1 September–20 February
Moorhen	1 September–31 January
Coot	1 September–31 January
Golden Plover	1 September–31 January
Snipe	12 August–31 January

Seasons   The tables opposite give the open and close seasons for game birds and deer. Apart from those mentioned in the tables, the other species in Britain's quarry list are, with the notable exeption of hares, considered to be vermin for which there is no close season. Although hares may be shot all year round, there is a ban on their sale from 1 March till 31 July inclusive.

Sewelling   Sewelling is a length of rope or stout cord on which is tied narrow strips of coloured plastic or other material so that the whole assembly resembles bunting. This is used by keepers on driven shoots to induce running pheasants to take to the air. If on a particular drive the standing guns have to be placed close to the edge of a patch of woodland which is then driven from the opposite end by a team of beaters, it is likely that the pheasants will run forward and flush at the wood's edge, i.e., too close to the guns. In this situation the guns will not be presented with high and fast birds, as the game will not have the space to climb and gain air speed.

To remedy this situation, on the morning of the shoot the keeper will lay a line of sewelling some distance back from the guns across the wood. With the rope suspended about one foot to 18 inches from ground level, many pheasants running before the beaters will stop at this unnatural line and flush at this point. Thus by the time they have cleared the trees and appear over the guns the birds will be both high and travelling quickly, offering far more testing and sporting targets.

Sewelling can also be laid parallel to the line of the drive on the edges of the wood in order to prevent birds slipping out sideways along hedge lines or ditches. In all instances the rope must be laid in position on the day of the shoot so as to present a strange and unnatural phenomenon to the running pheasant.

A good example of sewelling in the field

An open gun cannot be fired

Shooting Safety   All shooting accidents can be avoided if all sporting shooters use a combination of common sense and thought when handling weapons.

Just as safe car driving is a learned habit, so safe gun handling must become a subconscious habit through frequent and thoughtful practice.

All firearms are potentially lethal weapons, so safety must be a prime consideration whenever weapons are handled or stored. Thus, as well as general safety points detailed below, I have also listed more specific ideas about safe transit of weapons and safety in the home.

General Safe Handling

1   ALWAYS check that a gun is unloaded immediately you pick it up.
2   ALWAYS pass a weapon to another person stock first and with the breech open.
3   ALWAYS treat every gun as if it is loaded.
4   ALWAYS make sure that the barrels are pointing away from people and in a safe direction.
5   When in company ALWAYS keep the weapon unloaded and open.
6   Make a habit of checking the barrels are unobstructed whenever you load the weapon and at frequent intervals.
7   Develop the habit of slipping off the safety catch as you mount the gun to your shoulder.
8   Make a point of understanding the proof marks on a gun and use only ammunition that is compatible within the proof limits.
9   NEVER put a loaded weapon down and/ or leave it unattended.
10   NEVER leave a weapon where it can be knocked or fall over.

Weapons In Transit

1   NEVER place a loaded weapon in a vehicle.
2   ALWAYS transport a weapon in a protective case or sleeve.
3   Make sure the weapon is out of sight if you have to leave the vehicle.
4   ALWAYS lock the vehicle if you have to leave it.

Safety In The Home

1   NEVER allow unsupervised children access to guns or ammunition.
2   NEVER load a weapon indoors.
3   Keep weapons and ammunition separately.
4   Store both weapons and ammunition in secure locations.

If everyone followed these rules the 'thoughtless accident' would be a thing of the past.

Shore Shooting   To my mind, only two sports qualify for the term 'wildfowling': punt gunning and shore shooting. The shoreline of Britain varies considerably and a great proportion of it is of little interest to the wildfowler. The rocky shorelines, frequently backed by towering cliffs, and the wide sandy bays beloved of the holidaymaker do not usually hold any of the quarry species. The attention of the wildfowler is therefore focused on the mudflats and salt marsh of the many estuaries, from the great firths of Scotland to the deep and narrow river outlets of the south-west peninsula. It is these that offer both shelter and, to some extent, food for the thousands of wildfowl that migrate each autumn to their wintering grounds around Britain's coast. Twice each day the tide covers and uncovers large portions of these estuaries and the environment is in a state of constant change. The phase of the moon and wind direction dictate how much of the salt marsh is covered by each successive tide, and at low tide the deep creeks and gutters, the beds of reeds and spartina grass, and the soft exposed mudflats near the low water's edge all supply a variety of habitats that are attractive to wildfowl of many species.

The patterns of movements of the winter population of duck and geese are geared primarily to night and day, but they are also sensitive to the timing of high and low tide, and the established pattern is often broken by human disturbance or by rough weather. The habits of the wintering population on each estuary vary, and the more local knowledge the prospective wildfowler gains the better prepared he will be to take up the challenge of these wild places. Although to duck and geese an estuary offers comparative shelter and safety, to a human these areas are exposed and dangerous places. In the depths of a stormy December or January the wind strength on the coast is noticeably greater than inland, the temperatures are lower and the 'chill factor' is a much more important consideration. Any person who ventures out on to the foreshore without adequate preparation and detailed knowledge of the local conditions is foolhardy in the extreme; Britain's foreshores claim the lives of a number of these 'wildfowlers' every year.

The basic strategy of the shore shooter is to place himself under the flight lines of the dawn and evening flights of the wildfowl as they move from their estuary resting places to their feeding grounds. In order to have some hope of success it is essential that the shooter gets to know the area well. Preliminary daytime visits should start with observations from the safety of the sea wall of any marked bird movement over certain parts of the foreshore. The whereabouts of any creeks and gutters should be noted and memorized and the width of the different estuary levels recorded. From the sea wall the land will often be covered with short turf and rushes; this is the 'top level' of the salt marsh, as it is only covered by high spring tides. Below this lie the spartina beds, which begin roughly at the high-level mark of neap tides, and these will usually slope slowly down to bare muds and sands close to the low-water mark. The rate at which the incoming tide floods the estuary should be noted and safe escape routes from the racing tide carefully worked out.

As one gains more knowledge of the fore shore and the movement of the duck and waders the location of the flight lines will become clear and the places which could afford adequate concealment, or where hides could be built, can be worked out in more detail. The observer must also become familiar with the effect of wind on the tidal height and timing. On one Welsh estuary I know well, an onshore wind would flood the saltings one hour early and the tide could be nearly six feet higher than normal at the top end of the marsh. Failure to take this into account when shooting far from the

safety of the sea wall would have fatal consequences, particularly as the tide floods in faster than I could walk over the mud and through the spartina beds. At such times the known safe line of retreat must be adhered to at all costs. The creek that looked innocent enough at low tide will present a dangerous barrier of dark swirling water on a rapidly rising tide, and any attempted short cut may end on the banks of such a creek. The shock comes when you then attempt to retrace your steps back onto the safe escape route only to find that the water has risen in the meantime to cover the landmarks you used. The gathering dusk of a stormy winter's evening when the tide is flooding is not the best time to realize that you have forgotten your route to the sea wall which looks so tantalizingly close through the gloom.

Once you are confident that you know the layout of the estuary well and that you can predict the flight lines of your quarry with some degree of accuracy it is time to venture out for a dawn or dusk flight. On the wide flat landscape of a tidal marsh concealment is of the utmost importance, and a prepared hide can increase the success of the sortie. You may, on previous visits, have noticed little side-gullies and rills which gave adequate concealment; the important point to remember is that any visible 'lumps' on an otherwise level mudbank or bed of spartina will immediately arouse the suspicions of the birds, and it is therefore essential to sink your profile to the general level of your surroundings. Where no small rill or bank of a larger gully is available there are two alternatives: one is to use a portable screen and the other is to dig a pit.

As part of their standard kit many wildfowlers will carry a small roll of rigid plastic garden netting or chicken wire about six feet long and two feet wide. Through the mesh is woven a screen of rushes, spartina grass or driftwood and tidal flotsam. With such a screen the human outline can be effectively broken. If the screen is rolled around the lip of any slight depression in the sand or mud the fowler can lie prone and well-concealed, and as the screen is made of natural materials the wildfowl may take it for something left stranded by the previous tide.

Note how the trigger finger does not touch the trigger until the gun is shouldered

On wide expanses of bare mud close to the low-water mark even this type of screen hide can 'stick out' too much, and the only other method of concealment is to dig a grave pit. Using a lightweight shovel or other implement, a strip long and wide enough to take the wildfowler and his kit should be excavated and the loose sand and mud piled on the side from which the birds are expected to approach. There should be a gentle profile to the outer slope of the mound so that it is not too obvious. Behind this cover the fowler lies prone until the birds are within range, but sits up to take his shot. As may be imagined, wildfowling is a sport which does not require good footwork! Most of the shots will be taken from cramped and uncomfortable sitting positions while the fowler is encumbered with many extra thicknesses of clothes to keep out the extremes or the weather.

The evening and morning flights of wildfowl are the established routine that the wildfowler will attempt to intercept, and it is at these times that most of the fowler's activity takes place. If the shooter plans to stay on the salt marsh throughout the day, then the bulk of the daylight hours should not be wasted. If the weather is reasonably calm some time can be spent in walking up some of the larger creeks for the odd party of teal or mallard, an activity known generally as 'creek crawling'. It is surprising how well a small meander or sand bar in a creek can mask a flock of teal, and a careful approach will delay their 'spring' until they are within gunshot. At the top level of saltings there may be enough growth of rushes between small water flashes to attract snipe, and these may gather in some numbers in this sort of environment. As a consequence some part of the day may be given over to snipe shooting or, if the opportunity arises, trying to intercept flocks of golden plover as they commute from adjacent farmland onto the saltings.

Both these birds have unusual escape flights. The snipe's zig-zag flight when it is flushed is well known and it makes for a very testing target. Less well-known perhaps is the golden plover's escape tactic. When a flock of this species is shot at the birds will often go into a 'power dive' rather than trying to gain height. Close to the ground the birds

level out; at this stage the flock may well scatter in different directions, and the speed they gained during their dive assists their hasty low-level get-away. When shooting golden plover many experienced fowlers fire a 'waste' cartridge to bring the flock down, then try to pick off one bird with the second barrel – amid all the confusion a job easier said than done!

If the weather is blustery and the sea rough the day may be profitably spent trying to draw small parties of restless birds within shotgun range by the use of decoys. A pattern of duck decoys set out to be easily visible in a sheltered creek can sometimes attract duck from some distance away, particularly those trying to seek a calmer resting place. With duck decoying always a possible activity for a day spent on the marsh, it is always wise to include decoys in the wildfowler's basic kit.

There are, however, other items of equipment that are essential rather than optional. At the top of this list I would put a magnetic compass. I have seen a sea fog roll into an estuary in a matter of minutes, cutting visibility down to twenty yards and deadening the normal sounds of the surroundings. When this happens the fowler must get to safety as quickly as possible and, with no distant landmarks to go by, a compass is essential. Second only to the compass is a good torch, particularly if the fowler intends to stay on the marsh for the evening flight. The torch has a number of uses: searching for downed birds, helping to pick out the safe route to the sea wall in the gathering dark and, in an emergency, as a signalling aid. It must be remembered that the wildfowling environment is a remote one and help is often far away. A torch can be seen at a considerable distance and will guide help to you if you are in trouble. As an additional safety device I always carry a whistle which has a shrill, far-carrying sound, and I know of some fowlers who also carry small distress flares, which I think is an excellent idea. Finally, I always carry a small supply of emergency food in the form of glucose sweets and chocolate.

The main goose quarry species will vary in different parts of the country, but, although the identification of the individual species may be difficult in poor light, the greylag, pink-footed and white-fronted goose are easily distinguished from the protected 'black' geese like the brent or the barnacle goose. Not so the duck species. To an unaccustomed eye all flying duck look the same, but the wildfowler must learn to distinguish quarry species from protected species. In dim light he must be able to differentiate mallard from shelduck, and pochard from scaup. The time spent surveying the estuary prior to the first foray will also have been spent in watching the wildfowl and noting their particular characteristics in terms of their calls, their flight silhouette and their colour. The surface-feeding ducks are the main species that adhere to the pattern of morning and evening flights and the wildfowl observer must learn to identify mallard, teal, shoveller, pintail, gadwall and above all wigeon. The diving species such as pochard or tufted duck are more usually freshwater species although bad weather will drive them to the salt marshes and the wildfowler must be able to make a positive identification before raising his gun.

Above all other species, though, it is the wigeon which is the 'wildfowler's duck', and the whistle of the drake floating across a rising tide under a full moon is just as evocative as the loud pack calls of a skein of wild geese.

Shooting wigeon 'under the moon' is an accidental sport in that the conditions necessary for it to take place happen so infrequently that it can never be planned for.

Shore shooting, despite all our careful plans and observations and our own theories concerning wildfowl behaviour, is still largely a matter of luck in being in the right place at the right time. To my mind this only enhances the magic of being on the tide edge in a cold winter's dawn.

See also: **Wildfowling; Wildfowling Guns**

Shot 'Lead shot' is the term applied to the small spherical lead balls that make up the charge of a shotgun cartridge. Most shot is still made in the traditional way by dropping molten lead from the top of a tower so that it falls into a water bath. During its descent the molten lead forms into spheri-

cal droplets under the influence of surface tension, and these are chilled into solid lead on entering the water. They are then graded into different sizes and any non-spherical droplets are returned to the melting pot for another drop.

Commercial shot towers usually use 'hardened lead': lead to which antimony and other metals are added in small quantities in order to produce pellets which are less prone to deformation than pure (soft) lead.

For home loaders there are a number of 'shot-makers' on the market. Using scrap lead the amateur can produce quite good lead shot with these devices, but the product is often softer than commercially-produced shot. Nevertheless it is perfectly adequate for most sporting shooting purposes and there is some satisfaction in killing a bird with shot you have made yourself.

Dispersante cartridges: Some cartridges are loaded with square- or cube-shaped shot. These cartridges can be useful for close-range rabbit shooting where a maximum pattern

British Shot Size	No of Shot to oz	Diameter	
		in	mm
L.G. . .	6	.360	9.14
M.G. Mould .	7	.347	8.81
S.G. . .	8	.332	8.43
Special S.G. .	11	.298	7.57
S.S.G. . .	15	.269	6.83
S.S.S.G.. .	20	.245	6.22
S.S.S.S.G.	25	.227	5.77
S.S.S.S.S.G. or			
A.A.A.A. .	30	.214	5.44
A.A.A. . .	35	.203	5.16
A.A. . .	40	.194	4.93
A. or B.B.B.B.	50	.180	4.57
B.B.B. . .	60	.170	4.32
B.B. . .	70	.161	4.09
B. . .	80	.154	3.91
1 . . .	100	.143	3.63
2 . . .	120	.135	3.43
3 . . .	140	.128	3.25
4 . . .	170	.120	3.05
5 . . .	220	.110	2.79
5½ . . .	240	107	2.72
6 . . .	270	.102	2.59
6½ . . .	300	.099	2.51
7 . . .	340	.095	2.41
8 . . .	450	.087	2.21
9 . . .	580	.080	2.03
10 . . .	850	.070	1.78

spread is required at close ranges such as 10 yards. Other cartridges may be loaded with dispersante-type wadding, which when fired through tightly choked barrels will produce a wider pattern spread than achieved with normally loaded and wadded cartridges.

See also: **Steel Shot**

Shotgun Cartridge Design   Modern shotgun cartridge cases are made to two basic designs. The parallel tube case is one where the plastic or paper-tube is fitted to the base wad and this assembly is then fitted into the metal head. The case therefore is a three-piece construction. The base wad is made of fire-retardant paper or fibre and is cup-shaped so that the tube is sandwiched between the wad and the metal head. This design has been used ever since breech-loading cartridges were first made, and when the 'waterproof' cartridge first appeared in the 1950s the older varnished paper tube was simply replaced by a plastic one.

More recently the compression-formed cartridge was introduced. This is basically a one-piece plastic moulding which does away with the need for a base wad. Some cartridges even dispensed with a metal head, but due to extraction difficulties these have fallen out of favour with the users of pump-action and self-loading shotguns. Most compression-formed cartridges are therefore fitted with a metal head. Compression-formed cases have the advantage that they tend to allow the powder to burn more efficiently so that standard ballistics are obtainable using a smaller powder charge.

Both types are used in the manufacture of sporting shotgun ammunition and both have proved to be equally reliable.

Shot String   When the shot load is fired from a shotgun it will spread in two directions. The pattern is produced by the outwards spread of the pellets, and the shot string is the 'long' spread. Inevitably due to the pressure engendered when the cartridge is fired there will be a deformation of some shot pellets. These deformed pellets slow down more quickly and the charge of shot will string out in flight. The length of the shot string will vary from one cartridge to another but at 40 yards the string may exceed six feet even if the pattern spread may be no wider than a 40-inch circle.

A shot string of a reasonable length can be quite useful in increasing the effectiveness of the shot pattern. With some distance between the leading and trailing shot a bird flying into the pattern will be raked by the pellets, with the majority of strikes on the head and chest. This results in an instant and clean kill. Therefore those sportsmen who hold far enough forward when shooting live quarry, to allow the shot pattern to impact on the front end of the bird, will achieve cleaner kills due to the bird flying into the shot charge.

Shoveller   The shoveller (*Anas elypeata*) should not be confused with any other species. It is a medium-sized duck weighing about 1¾ lbs and measuring about 20 inches in length. The very obvious characteristic which instantly sets it apart from the other species is its enormous spoon-shaped beak, from which it gets its name. Even at a distance this feature is easy to pick out, particularly in silhouette. Its bill apart, the drake is a handsome bird. The deep bottle-green of the head gives way to a white neck and breast, which are also conspicuous in flight. The underparts are a rich rufous brown which gives way to white under the tail. The back is dark grey-black with white flashes at the base of each wing. The speculum in both sexes is a dark bottle-green edged in black on the trailing edge. On the drake, however, the speculum is preceded on the forewing by bright blue shoulder-patches.

Apart from its beak shape, the duck shoveller resembles a small female mallard in its brown and buff mottled plumage, and the underwing of both sexes is white. They are usually silent birds, but at close range the drake has a low double-note clucking sound and the female utters an abrupt quack.

The breeding population of this species in Britain is concentrated on the freshwater and brackish marshes of Eastern England. The low summer population is widespread in these environments and autumn sees the nesting birds migrating southwards to the Mediterranean. The winter population is made up of migrants from Iceland and Northern Scandinavia, some of which overwinter in

Britain, but the majority pass through on their way southwards. The main body of these migrants arrive in November and the main drift northwards occurs in late March.

The spatulate bill gives the bird a distinctive profile when swimming. The down-pointed head and large bill make the bird appear to swim 'bows down', and it feeds in the water margins by sifting plant and invertebrate food through its specialized filters. This method of feeding restricts the species to shallow-water environments, and it appears on many freshwater lakes and marshes as frequently as it does on the saltings. Unlike the other dabbling ducks it is predominantly a daytime feeder, moving about its habitat in pairs or small groups at any time of the day.

The flight of the shoveller is fast and direct, its rapid wing-beats producing a loud whistle, and the size of the beak and head makes the wings appear to be set well back on the body.

The shoveller cannot really be mistaken for any other species either in flight or at rest. At a distance their flock pattern in flight resembles the loose groupings of a teal flock, but even at long range the white breast of the drake and their heavy bills can be identifying features.

Often considered to be the least palatable of the duck quarry species, a carefully prepared shoveller makes very good eating.

See also: **Inland Waterfowl Shooting; Shore Shooting**

Side-By-Side A 'side-by-side' is the term given to any double-barrelled weapon in which the barrels are arranged alongside each other. Both shotguns and rifles are built to this design, and the side-by-side shotgun is commonly regarded as the 'traditional' English game gun. Side-by-side rifles tend to be built in the calibres where close-range shooting and great stopping power is the norm. Regulating both barrels so that the bullets fired from either barrel will hit the same mark is a very difficult process, and as a consequence side-by-side rifles tend to be very expensive.

See also: **Double Barrel**

Sidelock The term 'sidelock' is used to describe a double- or single-barrelled weapon of the 'drop-down' type on which the locks are mounted on the side of the action on the inside of the lock plate. It is usually possible to remove either one or both of these sidelock plates complete with their lock mechanism by the removal of one or two screw pins. Sidelock actions fall into two types depending on the location of the mainspring within the lock mechanism. The older 'back-action' sidelock, in which the spring is mounted behind the tumbler, has now been largely superseded by the 'bar-action' sidelock where the spring is located in the bar of the action in front of the tumbler.

See also: **Lock**

Sights – Rifle Rifle sights fall into three main categories. Open or 'iron' sights use a blade or bead foresight located at the muzzle of the rifle and a 'U' or 'V' notch rear sight which is mounted about halfway down the barrel. To aim the weapon the foresight is aligned in the notch of the rear sight and both are aligned with the target. Using open sights involves focusing the eye on these three separate objects in order to achieve a correct aim.

The aperture sighting system also uses a foresight but in this case the eye peeps through a very small hole of the rear sight which is mounted at the rear of the breech. In this case the eye needs to focus on two objects only, the foresight and the target, in order to achieve the correct aim.

Nowadays telescopic sights are by far the most popular choice of sighting system. The telescope is mounted at the rear of the weapon and the target is viewed through it. Within the sight there is an engraved reticule which the shooter places on the image of the target. In this way the eye is only focusing at one distance as both reticule and target appear at the same distance. Not only does this simplify the aiming process but the magnification of the telescope allows for more accurate bullet placement.

See also: **Aperture Sights; Bead/Blade; Foresight; Telescopic sight; Zero**

A trophy-quality sika stag shot in the New Forest

Sika Deer   The sika deer (*Cervus nippon*) is the third largest deer living in Britain. Although several sub-species exist, it is the Japanese sika which forms the bulk of the feral populations scattered about the country. The first sika was brought to this country in the mid-nineteenth century and many parks were stocked from the initial breeding herd at Powerscourt in Ireland.

The sika stag stands about 33 inches at the shoulder so it is somewhat shorter than a fallow. At the same time, however, both have a similar body length, and this gives the sika a stocky build. There is a greater difference between sika stags and hinds in terms of body weight than between the sexes of other species. Stags weigh between 150 and 200 lbs but sika hinds rarely reach 100 lbs live weight. Despite these differences, sika are perhaps the most frequently mis-identified of all our deer species. Their appearance in certain lighting conditions leads to sika being taken for either red deer or fallow, and to add to the confusion there are places in the country in which well-documented hybridization between sika and red have occurred.

The summer coat of a sika is a rich chestnut brown which is well covered with white spots, an obvious source of confusion with fallow. There are, however, distinctive features which help to differentiate between the two. Although white sika do occur, there is little variation in the colour of a normal group of this species. In groups of wild fallow several colour phases are usually evident. In addition, the tail of a sika is noticeably shorter than a fallow and is often completely white or white with a vestigial black line; the rump or caudal patch of sika is much more prominent than on a fallow deer. In the case of the sika it is larger, pure white and clearly bordered by black. The patch is enlarged still further if the deer is alarmed, which increases the prominence of the feature. The sika's face is quite distinctive. A 'U'-shaped crescent of light-coloured hair starts above the nose and extends to each eyebrow, giving the sika a permanently worried or annoyed frown, and the ears are smaller and more rounded than in other similar-sized deer.

The body colour of a sika can make it easily distinguishable from a fallow in that the underparts of a sika are not noticeably lighter than the flanks, and in the case of sika stags they are very much darker. Finally, the sika has a prominent white patch just below the hock joint on each rear leg.

All these features would serve to distinguish sika from fallow at any time of the year, but some additional difficulty may be caused by the colour change in the growth of the winter coat. In late September the rut will have begun and stags and hinds take on different colours. The stag's coat darkens considerably and the summer spotting disappears except for occasional relic spots along the backbone. Mature male sika grow a mane which, though not as long as that of a native red stag, is still a prominent feature. At this time of year a sika stag will appear to be almost all black apart from the features described above, and therefore is really unmistakable.

Hinds, on the other hand, change their chestnut and spotted summer coat for one of uniform grey-brown for the winter. Like the stags they are practically unspotted in their winter pelage, although some relic spots may still be visible along the spine. In their winter coat it may be very difficult, in some lighting conditions, to distinguish sika hinds from dark fallow does, yet the sika's white rump patch, the hock patch, small ears and facial frown can still be used as indicators to separate the two species.

The antlers of a sika are often confused with those of the red deer. Male sika calves grow their skull pedicles during their first winter and on these the first antlers will begin to develop by the time the animal is one year old. The first head consists of two spikes varying in length from two to ten inches, and very occasionally a good specimen will grow two points at the end of each spike. Under normal conditions, however, a pricket has unbranched spikes. By the third year this is replaced by six-point antlers, each side showing brow, trez, and top points; and it seems that six-point heads may be grown for two or three successive years until full maturity is reached and the stag grows an eight-point head.

Sika antlers are round in cross-section and generally form a steep-sided 'V' shape compared with the wide 'splay' of a red stag. The antlers of the smaller sika can at times, however, resemble a rather poor immature red deer's set of headgear, but the body shape, colour and other identifying features should aid a positive identification. Very occasionally a good specimen of a sika stag will produce a head of ten points. As in the other larger deer, the antlers are cast in April and the new set are cleaned of velvet by the end of August.

Sika deer cannot be readily distinguished by their gait. Their relatively short legs and stocky body give the impression of a heavy bounding gallop when the animal is moving at speed, but there is no really characteristic way of moving as found in some of the other species. Sika are agile and powerful. When alarmed their movements become concerted and unpredictable, with little of the doubt and indecision displayed by fallow.

It is only during the rut that sika stags justify the claim that they are the most vocal of all the deer species in Britain. Older stags begin to mark out their rutting stands during August, and much fraying serves the dual purposes of cleaning the antlers of velvet and marking out the stag's territory. In September and October the sika stag will hope to entice females onto his patch by calling, the main call being a most un-deer-like loud and piercing whistle repeated about three times and ending in a deep grunt. Here the sika resembles fallow in that he entices the females to him rather than gathering and defending a harem. In conflict with other stags it is his territory and rutting stand he will defend, rather than the hinds he has attracted, but a master stag may also attract and tolerate a number of younger males. Apart from the rutting whistle the sika stag will communicate with others through a wide range of barks, grunts, groans, bleats and lip blowing. For sheer variety of sounds the sika stag far surpasses other deer, yet none of these sounds have yet been interpreted with any certainty.

During the rut sika are violent and determined fighters, and a significant number of stags may be seen carrying broken antlers by the end of the season.

Sika calves are born in June and like other deer are heavily spotted at birth. Within eight weeks, however, the first winter coat has obscured the spotting and the youngsters will retain this dull grey pelage until the follow-

ing spring moult. Sika families tend to break up earlier than other species, with hinds chasing the female offspring of the previous year away in April. On a number of occasions stags have been observed to round up and separate yearling males from the hind herds before leading them off to join the 'bachelor' herd. This behaviour may also help to explain the master stag's tolerance of younger males on his rutting territory.

There is much about sika deer that we are still unable to explain with any certainty, and much confusion arises from the ability or readiness of the sub-species to interbreed with red deer. Sika deer come from the eastern seaboard and island arc of Asia. They are closely related to red deer despite the obvious physical differences, and hybrids of the two species are fertile. What cannot be explained with any certainty is why the two species should interbreed freely in some areas while remaining true to species in others. In many deer parks, in the Bowland area of Lancashire, in the southern Lake District and in the New Forest red and sika share the same territory. In most cases

Populations of sika in Scotland and northern England are spreading

The eyebrow marking on a sika gives its face a permanent 'frown'

each species lead separate lives yet in some areas hybrids are common. There are two possible explanations for this.

When sika were first introduced into Britain, two distinct races were imported: the Japanese sika (described above) and the larger Manchurian sika (*Cervus nippon mantchurius*). As the various park escapees or deliberate releases established themselves in the wild it seemed that the Manchurian sika would hybridize with red and the Japanese sika would not. This has led to the theory that the Manchurian sika as imported into this country was already a cross-bred animal, produced perhaps centuries earlier for a Chinese emperor's hunting. With an element of red deer already in its genes, Manchurian sika would naturally be more

likely to breed with red deer. Another theory is that cross-breeding, either by accident or by design, occurred at Powerscourt and Colebrook Parks in Ireland in the 1880s, and it is from these parks that many of the English deer parks subsequently received their sika. It is perhaps significant that deer originating from these sources display some traits of red deer behaviour in that stags at rut will gather a harem of hinds and the family groups among the hinds and offspring break up much later than in true Japanese sika herds.

It can therefore be seen that there is a great deal still to learn about this species, and even a description of its distribution in Great Britain cannot be as accurate as with other deer. Of all the deer species in Britain the sika is the most nocturnal and secretive. Throughout their existence in this country there have been numerous escapes from parks but in the majority of cases breeding in the wild has not been successful and the deer have died out. This is perhaps due to the fact that sika are more selective in terms of their ideal habitat, preferring damp and acidic woodland of coniferous or mixed type. They prefer dense cover, so new plantations often do not attract this species. At present the main population centres, where sika are thriving, are the southern New Forest, the Poole basin in south-east Dorset, the Bowland area of Lancashire and the Lune valley on the Lancs-Cumbria border. In the last area and in the south-eastern part of the Lake District there has been extensive hybridization with red deer so that few, if any, true sika remain.

In Scotland the species has extended its range through much of the Southern Uplands and border country, reaching down to the Kielder Forest to the south and to Galloway in the west. Further north, Kintyre has long held a population of sika and these are now extending their range in what is also red deer country. Curiously, only recently have there been reports of hybridization occurring. The other population centre in Scotland lies from central Sutherland to Loch Ness, and here again sika are on the increase. The re-afforestation of the Highlands with dense conifer plantations on acid soil seems to have provided an ideal habitat for this deer.

In the south of England the population in the Poole basin occurs on the low-lying and acidic marshes and conifer belts, and though they are now experiencing population pressure the sika seem disinclined to move out of the basin onto the chalk hills and deciduous woods further north. Other pockets exist in north Dorset, Kent and Essex, but their existence seems precarious. Nevertheless, where conditions suit this deer they will thrive to build up substantial populations, and wild sika deer are now a permanent addition to the British fauna.

See also: **Red Deer**

Sitty Tree

See: **Pigeon Shooting**

Sleeving   There are occasions when shotgun barrels may need replacing. This may arise through neglect, when the internal bores become deeply pitted by rust, or when the barrels receive a severe knock to the extent that the dents cannot be safely raised. In a single barrel shotgun it is usually a simple matter to fit a replacement barrel, and these are normally readily available. In a double barrel weapon the matter is more complicated. The shooter has a choice of two options. Either he can have the gun rebarrelled, or the existing barrels can be sleeved.

In good-quality double shotguns the former is preferable, and in the best-quality guns this should be carried out by the original gunmaker if possible. Rebarrelling a gun will not detract from its value and in some cases may even enhance it. Unfortunately, though, the process of fitting a new set of barrels to an existing weapon is very expensive and it is only when considering best-quality guns that the cost can be justified.

In many of the more moderately-priced shotguns the cost of fitting new barrels may well be more than the actual value of the gun, and this is where the shooter may choose to have the existing barrels sleeved. In terms of resale value a gun with sleeved barrels will command a lower price than one with original or new barrels, but this may be offset by the fact that perhaps an old and cherished gun can be made safe to use. In terms of safety, the sleeved barrels will have to undergo the same stringent proof tests as new barrels so the shooter may use a gun with sleeved barrels with the utmost confidence.

Basically, the process of sleeving involves cutting off and discarding the damaged barrels about 4 inches from the breech face. The remaining breech section, which includes the extractor mechanism and the barrel mounting lumps, is then reamed out to accept two new tubes. After these are fitted, the ribs, on each side in the case of an over-and-under, or the top and bottom rib in the case of a side-by-side, are silver-soldered onto the new barrels and married up to the existing top rib on the original breech section. At the appropriate stages the new assembly is proofed, bored to the desired choke and finished off. Unless the gun is

A gunsmith at work

*Walked-up snipe will test the skill of any
shotgun shooter*

sleeved by the original maker, the old top rib carrying the maker's name cannot be re-used and the barrels must carry information indicating that they are sleeved barrels. The flats of the barrels, carrying the original proof marks, are also stamped with new marks indicating the fact that the barrels are sleeved and must also carry the word 'sleeved'.

By this process many a moderately-priced and unsafe shotgun has received a new lease of life. In addition, the handling characteristics of any gun can be more easily matched to the individual shooter. A long-barrelled gun can have sleeved barrels of 25 or 26 inches to suit a short person, or the sleeved barrels may be made longer than the origi-

nal according to individual preference. When barrels are sleeved the customer also has the choice of top rib styles, be it narrow file-cut, concave or raised, according to preference, and it can be seen that the gun can easily be tailored to the individual. One limitation, however, is that it is more difficult and expensive to have the chamber altered and proofed for cartridges of a different length. As the breech ends of the original barrels are used, the sleeved barrels should only accommodate cartridges of the same specification as the original barrels. It would therefore be impracticable to re-proof a set of sleeved barrels for 3-inch magnum cartridges if the original barrels were chambered for standard game cartridges of 2¹/₂ inches.

The economics of sleeving: If a gun is in good condition (with the exception of damaged or rusted barrels), with lumps, joints, and lockwork in a sound, unworn condition, it will usually prove sound economics to sleeve such a gun. However, if the locks are well worn, the joint off the face, the lumps and their slots loose and worn, the action of sleeving is similar to replacing the cylinder block and pistons of a motor car engine whilst leaving the crankshaft, main bearings, etc. in a badly worn condition; in other words, the job is only being half done and will usually prove uneconomic. Any good gunsmith has the knowledge and will advise as to the best course.

Snipe   To many shooters, the snipe (*Gallinago gallinago*) is the ultimate test of skilful sporting shooting. It is a small brown wading bird with a distinctive long and straight bill. At close quarters the plumage is quite strikingly marked in various shades of brown and black. The upper parts have long yellow-buff stripes on the head and back with dark brown eyebrow and eye stripes. The underparts are paler but still barred with brown, except for the belly which is a grey-white. The upper surfaces of the tail feathers are strongly marked black and rufous red and the bird weighs a mere four ounces for its 10-inch overall length.

The snipe is a bird of the wetlands. In the spring its breeding habitat includes waterlogged moorland, wet lowland meadows and marshes. In the winter it frequents both fresh- and salt-water marshes, but it is predominantly a lowland species. By the end of September the arrival of overwintering birds and passage migrants from northern Europe and Iceland swells the numbers on any suitable marshland. Although large numbers may gather on one area of marshland, the snipe is not a 'flocking' bird and where groups are seen flying together (called a wisp of snipe) it is usually because a number of birds have been flushed simultaneously. It is generally a shy and retiring bird, resting during the day in thick cover and moving to its feeding grounds at dusk, but bad weather may alter these habits and indeed an inland freeze will move most of the population to coastal locations.

When disturbed a snipe will make its characteristic alarm note, which is short and grating – a good imitation can be made by striking the edges of two ten-pence coins together – and fly away from the disturbance in a low, fast, zig-zag escape. It feeds by probing soft mud with its long bill for molluscs and invertebrates, which form the greater proportion of its diet.

Snipe are shot by walking-up, driving and flighting. On one small marsh known to me the birds are walked up in the afternoon and the guns then return in the evening for the 'snipe flight'. This is very testing shooting as the snipe fly high and fast, dropping very steeply to alight again on their feeding grounds. The opportunity for a shot is often restricted to late evening twilight and it is at these steeply diving birds that I have experienced some of the most difficult shooting of all.

The snipe can be confused with the much smaller jacksnipe, which is a protected species. However, the larger bird is much more vocal and a much stronger flier. Once its alarm call is heard, identification is easy.

The snipe shooting season extends from 12 August to 31 January.

Soft Point   A 'soft-point' bullet is one which is designed specifically to deform and break up quickly on impact. To achieve this the hard gilding metal which is used to jacket the bullet lead is thinned progressively towards the point and the lead core is often exposed at the tip. This progressive thinning of the jacket towards the front produces a bullet with a 'delicate' nose. It is this front section which actually breaks up rapidly to cause the maximum of damage to the internal organs of a rifle shooter's quarry, which, if the bullet is placed correctly, produces an instantaneous and humane kill.

Soft-point bullets are designed for use against 'soft-skinned' animals and good penetration is achieved by the reinforced rear section of the projectile while the front section is disrupted.

See also: **Bullet**

Spitzer This term is used to denote a pointed or semi-pointed bullet. The aerodynamic shape of this type of projectile gives it good long-range accuracy and a predictable trajectory. On the other hand, it is far more prone to deflection by light obstacles such as a thistle stem or twig than a round-nosed bullet. Consequently, when shooting in heavy undergrowth, many European or American hunters would opt for a slower round-nosed cartridge rather than a high-velocity Spitzer.

In Britain, however, the vast majority of deer stalkers and centrefire fox shooters would opt for a Spitzer bullet for its greater accuracy and better down-range energy retention.

See also: **Bullet**

Sportsman's Library Published by A. & C. Black, the series of books making up the Sportsman's Library extended to about thirty volumes covering both field sports and competitive athletic sports. The series first appeared in the 1930s and the last reprints were distributed in the early 1950s. Compared to the other books published in Library form, the Sportsman's Library were smaller and more specialized in their subject matter. Thus game shooting was subdivided by publishing one volume for each game bird species in addition to more generalized titles on the various methods of sporting shooting.

All books were published in the same 7½×5 inch 'handbook' format and among the thirty or so titles were no less than thirteen of interest to the sporting shooter.

Vol. 4 **Gun Dogs and their Training**
H. Atwood Clark

5 **Making a Shoot**
Maj. Gen. Sir John Goodwin

8 **Big Game in Africa**
Maj. H.C. Maydon

9 **Deerstalking**
Patrick Chalmers

11 **Rough Shooting**
Yeates & Winnall

13 **Woodcock & Snipe**
Seigne & Keith

17 **Partridge Shooting**
Capt. J.B. Drought

18 **Pheasant Shooting**
Leslie Sprake

20 **The Shot Gun**
Purdey & Purdey

21 **Field Sports in Scotland**
Patrick Chalmers

22 **Wildfowling**
C.T. Dalgety

23 **Big Game of India**
Maj. H.C. Maydon

27 **Grouse Shooting**
Martin Stephens

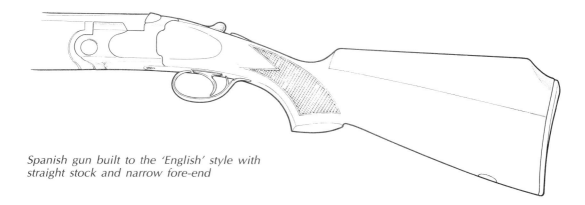

Spanish gun built to the 'English' style with straight stock and narrow fore-end

Written by recognized authorities in their own time, the series still has much which is relevant even half a century later. To the collector and reader of sporting books it also provides a fascinating insight into the way in which field sports were conducted in the years immediately preceding World War Two.

Stand

See: **Driven Game Shooting; Gamekeeping**

Steel Shot   In the past two decades research in North America pointed to the ingestion of lead shot as a cause of wildfowl mortality in many popular duck hunting environments. The lead shot that has been used by many generations of waterfowl shooters has scattered over the environment where it often lies in the first few inches of the soil or water margins of mudbanks. Here dabbling ducks are prone to ingest the lead during their feeding and this causes slow lead poisoning once inside the bird's digestive system. As a result of this research the use of lead shot was banned and many American cartridge manufacturers now use soft iron shot as a substitute.

In Britain the substitution of lead by iron shot (mistakenly called 'steel shot') is causing much controversy and many shooters are very concerned about the effect of using steel shot in finely tuned 'best' gun barrels. The barrels of these best British guns have for more than a century been designed and produced with barrel wall thicknesses to suit lead shot. To shoot steel shot through such best gun barrels will almost certainly result in such barrels being ruined and the choke constrictions lifted.

See also: **Shot**

A 'varmint'-style centrefire rifle uses a full pistol grip and Monte Carlo stock

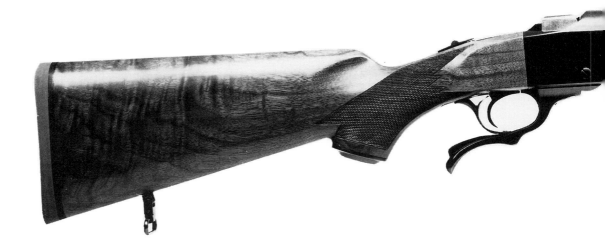

Stock   The stock is a piece of wood which makes the difference between a hand gun and a shoulder gun. It is the means whereby the weapon is mounted against the shoulder and on which the cheek rests while the shooter aligns the weapon with the target.

Ideally, the stock of any weapon should be tailored to fit the physique of the shooter and a person will usually shoot better and more consistently with a 'fitted gun' than with one which is 'off the shelf'.

Over the years a number of different styles of stock have evolved so that now there are clearly identifiable shapes which go with certain forms of sporting shooting.

In shotgun sports the traditional game or rough shooting side-by-side is fitted with a 'straight-hand' stock. Perhaps the lack of any pistol grip makes it easier to alter the grips of the hand slightly when the trigger finger moves from the front to the back trigger and this was the reason for the evolution of this stock shape. Nevertheless, many single-trigger game guns in both side-by-side and over-and-under configuration are still equipped with this straight stock.

Pistol-grip stocks, favoured by over-and-under users, are those which feature a grip reminiscent of the wooden grips of muzzle-loading pistols. The degree of curvature from the trigger guard gives the 'half pistol' or

'full pistol' grip, and the comfort these provide for the shooter depends to some extent on the size of the shooter's hand. A large-handed person would probably find a half pistol or even a straight-handed stock more comfortable than a full pistol grip. The 'Prince of Wales' stock is a variation on the pistol-grip idea, but the curve of the 'pistol grip' is extended further down the stock towards the butt end.

Swan-necked stocks are an elegant compromise between the straight and the pistol-grip stock in that the grip is curved as in a 'half pistol' but does not end in a grip cap but rather sweeps away towards the butt in one elegant curved line.

In order to shoot accurately the eye must be able to sight along the top of the barrel or barrels. To allow this the comb of the stock drops from the line of the barrels so that the shooter's cheek can rest on the stock in the normal shooting position. There are occasions when the shooter needs to be above the barrel sighting line, for instance when shooting at constantly rising birds in down-the-line clay pigeon shooting, or when using a telescopic sight on a rifle. For this purpose the shooter's eye may be raised to the correct level by using a 'Monte Carlo' stock. This stock has a parallel comb for 6–8 inches first used at Monte Carlo by

The Ruger No 1 International, a Stutzen-style rifle

pigeon shooters. The pigeons were normally shot on the rise, therefore the higher parallel Monte Carlo comb allowed the shooter to look slightly over and down the top rib, providing a better perspective and allowing the shooter to seemingly 'sit' the flying pigeon on top of the front sight as he fired. This meant he could see the result of the first shot more quickly and fire a quicker second shot than when shooting a gun with a lower comb, which required the bird to be 'blotted out' by the barrels at the moment of firing. Thus fitting a parallel comb on a gun correctly positions the shooter's eye in relation to the rib/front sight. The majority of rifles intended for use with a 'scope sight are built with a Monte Carlo stock.

The two rifle stock styles that have evolved can be termed 'classic' and 'American'! The classic stock of a British hunting rifle has a straight comb and full pistol grip, the woodwork is oil-finished and the pistol grip is often embellished with a discreet rosewood cap. The 'American' style of rifle has a Monte Carlo comb-piece, a full pistol grip and recoil pad, and the grip cap and pad are outlined by white spacers. In addition, the stock is often finished with skip-line chequering and a high gloss varnish.

Choice of stock style is, like so many other aspects of shooting sport, largely a matter of personal preference.

As long as the gun mounts easily and fits comfortably in the shooter's shoulder when mounted correctly, so that the gun points and shoots where the owner looks, and the shooter does not suffer from facial abuse when the gun is fired, stock design is immaterial. Some traditionalists hold that a Monte-Carlo-shaped stock looks out of place on a side-by-side game gun, just as a straight-hand stock would not seem right on a pump-action rifle. Even so, owners with guns stocked and fitted correctly should find such guns both a joy to own and very comfortable to shoot effectively.

Stop On a driven game shoot, a stop is in effect a 'static' beater. Before the commencement of a drive, the keeper may place stops at the points where hedges and ditches run into the ground that is to be covered by the beaters. By standing and quietly tapping his stick against a tree trunk or fence post the stop will effectively deter any game from running out of the side of the ground along these hedge or ditch 'escape routes'.

On more open ground, for example on grouse moors, the 'flagmen' fulfil the same function as a covert stop. By waving a flag at the right moment a flagman can make an airborne covey change course towards the guns rather than escaping out to the side of the line of beaters. Unlike stops, flagmen move in line with and some distance ahead of the end of the line of beaters.

Beaters working to the side and ahead of the main beating line are known as 'flankers' and, like stops and flagmen, serve to direct any game likely to break out sideways so that they fly over the guns.

See also: **Beater**

Strikers – Disc-Set   In many double barrel weapons the firing pins or strikers are tucked away within the action behind the standing breech. If a striker pin is worn or cracked replacing it is a job that involve stripping the action in order to gain access to the faulty part.

If, on the other hand, the strikers are set into the standing breech in screw-in discs, they can easily be removed for service or replacement. These are known as disc-set strikers, and they do make for easier maintenance of a double-barrelled weapon.

See also: **Firing Pin**

Stutzen   The Stutzen style of modern sporting rifle is one which evolved in continental Europe. In many German-speaking areas of the continent deer stalking and other rifle sports take place in dense woodland. Visibility is usually limited and most shots are taken at ranges below 100 yards. In addition, shots often have to be taken quickly, so the demand arose for a quick-pointing weapon. Reducing the overall length of the rifle was seen as an advantage as it increased the pointability of the weapon while at the same time reducing the risk of getting the barrel entangled in undergrowth. Under the conditions where shooting took place in dense cover, it was felt that the stock should

be extended to the full length of the shortened barrel in order to protect the barrel from knocks. The rifle which evolved is therefore 'full-stocked' and has a shortened barrel; the average length is around 18 inches. Mannlicher were among the first manufacturers to produce these full-stocked 'Stutzen' rifles and as a consequence the name has stuck. Modern Stutzens are also sometimes called 'Mannlicher-style' rifles.

The advantages of this design when shooting in close cover are such that it has become a popular choice among continental shooters, and its popularity in Britain is also increasing. There are, however, some disadvantages. The short barrel certainly increases 'muzzle blast' in some of today's calibres; and the high-frequency noise may cause some shooters increased discomfort, and in extreme cases causes 'gun flinch'. In addition, the short barrel also reduces the velocity of the bullet to quite a significant degree. While this is not an important factor in woodland stalking, where ranges are restricted, at the extended ranges of up to 200 yards that are sometimes required when deer stalking on open ground the trajectory of a bullet from a Stutzen is not as long as one from a standard rifle with a barrel length of 22 to 24 inches.

One sometimes sees Stutzen rifles chambered for magnum calibres, but the advantages of increased power and velocity from a magnum cartridge are virtually cancelled by firing it from a short barrel.

However, for woodland stalking the full-stocked Stutzen rifle is deservedly popular and the style has been adopted by many rifle manufacturers. As well as being produced by such makers as Mannlicher, Anschütz and Heym on the continent, Stutzen rifles are also made by Ruger and Interarms in the USA and until recently by BSA in Britain.

Teal The teal (*Anas crecca*) is Britain's smallest duck. Weighing up to 13 oz and measuring only 14 inches from beak to tail, the drake gives the impression of being an overall grey colour. Closer observation will distinguish a chestnut head with a broad bottle-green 'eye patch' extending from in front of the eye to the nape. This eye patch is separated from the chestnut by a pale yellow-buff line. The dark cream chest is spotted with dark brown or black and the underparts are a creamy white. The undertail feathers of the drake are yellowish bordered with black. The speculum of both sexes is a bright green and black and is bordered with a white line, and the base of the wing is striped black and white. The female is a dull mottled brown except for the speculum and the white underbelly. As with other dabbling ducks the drake goes into an eclipse plumage in the summer months when it more closely resembles the duck's colouring.

Teal are generally rather quiet birds but the drake has a low creaking whistle often repeated twice and the duck has a short and harsh quack, the call most often heard when a group of teal are flushed.

The breeding population of teal in Britain is quite large and they may be found in most parts of the country where the favoured nesting habitat of rushy and wet moorland exists. For feeding they require areas of shallow muddy water, which they sift for both vegetable and invertebrate food, and in winter they may be found on both freshwater and coastal marshes. There is, however, a general movement to the coastal marshes in autumn where numbers are greatly increased by a large influx of migrants from the Low Countries and the Baltic. These, and others from Iceland and Russia, begin arriving in October and the main return migration takes place in early April.

Because of their airborne agility, teal are my favourite duck. When disturbed they take off almost vertically and their incredible rate of climb has added the 'springing teal' to sporting clay pigeon competitions. When alarmed they really do seem to 'stand on their tail' and rocket skywards! When in level flight they behave more like waders than other duck, with much bobbing and weaving and rapid changes of direction. A flock of teal also resembles waders in that they fly in loose groups rather than in echelons and their flight is characterized by very rapid wingbeats.

Teal are gregarious by nature and they are often found feeding in small flocks, although they seldom congregate like wigeon into big packs. They are lovers of small creeks and water flashes, and parties of teal may be dispersed all over an estuary or salt marsh. On a marsh intersected by many creeks and channels, one of my favourite low-tide occupations is 'creek crawling' and 'teal jumping'. As a predominantly nocturnal feeder teal also take part in the morning and evening flights, but they seldom flight far inland from the coast, preferring to drop into some attractive muddy ditch or dyke near the marsh.

Because of their diminutive size and manner of flight teal can readily be identi-

Nowadays the sporting rifle seems incomplete without a telescopic sight. This example is a .22 LR fitted with a 4×30 'scope

fied, although in late summer they may be confused with the other small but protected duck, the garganey.

See also: **Inland Waterfowl Shooting**

Telescopic Sight   A telescopic sight is basically a small telescope which is designed to include within its construction a sighting device or reticule so that when mounted on a rifle it can be used for aiming the weapon.

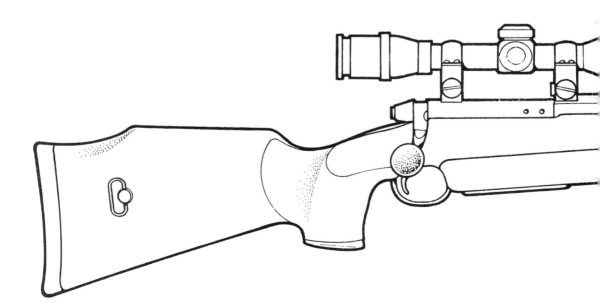

So great are its advantages over aperture sights and open sights that nowadays practically all sporting rifle users opt for a telescopic sighting system. It was not always the case. Before the Second World War telescopic sights were expensive or unreliable, but since the early 1950s there have been great advances in optical science and these have brought very reliable and inexpensive telescopic sights from American, Japanese, and European manufacturers.

The general acceptance and adoption of telescopic sights has led to some confusion in the terminology used in describing the specification of the sight. Telescopic sights are described by their degree of magnification and the diameter of the front lens, the objective. Thus a 6×42 sight has a magnification of 6 and a front lens diameter of 42 mm. In addition, these figures give an indication of the sight's performance in the poor light of dawn and dusk. This 'twilight factor' is calculated by dividing the objective diameter by the magnification, so 6×42 gives a twilight factor of 7. This means that the light passing through the 'scope comes to a focus in a circular area which is 7 mm across and this is also known as the exit pupil. In poor light the pupil of a human eye dilates to about 7 mm so a scope with a 7 mm exit pupil transmits as much light as the human eye can accept and is therefore an efficient device for use in poor light. By way of contrast a 6×30 'scope produces a 5 mm exit pupil so its twilight performance is not as good. By far the most popular choice of 'scope is the 4×40 which, although its exit pupil is greater than the eye can handle, is still a good performer in early morning or late evening. Zoom 'scopes are gaining in popularity as they have greater versatility than the fixed-power models. When stalking in thick woodland the sight can be set on low magnification for quick shooting but when in open country the power can be increased for deliberately aimed long-range shots.

When using a 'scope sight on a centrefire rifle the eye relief may become important. This term indicates how far behind the 'scope the eye must be to see the whole sight picture. In a heavy recoiling rifle a 'scope with too short an eye relief distance will result in the shooter's eyebrow being bruised and cut by the backward movement of the 'scope each time the rifle is fired.

Telescopic sights work well in lighting conditions which render other sighting devices unusable, they offer a picture of the sight and the target without the need for the eye to change focus, and the degree of magnification allows for much more precise

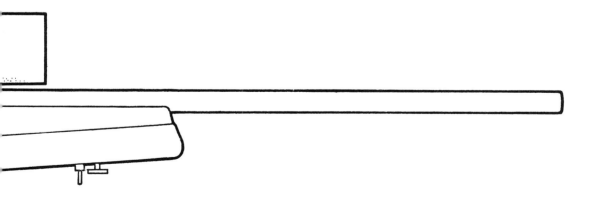

Though really a competition rifle, the Tikka M65 Sporter is often used as a hunting weapon

aiming than is possible otherwise. It is therefore hardly suprising that the telescopic sight is the first choice among air rifle and rimfire vermin shooters, and both woodland and highland deer stalkers.

Tikka Oy Tikkakoski Ab is a company founded in 1893 in Finland which in 1918 began manufacturing firearms for military purposes. Its expertise is reflected in the weapons sold under the Tikka brand name today. Concentrating on the manufacture of medium-priced weapons, Tikka produce two models of bolt-action sporting rifles together with a shotgun/rifle combination and one model of shotgun.

Unlike other gunmaking firms Tikka have designed their own bolt action for both their sporting and target rifles, and it is these weapons that have earned the good reputation this company enjoys. The two models of sporting rifle, the M55 and M65, are basically similar bolt-action magazine repeaters but the M55 has a short-stroke bolt for the short cartridge calibres and the M65 a long action. Each model is available in three grades. The 'standard' and 'deluxe' use different-quality timber in the stock with the latter bearing more embellishment. The 'Continental' model is the heavy-barrelled 'varmint' version of the rifle and is supplied without any form of open sights.

The long-actioned M65 is also produced in a short-barrelled model called the 'Wildboar' designed specifically for driven boar shooting on the European continent. It is normally used without telescopic sights as the sport requires very quick shooting at close range and a long-ramp rearsight is a positive aid in this form of driven shooting. The M65 is also available in a 'Sporter' version which is really a semi-target rifle. It is equipped with a heavy barrel and heavy shaped stock which is very comfortable for a right-hander but virtually impossible to use from the other shoulder!

All Tikka rifles are well-made and accurate and may be distinguished by a characteristic large knob on the bolt handle. In Scandinavian winter conditions this is very helpful when working the bolt through thick gloves, and it does demonstrate the thought that goes into their rifle production. For those with a liking for 'minority' calibres, Tikka production rifles are available for such rounds as the .17 Rem and the .25–06.

The Tikka M77K and MO7 are the shotgun/rifle combinations. Built on an over-and-under design, the upper 12-bore shotgun barrel has the rifle barrel slung underneath it. As with the bolt-action rifles these combinations are available in a variety of centre-fire calibres and they are much more widely used on the continent than in the British Isles. This is a reflection of the differences in the types of sporting shooting available in the two areas and also perhaps of British firearms legislation which raises administrative difficulties in the ownership of such a weapon.

The Tikka M77 over-and-under shotgun uses the same action as the combination weapons but has two shotgun barrels of 12 bore. By using the same components these can be interchanged with combination barrels, which gives the continental shooter some degree of latitude in the choice of weapon.

Trajectory The trajectory is the path followed by a bullet or a shot charge from the moment it leaves the barrel until it drops to earth.

In shotgun shooting the trajectory of the shot charge can be dismissed as unimportant. Within the effective range of a shotgun the influence of gravity on the individual pellets in the charge is effectively counterbalanced by the velocity of the charge and the spread of the pattern. Even at 50 yards the drop of the centre of the pattern is not really discernible, and the increasing spread of the shot renders the pattern ineffective well before gravity becomes significant.

In rifle shooting the trajectory assumes far greater importance. Gravity begins acting on a bullet as soon as it leaves the barrel but at the initial high velocity of the projectile the effect is minimal. As air friction slows the bullet down, however, so the effect of gravity's pull becomes more noticeable. The path or trajectory of a bullet can therefore be plotted as a downward curve of increasing gradient. To compensate for this curving trajectory the rifle's sights must be aligned to the point that coincides with the bullet's path at the optimum effective range. This process is known as 'zeroing'. However, not all shots are taken at the zero range and the shooter must be fully aware of how far the bullet will be above or below the line of sight at any shootable distance. If this is known the shooter may then compensate by aiming below or above the target to score a direct hit at the desired point.

Velocity plays an important part in the trajectory of any bullet – the lower the velocity the more quickly the bullet is pulled down by gravity. An air rifle pellet leaving the muzzle at about 600 feet per second will have dropped to the extent that it is beyond accurate range at 50 yards. A 48-grain bullet from a .220 Swift travelling at over 4,100 feet per second will have dropped only a few inches at 300 yards and will be effectively accurate even beyond that range. Generally, therefore, the faster the bullet the flatter the trajectory.

See also: **Zero**

Trigger   The trigger is the thin bar of metal which is connected to the mechanism that fires the gun. Thus squeezing or pulling the trigger activates the firing sequence.

The trigger pull, as this is called, is described in two ways. The weight of pull indicates the amount of force required on the trigger to fire the weapon, and this may vary according to the weapon and type of shooting. Some rifle shooters like a very light pull of about 2 lbs, and indeed a trigger pull of over 8 lbs may be a real hindrance to the accurate shooting of a rifle. If so much force is required to pull the trigger that the trigger hand has to change its grip the rifle will certainly not remain steady.

Shotgun shooting, on the other hand, is a sport in which the gun is swung rapidly to the shoulder and the finger finds the trigger whilst the gun is in motion. In this instance a very light trigger pull can constitute a real danger as the weapon may well be inadvertently fired before the shooter is ready. Shotguns therefore tend to have a trigger set at around 6 lbs to give sufficient safety margin and to allow a 'crisp' response to a

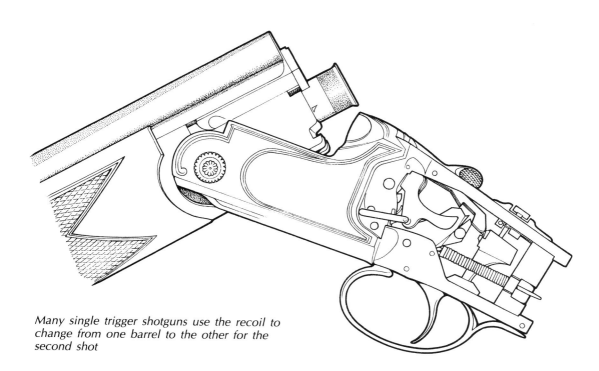

Many single trigger shotguns use the recoil to change from one barrel to the other for the second shot

determined tug on the trigger when the shooter wishes to fire.

The trigger pull is also described according to the movement of the trigger itself. If there is little or no movement of the trigger before its resistance is overcome and the gun is fired – a feeling likened to snapping a glass rod – then it is said to be a 'single-stage' trigger. Most shotguns and many centrefire rifles are fitted with this type of mechanism.

Air rifles and many rimfires are fitted with a 'two-stage' trigger. In this mechanism the trigger is first pulled a short way back against very slight resistance until the finger meets the more definite resistance of the second stage. Overcoming this then fires the rifle.

Trigger mechanisms are made to a very wide variety of styles in order to suit different shooting requirements. Most side-by-side shotguns are fitted with double triggers, one firing each barrel, so that the shooter has instant selection of possibly two choke borings as the gun is mounted to the firing position. However, single trigger mechanisms are more prevalent on over-and-under shotguns. In this type the trigger will fire both barrels in turn, and the gun is usually fitted with a barrel selector which is incorporated in the safety catch. Perhaps the most often used of these single trigger mechanisms is the type which uses the recoil of the first barrel to reset the device to fire the second. Obviously this inertia system will not work if the first cartridge misfires, but nevertheless it is a simple and reliable single trigger mechanism.

Double barrel rifles may, like their shotgun counterparts, be fitted with either single or double triggers. It is the single barrel rifle which shows a further variation on trigger mechanism design. Double trigger mechanisms are often seen on European rifles and these give the rifle shooter some choice in the way the rifle may be fired. For a quick 'snap' shot at an animal in dense cover one trigger may be pulled much in the same way as that of a shotgun. The trigger pull will be heavy but the rifle can be fired quickly. If, on the other hand, the opportunity for a carefully aimed shot presents itself, the shooter settles the rifle into the shoulder and pulls the 'setting' trigger. This changes the trigger pull on the other to a very light 'hair'

trigger: when the aim is settled and steady a slight touch on the hair trigger fires the rifle.

Different rifle manufactures use a variety of designs for this 'set' trigger mechanism – some with two triggers and some with a single trigger which is just pushed forward to 'set' it. In Britain the 'set' trigger has never been as popular as the single-pull trigger of the standard bolt-action stalking rifle.

Trigger Guard   The trigger guard is the roughly semi-circular strip of metal which encircles the trigger in order to protect it from being snagged or accidentally pulled.

In double shotguns the trigger guard is flattened in cross-section so that it presents a broader surface for engraving and some guards are extensively decorated. In rifles and some single barrel shotguns the trigger guard may also incorporate catches or levers that release the weapon's magazine, and they may also incorporate a safety catch to block the movement of the trigger. It must be remembered, though, that the trigger guard cannot possibly offer complete protection against accidental discharge and there are many instances of dogs standing on the trigger of a loaded weapon that has been carelessly laid in the back of a car.

Tufted Duck   The smallest of the diving duck in the British quarry species list, the tufted duck (*Aythya fuligula*) weighs about 1¼ lbs and measures about 17 inches in length. The drake is unmistakable. At rest it appears to be all black except for its white underbelly and flanks, and at close quarters its long drooping crest is obvious. In flight the upper surfaces of the wings appear to have black shoulders and a white wing bar extending from the body towards the wingtip; this impression is produced by the white colouring on the base of the primary and secondary feathers. At close quarters the female may also be identified by her short head 'tuft' and the plumage is really a dark brown copy of the drake, although the feathers around the base of the bill may be white.

The male has a soft and repeated whistling call and the female a rather harsh and rasping 'churr' but neither of these calls is used with any regularity outside the breeding season.

The tufted duck is very much a freshwater species and is usually seen on the coast only when driven there by hard weather. It frequents all manner of freshwater environments and may even be encountered on small rivers. Its preferred habitat, however, consists of reservoirs, large gravel pits, and natural lakes with reed-bed margins. In the winter months it may resort to the more open waters where it will sometimes congregate in substantial numbers. It is the most widespread of all British breeding diving duck and the gravel pit excavations in south-eastern England have readily been colonized by this species. At the moment the breeding population of tufted duck appears to be increasing rapidly and their distribution is being extended westwards and northward. In the winter their numbers are further increased by migrants from Iceland and many other parts of north-west Europe, the main body of arrivals appearing in October and departing in mid-March.

Like all the diving ducks, the tufted duck is mainly an aquatic feeder and the bulk of its food is gained by diving in water up to 20 foot deep. Its diet is varied, but molluscs and insect larvae are an important component. Its ungainly gait on land identifies the species as a 'diver', but it will take grass seeds and grain if they are available close to the water. Its take-off from water requires a pattering run to get airborne but once it has gained some height its flight is very fast and direct. Their relatively short wings, and rapid shallow wingbeats give the impression that they are 'frantic' fliers, particularly when a flock is seen beating across a strong wind.

Groups of birds tend to fly in loose formations and bunches with little tendency to develop into lines or 'V' formations, but as their roosting and feeding sites are often in the same place, they have little need to flight at dawn or dusk. Despite this, tufted duck are an important inland shooter's quarry if they can be intercepted on a line between two favoured stretches of open water. At first sight the drake can resemble a drake scaup (protected) but the latter has a grey back and lacks the tuft; while the females are even harder to distinguish from other female diving duck. Their flight characteristics make them a testing target for the shotgun shooter, and they are a good table bird when cooked carefully.

See also: **Inland Waterfowl Shooting**

Tumblers   The internal hammers of a 'hammerless' shotgun or rifle action are known as the tumblers. In the early version of the Anson & Deeley boxlock action the firing pin was actually an integral part of the tumbler, but on some guns the firing pin or striker may be a separate part housed behind the standing breech. The tumblers are set in the cocked position against the force of the main spring by opening the action. On pulling the trigger the bent on the tumbler is disengaged and the tumbler falls onto the firing pin.

Unlike guns fitted with external hammers, the tumblers of a hammerless weapon are almost always present in the cocked position.

See also: **Anson & Deeley**

U

Underlever The term 'underlever' denotes any weapon in which the breech is exposed for reloading by operating a lever on the underside of the action.

Most fixed-barrel and spring-operated air rifles are fitted with underlevers which are pulled downwards and backwards in order to cock the mainspring and open the loading point. Air rifle levers are long in order to achieve sufficient leverage to operate against a strong spring but, even so, on some underlever air rifles the reloading sequence requires some effort.

In the past many 'drop-down'-action double and single barrel shotguns and rifles were built with underlever mechanisms. These fell into two main types. The rotary underbolt lever was made to fit outside the profile of the trigger guard. The weapon was opened by pushing the lever sideways (usually to the right) and this movement removed the locking lugs which fitted recesses in the barrel lumps. The barrels were thus free to 'fall open'. In order to close and lock the breech the barrels had to be raised and the lever manually rotated back to 'locked' position. In the trigger-guard actions the opening mechanism was operated by pushing forward a thumb lever in the front of the trigger guard. In fact in many weapons this thumb lever was incorporated into the trigger guard itself by widening the section immediately in front of the loading trigger. Like the top and side lever actions, the thumb lever was spring-loaded so that the gun could be 'snapped' shut.

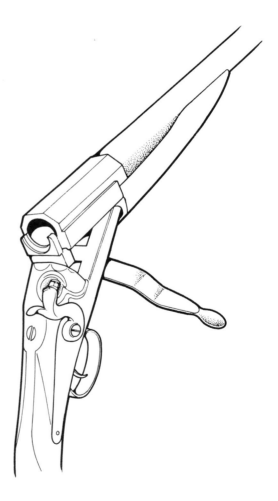

Underlever (rotary double underbolt) single 8 bore by Holland & Holland. 38 in barrel, weight 14 lbs, 3¼ in chamber

Underlever double-barrelled weapons had their heyday in the days of hammer guns as they could be safely operated without interferring with the external hammers. When hammerless shotguns took over the top lever quickly became the most popular style as it is both quicker and easier to use than either type of underlever.

Single barrel weapons, mainly rifles, with falling-block or tilting-block actions are also opened by underlever mechanisms. The 'Martini' action is operated by a lever which extends from immediately behind the trigger guard to form, in some weapons, a skeleton pistol grip. When the lever is pushed down the breech block tilts downwards to expose the breech, and returning the lever closes and locks the breech.

Falling-block actions such as the Sharps or the Farquharson are also operated by underlever mechanisms. The latter's lever folds back along the underside of the trigger guard with its operating linkage located in front. When pushed down and forwards the breech block 'falls' to expose the breech. Both the Martini and Farquharson mechanisms lock the breech very effectively and this positive 'lock-up' allows for greater accuracy. It is therefore not surprising that many target rifles are built on these underlever actions.

Perhaps the most familiar form of underlever action is the 'Winchester' lever action. Like the Martini, the lever extends to the rear of the trigger but in this case the trigger guard is an integral part of the lever. Throwing the lever down and forwards draws the breech to the rear to eject the spent case and exposes the breech for a fresh round. This design is ideal for low- or medium-powered repeating rifles but does not have the inherent strength to handle the heavy 'African' calibres.

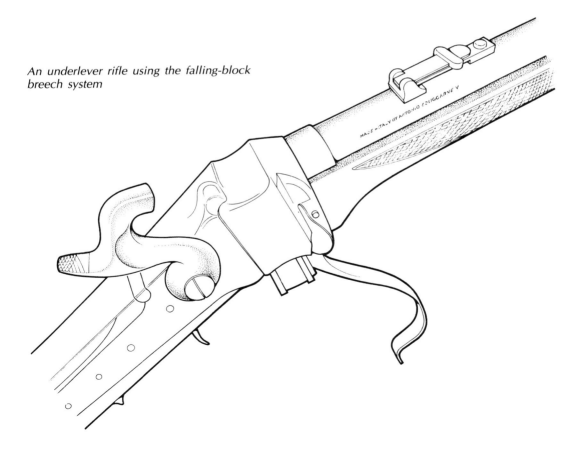

An underlever rifle using the falling-block breech system

Venison Although technically the term 'venison' should be only applied to the meat of the red deer, nowadays it is used to describe the meat of any deer species.

When a deer carcass is butchered and jointed, the prime cuts are normally considered to be the haunches (hind legs) and the saddle. Depending on the size of the species involved, the remainder of the carcass may be cut into a number of other joints. The forelegs are often used complete as one joint, although in fallow or red they may be further subdivided into shoulder and foreleg joints. The rib cage can be used for venison chops and spare ribs, and the neck is usually used for stewing venison or mince. The term 'venison' is also sometimes applied to the offal such as kidneys, liver and heart of deer, the organs that are usually considered to be the 'stalker's perks'.

Venison is a dark meat which is often described as halfway between beef and mutton in texture, and it has its own distinctive taste. Being the product of a wild animal it is almost fat-free and contains no artificial antibiotics or growth hormones.

Vermin In the world of sporting shooting, the term 'vermin' can be applied to any species that may cause unacceptable damage to agricultural or woodland crops or to species that may seriously deplete game, wildfowl or songbird populations through predation.

Among the species that cause a high level of crop damage are the wood-pigeon and the rabbit, and both are also noted for their culinary qualities to the extent that pigeon shooting and rabbiting are considered to be sports in their own right. Indeed, many shooters see these two as very sporting quarry and regard the fact that shooting them also serves the purpose of crop protection as of minor importance.

Until 1963, deer were also considered to be 'vermin' in many parts of the country for the arable and woodland crop damage they inflict. With the advent of the Deer Act in that year, however, all the less humane methods of deer control were made illegal. Today's increasing and spreading deer population now offers considerable scope for scientific and selective management and control of these, the largest British wild mammals, by a variety of stalking methods. No one but the most embittered forester would now consider deer to be 'vermin'.

Grey squirrels, on the other hand, are known to do considerable damage to both tree crops and the songbird population. In winter and early spring, bark is stripped off trees and saplings for the minerals it contains, and a substantial part of the squirrel's diet in late spring consists of songbird eggs and fledgelings. It is hardly surprising that the grey squirrel is actively controlled by forester and gamekeeper to the general benefit of all the wildlife.

Last on the list of agricultural pests is the collared dove. This lightly-built and elegant dove was practically unknown in Britain until the early 1960s, when a huge westward migration took place across Europe and this country was quickly colonized. Since then their numbers have increased to the extent that they do reach pest proportions in many districts, although they still do not create the same scale of crop damage as the wood pigeon.

A number of birds and mammals make up the list of predatory vermin. These are classed as a pest when their numbers are such that the 'normal' population of game and songbirds of a given area becomes depleted through their predatory activities. Many of these creatures cannot be classified as 'all bad'; in many instances a small and controlled population is actually beneficial to the balance of the wild ecosystem, and they are tightly controlled in order to maintain this balance.

Four species of the crow family, can, if kept in balance, fulfil a useful role. Magpies, for example, are excellent scavengers and make the most of clearing up roadside casualties. In this scavenging role they help to keep the countryside disease-free and clean, but any overpopulation will wreak havoc among game nests and songbird fledgelings. The jay is another corvid species which is a predatory pest; the damage to woodland bird populations can be quite significant if jays are allowed to increase in number.

Carrion crows and, in northern Scotland, the hooded crow affect ground nesting game birds and also may threaten animals as large as lamb, and they are species that are actively and ruthlessly pursued by the vermin controller. The rook, on the other hand, poses far less of a threat, and indeed there is much evidence that this species actually does more good than harm on arable land where soil and crop pests form a large part of its diet. However, rook numbers need to be controlled as overpopulation may encourage it to seek other food sources among ground nesting birds.

Last of the crow family in the lists of predatory vermin species is the jackdaw. Again, like the rook, it is highly sociable and omnivorous in its feeding habits. As such it will feed on nestlings, eggs and carrion wherever and whenever these are available.

On many freshwater ponds, lakes and waterways the coot can constitute a considerable threat to the natural balance. It is not really predatory in the same way as the corvids but its aggressive and territorial behaviour, and its prolific breeding potential, will serve to drive many other water birds from the area. It is for this reason that controlling the population of coots will be of benefit to the area's wildlife. A small pond on my shoot was once heavily populated with coots and very little else. One winter we reduced their numbers considerably and in the following spring we could add dabchick, teal, moorhen and water rail to our list of nesting birds for the first time.

The smallest of the mammal species of interest to the shooting vermin controller is the rat, and the list includes mink, weasel, stoat and the fox. While a shooter with a suitable weapon can go out specifically with the intention of ratting or fox shooting, the stoat, weasel and mink are often only shot when the opportunity presents itself. For these three species, trapping is usually a more efficient and time-effective method of controlling their populations.

Unlike the predatory bird species in the vermin list, the ground predators are all classed as carnivorous animals and actively hunt for their prey among smaller mammals and all kinds of birds. Consequently a small overpopulation of these ground mammals can inflict considerably more damage on the wildlife of an area than the same overpopulation in the corvid species.

See also: **Vermin Control; Vermin Shooting – Tactics; Vermin Shooting – Weapons**

Vermin Control Under the heading of 'vermin shooting' comes perhaps the greatest variety of different live-quarry shooting sports Britain has to offer. Depending on the species pursued and the time of year, the vermin shooter may be armed with shotguns of different calibres or a wide variety of rifled weapons from air rifles to the high-velocity .22 centrefires. With up to sixteen different species of birds or mammals to choose from, the vermin shooter has a greater variety of sports available than the deer stalker, the wildfowler or the game shooter.

As well as providing a wide variety of enjoyable shooting sport, vermin shooting has a serious function in that its main purpose is to reduce and control the population of these vermin or pest species. The need for this control differs with the species but may be categorized under three general aims. A number of vermin species inflict considerable damage on either agricultural or woodland crops. Shooting in order to reduce their population numbers therefore is a way of trying to reduce the scale of damage inflicted by these species, and in some parts of the country there are well-established crop protection syndicates and clubs run with this aim in mind.

On game and rough shoots, and in areas used as breeding grounds for waterfowl, a reduction in the number of predators will increase the survival chances of broods of game birds and waterfowl, thereby increasing the game or wildfowl stocks for the following season. Recent research has indicated that, without effective protection in this way, the wild stocks of pheasant, partridge or grouse would undergo a rapid decline as they are particularly prone to fall victim to ground predators such as fox, stoats, weasels and mink.

Finally, vermin shooting may maintain a more natural balance between the numbers of predators and their prey. For some reason not yet made clear, the magpie population in the British Isles has increased rapidly over the last few years. This increased population will result in increased predation on songbirds, their eggs and nestlings during the spring and early summer. This increased predation could spell disaster for the less common summer migrants of the warbler family and could well deplete the variety of British species. Much effort must therefore be expended in order to reduce magpie numbers and redress the natural balance. The aim of the vermin shooter in this case is not to kill all the magpies in an area but rather to reduce their numbers to the extent that the 'damage' they cause to other bird life is brought to a tolerable level. Magpies do, after all, act as very efficient scavengers and in this role small numbers are an asset to a wildlife ecosystem.

The style of shooting, the choice of suitable weapon, and the field tactics used in vermin control all vary with the quarry species pursued. The two most serious ag-

ricultural pests are the wood pigeon and the rabbit. The cost of the damage every year in Britain alone runs to millions of pounds and most farmers and land owners are very keen to allow vermin controllers access to their land in order to control these species. As well as being serious agricultural pests both wood pigeon and rabbit are valued for their sporting potential and for their culinary qualities. In many ways this has elevated them above the status of 'vermin' so that wood pigeon shooting and rabbiting have become respected sports in their own right and are dealt with as such in this book.

For most vermin-shooting situations, the shooter will require a far greater degree of field craft than would be demanded of any game shooter. Vermin species, both ground animals and the birds of the corvid group, are notoriously shy and alert. They will seldom come to the shooter unless a 'drive' has been successfully executed, and much of the vermin shooter's time will be spent in stalking the quarry. In the last 20 years there have been some dramatic advances in air rifle technology and this has led to the air rifle now being accepted as a valid and very effective vermin control weapon. Ranges, however, are still very restricted so that vermin control with a modern air rifle demands camouflage, stealth and field craft of the highest standard.

Moving up the 'power' scale, the .22 rimfire rifle is another effective vermin weapon, perhaps second only to the shotgun in its importance and in the number being used for this purpose. It is the prime weapon of the rabbit shooter and is versatile enough to kill close-range rats in enclosed barns using the 'bulleted-cap' load, while being capable of dealing with foxes effectively out to about one hundred yards with the 'hyper-velocity' long rifle ammunition.

Specialist fox shooters will take this a stage further in that they will emulate the North American sport of 'varminting'. Using centrefire high-velocity .22 rifles the accurate fox shooter can extend the effective range out to beyond three hundred yards with some calibres. The choice of calibre from the relatively sedate .22 Hornet to the extremely fast .220 Swift will dictate the shooter's maximum potential range, but the skill of being able to kill a fox at long range in open country will still rest with the shooter's steady hand and eye.

Vermin shooting allows for the use of a wider variety of shotgun calibres than any other general type of shooting sport. Even the tiny 9-mm 'garden gun' can be a very useful and effective shotgun for farmyard and rubbish-tip rat shooting, and the .410 and 28 bores are excellent calibres for close-range bolting rabbits, pigeon decoying or squirrel shooting. The larger 'small bores', the 20 and 16, can be employed as effectively as a 12 bore in shooting a wide variety of winged vermin species, especially in areas where the disturbance will not affect game birds or other wildlife to any great extent.

With the variety of weapons that can be used effectively for vermin control and the variety of sport available it is hardly surprising that the wealth of game and wildlife which inhabits Britain's countryside can be attributed in part to the numbers of shooters in this country who regard vermin shooting as an enjoyable sport which also serves a valid and useful purpose in crop protection and game or wildlife management.

See also: **Vermin**

Vermin Shooting – Tactics   Tactics used in vermin shooting will vary with the weapon employed, the quarry to be hunted, and the environment in which the shooting takes place. The essential difference between shotgun and rifle shooting tactics lies in the fact that the rifle user must rely on silence and concealment in order to shoot static quarry whereas the shotgun shooter will often seek to disturb the vermin species in order to shoot at a moving target.

Vermin control tactics for the rifle user can be divided into 'still hunting', stalking, lamping and, to a certain extent, decoying.

'Still hunting' is an American term which aptly describes the technique of sitting up and waiting for the quarry to come into range. There is, of course, much more to it than this simple description. The still hunter must learn to wait patiently and quietly for long periods of time without disturbing the wildlife around him. Fieldcraft plays an important part in concealment, and the ability to produce an accurate shot from different and often uncomfortable postures is essential. Reconnaissance of the area prior to a shooting foray is useful to identify the places frequented by the quarry and to find a suitable place for concealment which offers a clear and safe shot. Once this has been established the still hunter will be able to take the rifle out with more chances of success. Knowing the time the quarry are likely to appear, the shooter reaches his position as quietly and unobtrusively as possible in good time. Once concealed at the shooting position the shooter then waits for the targets to appear. Still hunting is a tactic that can be used to good effect to intercept a fox on its known round, and I have spent many hours in this activity. Rabbit shooting, when the shooter sits up overlooking a warren at first or last light, and shooting rats on a farmyard rubbish tip are also effective and enjoyable still hunting techniques that can be employed by both air rifle and rimfire shooters.

Vermin stalking relies on the same skills of silence and concealment as still hunting, only the shooter is mobile rather than static. At the appropriate time of day the stalker moves slowly and cautiously through the area known to be frequented by the quarry, wearing camouflage to help break up the human outline and using whatever cover is available to mask any movements. Essentially the sport is similar to woodland deer stalking. Each likely area is studied carefully with the naked eye and binoculars for signs of the quarry. Any detected movement should be studied in great detail as it may give away the presence of a potential target temporarily hidden behind grass or foliage. Once the quarry has been identified through binoculars and the possibility of a safe shot ascertained then the rifle should be brought to the shoulder for the final aim and shot. Most shots will be taken from a standing position and many vermin stalkers use a stalking stick to help steady their aim. A straight hazel stick of the same length as the distance from the eye to the ground will not only help to steady the rifle if held at arm's length with the fore-end of the rifle, but it can also be used to prop the binoculars for extended scrutiny of the surroundings. Very often the stalker will not account for as many head of vermin as the still hunter, but stalking is a sport which demands the utmost concentration and the most careful fieldcraft skills in order to achieve consistent success. As such it is perhaps the most satisfying of vermin-shooting sports.

Within the field of vermin-shooting sports, 'lamping' is one of the most specialized. Apart from the hare, no game species or deer may be shot during the hours of darkness, and, although wildfowlers are permitted to shoot 'under the moon', it is only vermin shooting that has stimulated the growth of lamping as a sport. Rats, rabbits, and foxes are the prime quarry species for this activity, and, although tactics may vary with species and environment, the general principles are the same.

Lamping is a sport which involves two people: one to hold and direct the lamp and one to shoot. Basically, an area known to be frequented by the quarry species is quietly patrolled in the dark and every so often the lamp is switched on to probe the surrounding area. Most animals, when blinded by the powerful beam, will 'freeze' for a moment, and this gives the shooter an opportunity for a shot. Often the lamp is mounted on a four-wheel-drive vehicle, but the rifle shooter should walk alongside, even though there is a strong temptation to shoot from the vehicle itself. The vibration and movement of the suspension do not produce as steady a shooting platform as when the shooter stalks alongside the vehicle and uses a stalking stick to aid accuracy. As with all other forms of shooting the quarry must be positively identified before the rifle is raised, because deer, badgers, dogs, cats and even courting couples are also encountered roaming the countryside in the dark.

One often sees 'solo' lamping outfits advertised in which the lamp is mounted on the rifle itself. I feel uneasy about this arrangement because in using the lamp to probe the surrounding darkness one is also pointing a loaded firearm, with the added risk this may entail.

When still hunting or stalking rabbits with a rifle the activity is confined to the few short hours around dawn and sunset, whereas the 'lamper' may be able to operate for far longer periods through the hours of darkness. Consequently lamping can be a far more productive and effective method of control and in areas well populated by rabbits it is not unusual to end a night with a three-figure bag. Lamping foxes using a centrefire rifle can also be very productive because of the extended time available for shooting and I know of one gamekeeper who shot over 100 foxes with his .22/250 rifle in his first year of lamping. Even more so than in daylight the shooter must be well acquainted with the lie of the land over which shooting takes place. Any potentially unsafe areas must be avoided and even greater care exercised in choosing the direction of safe shots, particularly if the shooter is armed with a rimfire or centrefire .22.

Decoying vermin for the shooter armed with a rifle must take secondary importance compared with decoying as a shotgun sport. Nevertheless, pigeons may be decoyed for the air rifle or rimfire user and the tactics followed will be broadly similar to those when using a shotgun. The main difference is, of course, that the pigeons must be brought in to land when using a rifle, and this may severely limit the size of the bag. However, there are instances where an air rifle is preferable to a shotgun. In late winter and early spring many pigeons can be drawn in to a patch of woodland by using 'lofted' decoys. At this time of year a shotgun may well cause unacceptable disturbance to nesting birds and other wildlife, and an air rifle can be equally effective and is much quieter to use.

Carrion crows and magpies may also be decoyed and this tactic is particularly useful if the shooter is seeking to eliminate one individual bird, or a family group. Basically the sport is similar to still hunting except for the fact that appropriate decoys are used to entice the quarry into range, and the same qualities of stealth and fieldcraft are required in this form of decoying.

Apart from pigeon decoying, a subject that is described separately, most shotgun vermin shooting is disruptive in that the quarry is flushed or disturbed so that its retreat offers the chance of a shot. Many head of vermin may be accounted for by simple walking-up tactics. A quiet walk through copses and along hedgerows can account for a variety of winged vermin as well as the occasional fox or other predators of the stoat family. Although the sport is 'disruptive', a walk around the shoot must not be noisy; after all, the quarry must be flushed within range of the gun. In fine weather rabbits will often lie up above ground during the day, concealed in tussocks of grass or other ground cover. In these circumstances rabbiting with a shotgun is not confined to dawn and evening and a bolting rabbit weaving between clumps of grass can make a testing target for the shotgun shooter. At other times rabbits can be dislodged from their burrows by using ferrets, and this has become a sport in its own right. Once a ferret has been released into the warren the shooter stands back, preferably behind some concealment, to await the appearance of the rabbits driven out by the carnivore in their midst. At times shooting can be fast and furious as rabbits bolt out of one hole and into another, but this form of shooting is an effective way of reducing the overall rabbit population in an area. Rabbits can be controlled without the use of a gun if the bolt-holes are covered with nets before the ferret is introduced. Any escaping rabbit is caught in the nets and quickly despatched, but this method is not considered to be a shooting sport.

Low-powered shotguns such as the 9-mm 'garden gun' can be effectively used against rats in confined spaces in and around barns and other farm buildings. Again, this is a form of walked-up shooting in that the disturbed rats present the shooter with a rapidly moving target. An even more effective variation on the theme is when the shooter enlists the help of a Jack Russell terrier to seek out and flush the rats. Great care must be exercised, however, because these enthusiastic dogs may be following hard on the heels of their adversary and the risk of shooting the dog by mistake is quite high. The shooter must stay calm and cool even though the action may be frenetic.

Vermin-shooting tactics possess much greater scope for variation and adaptation than any other form of live-quarry shooting. Due to the wide variety of species that feature in the vermin list, the variety of weapons that may be effectively used, and the different environments and times of day in which the shooter may operate, vermin shooting in Britain has a greater number of participants than any of the other shooting sports. As well as being an enjoyable activity, the shooter is providing a very valuable service to both the agriculture and wildlife management of Britain's countryside.

See also: **Vermin**

Vermin Shooting – Weapons The correct choice of weapon for vermin control depends on a number of factors. The size of the species to be hunted is the most obvious of these. As a general rule, the larger the quarry the more powerful the weapon required. This certainly holds true when selecting the type of rifle, and is to a lesser extent valid in determining the ideal shotgun calibre. As a result I would not wish to shoot at a fox with a shotgun smaller than an 20 bore or a rifle less powerful than a .22 LR loaded with high-velocity long rifle hollow-point ammunition. By the same token I would not go ratting armed with a 12-bore shotgun.

The anticipated range at which the quarry will be shot is another factor. Close-range work would dictate the use of a small-calibre shotgun or an air rifle, while the larger or more powerful calibres may be reserved for longer ranges. Thus I consider a 28 bore ideal for pigeon decoying yet would opt for a larger shotgun for shooting flighting or roosting pigeons.

The environment in which the shooting takes place is a very important consideration in determining the correct weapon. Safety is, of course, of the highest importance and it would be irresponsible folly to use a high-powered weapon, either rifle or shotgun, close to human habitation or busy roads and paths. The shooter must therefore tailor the power of the weapon to the surroundings. For rat or collared dove shooting in enclosed areas and farm outbuildings an air rifle is the obvious choice if a single projectile is deemed sufficient, although a bulleted cap in a .22 rimfire rifle will also eliminate the risk of ricochets or minor structural damage!

The .22 rimfire is the ideal weapon for rabbit control

As one moves away from other human dwellings, so the power of the weapon may be safely increased. This not only pays due regard to safety but also minimizes the risk of noise disturbance. Low-powered weapons usually have a quiet discharge and can be used among farm buildings without causing undue alarm.

Finally the question arises of the anticipated stance of the target. If it is expected that the quarry will be shot while it is standing or sitting still then a rifle of some description will fulfil the task. If, on the other hand, the target is expected to be moving – either running, climbing or flying – then the shotgun firing a pattern of pellets is the obvious choice.

Careful application of these points to any vermin-shooting situation will usually identify the best weapon for that particular task, and the range from which to choose is greater than for any other form of sporting shooting.

'Hunting' air rifles, those that are designed for live-quarry shooting, come in a choice of four calibres and a wide variety of designs.

The advancement in the designs of barrel locking mechanisms has contributed to the acceptance of the break-barrel design as a good reliable hunting weapon. In this design the barrel is broken to cock the spring and the breech end is thus exposed for loading. Break-barrel rifles are perhaps the easiest to load, particularly in winter when the shooter may be wearing thick gloves, and they have the additional advantage of a simple cocking mechanism. In the past a criticism has been made that when the barrel was closed after loading any looseness in the barrel locking catch would make break-barrel air rifles too inaccurate for hunting purposes. Nowadays all hunting air rifles of this design feature a positive lock-up for consistent accuracy.

The fixed-barrel underlever design overcomes any problems with the breech lock. The mainspring is cocked by pulling back a lever under the barrel and cylinder and the pellet is loaded through a loading point at the breech end of the barrel. In some designs the loading process can be fiddly but the fixed-barrel design has much to commend it for hunting purposes. Both the break-barrel and underlever suffer from the disadvantage

that they are inconvenient to reload when the shooter is lying prone; the rifle has to be raised or canted to the side in order to achieve the clearance for the arc of the barrel or underlever. When stalking through undergrowth this can pose quite a problem.

One air rifle design which overcomes this uses the sidelever cocking mechanism. Similar in principle to the underlever, the sidelever rifle gains in performance what it loses in elegance; it is difficult to conceal a lever strong enough to cock the main spring on the side of an air weapon, but the sideways arc of the lever makes reloading when lying prone that much easier and quicker.

Pneumatic or 'pump-up' rifles have always had their supporters, and weapons of this type may also be used for vermin control. The gas cylinder is pre-charged by pumping air into it using a number of pump strokes on a lever. In many ways this makes the weapon more versatile as the power can be varied by varying the number of pump strokes and without a mainspring housing the pneumatic air rifle can be made much lighter than 'spring' air weapons. For the younger shooter the weight factor can be a very important consideration. There are times, however, when the time it takes to recharge the cylinder and the noise this makes is a decided disadvantage. If speed of reloading is important then a pump-up air rifle scores rather badly compared to the spring-powered weapons.

In recent years the 'bolt-action' air rifle has made an appearance. The pellet is powered by an air cartridge which is inserted into the rifle much in the same way as a centrefire rifle round. Like the pneumatic weapons, the lack of mainspring housing gives these weapons the advantage of lightness, and they are very accurate. However there are distinct disadvantages. Each shot uses one compressed air cartridge and therefore cannot be wasted in the field. The cartridge itself is bulky and carrying enough for, say, twenty shots can pose a problem.

In addition, reloading a supply of used cartridges may mean some time spent in laborious pumping to achieve the desired pressure to deliver around 12 ft lbs energy. Nevertheless, if few shots are expected per outing and if the look of the weapon is important (these bolt-action air rifles more closely resemble centrefire hunting rifles) then an accurate cartridge-fed bolt-action air rifle may be a good choice.

Within these five types of air weapon there is a very wide selection of good, accurate and reliable models on the market. The ultimate choice may therefore rest on weight, cost, or appearance.

Of the four air rifle calibres available, the two most popular are the .177 and .22. The .177 calibre uses a pellet whose weight averages around eight grains. It is therefore a small and lightweight projectile which possesses the advantage of higher velocity and better penetration than the larger calibre. The legal limit for air rifle power is set at 12 ft lbs muzzle energy. An air rifle delivering close to this limit will drive a .177 pellet out at about 850 fps. At this velocity the trajectory is flatter than a comparable .22 calibre air rifle and the smaller surface area of the pellet head produces better penetration than the larger calibre. Against these must be set the fact that .177 calibre pellets do lose their momentum and velocity through the air more rapidly and the 'shocking power' is considerably less than a .22 air rifle pellet. Nevertheless the .177 calibre has many supporters among vermin hunters and its increased penetration can be used to good effect on feathered vermin.

The .22 calibre air rifle with its 14-grain projectile is the best all-purpose choice for the air rifle hunter. Although at the 12 ft lbs legal power limit the velocity of the .22 is only around 620 fps, it still retains enough energy to pass straight through the chest cavity of a rabbit at up to 30 yards while at the same time delivering sufficient shock to knock the animal over. In a well-built and reliable rifle the round is sufficiently accurate to consistently kill rabbits out to about 40 yards providing the weapon is accurately zeroed and the shooter's hand is steady. Within this range it will deal effectively with all vermin species except the fox and is generally acknowledged to be the best 'all-round' calibre for the vermin shooter who wishes to use an air rifle.

The two other air rifle calibres are the .20 and the .25. The former was pioneered by Sheridan in the USA in the early 1960s and this company still manufactures large quan-

tities of .20 pneumatic air rifles for the world market. Coming somewhere between the .177 and .22 in its characteristics, the Sheridan produces around 700 fps from its 11 grain pellet at the British legal power limit. To its devotees the .20 calibre possesses the best of both worlds, but it remains a minority calibre and the lead taken by both .177 and .22 is unlikely to be eroded by the Sheridan .20 calibre.

In recent years there has been a rekindling of interest in the .25 calibre air rifle. Air weapons in .25 were produced in some quantity between World Wars One and Two, but the calibre was all but obsolete until the air rifle 'revolution' began in the late 1960s. Since then a number of air rifle manufacturers have introduced .25 models, claiming that the larger pellet delivers even more shock than the .22 air rifle. The increased surface area of the pellet does have an improved 'knockdown' effect, but in order to keep the weapon within the legal power limits the heavier 18-grain pellet must not exceed, about 520 fps. To a shooter used to firing .177 or even .22 air weapons, the trajectory of the .25 is inferior. A slowly growing number of vermin hunters are prepared to tolerate this in order to benefit from the increased shock sustained by quarry hit with this 'big-bore' air rifle pellet.

The advances made in air weapons technology over the last twenty years have been matched by the development of inexpensive telescopic sights of good and reliable quality. Thus most air rifle hunters would nowadays fit this type of sight to their weapon in order to achieve greater precision and accuracy within the air rifle's effective range. The standard air rifle telescopic sight is parallax-adjusted to 30 yards rather than the 100-yard fix for rimfire and centrefire weapons, and sights range from small 4×15 scopes to the 'large-optic' scopes for dawn and dusk shooting.

To be of use to the vermin shooter a hunting air rifle must fulfil a number of criteria. It must be powerful enough to be effective up to 35–40 yards. It must be consistently accurate and reliable in operation, and its loading cycle must be reasonably straightforward and quick. There are a great many air rifles on the market today that fulfil these criteria very well indeed and the sporting air rifle is now a serious weapon in its own right.

Of all rifle calibres employed in vermin control, the .22 rimfire is the most versatile and therefore the most useful. While the air rifle hunter can perform a very useful task he will nevertheless be limited by the range and energy of the air-powered rifle he uses. The rimfire user, on the other hand, is able to select from a wide range of ammunition in order to exceed the capability of the air rifle and extend the effective range out to beyond 100 yards. Even close to farm buildings and in enclosed spaces the low-powered bulleted-cap ammunition may be used for ratting and for controlling collared doves, while at the other end of the scale foxes are well within the capability of the rimfire user. Rimfire rifles in .22LR calibre are available in a wide variety of styles and mechanisms. Providing the rifle is accurate and reliable there is no restriction on the type of weapon that can be used.

Many gamekeepers and vermin controllers opt for an auto-loading .22 rifle. These weapons gain in firepower what they lose in long-distance accuracy and for situations that may require rapid shooting they are ideal. In addition, models such as the Remington 'Nylon 66' are very light and easily handled. Most auto-loading designs nowadays are reliable, but the reloading cycle does depend on the power of the cartridges that are being used. Auto-loading mechanisms on .22 rimfire rifles are based on the 'blowback' principle in which the recoil of a cartridge being fired pushes the bolt backwards to eject the spent case and chamber a fresh round. Reliable though this system is with standard long rifle ammunition, the .22 short and bulleted caps may not activate the reloading cycle because they generate less recoil and may need to be loaded singly. This rather defeats the object of using an auto-loader. The blowback system also produces less accurate results than mechanisms which feature a solid 'lock-up' of the bolt, but this only becomes critical over the longer distances. Nevertheless a vermin controller using this type of weapon can take great toll on a heavy population of rabbits.

Lever-action and pump-action repeating .22 rifles are also suitable and possess more inherent accuracy than the auto-loader. Their

A .22/250 heavy-barrel Ruger No 1 rifle – a potent long-range fox killer

one disadvantage lies in the fact that they generate more noise than other designs. The slide and fore-end of a pump action are prone to rattle when one is creeping through cover, and such metallic noises will alert any quarry; and many lever actions clatter when the rifle is reloaded, again with the same effect. Nevertheless these mechanisms are reliable and the rifles are accurate – two of the main criteria for a good vermin rifle.

Perhaps the most popular choice of .22 rimfire rifle is the bolt action. Its chief advantages lie in simplicity of design, ease of maintenance and excellent accuracy. It is not surprising that most target-competition rimfire rifles are built around a bolt action. Though lacking the firepower of the other designs, the bolt action is more silent to operate, less likely to rattle at a critical moment and more likely to produce precise hits at long range. Models such as the Brno No 2, the Anschütz range and others have established fine reputations as excellent hunting rifles.

Ammunition for the .22 rimfire comes in a wide variety of shapes and sizes. From the lowest-powered bulleted cap, useful for close-quarters ratting, to the recently introduced hyper-velocity rounds travelling at a muzzle velocity of around 1,500 fps, the shooter is presented with a selection of 'short' and 'long' rifle ammunition with high velocity, standard and 'subsonic' velocities. Bullet types available include solid, hollow-point and truncated-cone designs. For live quarry the last two are to be preferred as the deformation they sustain when striking any object makes them far less prone to ricochet. Solid bullets, though more accurate, may 'bounce around the countryside' after passing through an animal.

Many .22 rifles have muzzles that are screw-cut to accept a silencer, and fitting one of these devices does bring certain advantages. When suitable ammunition is used the normal 'crack' of a rimfire is reduced to a dull 'plop'. The advantage of this is obvious to a shooter sitting up overlooking a rabbit warren on a warm summer's evening – a time when the rifle's normal report would keep many underground. There are many other situations when a silenced rifle is more effective than the noisier unsilenced weapon but using a silencer does limit the choice of ammunition. A .22 silencer is designed to muffle the 'subsonic' noises of a rifle being fired and cannot absorb the supersonic crack of a bullet as it exits the muzzle above the speed of sound. Therefore, to be really effective only subsonic ammunition should be used. Travelling at about 1000 fps the subsonic trajectory is more curved than the higher-velocity cartridges and accurate range is consequently limited to about 75 yards. Within this distance, however, the silenced .22 rimfire is a quiet and accurate weapon suitable for all but the largest and smallest of the vermin species.

The great majority of .22 rimfire shooters fit a telescopic sight to their weapon. The mild recoil of even the lightest rifle allows a wide range of expensive sights to be used without the risk of recoil throwing the sight off zero. However, in order to make best use of the calibre's accuracy, a scope sight of at least 4×32 should be fitted. Specialist users may increase the magnification to 6× or even, for night-time 'lamping' of rabbits or foxes, the massive 8×56. As a general rule, the better the quality of scope sight the more accurate will be the rifle.

Nowadays a number of rifles are chambered for the .22 WRF Magnum cartridge. With a longer cartridge case this calibre drives a 40-grain bullet at 2,000 fps. It is an effective intermediate calibre between the .22 LR and the mildest .22 centrefire, the .22 Hornet. Its use for vermin control rests with long-range rabbit shooting and fox control. Certainly, with rabbits the cartridge often produces unacceptable meat spoilage at distances below 60 yards but will kill with reasonable certainty out to about 130 yards. With these characteristics it is a good fox-shooting weapon if the ranges do not demand the use of a centrefire.

The ultimate weapon for the specialist fox shooter, however, remains the .22 centrefire. A choice of five calibres gives the shooter added versatility and he can tailor the choice to the anticipated average range. The .22 Hornet will enable a good shooter to kill foxes cleanly at 150 yards while the .222 Remington and the .223 Remington will both extend the useful range to over 200 yards. The two 'hot' calibres in this group extend the range out to beyond 300 yards, and the .22/250 Remington and the .220 Swift produce startling velocities to maintain accuracy at these very long ranges. Shooting long-distance 'varmints' in North America has caused a specialized 'varminting' style of rifle to evolve. Whether built around a bolt action or a single-shot mechanism, a 'varmint-style' rifle is fitted with a plain heavy target barrel without iron sights. The stock is fitted with a raised comb and full pistol grip and the design is intended to be used in conjunction with a telescopic sight. Skip-line chequering and white line spacers are other embellishments expected on a varmint rifle and the weapon is deliberately built heavier than a standard sporting rifle.

Many fox shooters use this style of rifle for their long-distance shooting and I have seen foxes killed at over 400 yards with such weapons. The weapons currently offered on the market are generally bolt-action variants of the standard sporting rifle, although Ruger produce a heavy-barrel edition of their single-shot No 1 rifle. Standard sporting rifles, though not designed for extreme-range shooting, are also quite suitable for fox shooting and even at very long distances are sufficiently accurate to be effective – it is after all the first shot which is important, and the heavy-barrel model only scores over the standard weight when the barrel heats up.

Long-distance fox shooting demands a telescopic sight of moderately strong magnification and of the best optical quality. Large optics also help in poor light and the specialist fox-shooting centrefire should be fitted with a 6× or 8× scope with as large an objective lens diameter as possible. An 8×56 scope gives good long-distance magnification and excellent light-gathering power in poor light. Some of these centrefire rifles produce a sharp recoil, and a telescopic sight should be well built and sufficiently robust to remain unaffected by the jolt of the recoil. This is particularly important when the weapon is zeroed for 250 or 300 yards. At that distance the slightest movement of the scope reticule as a result of recoil shaking will place the bullet well away from the mark and render the weapon unusable. It is for this branch of rifle shooting that a top-qual-

The .22 centrefire cartridges most often used for fox shooting (left to right): .22 LR (for comparison), .22 Hornet, .222 Rem., .22/250 Rem., .220 Swift

ity telescopic sight is considered to be essential rather than desirable, as the top manufacturers design their scope sights specifically for recoil resistance.

As stated previously, rifles of any type used for vermin shooting are intended for static quarry. When the quarry is moving, a shotgun rather than a rifle should be chosen. A shotgun is therefore a valuable part of the vermin shooter's armoury for use particularly against birds, treed squirrels and bolting rabbits. In terms of selecting the type of shotgun, a game shooter will experience considerable social pressure from his fellow sportsmen to conform to 'tradition' in his choice of a game gun. Not so the vermin shooter, a person who has available a wider selection of shotgun types and calibres than even the rough shooter.

Double barrels in both over-and-under and side-by-side configuration, single shots, pump action, bolt actions and auto-loaders may all be employed in vermin control. The main criteria in selecting a shotgun lie with matching the weapon's power to the quarry species and the environment in which the shooting takes place. Chasing rats around barns and farm outbuildings, in the company of a small terrier, when armed with a 9-mm shotgun is a very effective way of controlling these rodents. The speed of the rats requires very quick reflexes and the presence of a ratting dog demands great care and a 'cool head'. The 9 mm is a calibre which has a quiet report and very limited range; hence its use in buildings and enclosed surroundings.

Moving up the scale to the .410 and the 28 bore we come to guns that are light and handy enough to be used for close-range bolting rabbits and pigeon decoying. These shotguns, if well bored, are a delight to use and their reports and recoil are considerably less than the normal 12 bore. In terms of effective range a 28 bore loaded with No 7 shot will throw good patterns even at the 'standard' 40 yards, although shots should be taken at closer range with the .410.

The 12, 16, and 20 bores can be termed the 'general-purpose' shotgun calibres for vermin control. Careful selection of shot load and size can virtually eliminate the differences in their performance and, suitably loaded, they can tackle anything from a fox downwards.

The choice of shotgun type for vermin shooting rests with the personal preferences of the shooter and while one may use a side-by-side double for this purpose an auto-loading gun is equally as efficient, and probably more so when used for flocks of pigeons.

The wide variety of vermin shooting that exists in Britain allows the shooter a far greater choice of weapon than any other shooting discipline and, paradoxically, it is through the activities of a great many vermin shooters that the wildlife of the countryside flourishes.

See also: **Vermin**

Voere The Voere Jagd und Sportwaffenfabrik is a German arms manufacturer that specializes in the production of hunting rifles. Based at Vohrenbach, this company has become known in Britain for the production of well-made and accurate bolt-action centrefire rifles in the medium-price range.

The two principal weapons of interest to the British shooter are the 'Titan Menor' and the 'Titan II' models. Both are bolt-action magazine-fed repeating rifles of good quality; the former is the short-action model for the .22 calibre centrefires and the latter model accommodates a wide variety of the larger calibres.

The .22 centrefire 'Titan Menor' has an enclosed action with a side ejection point for the spent cartridge. This design helps to produce a smooth reloading cycle by reducing the free play of the bolt when it is withdrawn from the breech face. Chambered for four .22 calibres from .222 Rem. to the 5.6×50 Magnum, the 'Titan Menor' is available in three models. The standard is a plain workmanlike rifle, the deluxe adds further embellishment to the stock and the competition model is available with a high comb 'semi-target' stock and heavy barrel.

The 'Titan II' is available in no less than 23 calibres from the 5.6×57 RWS to the .458 Win. Magnum. This range includes some of the less well-known calibres such as the 7.5×55 Swiss, the 25–06 Rem. and the .308 Norma Magnum – calibres that are only available from other manufacturers to special order. Like the 'Menor' model, the 'Titan II' is supplied in three grades; standard, deluxe, and heavy barrel. Voere have an unusual method of allowing the shooter to 'customize' his own rifle. Silver pistol-grip caps are available with a variety of engraved scenes, and a factory custom rifle is sold with deep chiselled engraving on the action and magazine floor plate. Custom models are available with both silver and gold inlay, but even the standard rifle has gained acclaim as a well-made and smooth-operating weapon.

Wad The wad in a shotgun cartridge serves two main purposes. Placed between the propellant powder charge and the shot load it protects the lead shot from the high temperatures of the igniting powder and it provides an efficient gas seal, thereby using the force of the explosion to drive the shot load through the barrel. In order to do this many game-shooting cartridges use a column of three wads between powder and shot. Immediately above the powder is a thin card 'over-powder' wad which is relatively flameproof and provides protection for the thick 'felt' wad above it. This fibre wad provides an efficient gas seal and its thickness is such that this seal is maintained even when it passes through the chamber cone. A good gas seal (also known as obturation) is maintained through the length of the barrel because the thick felt wad deforms slightly under the pressure of the exploding gases to fill the barrel and produce a 'piston' action.

In order to prevent pellets at the bottom of the shot load embedding themselves in the felt when subjected to the violent acceleration of the cartridge being fired, another thin card 'undershot' wad is placed between the felt wad and the shot load. This column of three wads has proved to be reliable and is still frequently used in cartridges loaded for sporting shooting. The paper and fibre material are biodegradeable and this construction is therefore to be recommended on land which is also used by livestock. Each cartridge manufacturer will vary the properties and material in their own wads in order to impart some additional advantage to the

wad's function. Eley, for example, devised their 'Kleena' wads which, as well as their two main functions, also remove excess lead and powder fouling from the interior of the barrel.

On cartridges closed with a rolled turnover or a wax seal, an 'overshot' thin card wad prevents the shot being lost from the cartridge case. The size of shot and other information is often printed on the overshot wad.

In the last twenty years a revolution has taken place in the way cartridges are produced and in the new types of wadding that have been developed. Originally designed for competitive clay pigeon shooting, the new-style one-piece wad has also replaced the card and felt wads in some sporting cartridges. One-piece wads are usually made of nylon or plastic – materials which are flexible enough to provide a good obturation under the pressure of discharge. In addition, the front end of the wad is usually extended to provide a thin protective 'shot cup' in which the pellet load sits. When the shot charge and wad exit the muzzle, slits in the shot cup cause it to open and as the shot charge continues unhindered the wad quickly falls to earth.

This revolutionary design yields a number of benefits. As there is no contact between the pellets and the barrel wall, fewer are deformed and the percentage of effective pellets in the pattern increases. This effectively produces a denser pattern, and selective loadings can throw, for example, a full-choke pattern from a quarter-choke-bored barrel. It is for this reason that some cartridges intended for use against high pheasants use one-piece shot-cup wads in their construction. The lack of contact between the lead shot and the barrel wall also eliminates lead fouling in the bore.

Shot-protecting one-piece wads are available in a variety of designs so that careful selection of different cartridges and loads will greatly extend the versatility of the shotgun. By checking the pattern of each load on a pattern plate the shooter may be able to identify the cartridges to use for tighter (more heavily choked) patterns, which ones throw 'standard' patterns from the barrel choke, and any cartridges that may even throw more open patterns. Such versatility is just not possible with the traditional wad column, but there are disadvantages inherent in the design of the plastic wad.

While eliminating lead fouling, some plastic wads are prone to leave a plastic residue in the barrel which is often much more difficult to remove. Again, sporting shooting often takes place on the foreshore, on high moorland and in environmentally sensitive areas, and plastic wads can cause unnecessary litter, while on farmland there is a risk of ingestion by livestock. The length and thickness of the piston 'skirt' at the base of the wad is critical to producing a good gas seal and poorly designed wads are more prone to leakage than the traditional fibre.

Present developments: a new cup-type wad, similar in shape to the plastic cup-type wad but made of biodegradable material, is now on the market. Tests seem to show this wad can replace the present plastic cup-type wad giving the shooter a viable alternative.

If in the future the use of steel shot becomes mandatory there will be those who

A brace of walked-up grey partridge

own 'best' guns and who may be tempted to use steel-shot loaded cartridges with one of the above cup-type wads. Before they shoot any steel-shot loaded cartridges, it is strongly advised that they seek expert advice from the makers of their 'best' gun. The results of tests on steel-shot cartridges in the USA seem to show that it is very unwise to shoot steel-shot cartridges through the barrels of a 'best' gun, most of which to date have been designed to shoot cartridges loaded with lead shot.

See also: **Ammunition Reloading;**
           Obturation

Walked-Up Shooting   The term 'walked-up' shooting is self-explanatory. Basically a team of guns walk in line over an area of ground in order to flush game which is then shot. The term, however, covers a wide variety of different shooting sports and quarry species. Walked-up shooting can be almost as formal as driven game shooting at one end of the spectrum and take in any informal dog-and-gun sport at the other.

Perhaps the most formal of all walked-up shooting involves shooting grouse over pointers. It is one of the oldest and best-established forms of game bird shooting, and it has in the past caused the development of a variety of breeds of 'pointing' or 'setting' dogs. Before the development of driven bird shooting all game was pursued 'over dogs'. It was only with the development of percussion-cap shotguns and later breech-loaders that guns could be fired safely at a high angle, and it was only with these developments in shotgun design that the overhead driven bird became shootable. Nowadays shooting grouse over dogs does not have the prestige of a day's driven grouse shooting, but it remains a very rewarding and enjoyable method of shooting.

The most popular dog breeds used for grouse include the English pointer and the three breeds of setter, the Irish, the Gordon and the English. The arrangement of the dog is rather free-running in that much depends on the scenting ability of the dogs used. However, the area of ground to be covered is often walked over in a circular general move-ment, ending up at the starting point after spending from four to six hours in the field. At the start of the proceedings the dogs are allowed to range over the moorland, some-times at a good distance from the guns, and even at a range of 300 yards or so providing the dogs are still visible! The role of the guns is a passive waiting one until the dogs indicate that they have located grouse. The experienced gun will note the dog's change of pace or a slight falter as the first faint scent is caught, and the dog will slow down and freeze into sudden immobility as it locates and 'holds' the birds. Often a second dog will 'back the point' if it is downwind of the leading animal and they will hold this motionless stance.

Once the dogs have made a 'find' the guns will approach carefully and take up positions on either side and downwind of the anticipated flushing point. On the command to 'road in', the dogs flush the game and flatten to the ground while the guns try to take a toll from the covey. It can be seen that an unruly or jealous dog can ruin an area of moorland by failing to hold point at the initial time or final approach by the guns. However, over well-trained setters there can be no finer way of covering an area of moorland on a sunny late summer day. Although the bags are considerably lighter than in a driven grouse shoot, the joy of working closely with keen and elegant gundogs holds an unique pleasure. Incidentally, a further refinement and even older sport is a variation on this theme: a small number of falconers fly peregrines at grouse 'over dogs'.

Guns shooting over dogs must always be aware of the risk of hitting the dog with a hasty and careless shot, and should also avoid shooting when the dogs are close, in order to avoid damaging the dogs' hearing with muzzle blast. After taking off, the grouse will be flying very low, and it is a wise dog trainer who trains his setters to 'drop to flush'.

Shooting partridge and pheasant over dogs is also practised in many lowland parts of Britain, but the birds really have to lie well. Grey partridge will do this, but red-legged partridge and pheasant tend to run on which will unsettle a good pointer or setter. Lowland shooters therefore tend to use multi-purpose or 'HPR' breeds for lowland work. These hunter/pointer/retriever breeds include the German short-haired pointer (GSP), the

Munsterlander, and the Weimaraner, all of which will seek, point, flush and retrieve the quarry. On moorland, however, grouse shooters working over dogs often use setters to point and flush the birds and spaniels or labradors to retrieve the shot game. In either environment a great deal of satisfaction and enjoyment is derived from watching good dogs working the wind for any scent of game, and the relaxed pose of the shooter changes to excited anticipation as the nerves are keyed up when the dogs on point are ordered in to the flush.

Other forms of walked-up shooting also involve the use of gundogs, but not in the same way as when shooting 'over dogs' as described above. The term 'walked-up' shooting usually implies a team of guns walking in line rather than an individual, and this method is also used early in the grouse season. Unlike the sport of shooting over dogs, it is the line of guns, helpers and dogs which flushes the grouse from the heather. Similarly, walking the September stubbles for partridge is also a well-established sport in many parts of Britain. When using spaniels, these must be trained to quest and flush birds close to the line and well within shotgun range – far too many dogs range too far ahead of the line and flush birds well beyond shot, and I have seen a line of angry guns trying desperately to keep up with unruly and 'deaf' dogs. Later in the season both partridge and pheasant can be walked-up in clover, beet and kale fields or through strips of game cover or set-asides. Again it is the line of walkers and their close-ranging dogs that flushes the birds.

Although the sport is less regimented than a driven shoot, it is imperative that in walked-up shooting a certain discipline is maintained. The guns must walk in line; this sounds a simple task but in woodland, marshy or rocky ground it is very difficult to maintain the line consistently. Each gun must be constantly aware of the whereabouts of the other guns, walkers, and dogs, to minimize the risk of an accident. Without a good line a quartering shot ahead or behind carries a risk of horrendous consequences.

In addition the pace of the walking line must be slow and measured. All too often I have seen a walking gun rush through some cover and fail to dislodge a bird that is 'sitting

tight'. A slow and deliberate pace is more unnerving and far more likely to flush game. The pace must also be kept in check to allow the guns and other walkers to maintain the line and their own composure. A gun breathless from a rushed pace is more likely to result in a fall in boggy or rough ground – quite undesirable when one is carrying a loaded shotgun.

Finally, when any game is flushed the line should halt immediately. If any birds are dropped these must be retrieved before the line moves on again, and even if no shots are fired the retreating partridge or pheasant may be watched until its landing is observed and noted.

Where more than a handful of guns are taking part in a walked-up shoot, the pattern may be modified to form a wide 'U' shape rather than a straight line. The forward guns on the flanks are then able to deal with any quarry that is flushed well out and breaks to the left or right. The walking guns in the centre of the line must ascertain their safe shooting arcs in order to avoid putting the flanker at risk. Thus, in the centre of the line the only safe shots may be dead ahead or in an arc behind the line. Those at the corners of the 'U' shape can cover birds breaking out sideways and those breaking back, and all guns must exercise the utmost care and consideration when walking in this formation.

Another alternative strategy when guns can be spared from the line is to send two or three forward to act as 'standing guns'. These will hopefully receive driven birds much in the same way as on a driven shoot, but with care and planning the walking guns may also enjoy considerable sport before being called to stop 'firing forward' towards the standers.

All species of lowland game may be pursued by walking-up methods and even on the best driven shoots the boundaries are often walked-up to push the birds back into the shoot lands. In other instances water-meadows and marshes may be walked-up for snipe and duck in the wooded valleys of the south-west and Wales – this is the favourite method of shooting woodcock. In such wooded country it is even more important to be aware of maintaining the line even though the neighbouring gun may be frequently obscured by trees and bushes.

Cut-away of the Weatherby action – strong enough to withstand magnum pressures

This form of woodcock shooting can be exhilarating and exhausting sport even though the bag returns may be light. Where numbers allow it, the last shoot of the season is often a walked-up hare shoot in which up to thirty guns normally split into two teams, who act alternately as walkers and standing guns. Hare shoots often cover a great deal of land and serve to thin out any surplus hares before the breeding season. In a number of areas, however, the lowland brown hare is a declining species and end-of-season hare shoots have been suspended.

The most informal of walked-up shooting is the sport of two or three guns 'dogging' the hedgerows for the odd late-season pheasant, or walking a small salt-marsh for snipe between the morning and evening flights. Even here the general discipline and

safety procedures described earlier are essential for the well-being of the participants. Even though this may be second nature to an experienced shooter, the novice must be instructed and helped in such a way as to ensure that silly errors are prevented. There is, to my mind, no better way of instructing the new entrant in the basics of safe gun handling in company than on an informal walked-up shoot.

See also: **Game Shooting; Game Species**

Weatherby In 1945, Roy Weatherby began producing rifles in America that were characterized by high-velocity ballistics. Producing only bolt-actioned rifles of 'custom' quality, Weatherby designed a series of magnum rifle calibres which would suit any

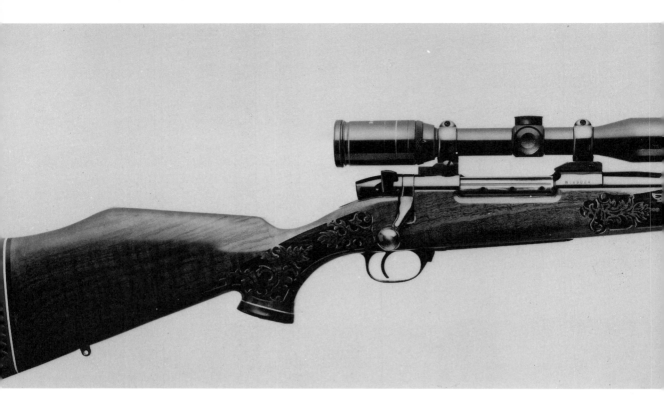

Weatherby magnum rifles with lazermark chequering

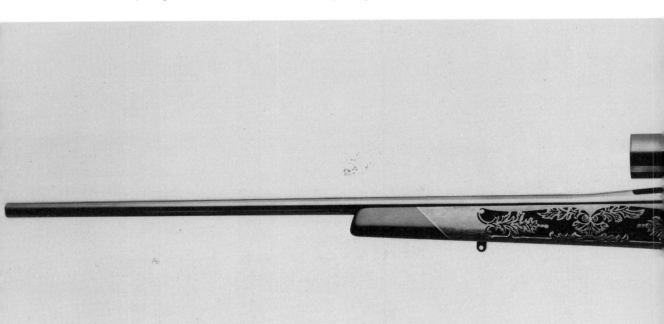

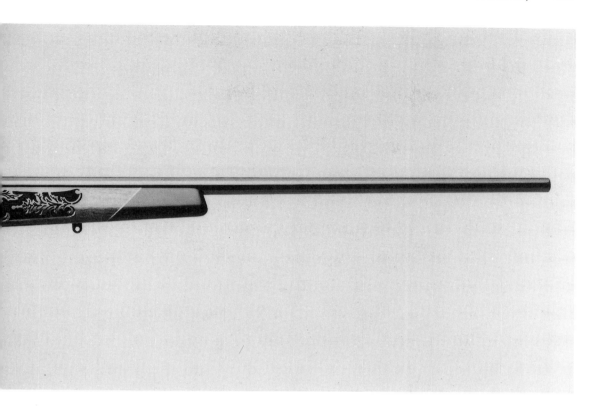

form of shooting from long-range 'varminting' to hunting Africa's largest and most dangerous game.

In doing so, Weatherby pioneered a number of innovations which have subsequently been copied by many other manufacturers. It was he who first popularized what is now called the 'American' style of rifle stock. This style has a raised 'Monte Carlo' cheekpiece to lift the shooter's eye level to the plane of a telescopic sight, a full pistol grip and a squared fore-end, both of which are embellished by a white spacer and a rosewood cap. Weatherby rifles were designed at the outset for use with a telescopic sight, so the barrel was left 'clean', i.e., without any iron sights. In terms of barrel production, Weatherby also contributed much to the modern process of hammer-forging rifle barrels to the very fine tolerances required for accurate shooting.

The innovations so far mentioned are concerned with production techniques or the finished weapon's appearance. What really made Weatherby rifles different to others was the development of unusually powerful ballistics.

In order to do this the rifle's bolt was re-designed to accommodate nine locking lugs. This increase in bolt strength adequately compensated for the increase in chamber pressure of the powerful cartridges. The shape of the cartridge was changed, making the shoulder angle on the brass case steeper, increasing the potential powder capacity, and the use of a 'belted magnum' case for all Weatherby magnum calibres increased the safety margin of the cartridges.

Weatherby magnums now come in nine calibres: .224, .240, .257, .270, .7 mm, .300, .340, .378, and .460. These calibres are all characterized by a significant increase in muzzle energy and velocity over comparable 'standard' calibres, using steeply shouldered belted magnum cartridge cases to achieve this higher performance.

Weatherby has always championed the principle of 'lighter bullet and high velocity' in hunting calibres, and until recently the .460 WM was the world's most powerful rifle cartridge, with a 500-grain bullet generating 8,100 ft lbs energy at a velocity of 2,700 fps. As such it uses a relatively light bullet for the energy generated, and is a direct contrast to its successor in the 'most powerful' claim – the new Holland .700 Nitro Express, which uses a 1,000-grain bullet at 2,100 fps to generate 9,500 ft lbs. Big-game-rifle users tend to polarize into two 'camps' – those who adhere to the 'light and fast' philosophy of Roy Weatherby and those who believe the 'heavy and slow' calibres are more effective.

The Weatherby Mark 5 rifle is the basic bolt-action model chambered for the Weatherby magnum calibres, and various degrees of 'customizing' are available to suit a purchaser's taste and preferences. In addition, Weatherby also produces Vanguard bolt-action rifles chambered for standard calibres, a .22 rimfire auto-loading rifle and an over-and-under 12-bore shotgun. However, the name Weatherby will always be associated with the development and production of high-velocity magnum bolt-actioned rifles.

Webley & Scott   The history of Webley & Scott is more diverse than many sporting gunmakers in that the Birmingham firm was established as the 'Webley & Scott Revolver and Arms Co. Ltd', in 1898.

In addition to large-scale government contracts to manufacture service revolvers, Webley & Scott also produced sporting guns and their components for a wide range of other gunmakers who then sold the weapons on under their own name. As a consequence Webley & Scott could not apply the same production-line techniques to the manufacture of shotguns as they did to their revolvers because each gunmaker demanded a wide range of variations to the 'basic' gun. There were even occasions when guns made for another maker by Webley & Scott were proved in the London proof house to give the impression that they were a London-made gun.

After the First World War the firm began marketing shotguns under their own name, producing both sidelocks and boxlocks of a good sound quality. In the post-war period Webley & Scott produced a range of sporting shotguns under their own name and the 700 series did much to enhance their reputation as makers of good-quality and robust boxlocks.

W.C. Scott side-by-side boxlock hammerless ejector gun

In the same period Webley & Scott also began making air rifles, and today a range of these weapons is still sold under the name of Webley. In 1965 the firm bought out W.W. Greener and for a time continued the production of the single barrel Greener G.P. under the name of Webley–Greener. Competition from European shotgun manufacturers forced the cessation of shotgun production in the 1980s, although the firm was re-established as W.C. Scott to produce a range of boxlock shotguns. Recently the firm of W.C. Scott has been bought by Holland & Holland. At the time of writing W.C. Scott are producing fine-quality boxlock guns for both firms. They also produce chopper lump barrels for the 'best' gun trade. In addition, they repair, re-barrel and restock shotguns. Today the name of Webley continues in the production of a variety of sound and moderately-priced sporting air rifles.

Westley Richards Though based in Birmingham rather than London, the gunmaking firm of Westley Richards has played a leading role in the development of the modern sporting firearm. The firm was established in 1812 by William Westley Richards and quickly gained a good reputation for the consistent quality of their products,

indeed Colonel Peter Hawker wrote favourably about their guns in his famous book.

Westley Richards took a lead in the development of both breechloading rifles and shotguns, collaborating with Captain Minie and with Whitworth in the design of their rifle mechanisms. Among their achievements was the production of the solid-drawn brass cartridge case and their falling-block rifle action which led eventually to the underlever Martini rifles.

On the shotgun side their most notable contribution was the Anson & Deeley boxlock action, which is little changed today. This first appeared in 1875 and a further refinement came in 1898 when Westley Richards boxlocks were fitted with detachable locks which were removed by unclipping the floor plate of the action. In addition the firm devised a reliable ejector mechanism for double guns and a device to prevent double discharge in heavy rifles. In 1901 Westley Richards offered their own single selective trigger mechanism and they took a lead in the design of medium and heavy rifle calibres. Although their .318 Accelerated Express and the .476 are now obsolete, new rifles are still built in the .425 Westley Richards calibre, since cartridge brass is now available from American sources.

Unlike the prestigious London gunmakers, Westley Richards produced a range of 'off-the-shelf' guns in a range of qualities from 'best' sidelocks to simple and robust box-locks. Today Westley Richards continue to produce good English double shotguns and rifles at their Birmingham plant, although most new guns are now made only to order.

Westley Richards continue their long tradition and remain probably the most respected of the Birmingham gunmakers.

White-Fronted Goose   Two races of the white-fronted goose (*Anser albifrons*) are regular winter visitors to Britain. Land north of a line from the Dyfi Estuary in Wales to Scarborough receives white-fronts of the Greenland race, the main concentrations occurring on the Solway Firth, in Ireland, and in north-west Scotland. White-fronts wintering south of the line are of the European race. Both are medium-sized grey geese with an overall grey plumage which becomes more brown-grey on the neck and head. Adult birds have a white patch on the forehead and around the base of the bill from which the name is derived, and the underparts are strongly barred with bold black markings. The Greenland race is protected for much of its range in Scotland, and only the more southerly European white-front is listed as a quarry species in England. The feature that distinguishes the two races is the bill. In the protected Greenland race the head is a darker colour and the bill a bright orange-yellow, while the bill of the European bird is a pale fleshy pink.

The white-front is a noisy species with a characteristic high-pitched cackle and metallic three-syllable flight notes which resemble the sound of a 'squeaky' wheel. The birds arrive from their northern breeding grounds in October and depart on the return journey in March. More than any other species this goose is a bird of wet lowland pasture, and large numbers may congregate in such areas during the winter months. Their food includes grass and clover, seeds and corn stubble, although in hard weather they will also visit potato and other root-crop fields.

The white-front is an agile and swift flier and often performs startling aerobatics for so large a bird. Although they may flight in large 'V'-shaped skeins they quickly split into family groups when feeding. When disturbed they can spring almost vertically into the air and climb at a steep angle to gain height rapidly.

With its white-fronted face and strongly barred underparts the adult is easily recognizable. The immature bird, however, lacks these markings and can easily be confused with the pink-footed and the protected bean goose, but its small size and distinctly musical call note do help towards a positive identification of the young white-front.

White-fronted geese are daytime feeders but their flighting is more unpredictable than other grey geese. Indeed, on undisturbed sites they will roost on their feeding grounds or very close by and this minimizes their daily movements at dawn and dusk.

Where the shooting of this species is permitted, they are normally intercepted somewhere on the short flight lines. The white-front is an excellent table bird.

See also: **Inland Waterfowl Shooting; Wildfowling**

Wigeon   The wigeon (*Anas penelope*) is perhaps the duck species dearest to the heart of any wildfowler. It is a medium-sized duck weighing up to 2 lbs and measuring 18 inches long in an adult bird. Its rather short neck and small bill give it the appearance of having a stocky build. The plumage of the male is quite distinctive. The head is chestnut with a clear buff patch on the forehead and crown, and the short beak is a slaty grey ending in a black tip. The chestnut-pink upper chest gives way to all-white underparts and underwings. Even at a distance the large white patches on the upper wing are clearly visible and these makes it easy to identify in flight. The speculum on the trailing edge of the wings in both sexes is a deep green, which in the drake is bordered in black and in the duck has a white surround. The female is a dull mottled brown with a clear white belly, and the tail of both sexes appears short and pointed in flight.

The call of the drake wigeon is a 'whee-oo' whistle which once heard on the saltings will never be forgotten. The drakes are quite vocal and flocks are often detected by their calling before they come into view in the murky light of a winter's dawn. The female is a quieter bird, but its characteristic noise – a loud purr – can carry quite a long way.

Like all dabbling ducks, the wigeon will jump from a flush and gain height rapidly. They fly fast and often flight in parties ranging from a dozen or so birds to great flocks of several thousand. When flying in a pack they tend to develop an 'echelon' flock shape rather than the more formal 'V' of a skein of geese, and they are very acrobatic fliers, often using a strong wind to tumble and jink.

A small number of wigeon breed within the British Isles, and these are restricted to the upland lochs and willow-fringed moorland bogs of Scotland. Outside the breeding season they are chiefly a coastal species. Here their numbers are greatly augmented by the huge number of migrants from Iceland, Scandinavia and Northern Russia. These arrive in October and depart on their northward migration in March. In winter every salt marsh will have its own population of wigeon and in some areas on the east coast of England they gather in enormous numbers. I have witnessed over ten thousand wigeon in the air at one time, and the sight and sound are unforgettable.

The wigeon is chiefly a grazing duck. In times past its chief food source was the *Zostera marina* seaweed which once flourished in huge beds at the lower end of the tidal range. Since the mysterious disappearance of this plant from much of the British coastline the species has taken to grazing on the saltings and on inland pasture. A nocturnal feeder, the wigeon can be flighted in moonlight if the cloud conditions are suitable, and its gregarious nature will tempt it to decoys of its own species and others, particularly mallard.

Although the female resembles the females of the other dabbling duck species, its green wing speculum, short neck and short bill will allow it to be identified at close quarters. The drake, with its distinctive white wing patches, its chestnut head and its distinctive whistle, should not be confused with any other species.

See also: **Shore Shooting; Wildfowling**

Wildfowl 'Wildfowl' is the term given to all the wetland bird species that may be shot in Britain. All the quarry species of wild geese, duck, waders and gallinaceans come under this general heading.

Of the wild geese, the species that may be pursued include greylag, the white-fronted goose and the pink-footed goose. In addition to these grey geese the Canada goose is also a quarry species but the brent and the barnacle goose are excluded.

The wild duck that may be shot include mallard, wigeon, teal, pintail, shoveller and gadwall of the surface-feeding species, and pochard, goldeneye and tufted duck, all three of which are 'diving ducks'. All other species of ducks are protected. The shooting season for all the geese and duck mentioned as quarry so far varies with the location of the sport. On the foreshore the wildfowler's season opens on 1 September and continues until 20 February. In all other locations the season also opens on 1 September but closes on 31 January.

Of the other wildfowl quarry species, golden plover may be shot from 1 September until 31 January, and this season also applies to coot and moorhen regardless of the location. Snipe on the other hand have their open season extending from 12 August until 31 January, and woodcock are considered to be a game, rather than a wildfowl, species.

When one considers that the sport of wildfowling usually takes place in conditions of poor light and rough weather, correct identification of the quarry is vital. A shooter may well encounter many species of duck that are protected and shooting one through faulty identification is inexcusable. The main recognition points of each of the quarry species appear under their individual headings.

Wildfowl Decoying   In America the sport of decoying waterfowl has developed almost into an art form. On that continent the skill in deploying an attractive pattern of decoys and in calling in the quarry species has become highly refined, but in Britain the use of decoys is looked on as a fringe sport compared to flighting and walking-up. There are times, however, when a good pattern of decoys can greatly increase the chances of birds coming within range of the gun, and a few decoys are a useful addition to the duck and goose shooter's accessories.

There are many different types of wild-fowl decoy on the market nowadays. Duck decoys are usually of rubber and are designed to float. They all have loopholes so that an anchor of some sort can be tied to them on a length of strong cord and they are designed to sit on water. Most duck decoys are full-bodied and come in two forms. The rigid decoy is the most resistant to hard wear but it has two disadvantages: it is the most expensive of the types available and it takes up a great deal of space in a shooter's bag. Rigid duck decoys are available in different sizes and are painted to represent mallard, wigeon, teal, pochard and tufted duck. Although there are some variations, most are shaped to depict a duck with head up and at rest.

Collapsible duck decoys are made of a thinner latex rubber and have the advantage of taking up less space than the rigid decoy. Consequently a shooter can carry and use more of these than the rigid variety. On the other hand, they are more prone to perishing and punctures than the rigid variety and they require more careful handling. One of the most successful of this type of decoy has a weighted ring base so that when the decoy is thrown onto water it rights itself and the trapped air inflates the decoy's body. This pattern of decoy has much to commend it, but of course it can only be used on water. As far as I am aware these collapsible decoys are only available for mallard, but this is of little consequence as a pattern of mallard decoys will also attract other species of duck.

Many duck shooters produce their own handmade silhouette duck decoys. An hour's work on a jigsaw will allow the shooter to cut out a good number of duck profiles from three- or five-ply wood. Each one is then screwed onto a flat board which acts as a raft; the profile can then be painted to resemble the desired species. As the bulk of inland duck decoying takes place in the early morning or late evening when the light is dim, painting is not really necessary. It is the profile of the duck on water which is important and many shooters merely varnish the cut-out in order to waterproof the wood. A hole drilled in the base to take the anchor string completes the decoy. The two main disadvantages with profile decoys are that they are invisible from an overhead in-spection by a high duck, and that they can only really be used in relatively calm water unless they are elaborately weighted to make them self-righting. Nevertheless on a dark winter evening when the birds are flying low they can be every bit as effective as a full-bodied decoy.

The great majority of duck decoys are designed for sitting on water, but goose decoys, on the other hand, are usually designed for land use. Full-bodied decoys are available for both greylag and Canada geese, although the greylag can be used with equal success for pink-footed and white-fronted geese.

Goose decoys are usually made of plastic or fibre-glass and are non-floating. They are supplied with a peg for staking into the ground to give the appearance of a standing goose. Many of the decoys available can be changed from a 'head-up' sentinel to a 'head-down' feeding posture by detaching one neck and fitting another. There are also a number of silhouette goose decoys available, and these can be used with good effect providing the wind is not strong enough to blow them over. Again, it is a simple matter to make your own 'silhouette' goose decoy from plywood, but these suffer from being far heavier than the plastic models commercially available.

Unlike the silhouette duck decoys, goose decoys should be painted to resemble the species because decoying often takes place as the light is strengthening in the morning – colour thus becomes almost as important as shape in a goose decoy. Research has shown that geese are not good discriminators of size thus decoys can be made larger than life in order to increase their visibility; in America they have even taken to building Canada goose decoys large enough to accommodate a seat for the shooter! To my knowledge these giant decoys have not been used in Britain although most commercial goose decoys are larger than life-size.

Although wildfowl decoying is essentially an inland sport there are many occasions when the foreshore wildfowler can use decoys to good effect. On the coast the morning and evening flights form a regular pattern of bird movement, but during the day small parties of duck may well move about the shoreline. In rough weather especially the birds will move from the open water to seek the more sheltered creeks and water flashes of the saltings. On a number of estuaries I have noticed quite regular movements of duck around mid-day or when the tide turns from its lowest ebb. At times like these a small group of decoys set out so that they are visible to the passing traffic will often draw duck within gunshot.

On some of the northern firths rough or foggy weather will have a disruptive effect on the general pattern of movement of the wintering population of wild geese. In these conditions small parties of geese may be tempted to investigate a pattern of decoys on the saltings, and the chances of bagging a goose over decoys may be quite promising if the site is chosen carefully and the shooter well concealed.

However, coastal wildfowling is predominantly a sport of flight shooting and decoying is only a minor tactic for the daytime. Inland, however, decoying can take on more significance. For duck, a known favoured area on a river or pond can be set with decoys in anticipation of the birds returning for their evening 'wash and brush-up' after a day on the feeding grounds. On larger expanses of fresh water, decoying can approach the scale used in America, in that upwards of twenty decoys can be set out in an attractive formation and will sometimes draw birds from a long way away. The most favoured patterns are called the 'V' and 'J' rigs. In the former the decoys are set out on the water in a 'V' shape with the apex of the 'V' touching the bank. This is particularly effective when the wind is blowing offshore and the bank affords most protection. Any birds drawn to the decoy pattern will swing into the wind and drop into the centre of the 'V' shape. When on their final approach they offer on-coming targets as they side-slip to lose height. The 'J' pattern is more effective if the wind is parallel to the water's edge. The curl of the 'J' is closest to the land and the stem trails away downwind further from the bank. Approaching birds will hopefully drop into the space between the stem of the 'J' and the bank. A gunner concealed nearby will then be presented with crossing birds as they make their approach. Of course, any shot birds will drop into the water and a good water dog or boat

is essential for their retrieval, unless the shooter can be so placed to shoot birds only when they cross over onto land. Birds that are attracted to a decoy pattern will often make a couple of low-level passes before committing themselves to landing, and it is during these passes that they present good targets within the shotgun's range.

Decoying geese is a tactic used by the shooter on or near their feeding grounds, although at times geese can be tempted from their flight line by a 'flock' on the ground some distance from their favourite potato or corn stubbles. It is a sport of the early morning, with the decoys set out and the shooter well hidden before the arrival of the early birds. If these can be diverted by a combination of the decoy pattern and skilful goose calling, then the prospects are good for the main body of the flight. In setting out a pattern of goose decoys many shooters opt for placing 'feeding geese' towards the centre of the pattern with occasional 'sentinels' around the edge to give the impression of a flock busily feeding. Both wild grey geese and Canada geese can be decoyed in this way, and a set of decoys can add to the chances of success in what is a very unpredictable sport. Every shooter of waterfowl, whether an inland shooter or a coastal wildfowler, will find that a few decoys will not guarantee success but can certainly improve the odds of putting a bird or two in the bag.

Wildfowling Although wildfowling may simply be defined as the sporting pursuit of the geese, ducks and waders that appear on the quarry list, I would take this a stage further and claim that true wildfowling takes place on the coast in the form of shore shooting or punt gunning. Of course, a great many wildfowl are shot inland – geese and duck flighting to their feeding grounds or stubble fields, duck walked-up on rivers and flight ponds – but I do not consider this to be true wildfowling.

Many shotgun shooters would agree that it is not the quarry species but the environment and weather conditions that really earn the sport the term 'wildfowling'. Although the shooting season for wildfowl opens on 1 September, the shore shooter does not really make serious wildfowling trips until the arrival of the migrating species of geese and duck on their coastal wintering grounds in Britain. To my mind, therefore, true wild-fowling begins in November and continues until the end of the season, and even the end of the season indicates the different nature of inland and coastal shooting. Above high-water mark of spring tides the wildfowl season ends on 31 January, but below the mark it is extended to 20 February. The coastal wildfowler thus has a longer active season than his inland duck-shooting count-erpart.

Wildfowling is a romantic sport. It takes place in some of Britain's wildest and most remote places and in the most rigorous weather conditions this country can offer in the depths of winter. It is not a sport for the weak or foolhardy, as the estuaries and salt marshes are treacherous places for the unwary and the exposed nature of the en-vironment has resulted in deaths from drowning or exposure. It is a sport which pits the skills, knowledge and stamina of the shooter against Britain's wildest and most wary bird species, and the returns in terms of birds killed are small.

Most of the land lying below the tidal high-water mark belongs to the Crown and is known as 'Crown foreshore'. In times past this land was open to any shooter to pursue the sport, but nowadays a good proportion of Crown foreshore is leased to local wildfowling clubs and shooting syndicates. Access to much of Britain's best wildfowling is now only possible through these clubs or through a permit scheme run by the BASC on the clubs' behalf. Although the image of the 'lone fowler' with freedom of access to our estuaries and coastline belongs to the past, wildfowling today is still a rigorous and testing sport.

Wildfowling Guns In choosing a shotgun suitable for wildfowling, the shore shooter is faced with a different set of criteria to the game shooter and other inland shooters. Generally speaking, the average game-shooting range is around 35 yards, but in coastal wildfowling shots are more often taken at longer ranges between 40 and 50 yards. The shotgun therefore needs to be able to throw dense patterns to these greater distances, and most wildfowling guns tend to be more heavily choked than their game-shooting counterparts. The striking energy of

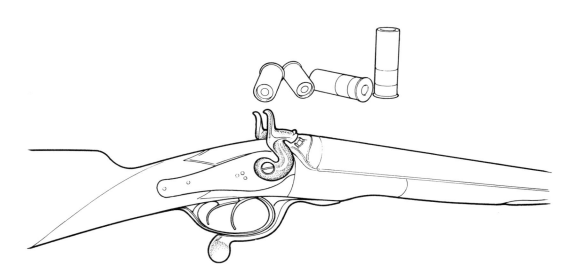

A double 8-bore underlever hammer gun by William Moore & Grey

the individual shot pellets in the pattern also needs to be maintained at these longer ranges, and geese in particular need a heavy pellet strike in order to kill them cleanly. The solution is to increase the shot size in the cartridge, thereby ensuring that the shot retains sufficient energy and penetration, so No 4 and even No 1 shot are most often used for duck and geese respectively. The problem then arises in maintaining a dense and killing pattern with fewer of these large pellets per charge, and the solution is to increase the weight of the shot load in the cartridge. Thus the coastal wildfowler will usually resort to heavily-loaded cartridges in the large shot sizes for his sport.

A wildfowler's gun will have to be proof-tested to accommodate heavily-loaded cartridges and be of sufficient weight to absorb much of the increased recoil. The conditions encountered by the coastal wildfowler demand other qualities of the gun. Shooting from concealment among spartina grass and soft estuary mud demands that the gun should have a minimum of its working parts exposed to the elements, thereby minimizing the ingress of mud and grit to the gun's mechanism. Auto-loading and pump-action guns are not ideal for this reason as estuary mud can quickly jam up the mechanism and render them unsafe or unusable. Salt water and sea spray also take a heavy toll on exposed mechanisms, so that even an over-and-under double can encounter problems with clogged extractor and ejectors on either side of the breech, and the style of shotgun best suited to coastal fowling is therefore the side-by-side double, as the minimum of its working parts are exposed to risk.

It would be foolish to expose best-quality guns to this type of sport, not because of any fear of malfunction, but because the risk of damaging a fine-quality weapon would be too great. Most wildfowlers would therefore choose a strongly-built and relatively inexpensive boxlock side-by-side for their sport. In days gone by the British foreshore often echoed to the sound of the large-calibre shotguns, but in the immediate post-war years the 4-, 8- and 10-bore wildfowling shotguns declined as ammunition became increasingly expensive and scarce. In recent years, however, there has been a rekindling of interest in the big bores for

wildfowling, and even though the 12-bore magnum remains the wildfowler's 'maid of all work' an increasing number of the larger shotguns are appearing on British coastlines.

The 4 bore is the heaviest shoulder gun used for sporting shooting in Britain. Its cartridges are loaded with between 3 and 4 oz of shot and the effective range of a well-bored gun may extend out to about 75 yards. Although in the past double barrel 4 bores were made, their weight of up to 25 lbs made them impractical for flying shots and they were more often used as light punt guns. Single barrel guns in this bore are still, however, being produced in small numbers. They weigh between 15 and 19 lbs and are wielded by some wildfowlers for long-range goose flighting. All the large-bore shotguns tend to be built with long barrels and 4-bore singles often have barrels of 40 inches. Not only does this add to the weight of the gun, but it also helps to counteract the weighted stock in order to improve the gun's balance and handling. In the past these weapons were built on the underlever drop-down action, but more modern guns have top-lever opening. As a single-shot gun the 4 bore does have its limitations, and it is questionable whether its increased range over the 8 bore is adequate compensation.

The double 8 bore, on the other hand, is seen by many wildfowlers as the ultimate goose gun. Firing shot loads of 2 oz to $2\frac{1}{2}$ oz, each load carries enough No 1 size shot to give a good killing pattern up to about 65 yards and the 8 bore is by far the most popular of the 'big guns'. In the past 8 bores were made in some quantity by the gunmakers specializing in wildfowling guns, and examples by Holland & Holland, Bland and Tolley today command high prices. For some time I used a double underlever hammer 8 by William Moore & Grey and despite weighing $13\frac{1}{2}$ lbs it balanced well and was a delight to use. The resurgence of interest in the 8 bore came with the availability of Remington industrial cartridge cases in this calibre. The plastic compression-formed case with a long brass base proved easy to reload and those guns that had been made redundant through lack of ammunition were quickly put back into use. More recently still a number of new double hammerless 8 bores have appeared on the market. These are of Spanish origin and weigh about 12 lbs. Their barrels are usually 32 to 36 inches long and are well-bored and tightly choked, and the guns have been well received by today's wildfowler for coastal goose flighting. Because they handle a 2 oz load more efficiently than the 10 bore, their patterns are generally superior and their only real limitation lies in the shooter himself. To swing the gun into a goose at 60 yards and kill it cleanly demands great skill, particularly if the wildfowler is up to his ankles in estuary mud at the time!

The 10 bore never really declined to the same extent as the 8 and 4 bores. Even though cartridge production ceased in Britain at the same time as its larger cousins, American 10-bore cartridges have always been available. In the United States the 10 bore is the largest permitted shotgun calibre and it has a strong following among the flyway goose hunters. In American-made guns the chamber length was extended to $3\frac{1}{4}$ inches and the 'magnum' 10-bore loads contained 2 oz of shot or more. While this theoretically gave equal performance to an 8 bore, the narrower diameter meant that there was a correspondingly longer column of shot being driven up the barrel. A long shot column brings a higher proportion of shot into contact with the barrel wall when the cartridge is fired, and these shot are deformed to such an extent that they quickly fall out of the pattern. A pellet count of a 2-oz load fired from a 10 and 8 bore would show the superior consistency from the 8.

Nevertheless the availability of factory-loaded 10-bore cartridges has ensured that this calibre is probably more frequently seen than the larger 8. The British 10 bore was rather a compromise gun. Chambered for either $2\frac{5}{8}$-inch or $2\frac{7}{8}$-inch cartridges it carried heavier loads than the 12-bore game gun and was popular as a live pigeon competition gun as well as for wildfowling. When the 12 bore was adapted to shoot 3-inch cartridges the 10 lost its advantage although it still threw sweeter patterns than the corresponding 3-inch 12 bore. Ammunition for the 10 bore was, however, more expensive and it quickly lost favour to the magnum 12. It was only with the development of the American 10-bore $3\frac{1}{2}$-inch magnum that this calibre regained an advantage over the 12

bore, and over the last twenty years 10-bore shotguns have been reintroduced by manufacturers in southern Europe and in the USA. For some time double barrel side-by-side 10 bores had been exported in small quantities to America from Spain, and while some of these are now diverted to the British market, American manufacturers began producing their own variety of 10-bore guns. In 1974 Ithaca produced the first gas-operated semi-automatic 10 bore as their 'Mag 10' model. Shortly after, Marlin produced a 10-bore bolt-action repeating shotgun known as their 'Super Goose', and Harrington and Richardson another single barrel single-shot weapon in this calibre.

All these new 10 bores are chambered for the magnum $3\frac{1}{2}$-inch cartridge firing 2 to $2\frac{1}{4}$ oz of shot, and they are all available in Britain. It does seem that, perhaps due to traditional British taste in shotgun design or to the rigorous conditions experienced on Britain's winter foreshore, the Spanish-built side-by-side boxlock double is by far the most popular choice as a long-range wildfowling gun in Britain. Its cartridges are readily available and the guns themselves weigh between $9\frac{1}{2}$ and 11 lbs so that they can be carried and used comfortably by the majority of shooters.

One of the criticisms one hears levelled at the users of these large-bore guns is that they are 'unsporting' and cause too much disturbance on a salt marsh. To this I can only reply that shooters are just as prone to 'stretch' the range of a 12 bore as any other calibre, and, due to the cost of these larger cartridges, a big-bore user is far less likely to squander his shots than a 12-bore user. After all, a single 4-bore cartridge can cost the same as 50 for a 12 bore!

Despite all I have said about the rebirth of the large-bore wildfowling guns, 90 per cent of all today's British shore shooters arm themselves with a 12 bore. The 3-inch chambered 12 bore appeared in Britain in the 1920s, and with its $1\frac{1}{2}$-oz shot load it competed favourably with the 10 bores of the period. In addition, the 12 bore was a considerably lighter and handier weapon of only about $7\frac{1}{2}$ lbs and it became known as the 12-bore 'duck gun'. American arms manufacturers were quick to see the potential of the long 12-bore cartridge. By varying the wadding thickness and the propellant powders the shot capacity could be increased to $1\frac{7}{8}$ oz, nearly the equivalent of an 8 bore from a 12-bore shotgun. In order to limit the effects of recoil from these heavy cartridges the weight of the double 12 was increased in some cases to $8\frac{1}{2}$ lbs and the 12-bore 'magnum' was born.

Most wildfowlers nowadays would recognize that these very heavy 12-bore loads result in a high degree of pellet deformation in the barrel and the patterns suffer in consequence. A great many will select the $1\frac{1}{2}$-oz 'semi-magnum' cartridge as a good wildfowling load which is effective against duck and geese out to 50 yards and will throw reliable patterns even in tightly choked guns. Although most 'wildfowling' guns are sold with tightly choked barrels there have been many advocates of more open borings on the grounds that the better quality of the patterns makes up for the wider spread of shot. From my own experience my shooting certainly improved when I had the full and three-quarter chokes on my Zabala magnum 12 opened out to half and quarter choke.

The 12-bore 3-inch magnum shotguns are available in a far greater variety of types than any of the heavier calibres, and the wildfowler can choose from self-loaders, pump-actions, bolt-actions, over-and-unders and side-by-sides. In addition, ever greater versatility can be gained if the weapon is fitted for screw-in choke tubes, and of course, the 12-bore magnum loaded with standard cartridges will cope adequately with any other shotgun quarry or shooting method – I have quite happily used 1-oz loads in my magnum for driven partridge. The fact that this versatility is possible only in the 12 bore will ensure its continued dominance as the calibre most often used by today's wildfowlers.

See also: **Calibres – Shotgun**

Windage   The path of a bullet through the air is affected by any wind which blows across it. The effect of this crosswind is to blow the bullet off target on the downwind side of the intended point of impact. This lateral movement of the point of impact can be compensated for in two ways. The shooter can deliberately offset the aim of the rifle to the upwind side of the desired impact point or he can move the lateral adjustment of the rifle's sights in order to compensate for the effects of wind. The lateral adjustment of the sights is known as 'windage'. Telescopic sights have a windage adjustment ring on the side of the scope tube, and turning this moves the graticule from side to side. Most aperture sights and rear 'iron' sights also have some form of windage adjustment to produce lateral changes in the impact point.

Understandably most rifle shooters are reluctant to adjust the sights of a carefully zeroed rifle in order to compensate for an occasional crosswind shot and would prefer to compensate by an offset aim. To make an accurate shot in this situation the shooter must be aware of how much wind affects the bullet that is being used, and this knowledge can only come from target practice in windy conditions and experience gained in the field.

Woodcock   Although considered to be a game bird, the woodcock (*Scolopax rusticola*) is really a wader which has forsaken the open wetlands for woodland habitat. Measuring up to about 14 inches in length, it is a medium-sized and dark-coloured bird with a long straight bill. The plumage is an intricate and richly-marked pattern of black, brown and cream with a lighter shading on the underparts. This pattern camouflages the bird so well that it is often virtually invisible when at rest on a woodland floor. In flight the bird appears rather stout, an appearance accentuated by its short tail and its downward-pointing bill. The high forehead gives the head an angular shape and the eyes are set high on each side of the head. These high-set eyes result in a quite unique flight pattern in woodland, because, while they give the bird excellent all-round vision, its vision straight ahead is slightly impaired. When flushed in thick woodland, therefore, it will dodge around trees at the last moment, thereby offering a very erratic target. In the open its flight is swift and direct on rounded wings which produce a distinctive 'swishing' sound. The plumage of both sexes is similar and the young resemble the adult bird to the extent that they are virtually indistinguishable in the field.

The woodcock is essentially a forest wader, with residents nesting in their preferred habitat of dry, mature deciduous woodland adjacent to damp pasture in which they feed. They are nocturnal feeders, spending much of the day resting among dead leaf litter on the woodland floor, where their camouflaged plumage offers them the greatest protection, and flighting out to the adjacent pastures to feed in late dusk. In poor weather these habits may be changed so that woodcock may be observed feeding during the daylight hours. Its diet is mainly of earthworms and other soil larvae which it obtains by probing in the soft earth with its long beak.

Although there is a resident breeding population in Britain, the numbers increase rapidly in October and November as the influx of migrants from Scandinavia and Western Russia arrives. Many of these move to the western margins of Britain, and there are years when the deep wooded valleys of Wales and the south-west peninsula hold substantial numbers of these birds.

The return migration takes place in March and April, leaving the males of the resident population to mark out their breeding territories with their characteristic 'roding' flight. Although usually a silent bird the male utters a 'tswisk' call whilst roding in April and May.

Woodcock shooting as practised in Wales and the West Country usually takes the form of walked-up shooting in dense woodland, although a 'woodcock drive' may add variety to many driven shoots in these areas. As a game bird, the woodcock season conforms to other game species in that the season ends on 31 January. However, the opening date varies, with woodcock shooting in Scotland beginning on 1 September, but this is delayed until 1 October in England and Wales. The woodcock may be confused in flight with a snipe, but it is altogether a heavier and larger bird which is normally found in very different environments.

See also: **Walked-Up Shooting**

Wood-Pigeon   The wood-pigeon (*Columba palumbus*), although classified as an agri-

cultural pest, is one of the prime quarry species in the British Isles. As birds of the pigeon and dove family go, the wood-pigeon is a heavy and large species with an overall length of about 16 inches and weighing up to 2 lbs. Its most conspicuous identifying feature are the large white wing bars between the dark grey/black primaries and the pale grey shoulders. These wing bars are easily seen in flight. At a distance the overall im-

The woodcock is perfectly camouflaged against a woodland floor

pression is of a blue/grey bird, but closer observation will pick out other distinguishing features. Adult birds have a white patch on either side of the neck adjacent to a small purple-green group of feathers which may extend to the nape. The breast has a distinctly pink shade and this merges into a pale off-white underbelly. The upper surfaces are a blue-grey which is paler on the rump and darkens to a sooty grey-black on the tail. Immature birds are browner and lack the white neck patches, although the white wing bars are still conspicuous.

The wood-pigeon occurs in all areas of the British Isles, although the population is not evenly distributed. Some of the upland areas are fairly thinly populated whereas very heavy concentrations of birds may occur where the food supplies are abundant. The ideal wood-pigeon habitat is a mixture of cultivated farmland and woodland. However, it will also colonize the wooded fringes of high moorland and has adapted well to life in city parks and gardens.

The rural wood-pigeon population makes use of the farmland for feeding and the woodland and hedgerows for roosts and nest sites. The British population is mainly resident and sedentary but an influx of birds from the European continent does occur from October into the winter. These European birds tend to remain on the low farmlands of eastern England until they depart in March.

The wood-pigeon is a daytime feeder, feeding mainly on the ground and making extensive use of any arable crops. In autumn and winter they frequently feed in large flocks on newly sown grain, brassicas, and clover. Spring-sown grain crops, peas, beans, and other crops are taken from March through to July when the ripening grain fields become the main target. However, at the appropriate times of the year wood-pigeons will feed extensively on acorns, beech mast, ivy berries and tree buds.

Woodlands are used for large communal roosts in the colder months but in spring and summer the flocks split up into breeding pairs. Nest sites are rarely more than 20 feet from the ground in trees and hedgerow bushes, and up to three broods may be raised each year.

The wood-pigeon is a strong and agile flier. When disturbed it takes off amid a loud clatter of wings which serves as a danger signal to others. Flight is rapid and direct, although it will find any easy path into a strong headwind by slipping behind any sheltering hedges or banks. It flies downwind at an amazing speed and a high downwind pigeon is perhaps the most difficult of all overhead shots.

Most pigeon shooting exploits the fact that the wood-pigeon is a very gregarious bird and will be readily attracted by decoys. At other times they may be shot when flighting to or from their feeding grounds or may be intercepted when coming in to roost.

In addition to being Britain's most damaging agricultural pest, the wood-pigeon is a very sporting quarry and, if carefully cooked, a gourmet's delight. Because a pigeon shooter is providing a valuable 'crop protection' service, the sport of pigeon shooting is usually available free for the asking from the majority of farmers and landowners, and it is not surprising that, of all the shotgun sports, this is the one with the highest number of participants.

See also: **Pigeon Shooting**

Woodward The gunmaking firm of J. Woodward was established as Woodward & Moore in London in 1800, but by 1851 the 'Moore' had been dropped from the company name. In 1877 Woodward produced their first hammerless gun and they established a high reputation for the quality of finish and the elegance of their guns and rifles.

Perhaps their most important contribution to the development of modern sporting guns was their over-and-under gun, first introduced in 1913 and further refined in 1921.

In 1949 the firm of J. Woodward & Sons was bought out by James Purdey, who continue to service and maintain Woodward guns to the high standard which befits guns of this quality.

See also: **Purdey**

Zabala The Zabala Brothers gunmaking factory is one of the most highly mechanized in Spain. This company has specialized very successfully in the production of low-cost but reliable shotguns for a number of British arms importers. The vast majority of Zabala's output is in 12-bore side-by-side built on the Anson & Deeley boxlock action, although they also produce the complete range of centrefire shotgun calibres from 12 bore downwards. A smaller number of sidelocks are also made.

These shotguns are styled to suit British taste, with concave ribs and straight stocks, although some variations do exist. In the Zabala factory costs are cut by forging the barrels to a demi-block pattern rather than the more expensive chopper lump system, and the high degree of mechanized production reduces skilled labour costs. Engraving is also kept to a minimum and the resulting gun, although lacking in elegant embellishments, is a thoroughly reliable and hard-working weapon.

Zabala shotguns are marketed by a number of arms importers in Britain. The wildfowling model I owned in the 1960s came from the Grange Gun Co., and nowadays perhaps the best-known of the Zabala range is marketed as the Gunmark Kestrel series of shotguns.

Zero A rifle is said to be 'on zero' when the impact point of the bullets coincides with the sighting line at a given distance. Hence an air rifle may be on zero at 30 yards if the pellets impact on the aiming point at this distance, and a .270 stalking rifle may be zeroed for 200 yards if the main point of impact coincides with the sighting mark at that range.

Normally there are two zero points for any given rifle's trajectory. Regardless of whether open, aperture, or telescopic sights are used, the line of sight is placed vertically above the bore of the rifle and in order to obtain a zero at a given range the line of sight and the alignment of the bore must converge. Thus the trajectory of the bullet will cross the line of sight in two places, once as the bullet rises above the line of sight and again further away, when it falls below it. These two intersections are sometimes known as 'close zero' and 'distant zero'. Between the two the bullet is travelling above the line of sight. Some air rifle shooters, however, adjust their sights to achieve a single zero point, the pellet rising to the sighting plane then falling away again without crossing it. Thus in this case at any range other than the zero point the impact point of the pellet lies below the sighting plane.

Zeroing a Rifle A rifle is useless unless it is dependably accurate, and the process of zeroing a rifle is the process of adjusting the rifle's sights in order to bring the point of bullet impact to the point of aim at the optimum distance for effective hunting. On a few rifles, the sights are fixed and therefore zeroing adjustments cannot be made. The only answer in this case is to practise sufficiently at targets in order to get to know exactly where the rifle shoots at a variety of ranges and to compensate for this when aiming. The vast majority of rifles, however, have adjustable sights.

The basic process of zeroing a rifle is the same regardless of the sighting method used. Firstly the 'close zero' is obtained and then the final adjustments are made to obtain the 'distant zero'. When zeroing a rifle for the first time a zeroing frame or vice is a valuable and time-saving accessory as it allows the rifle to be held steady while the sights are adjusted.

Before commencing the process of zeroing a weapon the shooter must ascertain that the sights are secure and firmly mounted; this will prevent any movement in the sights each time the weapon is fired. Zeroing is also a pointless exercise if the shooter is incapable of mounting and firing the weapon consistently enough to put the bullets close together at a given distance.

Failure to achieve a consistent close grouping of bullet holes on a target is usually attributable to loose sights, a loose barrel mounting screw on the rifle, or an unsteady aim. In order to eliminate the first two the sights need to be inspected and the barrel mounting screw, usually found under the barrel just in front of the trigger guard, should be checked for tightness. At the same time the barrel and fore-end of the rifle must be checked for any grit or other obstruction. Many rifles these days have a 'floating' barrel, i.e., the barrel is securely welded into the stock close to the breech, but forward of this it does not come into contact with the stock at all. When the rifle is fired the barrel vibrates much in the same way as a tuning fork and the weapon's accuracy is dependent on the barrel being allowed to vibrate in a consistent way. A twig or grit lodged between the fore-end and the barrel would interfere with the barrel's natural vibrations and this would have a detrimental effect on accuracy.

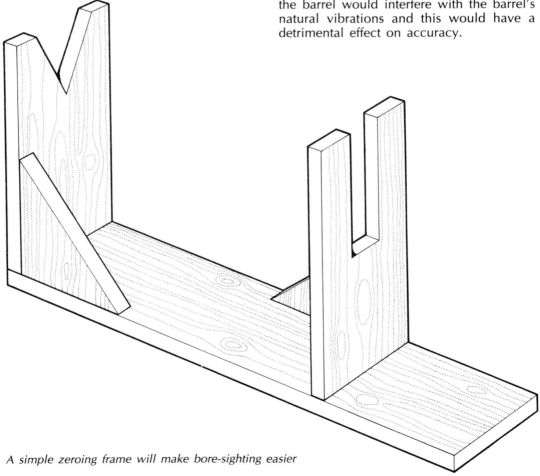

A simple zeroing frame will make bore-sighting easier

Unsteadiness in aiming can be virtually eliminated by shooting from a prone position or from a bench rest. In both instances the fore-end of the rifle should be rested on a sandbag or firm cushion to eliminate 'leading-hand' wobble. Resting the rifle on a hard object should be avoided as this tends to make the rifle 'jump' when it is fired, so the sandbag or cushion should have a certain amount of 'give' for consistent shooting.

Holding the rifle only by the stock on his shoulder and by the trigger hand, the shooter, whether prone or at a bench, must be both comfortable and relaxed. Any tension in the body will be reflected in unsteadiness of aim. Having checked the rifle and made sure of a comfortable and steady firing position, the shooter can then begin zeroing the weapon.

The first stage is to 'bore sight', i.e. to align the sights with what can be seen through the barrel. Using a vice or a zeroing frame the rifle is pointed at a mark about 30 yards away. The precise aim is checked by looking through the barrel at the aiming mark. On a bolt-action rifle this is a relatively easy procedure. The bolt is simply removed and the vice or frame moved until one can see the mark through the barrel. In other types of rifle a small mirror must be placed into the breech in order to see up the bore. Once you can see the mark through the barrel the sights are carefully adjusted until they also point to the mark.

The rifle can now be removed from the vice or zeroing frame and the first shots fired at this range in order to achieve the 'close zero'. Fire a group of five rounds at the target, using the same aiming point for each shot regardless of where the bullets may be striking. When zeroing a rifle one should not fire more than five rounds at a time as the barrel heats up rapidly and tends to produce erratic results in its heated state. Allow the barrel to cool down between each group of shots. With careful shooting the first five shots should form a tight group, but the point of impact may not be on the aiming mark. Place the rifle back in the frame and align it so that the sights are aligned exactly at the aiming mark. Now, with the rifle securely held, adjust the sights until they point to the centre of the group of five bullet holes.

Again, fire a string of five shots and the impact of the shots should be very much closer to the aiming mark. Repeat the process until the bullets are grouping on the aiming mark, i.e., the rifle is shooting exactly on the point of aim at about 30 yards.

With the 'close zero' achieved the shooter then selects the appropriate range for the calibre and quarry, perhaps 60–70 yards for a .22 LR or 100 yards for a woodland stalking rifle, and repeats the process at this range. Firing off groups of five shots and 'fine tuning' the sights to the long range will achieve the 'distant zero' very quickly.

This is the basic process of zeroing, and it is probably the most precise method of producing a well-zeroed, accurate rifle. It can, however, be quite expensive on ammunition if using a centrefire rifle and to compensate the groups may be reduced to three shots each. When the rifle needs to be zeroed at a longer range this basic method becomes impractical; the longer the range the more widespread the grouping becomes, and the more prone each bullet is to wind. Even a light crossing breeze can spread bullets over six inches at 150 yards, so another method must be used. Here the knowledge of the trajectory produced by one's selected brand of ammunition is essential. I know, for instance, that my favourite brand of .270 ammunition will shoot $1\frac{1}{4}$-inches high at 100 yards if the rifle is zeroed for 200. I therefore zero the rifle to shoot $1\frac{1}{4}$-inches high at 100 yards. On a calm day I then check the point of impact on safe ground at 150 yards and 200 yards, carrying out any minor adjustments that are necessary. As I use this particular rifle for deer, having it zeroed for 200 yards means that I know exactly where the bullet will strike the target at any distance out to the zero, and the differences in the bullet's trajectory can be allowed for. In deer stalking terms these differences are so small as to be of little importance.

Finally, if, due to the design of the rifle's breech, bore sighting is impractical, a telescopic sight can still be roughly aligned using a collimator to achieve the same effect as bore sighting.

See also: **Collimator; Telescopic Sight**

APPENDIX 1

USEFUL ADDRESSES

Sporting organizations

The British Association for Shooting and
    Conservation (BASC)
National Headquarters
Marford Mill
Rossett
Clwyd LL12 0HL

The British Deer Society (BDS)
Beale Centre
Lower Basildon
Reading
Berkshire RG8 9NH

The British Field Sports Society (BFSS)
59 Kennington Road
London SE1 7PZ

The British Shooting Sports Council (BSSC)
Pentridge
Salisbury
Wiltshire SP5 5QX

The Game Conservancy
Burford Manor
Fordingbridge
Hampshire SP6 1EF

The Game Farmers Association
Oddington Lodge
Moreton-in-the-Marsh
Gloucestershire

The Saint Hubert Club
The Old Manor House
Hinxton
Saffron Walden
Essex

Proof houses

The Birmingham Proof House
Banbury Street
Birmingham B5 5RH

The London Proof House
The Gunmakers Company
48 Commercial Road
London E1L 1LP

Gun and rifle makers

Boss & Co
13 Dover Street
London W1X 3PH

John Dickson & Son
21 Frederick Street
Edinburgh EH2 2NE

William Evans Ltd
67a St James Street
London SW1A 1P

Holland & Holland Ltd
33 Bruton Street
London W1X 8JS

David Lloyd
Pipewell Hall
Kettering
Northampton NN14 1QZ

Parker Hale Ltd
Golden Hillock Road
Birmingham B11 2PZ

William Powell & Son
35–37 Carrs Lane
Birmingham B4 7SX

James Purdey & Sons Ltd
Audley House
57–58 South Audley Street
London W1

John Rigby & Co
13 Pall Mall
London W1

Westley Richards & Co
Grange Road
Bournebrook
Birmingham B29 6AR

I must point out that this is a short list of those gunmakers mentioned in the text. In addition to these there is a large number of small provincial gunmakers who continue to make weapons of a very high quality to order.

The sporting press

Airgun World
Burlington Press
10 Sheet Street
Windsor
Berks' SL4 1BG

Air Gunner
2 The Courtyard
Denmark Street
Wokingham
Berks RG11 2LW

The Field
10 Sheet Street
Windsor
Berks SL4 1BG

Shooting Gazette
2 West Street
Bourne
Lincs PE10 9NE

Shooting News
Unit 21
Plymouth Road Industrial Estate
Tavistock
Devon PL19 9QN

Shooting Times and Country Magazine
10 Sheet Street

Windsor
Berks SL4 1BG

Sporting Dog
Press and Television Ltd
Yelverton
Devon PL20 7PE

Sporting Gun
Bretton Court
Bretton
Peterborough PE3 8DE

Stalking Magazine
  (Available on subscription only)
Field Sport Publications Ltd
48 Queen Street
Exeter
Devon EX4 3SR

Contacts for shooting overseas

AFRICA

Cape Safaris
PO Box 2501
PAARL
S. Africa

Ecosafaris (UK) Ltd
146 Gloucester Road
London SW7 4SZ

Hunting Safari Consultants
83 Gloucester Place
London W1H 3PG

Selous Hunters
Horsted Keynes
Sussex

UK Field and Stream
Birchensale Farm
Salters Lane
Redditch
Worcs B97 6QB

FRANCE

The French Government Tourist Office
178 Piccadilly
London W1

GERMANY

The German Hunting Association
Deutsches Jagdschutz Verband
Schillerstrasse 26
D-5300 Bonn
Germany

German National Tourist Office
61 Conduit Street
London W1R 0EN

HUNGARY

Danube Travel Agency Ltd
6 Conduit Street
London W1R 9TG

The Hungarian Hunting Bureau
MAVAD
1014 Budapest
Uri Utca 39
Hungary

NORWAY

The Norwegian Government Agency
Direktoratet for Vilt og Ferskvanfiske
Trondheim
Norway

The Norwegian Hunting Association
Norges Jeger og Fiskerforbund

Hvalstadasen 7
Norway

POLAND

The Polish Hunting Association
Polski Zwiazek Lowiecki
00–029 Warsaw
Nowi Swiat 35
Poland

Polish Travel Office
313 Regent Street
London W1R 7PE

SPAIN

Istituto Nacional para la Conservacion de
  la Naturaleza
(ICONA)
Madrid
Spain

Spain Safaris
Box 752
Santiago
Spain

WORLDWIDE

Worldwide Hunting Ltd
88 St Clements Street
Oxford
OX4 1AR

APPENDIX 2

SUGGESTED FURTHER READING

General

Backhouse, Eliot et al *The Complete Book of Shooting* (Octopus 1988)
Begbie, Eric (ed) *The Sportsman's Companion* (Saiga 1981)
Coles, Charles (ed) *Shooting and Stalking* (Stanley Paul 1983)
Falkus, Hugh *Nature Detective* (Gollancz 1978)
MacPhail, Roger *Open Season* (Airlife 1986)
McKelvie, Colin *A Future for Game?* (George Allen and Unwin 1985)
Taylor, Fred J. *Reflections of a Countryman* (Stanley Paul 1982)
Various authors *Hunting* (Nordbok 1980, Sweden)
Willock, Colin (ed) *ABC of Shooting* (Andre Deutsch 1975)

Wildfowling and wildfowl

Begbie, Eric *Modern Wildfowling* (Saiga 1980)
Gresham, Grits *The Complete Wildfowler* (Stoeger 1975, USA)
Jarrett, Alan *Wildfowling, One Winter's Tale* (Dickson Price 1988)
Ogilvie, M.A. *Wild Geese* (Poyser 1978)
Scott, Peter *Wild Chorus* (Country Life 1938)
Sedgewick N.M. et al *The New Wildfowler* (Herbert Jenkins 1961)
Soothill & Whitehead *Wildfowl of the World* (Blandford 1978)
Swan, Mike *Fowling for Duck* (Crowood 1988)

Sporting weapons

Akehurst, Richard *Game Guns and Rifles* (Bell 1969)

Burrard, Sir Gerald *Notes on Sporting Rifles* (Arnold 1920)
Burrard, Maj. Sir Gerald *The Modern Shotgun* (3 vols) (Herbert Jenkins 1931)
Cradock, Chris *Cradock on Shotguns* (Batsford 1989)
Garwood, G.T. *Gough Thomas's Gun Book* (A & C Black 1969)
Marshall-Ball, Robin *The Sporting Shotgun* (Saiga 1981)
Marshall-Ball, Robin *The Sporting Rifle* (Pelham 1986)
O'Connor, Jack *The Hunting Rifle* (Stoeger 1970, USA)
Taylor, John *Big Game and Big Game Rifles* (Herbert Jenkins 1948)
Tegner, Henry *The Sporting Rifle* (Herbert Jenkins 1962)

Deer

Cadman, Arthur *Dawn, Dusk, and Deer* (Sportsmans Press 1989)
de Nahlilk, A.J. *Wild Deer* (Faber 1959)
Elford, Colin *Practical Woodland Stalking* (Crowood 1988)
Hudson, David *Highland Deer Stalking* (Crowood 1989)
MacNally, Lea *Highland Deer Forest* (Dent 1973)
Prior, Richard *Living with Deer* (Andre Deutsch 1965)
Prior, Richard *Trees and Deer* (Batsford 1983)
Prior, Richard *Deer Watch* (David & Charles 1987)
Prior, Richard *Deer Management in Small Woodlands* (Game Conservancy 1987)
Whitehead, G. Kenneth *Hunting and Stalking Deer Throughout the World* (Batsford 1982)

Whitehead G. Kenneth *Practical Deer Stalking* (Constable 1986)

Shotgun sports

Brook, Michael *The Gameshooter's Pocket Guide* (Batsford 1990)

Carlisle, G. L. *Grouse and Gun* (Stanley Paul 1983)

Rice & Dahl *Game Bird Hunting* (Harper & Row 1965, USA)

Smith, Guy N. *The Rough Shooter's Handbook* (Boydell 1986)

Turner, Gerry (ed) *Handbook of Shooting* (Pelham 1985)

Willock, Colin *Town Gun* (Andre Deutsch 1973)

Willock, Colin *Town Gun 2* (Andre Deutsch 1981)